HYPATIA REBORN

HYPATIA REBORN

Essays in Feminist Philosophy

EDITED BY

AZIZAH Y. AL-HIBRI

AND

MARGARET A. SIMONS

INDIANA UNIVERSITY PRESS

Bloomington and Indianapolis

The paper used in this publication meets the minimum requirements of American
National Standard for Information Sciences—Permanence of Paper for Printed
Library Materials, ANSI Z39.48-1984.
⊗™

Manufactured in the United States of America

Library of Congress Cataloging-in-Publication Data

Hypatia reborn : essays in feminist philosophy / edited by Azizah Y.
al-Hibri and Margaret A. Simons.
p.   cm.
Includes bibliographical references.
ISBN 0-253-32744-X (alk. paper). — ISBN 0-253-20585-9 (pbk. :
alk. paper)
1. Feminism—Philosophy.   I. Hibri, Azizah.
II. Simons, Margaret A.
HQ1206.H94   1990
305.42′01—dc20   89-46334
                                                           CIP

1 2 3 4 5 94 93 92 91 90

CONTENTS

Contents   vii

FOREWORD

The essays in this volume are from the first three issues of *Hypatia: A Journal of Feminist Philosophy*, which appeared annually as a special issue of *Women's Studies International Forum* from 1983 through 1985. Now that *Hypatia* is firmly established as an independent journal, essays from the first three issues are being published in book form to make them more readily accessible to the large audience that has developed for feminist philosophy.

Hypatia is rooted in the Society for Women in Philosophy, or SWIP, an organization of mainly faculty and student women that was formed in several regions in the United States and Canada in the early 1970s. As Kathryn Morgan of Canadian SWIP writes, "the formation of SWIP and the development of *Hypatia* were parts of a movement of women in philosophy from silence into feminist speech and . . . from a status of philosophical marginality to a place of public legitimacy that was of our *own* creation, where not only the topics but also the methodology . . . served feminist goals of political and intellectual empowerment of women and not the death-oriented adversarial models of the patriarchal paradigms."*

Almost as soon as SWIP was formed, members began to discuss the idea of a journal. Jacqueline M. Thomason, then a member of Eastern SWIP, recalls:

> I particularly remember a SWIP meeting at my house in the spring of 1972. . . . We talked about the journal, what it meant, what we wanted from it. Not an academic journal, but something living and breathing, a place to create and develop ideas. A place to try things out and not have them forever cast in stone. A place to be wrong with impunity and to learn from it. Where being first and being right were less important than learning something new. Where the process was more important than the product. We joked (but with a lot of seriousness) about calling it *The Journal of Half-Baked Ideas*.

The journal was discussed at SWIP meetings in the United States and Canada for several years. By mail, by telephone, and in person women worked through ideas about how decisions should be made for the journal and what its content should be. One focus of concern was the name. Linda Lopez McAlister writes: "My earliest recollection of a full-blown discussion of a journal is at the second Eastern SWIP meeting held at Barnard in, I believe, Spring 1973. . . . It was in a sunny fourth-floor room called the James Room, late one after-noon. . . . That's where the idea of calling the journal *Hypatia* first surfaced; I think that the actual suggestion came from Sue Larson." Although many of the Board members were immediately committed to naming the journal after the fourth-century Alexandrian woman philosopher and mathematician Hy-

---

*All quotations in this foreword are from correspondence in the files of Joyce Trebilcot.

patia, others suggested alternative names, for example, *Conceivings*. It was not until 1980 that the name *Hypatia* was finally agreed upon.

The first formal steps toward publication of the journal were taken by Jackie Thomason and Ann Garry, then both members of Pacific SWIP, when they issued a call for volunteers for the Editorial Board in 1977. Ann recalls: "Jackie and I picked the Board from the *vitae* that were sent to us. We spread the *vitae* on the floor by geography, and then sought balance also in terms of feminist and philosophical interests, lesbianism and heterosexuality, and so on." That original Editorial Board consisted of Sandra Bartky, Ann Garry, Candace Groudine, Sandra Harding, Sarah Lucia Hoagland, Alison Jaggar, Helen Longino, Linda Lopez McAlister, Kathryn Morgan, Janice Moulton, Connie Price, Jacqueline M. Thomason, Joyce Trebilcot, and Jane Upin.

The Board members began working on the various tasks involved in getting the journal started. Sarah Lucia Hoagland coordinated the development of policy, writing to the other Board members with questions and suggestions about the form, content, and politics of *Hypatia*; Sandra Harding worked on budget and funding; Janice Moulton investigated legal issues; Ann Garry and Jackie Thomason undertook the difficult task of getting a publisher interested in a new journal in feminist philosophy, a field that many thought merely a fad; Sandra Bartky and Joyce Trebilcot arranged a weekend meeting in Chicago for the Board but, primarily because most Board members received no financial or other support for work on a feminist philosophy journal from their academic departments (in many cases, quite the opposite), the meeting was not held. The women on the Board continued, however, with the planning for the journal.

In 1978 it came to the attention of some of the Board members that Azizah al-Hibri, a skilled philosopher and dedicated organizer of Southwestern SWIP, might be able to arrange for publication of *Hypatia* through her contacts in publishing. As Board members discussed this possibility with Azizah, it became clear that she had the resources and commitment needed to guide the journal into print. Accordingly, at a Board meeting in Denver in April 1979 (held in conjunction with a meeting of the American Philosophical Association), it was decided that Azizah would be invited to be the first editor of *Hypatia*.

Azizah's acceptance of this invitation meant that *Hypatia* would finally become a reality. By fall 1982 she had made arrangements with Pergamon Press for publication and was setting up an office for the journal at the University of Pennsylvania. In the meantime, however, Azizah had decided to supplement her Ph.D. in philosophy with a law degree, so she was in the unusual and difficult position of starting the journal while also a law student. Despite this double demand on her energies, Azizah did much of the organizing and decision making required for a new publication and produced three fine issues of *Hypatia*. Her dedicated efforts, along with those of the students who worked with her, were essential to the realization of the SWIP dream of a feminist philosophy journal. Indeed, the work of all the founders turned out to be worthwhile, for *Hypatia* is now a flourishing contributor to the well-being of women.

JOYCE TREBILCOT

PREFACE BY FOUNDING EDITOR

Only a decade ago the possibility of bringing *Hypatia* into being was becoming increasingly remote. The market for new journals had soured, and publishers decidedly viewed the launching of a feminist journal as a risk. But some of us feminists simply did not get the message. Pooling our resources and energies, we were able to devise an innovative approach to publishing *Hypatia*. The centerpiece of this approach was a "piggyback" publishing arrangement worked out with Dale Spender, editor of *Women's Studies International Forum* (*WSIF*). Under this approach, Pergamon Press would absorb *Hypatia*'s publishing and advertising costs. In return *Hypatia* would appear, first annually and later more frequently if so desired, as a special issue of *WSIF*.

The arrangement, which was viewed by all concerned as temporary, provided *Hypatia*'s Editorial Board with a unique opportunity to prove to future publishers that it was capable of producing a scholarly feminist journal with a sizable audience and a market niche. In negotiating this novel arrangement, I had the firm conviction that once given the opportunity, *Hypatia* would rise to the challenge and readily attract publishers' attention. This, in fact, is what transpired.

Producing the first few issues, however, required additional creativity. The journal had no budget, no staff and no headquarters. Earlier, I had not concerned myself with this aspect of the problem, since I expected the university I was teaching at to provide me with at least some of these items. But my agreement with Pergamon Press was reached just as I was heading to law school at the University of Pennsylvania. Hence I turned to that university's Department of Philosophy and Women's Studies Program. Their combined efforts provided *Hypatia* with a home, an operating budget, a work-study student and many graduate and undergraduate student volunteers. Of these, Donna Catudal edited the first issue and Ruth Schwartz the second.

Nothing came easy, despite the nationwide surge of support. We were but a handful of committed women, mostly novices, working against all odds to bring to life SWIP's decade-old dream. The pressure at times was unbearable, the work too demanding. There were tears, but there was also laughter. Then the *Hypatia* staff evolved into the *Hypatia* family, and the office metamorphosed into a home. As the first issue was completed there was joy, pride and relief. The issue was well received, but the *Hypatia* family did not await the market response. Preparations for the second issue began even before the first issue was out, for we had faith that if we did our best, *Hypatia* would succeed. By the third issue, the journal was achieving broad academic recognition and was well on its way to prosperity and independence.

Our modest resources were being outstripped by the new demands of a growing *Hypatia*. Concurrently, various parties with greater resources were contacting us to inform us of their readiness to house, edit and finance the

journal. The *Hypatia* family decided that it was time to let *Hypatia* go. In consultation with us, the Board of Associate Editors of *Hypatia* chose *Hypatia*'s second editor and second home. As *Hypatia*'s files were being packed and mailed, sadness was mixed with the joy of achievement and with satisfaction. The new editor, Margaret A. Simons, was someone who had worked closely with us during the difficult early days. We had asked her to edit our special issue on Simone de Beauvoir. *Hypatia*, we felt, would be very much loved in her new home—and, at last, independent.

With this publication of selections from the first three issues of *Hypatia*, I would like to thank all those who helped bring *Hypatia* into being. Among them are Elizabeth Flower (Department of Philosophy) and Joan Shapiro (Women's Studies Program); both are faculty members at the University of Pennsylvania who supported our cause, carried it to their colleagues and translated the support into office space and a budget. I would like also to thank Dale Spender, who sold Pergamon Press on the "piggyback" arrangement, and Phyllis Hall (Pergamon Press), who made the transition to *Hypatia*'s second publisher and this book possible. Also, I would like to thank members of SWIP and the original Editorial Board, who gave us our national grass roots and reservoir of energy. But most of all, I would like to thank the students of the University of Pennsylvania—Donna Serniak-Catudal, Ruth M. Schwartz, Melissa Marmalstein, Susan Feathers, Pat Carroll, Ralph Murray, Sylvia Hernandez, Lori Klein, Sally Fowler and Ann Dibble—for their selfless commitment and the numerous hours they expended making a dream come true.

Azizah Y. al-Hibri

Part I

Feminist Philosophy
Analysis and Recovery

Introduction
Donna Serniak

These selections from the inaugural issue of *Hypatia* offer a rich array of examples of feminist philosophy. Though the examples do not designate rigid boundaries for a definition of feminist philosophy, they do suggest a characterization of the personality of feminist philosophy. Where traditional philosophy seems enamored of the scientific stance of the detached observer, feminist philosophy seems almost moralistic in its quest for truth. The analyses of epistemological and metaphysical endeavors, as well as those of ethical inquiries, are circumscribed by social and political considerations. Because all philosophical criticism takes on a decidedly moral tone in the hands of feminist thinkers, feminist philosophy struggles with the demand for fundamental social change. Moreover, feminist philosophy must itself be held accountable to its criticism, even though its own history and position may make it difficult to do so.

This predicament of feminist philosophy is never far from the surface in *Hypatia*. It situates feminist philosophy in a somewhat awkward context, a context of theoretical resistance. Even as the essays in this part employ the methods of analysis, they seek to undermine the ideology associated with such methods. Thus *Hypatia*'s overall gestalt is one of intellectual tension, a tension rich with both understanding and suggestions for change. While the methodology and style of most of these essays connote epistemological authority, the conclusions drawn and ideas proposed are far from comforting. Most end with provisions and qualifications, difficulties and problems.

María C. Lugones and Elizabeth V. Spelman's essay is exemplary in this regard. Having identified friendship as the only possible context in which voices of women of color might be heard, they end by warning against the use of

friendship for the sake of constructing theories. Taken seriously, such a warning creates a problem for any antiracist account that is not already independently grounded in and motivated by genuine interracial friendship. Lugones and Spelman argue that feminist theory is seriously implicated in this regard, since it has presumed both that discrimination and oppression are intolerable on moral grounds and that (problematically) the concerns and perspectives of white middle-class feminist theorists adequately represent everyone else's. Their criticism hits hard against feminist theory, since the objectives of theory cannot themselves sustain friends through the necessary pain, sadness and shame brought by interracial friendships between white women and women of color.

The customary detachment and cool light of Reason traditionally associated with the philosophical method is challenged by the passion and political commitment in Terry R. Winant's essay. Winant undertakes the feminist critique of patriarchy in a nonacademic context, the ordinary language of advertising. Her analysis focuses on the controversial media advertisement for *Sidney Sheldon's Bloodline*. Winant uses this ad to demonstrate how our acculturation as women undermines the very possibility of feminist criticism—in this instance, of the juxtaposition of women, sexiness and violence. Central to her analysis is the pragmatic conception of discourse as productive and goal directed. Winant examines how the ad works—how it gets us to want to see the film—by suggesting that the ad functions like the grammatical object of a statement in the passive voice. In this analysis the subject—the viewer of the ad—is invisible. Since (1) the object is ambivalent, somewhere between a woman in ecstasy and a woman in pain, and (2) in our culture men are the subjects producing such states in women, the viewer is forced to take the male point of view: sex as violent and violence as sexy.

Jo-Ann Pilardi traces twentieth-century international politics back through Freud to Hegel's conception of the individual. She suggests that the conflict and inevitable hostility that is definitive of the Hegelian self is psychologized by Freud's dualistic characterizations of life and death. Employing Nancy Chodorow's object-relations theory, Pilardi diagnoses a gender bias in our international relations due to the partiality and incompleteness of what was for Hegel ontology, for Freud human nature. She then recommends the values left out of their accounts: the connectedness and caring that are fostered in the development of female identity as the basis for international relations.

Psychoanalytic theory also underlies Christine Di Stefano's political analysis. Di Stefano argues that both the substantive content and the methodological style of Hobbes's *Leviathan* gain in clarity and intelligibility when understood against the background of object-relations theory. Di Stefano unpacks Hobbes's metaphor of men "sprung out of the earth . . . like mushrooms" in terms of a psychoanalytic denial of the mother. Hobbes's conception of civil society as a delicate contractual balance between competing egoists becomes an inevitable outcome of the defensiveness definitive of male children toward their mothers. Di Stefano concludes her reading of Hobbes by placing *Leviathan* within the epic tradition, the heroic nature of which serves men to overcome their vulnerability in relation to their mothers.

Feminist work in the history of philosophy is not, however, wholesale rejection and criticism. For example, Janet Farrell Smith's essay defends Plato's discussion of women guardians in the *Republic*. She suggests that hindsight has led us to criticize Plato's views on women according to contemporary feminist issues, the end result of which is an ahistorical reading of Plato's thought. Conceding that Plato does objectify women, Farrell Smith commends him for his awareness of the social composition of natures by showing that he realized there is a greater difference between individuals of the same gender than between individuals of different genders. Thus she warns against too hasty a criticism of Plato's recommendation of the same educational opportunities for men and women.

Nancy Tuana also defends a view frequently attacked by feminists, the distinction between the concepts of nature and nurture. She proposes a vindication of the nature/nurture distinction and explains its apparent shortcomings in terms of the ideologies of mechanism and determinism. Updating what is essentially a seventeenth-century conception of matter with a twentieth-century conception of energy, Tuana outlines what she calls a process view of the nature/nurture distinction. This process view promises to avoid realist assumptions about the fixedness of nature. Tuana further contends that such a reconstruction of the distinction is necessary for feminist theory because previous criticism has only succeeded in further legitimating the conceptual dichotomy of nature and nurture. She maintains that external criticism, criticism of the very conditions under which the nature/nurture distinction is conceptualized, is found to be less effective than a recovery of that distinction within a feminist conception of reality.

Thus, given social and historial change and the attendant availability of a new conception of scientific reality, the possibility of a viable nature/nurture distinction emerges. Tuana's proposal illustrates what I earlier identified as a personality trait of feminist philosophy: its socio-political attentiveness. In *Hypatia*'s hands, feminist philosophy insists on serious consideration of social realities and the way they influence the production of knowledge.

ON THE WAR PATH
AND BEYOND

HEGEL, FREUD AND FEMINIST THEORY

Jo-Ann Pilardi

'But the state is an individual, and individuality essentially implies negation.
Hence even if a number of states make themselves into a family, the group as
an individual must engender an opposite and create an enemy.' (Hegel, 1967:
295)

'If willingness to engage in war is an effect of the destructive instinct, the most
obvious plan will be to bring Eros, its antagonist, into play against it. . . .'
(Freud, 1963: 144–146)

Feminist theory has moved beyond the critiquing of existing patriarchal thought
and is now proposing new questions. This paper proposes new questions about
wars between nations, by searching for the mechanisms of the patriarchal mind,
a mind which engenders states and conceptions of states which in turn engender
war, or make it almost inevitable. In searching for the mechanisms of the
patriarchal mind, a comparison of Hegel and Freud is fruitful, since each of
these thinkers develops an analysis of the human mind which stresses its definitive hostility. From this starting point, it becomes easy for them to provide
a justification for the existence of social-political hostility, and such justifications
become, in their turn, renewals of certain patriarchal assumptions.

My method will be, first, to provide a critical rereading of Hegel and Freud
on war, and then to incorporate ideas from feminist thinkers in regard to other
subjects into this investigation of war; from this incorporation I draw new feminist inferences. The feminist theories and principles to which I refer here are
those which describe the differences between the development of female and
male gender identity and those which make connections between male ego
development and sexual violence.

Specifically, this paper will show first how one thinker, Hegel, conceptualized
the state in a way that *necessarily* connects the individuality of the state to

For generously helping me rethink and revise this paper from its original form, I want to thank:
Sarah Begus, Sandra Harding, Nancy Hartsock, Nancy Hirschmann, George Armstrong Kelly,
Karen Maschke, and the editors of *Hypatia*. Thanks too to Rita Mowery.

opposition, a definition through negation, a path that leads him to insist on the necessity of international violence—war. Then it will turn to Freud who asserted that war would be inevitable as long as the destructive or death instinct were not controlled by the erotic or life instinct. Freud is an instructive counterexample to Hegel, since though he posited a dualism within the psyche (an opposition of destructive and erotic), the opposition was a parallel one and not a dialectical one. Thus though he believed that an aggressive instinct would always be present in human beings, he also believed that it could be checked by its counter-force: the erotic, the activity of binding. This thought is echoed in current feminist work which attempts to draw the outlines of female experience, like Mary O'Brien's *The Politics of Reproduction* (1981), Carol Gilligan's *In a Different Voice* (1982), or even the earlier *Toward a New Psychology of Women* by Jean Baker Miller (1976). So too, Nancy Chodorow's work (1978) has shown that while the path of gender identity for males is one of a separation from the original love object, the mother, that of girls is one of more-or-less continual relations. In addition, Jessica Benjamin (1980) has argued that the male path of identity through differentiation is what leads to violence, in particular the erotic violence of men against women.

In works such as these, important pieces of an account of patriarchy are beginning to fall into place; while we see a picture emerging of girl-woman as an affiliating, relating, caring, binding being, we also know that she is only one half of the picture of a patriarchal universe which has demanded highly structured gender roles, and which has promoted a metaphysics and psychology of separation, of negative/hostile opposition, for the male half. The achievement of masculinity, burdened as it is with defining boundaries in order to define the self, is played out repeatedly on the international level. The present grisly reality, the stockpiling of nuclear weapons—international relations as the science of one-up-man-ship—is the logical but irrational outcome of the patriarchal mind. But we are in advance of our paper. We need to look in some detail at the war path created by Hegel, and the different version proposed by Freud; then we need to move beyond it with the help of feminist thought.[1]

HEGEL ON WAR

In his *Philosophy of Right*, Hegel tied the issue of international war to his conceptualization of the state and the related notion of sovereignty.[2] He con-

---

[1] This paper focuses on international conflicts, not internal ones. If anything, it is an argument against the existence of standing armies. It is not meant to be an argument in favor of pacifism nor against national liberation movements. On the other hand, I no longer reject the former outright nor support the latter without regarding methods. A just cause, a just war, should be undertaken with attention paid to the use of humane tactics so that the liberators not become indistinguishable from the oppressors.

[2] In eighteenth century Germany, the term 'state' did not refer to a specific political organization, but it had begun to be used to name a web of executive, bureaucratic, military and legal functions. Cf. Kelly (1978: 94).

ceived of the state 'philosophically', which for him meant as a unified whole, and specifically, as an individual. The state derives its sovereignty from its unity as a single self (Hegel, 1967: 179–180).[3] Hegel underscores this individuality by claiming that it can be realized only through an actual person, i.e. a monarch, whose signature reveals reason in actuality (*ibid.*: 289).

The state's interest in other nations is in fact a result of its individuality and, in turn, its individuality is realized in the sphere of international relations: 'A state is as little an actual individual without relations to other states . . . as an individual is actually a person without *rapport* with other persons . . . ' (*ibid.*: 212). But as we will see, Hegel's *rapport* is negatively conceived as opposition. Maintaining its 'substantive individuality', i.e. its independence and sovereignty, will require negation, since all individuality is based on negativity in the Hegelian schema. And though the sovereignty of a state is the basis for its relations to other states, it is this very sovereignty which gives no legitimate basis to the *relations* between states. International treaties and international law only provide guidelines for the coexistence of states, guidelines which have no real legitimacy and are binding only by the fact of their acceptance by all the states.[4] Thus international relations take place on a see-saw where relations continually alternate with the severing of relations in 'a maelstrom of external contingency and the inner particularity of passions, private interests and selfish ends, abilities and virtues, vices, force, and wrong' (*ibid.*: 215). And with the severance of relations often comes war.

Thus the state as conceived by Hegel engenders problems. Dependent upon other states for the full definition of its sovereignty, the Hegelian state nevertheless requires for this definition of sovereignty a separation from other states, a definition which proves its difference from, rather than its similarity with, the others. This negative separation is what makes war possible, even likely, and perhaps inevitable in the Hegelian schema. The Hegelian state arises from (and in fact demands) negativity, so that it most fully realizes itself in regard to other nations through war. Averini has said it well (Averini, 1972), paraphrasing Hegel: 'War is the power of negativity'. Because it is fundamentally conceived out of a notion of identity as negative opposition, the Hegelian state is egging for a fight.

War performs a dual work: it works upon the state itself, as well as upon its neighbors. The sacrifice of one's life on behalf of the achievement of this individuality becomes the tie which binds the members of the state. Thus war does its work through this sacrificial binding, to unify the whole, to create a 'one from many'. This leads Hegel (*ibid.*: 210) to maintain that war is healthy

---

[3] This notion of sovereignty as individuality, as single-selfness, is not unique to Hegel. For example, it is reminiscent of Rousseau's notion in *The Social Contract* that 'the sovereign' is an 'artificial' and 'public person', the 'body politic', which has 'members', an 'ego', a 'will', and a 'life'. Cf. Rousseau (1968: 61–62).

[4] One could argue that international diplomacy operates on such a Hegelian notion of sovereignty as negative identity, as pointed out to me by Sandra Harding. In his article on Sovereignty in the *Encyclopedia of Philosophy*, Stanley Benn points out that article two of the United Nations Charter states that the organization is based on the sovereign equality of all its members (1967: VII 504).

for the state for a variety of reasons, the most striking being that there are benefits provided to a society by a good 'cleansing' from war, since peace is a state of stagnation; 'just as the blowing of the winds preserves the sea from the foulness which would be the result of a prolonged calm, so also corruption in nations would be the product of prolonged, let alone "perpetual", peace', he says, in a biting reference to Kant's essay, 'Perpetual Peace'. Elsewhere Hegel (*ibid.*: 295–296) repeats the claims of the stagnation which peace represents, so that the reader is once again presented with the notion that a peaceful world would be an ethical cesspool, cultivating the pesky mosquitoes of assorted socio-political horrors, needing the cleansing winds, the purgative, the bloodletting of war. Wars will occur when necessary, he concluded, for insofar as they are individuals, states have wills, and when those wills cannot agree, when there is a collision of wills, which there will be, war may be the outcome.[5]

The analysis of consciousness in Hegel's earlier *Phenomenology of Spirit* (Hegel, 1977) provides a foundation for the later discussion of the state and war. That analysis is provided in the famous master—slave passage which expresses Hegelian notions of the achievement of consciousness and self-con-sciousness, connecting it to the negative definition of the individual, in a life and death struggle of two consciousnesses which shows the dialectical inter-relation of the two, and ending with: 'one individual is confronted by another individual . . . each seeks the death of the other . . . (and this) involves the staking of its own life' (*ibid.*: 111–114).[6] This Hegelian dialectic of self-identity through a struggle for domination, even destruction, of an other has been used in a variety of places: Marx used it to describe the class struggle; Bataille found it useful to understand erotic violence; Beauvoir used it to describe the unusual structure of relationships which exist between the sexes, unusual because the struggle of self-other never became reciprocal, so that women were, suppos-edly, forever Other. Insofar as it is essential to the Hegelian system to claim negation to be the machinery of individuality, the state—as is true of any individual—always needs to push against its borders, to find out who and what it is. We will see later that self-definition through negation of the original love object, the mother, has been shown to be the psychosocial process of separation necessary for the achievement of masculinity. Hegel's theory of the state and war itself can be read as a reflection of his phenomenology of mind and, I would

---

[5] Cf. footnote and remarks on Pitt in Hegel (1967: 295–296, 214).

[6] The complete passage reads: 'Self-consciousness exists in and for itself when, and by the fact that, it exists for another; . . . Self-consciousness is faced by another self-consciousness; it has come *out of itself.* This has a twofold significance: first, it has lost itself, for it finds itself as an *other* being; secondly, in doing so it has superseded the other, for it does not see the other as an essential being, but in the other sees its own self . . . it is an individual. What is "other" for it is an unessential, negatively characterized object. But the "other" is also a self-consciousness; one in-dividual is confronted by another individual . . . each seeks the death of the other . . . (and this) involves the staking of its own life.' (Hegel, 1977: 111–114). This work was originally published in 1807). As George A. Kelly has pointed out to me, Hegel would not allow the juxtaposition between this lower level of self-consciousness on which the master-slave dialectic takes place, and the higher one of objective spirit, Right, where the realization of spirit as the state takes place. Cf. section 57, *Philosophy of Right*. With some trepidation, I nevertheless make the juxtaposition.

contend, represents an elaborate version of that psychosocial process, a meta-physics of separation to suit a psychology of separation. Accompanied by the feminist theories of gender development to be discussed later in this paper, it becomes increasingly difficult to overlook, in the thought of philosophers like Hegel, certain of the themes of male psychosocial development, raised to the standpoint of absolute truth.

FREUD ON WAR

Turning to Freud's work now, I will be viewing him not as a scientist who had discovered 'objective' truth, but as a speculative thinker, as Hegel was. Freud's dualistic theory of the life and death drives, or the erotic and destructive (aggressive) instincts, as he called them at another point in his career, offers a path by which to pursue those mechanisms that engender war. Reading Freud, however, is never to follow a simple path.[7] Freud asserted the existence of an aggressive instinct from 1905 at least, in the *Three Essays on the Theory of Sexuality* where he discussed sadism and masochism, but he specifically pre-sented his notion of the death drive, which he named 'Thanatos' in *Beyond the Pleasure Principle*, written in 1920 (Freud, 1961). In this work, he claimed that the pleasure principle is always accompanied by an equally powerful death drive which is as basic to the individual psyche and the race as the pleasure principle. In *Civilization and Its Discontents*, 1930 (Freud, 1961: 59), he made detailed remarks on the existence of an aggressive or destructive drive as a hindrance to the unification of humanity, and claimed that, *while society was structured into the family (ibid.: 79)*, this instinct would arise from the guilt fostered by the Oedipus complex.[8] Earlier, in *Totem and Taboo* (Freud, 1950), published in 1913, he had detailed a phylogenetic explanation of this via the 'story' of the parricide of the primal father by the sons. Freud needed the

[7] For an excellent new reading of Freud, see Weber (1982). I am indebted to Samuel Weber's insightful courses on Freud at Johns Hopkins University.

[8] Freud (1961). (Originally published in 1930.) The history of Freud's use of dualisms is complex and involves an original dualism, in the pleasure principle and the reality principle formation, which was eventually superseded in *Beyond the Pleasure Principle* by another dualism, the life and death drives, which he names mythologically as Eros and Thanatos. In his first set of forces, sexuality bears out the pleasure principle of free energy, unbounded, while the reality principle is the seat of a binding/bonding/bounding activity. Later, after *Beyond the Pleasure Principle*, sexuality is part of the erotic or life instinct, thus it is what binds, what forms unities, and the death instinct is what destroys unities, first within the organism itself, trying to bring its own life to a halt, and also within the larger social arena. Freud held to this later notion until his death, though it has not been greatly accepted by the psychoanalytic community. So sexuality, at first seen as 'free' energy, later came to be conceived as part of the erotic drive whose goals were self-preservation and binding or forming unities. In Laplanche and Pontalis (1973), see entries for: Aggressive Instinct, Destructive Instinct, Death Instincts, Eros, Libido, Life Instincts, Pleasure Principle, Reality Principle, Sexuality—to understand the interplay of these notions in Freud's writings. Also, note: the translation of *Trieb* as 'instinct' is controversial; the English 'drive' is more appropriate in most instances, and I usually use that. See S. Weber's book, cited in footnote [7], for discussion of such terms in the English edition of Freud.

Oedipus complex to explain male hostility toward the father, due to the son's love of the mother which must be relinquished. A successful Oedipus complex resolution would require the relinquishment of the mother, the original love object, since she was the father's love object.

I have chosen to use Freud's essay, 'Why War?,' (Freud, 1963), a late piece in which he popularly summarized his earlier notions of the aggressive instinct, which he ultimately transformed into the death drive. In this essay Freud claimed that wars are the result of a drive for hatred and destruction, one of the pair of drives for life and death (*ibid.*: 141):

> 'According to our hypothesis human instincts are of only two kinds: those which seek to preserve and unite—which we call "erotic", exactly in the sense in which Plato uses the word in his *Symposium*, or "sexual", with a deliberate extension of the popular conception of "sexuality"—and those which seek to destroy and kill and which we class together as the aggressive or destructive instinct'.

Freud maintained that the death drive, as lived out in the social realm, is responsible for the human race's continual capacity for war. It becomes the 'destructive instinct' when it is directed outwards, toward objects, rather than turning inward onto the individual, which is its original 'in-tention'. Freud (*ibid.*: 141–144) is forced to maintain that external destruction, e.g. war, assures the continuance of individual psychic health; internal, psychic war is avoided by the creation of external, inter-national war. Hence there will always be an internal psychic reason for war, in the makeup of human beings, regardless of how many external socio-political reasons there may or may not be.[9] Though Freud does not make a gender distinction on this point to stipulate that men are more likely than women to externalize the destructive instinct through war, his thinking in *Totem and Taboo* and *Group Psychology and the Analysis of the Ego* suggests this. These works, in turn, had been founded on his theory of the Oedipus complex as first developed in 'Analysis of a phobia in a five-year-old boy', 1909 (Freud, 1963).

In the Freudian Schema, this hostility can be counteracted and neutralized by the binding process of Eros, whereas in the Hegelian schema, since self definition required opposition and opposition required dialectical negation from the other, enmity was a necessity, on the level of consciousness and war a necessity in the development of objective spirit (*Geist*). Though the formation of an international body like the League of Nations (for which Freud wrote the essay, 'Why War?') might be a 'binding', the effectiveness of such a binding would really require *prior* relinquishing of notions of sovereignty by the states. The formations of an international body and the necessary voluntary surrender by each nation of its sovereignty would be an 'erotic' binding: 'If willingness

---

[9] Yet Freud's topography of the mind, of ego, id, and super-ego, which this paper cannot develop, belies this notion of possible psychic peace. Eros may bind us to others, but our psyche, always the scene of conflict, is continually bound and unbound, stablized and destabilized. See S. Weber's book in footnote [7].

to engage in war is an effect of the destructive instinct, the most obvious plan will be to bring Eros, its antagonist, into play against it (*ibid.*: 144). Never to be overcome, Thanatos can at least be diverted away from war by Eros.

The work of Eros, the life instincts, is twofold. First, it creates ties, either in specifically sexual or non-specifically sexual ways, since, Freud claimed, any effort to encourage *emotional* ties between human beings would perform an anti-war work as well. These emotional ties could be similar in quality to those toward a loved object, or they could be ties created through identification with others: 'Whatever leads men to share important interests produces this community of feeling, these identifications. And the structure of human society is to a large extent based on them' (*ibid.*: 144). Hence, sharing, tie-ing, binding, identifying with, in a word, attachment, are all aspects of Eros; attachment is the law of Eros, either individually or communally realized attachment. (We will see later that attachment is also the quality of mother-daughter relationships, as Chodorow describes them, whereas separation is the distinctive quality of the male psychosocial development of gender. When Freud describes Eros, it sounds like the history of female maturation.)

Secondly, Freud (*ibid.*: 146) maintained that Eros's work is literal self-preservation.[10] The organism's instinct to preserve itself, the race's instinct to preserve itself, the use of Eros against Thanatos, is a 'natural' tendency; pacifism is a part of this natural tendency toward self-preservation, carried out on the level of the species, rather than on the level of the individual organism.

But Thanatos is as natural a tendency as Eros, so that a death drive, the opposite of a life drive, is equally present. In its outward turning, Thanatos seeks its victims outside the psyche, on society's battlefields, domestic and international. Engaged in permanent conflict due to the co-existence of life and death drives, the psyche is condemned to a battle, as is the human race.[11]

But the erotic building of an international organization of nations will be no guarantee of peace, since the existence of Thanatos is not the only force working against it. In the Freudian schema, Eros itself can work as a counter-force to Eros. In *Group Psychology and the Analysis of the Ego*, published in 1921, Freud explained (Freud 1959) that the formation of groups was a result of an erotic bonding, libidinal, in other words, the focus of which was a leader or a cause—a father or *ersatz* father. Of the two great artificial groups Freud mentions, the Church and the Army, it is the Army which, we can add, is the arm of the state and a war machine, at a position intermediate between the state and war (*ibid.*: Ch. V). Though he had already posited the death drive a year earlier in *Beyond the Pleasure Principle*, and had acknowledged an aggressive instinct since at least 1905, Freud does not claim that the creation of this artificial group, the Army, arises from the death drive; rather, he claims, it is Eros which calls it into existence, since it is Eros which brings together (*ibid.*:

---

[10] Hence his remark, 'We are pacifists because we are obliged to be for organic reasons'. (Freud, 1963: 146).

[11] Here too we need to call upon the topography mentioned footnote [9] to do a thorough discussion of these issues.

24). He does maintain that the aggressive instinct exists, but with the formation of a group, the aggression is directed outward, away from those whom one loves and binds to, and toward the enemy (*ibid.*: 34–35). The question arises: does the existence of the erotically-formed Army react to an enemy—or create one? We recall that Hegel had claimed that war could bind the members of the state. Freud similarly insists that binding is an act of the erotic drive, which is the counter-force to the destructive drive; the Army is bound internally by its external enemy.

What Hegel and Freud were both burdened with, I contend, was a notion of identity which defines it as oppositional, and which was derived from the psychosocial development of male children, which requires, in a patriarchal society, separation from the original love-object, the mother, for, as Freud claimed in *Civilization and Its Discontents*, 'so long as the community assumes no other form than the family, the conflict is bound to express itself in the Oedipus complex', with its attendant hostility of male against male, and separation from the (m)other as a measure of self identity (Freud, 1961: 79–80). This is the family, assuredly, but the patriarchal family, and the patriarchal state. Thus, erotic binding to the original love object is confusedly accompanied by the need for separation from the loved object, in a psyche torn by internal strife in order to achieve its identity—which requires the achievement of gender identity as well as directly 'personal' identity. This Freudian notion of the psyche is patriarchal by genus, male by species.[12] The patriarchal family, and patriarchal society, with their inescapable foundation in an original love of the mother as the exclusive nurturer, brings with it a devaluation of women, and a love and hate of the intruder father. This, then, is the arena of dominance and violence against women, as well as the arena of hostile and paranoid groupings of men against men, on domestic, national and international levels.

THE THERAPEUTIC VALUE OF
FEMINIST THOUGHT

The relationship that has held between the sexes has been male-dominant.[13] In these patriarchal relations, sexuality itself will harbor domination—sometimes to the extent of psychological and physical violence, destruction or death. It is not surprising that Freud was haunted by the issue of the placement of sexuality within his basic dualism.[14] Beginning with his study of sadism and

---

[12] Juliet Mitchell's contention that Freud was analysing, not recommending, a patriarchal universe is correct, at least in this instance. Freud seems sometimes aware of this and sometimes forgetful of it. Cf. Mitchell (1975: xiii).

[13] As mentioned earlier, Beauvoir's *The Second Sex* begins with an 'Introduction' in which she uses Hegel's master-slave dialectic to found her analysis of western culture, a culture in which woman is Other, inessential, the 'slave' in a dialectical relationship wherein master and slave need each other, but wherein one is indisputable 'self', master. This otherness of woman is borne out in sexual relations, as it is throughout the culture.

[14] Here see remarks in footnote [8].

masochism he was on the track of an Eros which, at least as heterosexually constituted, demanded a domination of the other's subjectivity to achieve its own identity, of an Eros in which eroticism often required some form of domination, arising as it did from tremendous conflict between a self and an other, a master and a slave—a patriarchal Eros, which requires opposition within and toward the other to make its 'bind', much as Hegel's state required a negative opposition in order to achieve its identity: a masculine erotics.[15]

In 'The bonds of love: rational violence and erotic domination', Jessica Benjamin offers an analysis which connects the domination theme of Hegel's master-slave passage with the work of Bataille on erotic violence (Benjamin, 1980: 150–155). Through the use of Freud, as well as the work of feminist psychologists like Nancy Chodorow, Benjamin draws out the important beginnings of a theory of the sources of male domination and violence against women. Her thesis is centered on male identification/separation issues. She uses the Hegel of *Phenomenology of Spirit*; we can extend this to his *Philosophy of Right*, and issues of state sovereignty and war.

Benjamin reminds us that early psychoanalytic theory had maintained that a radical separation was necessary for the child to achieve self-identity. But Chodorow showed that these earlier psychoanalytic conceptions of identity were reflections of male experience, which stresses separation by a rejection of the mother: 'Thus male identity emphasizes difference from the nurturer over sameness and separation from the mother over individuation' (*ibid.*: 147). Differentiation plays a greater role in the character formations of males than it does in that of females. This emphasis on separation from the mother, the original love object, is magnified in certain theories of sexuality like Bataille's, which follow Hegel's analysis of the master-slave relation (*ibid.*: 154–155).

Benjamin uses Hegel/Bataille to suggest a new way to look at erotic domination; Hegel's master-slave dialectic clearly expresses the unhappy and ironic requirement of an interrelation, a dependence upon the other, in the attempt to achieve independence-self identity. But this can only be brought about by a confrontation with an other which is really a subject, a person in her or his own right (*ibid.*: 151). If the other to whom I relate is totally within my control, they are no longer 'there', for themselves, and they do not afford me the differentiation I need; my identity is not achieved because there is nothing against which to achieve it (a claim with which de Sade would be in agreement). In order to prove his own existence, the erotic master must dominate the other, and this must be the unwilling domination that physical violence expresses, in which the other, subject-to-become-object, is dragged, kicking and screaming, into domination. This is most often borne out heterosexually as the 'male-master', 'female-victim' system, within pornographic literature and materials (*ibid.*: 154). For Bataille, as for Hegel, since self-identity required the con-

---

[15] Freud had said that female sexuality was 'a dark continent' to him. But in many places, he forces a masculine erotics into an analysis of the sexuality of female patients and issues of femininity. Cf. his *Dora: An Analysis of a Case of Hysteria* as well as the essay, 'Femininity', in *New Introductory Lectures on Psychoanalysis*—and elsewhere.

frontational recognition of an other with the goal of domination, erotic violence
is as unsurprising as international violence. War becomes the international
living out of the erotics of patriarchy.

Benjamin's reliance on the work of Nancy Chodorow allowed her to make
an important connection between individuation and separation within the male
experience, and domination within sexuality. She speculates that it is the
thwarting of affiliation, the denial of physical and emotional ties, relationality,
which a rationality of erotic violence is constructed to satisfy—such as Bataille's.
Chodorow's book had argued that mothering is reproduced through socially
structured and induced psychosocial processes, whereby mothers reproduced
mothers, via the mother-daughter relationship, in a society in which woman-
as-mother is relegated to the domestic sphere, a devalued arena.

Importantly, by her use of an object relations psychoanalytic approach, Chodorow critiqued what she calls Freud's 'instinctual determinism'; though she
claims the drives of life and death are there, she says they do not determine
our behavior (Chodorow, 1978).[16] She questioned how family structure and
process affect unconscious psychic structures and processes, which led her to
claim that the positions in the Oedipal drama—mother, father, son—were acted
out according to a certain 'practice', not to any eternal psychic truth. The
practice is that of asymmetrical parenting, and an 'exclusive mother' and 'absent
father' pattern. Through this practice, the patriarchal family developed relationships which devalued women's work, fantasized the father as a role model
for the son, set up a system of gender development which required separation
by the male child from the mother, yet encouraged a continuing relation from
the female child to the mother—in order that mothering be reproduced. Chodorow spells out a different Oedipus complex for girls and boys, since the nature
of the attachment of boys to the mother is different than that of girls.[17] As a
result of the difference in movement from the preoedipal stage to the Oedipal,
and the difference in the Oedipus complex for boys and girls, the achievement
of masculinity involves the repression of affiliation in boys. Masculinity involves
the repression of the female, hence it is a psychological state which is negatively
achieved (*ibid.*: 181–182). We can add, if 'war is the power of negativity',
(Avineri, 1972: 198) so is masculinity. It is a quality to be 'won' by separating
from the female and engaging with other boys and men in puberty rites, sexual
rivalries—or by joining the Army.

Chodorow's argument has been borne out in Carol Gilligan's work, *In a
Different Voice*. Though at this point Gilligan's studies are more suggestive
than conclusive, they do strengthen the arguments and claims of Chodorow,
as to the differences in psychosocial development in individuals of masculinity
and femininity—i.e. that male development requires more individuation

---

[16] I have some disagreement with Chodorow's reading of Freud, for example, in straightforwardly
rendering him an 'instinctual determinist'.

[17] Freud spelled out a different Oedipus complex for girls; in his forced explanation, he posits
'penis envy'.

through boundary-making and repression of affiliation, and female development is more continuous with others, more relational.

When Gilligan turns to the development of morality in girls and boys, she finds that there is more importance given by girls to attachments. Her investigation turns into a critique of certain current psychological theories, in that they are based on the male model unself-consciously. Erikson, among others, had claimed that the development of maturity means a process of separation, one in which attachments are impediments to the development of maturity, i.e. maturity means separation instead of relation; girls and women fare badly on the male models of maturing (Gilligan, 1982: 11–12). As a graphic demonstration of her claim of psychosocial development on the male-separation, female-relation models, Gilligan discusses studies in which men and women were given the same pictures; men perceived danger in the pictures in connections; women perceived it in separations (*ibid.:* 42–43). Freud's remark in *Civilization and Its Discontents,* that our feeling of our self 'appears autonomous and unitary, marked off distinctly from everything else', becomes for Gilligan a perfect example of a masculine conception of the self (Freud, quoted in Gilligan, 1982: 46).

In addition to differences between girls and boys in conceptions of the self, there are differences in their conceptions of morality.[18] For women, morality involves responsibility to others; their moral dilemmas arise over conflicting responsibilities (Gilligan, 1982: Ch. 3, 5 and 6). Gilligan claims this represents the outline of a morality of responsibility and care, or relations, rather than separation. On the other hand, boys develop a morality of rights, in which issues of justice, equality, and fairness predominate. This requires a notion of people as isolatable, equal units, which co-exist but do not overlap—a metaphysics of separation, we might add. Gilligan's research shows the danger of describing women's experience or judging women's morality by male models.

The notions of a metaphysics of separation and a patriarchal eros that I have suggested here through a reading of Hegel and Freud overlap with the delineation by Benjamin, Chodorow and Gilligan of the psychosocial development of gender. Freud's contention, in *Totem and Taboo* and *Group Psychology and the Analysis of the Ego,* that male bondings—whether pre-historic primal herds of brothers or later groups like the Church and the Army—operate largely by exclusion and permit great cruelty to those who lie outside the borders of the group, adds another dimension to this picture, though Freud himself called less attention to 'male' and more attention to 'bonding' in these works than I now do.

In a patriarchal society, wars are also fought on the home front, through the male group's struggle against the enemy within its own borders, the Other, womankind. For Hegel, womankind was that force which strengthened the family as it weakened the larger whole, the community, and ultimately, the

---

[18] L. Kohlberg's structure of moral development, with its placement of women at mid-levels, is well known. Gilligan points out the bias in this (Gilligan, 1982: 18).

state. Freud's woman, the mother—also the erotic object possessed by the father—was the nucleus of that 'nucleus of the neuroses', the Oedipus complex. Rather than bringing Eros into play against Thanatos to end war, as Freud suggested, the twentieth century may be seeing the progressive movement of the patriarchal erotic toward death, in the practice of violence against women. (I am thinking of the great popularity of bondage themes in pornography, the actual commission of murder of some model-victims, in the making of 'snuff' movies, and the rise in popularity of Nazi themes within pornography, as well as more standard forms of erotic violence against women.) If so many men want to kill or harm their 'lovers', either in reality or fantasy, where will they ever find the strength and control to love their (global) enemies, or even let them live?

The conclusions I formulate from this material are: (1) Hegel's theory of the state and war is a rational rendering of male psychic needs for differentiation as a mode of achieving identity, i.e. a reflection of the fact that masculinity means separation from the primary other;[19] (2) we can maintain dialectical conceptions of relationships by focusing them not on opposition but on binding, i.e. we can replace a patriarchal erotics with an erotics of affiliation; (3) we should try to determine how to allow conflict with others without turning it into opposition, aggression and destruction.

Building on this knowledge, we can proceed to an important new question: how to conceptualize a feminist world, beyond a metaphysics of separation and beyond a patriarchal Eros.

> 'Last night I had the strangest dream
> I'd never dreamed before.
> I dreamed the world had all agreed
> to put an end to war. . . .
>
> And the people in the streets below
> were dancing round and round.
> While swords and guns and uniforms
> were scattered on the ground'.
> (McCurdy, 1960: 168–169)

REFERENCES

Averini, Schlomo. 1972. *Hegel's Theory of the Modern State*. Cambridge University Press, Cambridge.

---

[19] This question is really a repetition of Jessica Benjamin's questions on erotic rationality and violence and domination, but carried into the political arena.

Benjamin, Jessica. 1980. The bonds of love: rational violence and erotic domination. *Feminist Studies* **6** (1): 144–174.

Benn, Stanley. 1967. Sovereignty. *Encyclopedia of Philosophy* VII. MacMillan, New York.

Chodorow, Nancy. 1978. *The Reproduction of Mothering: Psychoanalysis and the Sociology of Gender*. University of California Press, Berkeley.

de Beauvoir, Simone. 1952. *The Second Sex*. (Parshley, H. M., trans.) Bantam Books.

Freud, Sigmund. 1909. Analysis of a phobia in a five-year-old boy. In *The Sexual Enlightenment of Children*, Rieff, Phillip, ed. Collier Books, New York (1963).

Freud, Sigmund. 1913. *Totem and Taboo*. (Strachey, James, trans.) W. W. Norton, New York (1950).

Freud, Sigmund. 1920. *Beyond the Pleasure Principle*. (Strachey, James, trans.) W. W. Norton, New York (1961).

Freud, Sigmund. 1921. *Group Psychology and the Analysis of the Ego*. (Strachey, James, trans.) W. W. Norton, New York (1959).

Freud, Sigmund. 1930. *Civilization and Its Discontents*. (Strachey, James, trans.) W. W. Norton, New York (1961).

Freud, Sigmund. 1932. Why war? In *Character and Culture*, Rieff, Philip (ed.) Collier Books, New York (1963).

Gilligan, Carol. 1982. *In a Different Voice: Psychological Theory and Women's Development*. Harvard University Press, Cambridge, Mass.

Hegel, G. W. F. 1807. *The Phenomenology of Spirit*. (Miller, A. V., trans.) Oxford University Press, Oxford (1977).

Hegel, G. W. F. 1821. *Hegel's PHILOSOPHY OF RIGHT*. (Knox, T. M., trans.) Oxford University Press, Oxford (1967).

Kelly, George Armstrong. 1978. *Hegel's Retreat from Eleusis*. Princeton University Press, Princeton.

Laplanche, J. and J.-B. Pontalis. 1973. *The Language of Psychoanalysis*. (Nicholson-Smith, Donald, trans.) W. W. Norton, New York.

McCurdy, Ed. 1960. Last night I had the strangest dream. In *The Weavers' Song Book*. Harper and Row, New York.

Miller, Jean Baker. 1976. *Toward a New Psychology of Women*. Beacon Press, Boston.

Mitchell, Juliet. 1975. *Psychoanalysis and Feminism*. Vintage Books, New York.

O'Brien, Mary. 1981. *The Politics of Reproduction*. Routledge and Kegan Paul, Boston.

Rousseau, Jean-Jaques. 1968. *The Social Contract*. (Cranston, Maurice, trans.) Penguin, Harmondsworth.

Weber, Samuel. 1982. *The Legend of Freud*. University of Minnesota Press, Minneapolis.

HAVE WE GOT
A THEORY FOR YOU!

FEMINIST THEORY,
CULTURAL IMPERIALISM
AND THE DEMAND FOR
'THE WOMAN'S VOICE'

María C. Lugones and Elizabeth V. Spelman

Prologue

(*In an Hispana voice*)

A veces quisiera mezclar en una voz el sonido canyenge, tristón y urbano del porteñismo que llevo adentro con la cadencia apacible, serrana y llena de corage de la hispana nuevo mejicana. Contrastar y unir

> el piolín y la cuerda
> el traé y el pepéname
> el camión y la troca
> la lluvia y el llanto

Pero este querer se me va cuando veo que he confundido la solidaridad con la falta de diferencia. La solidaridad requiere el reconocer, comprender, respetar y amar lo que nos lleva a llorar en distintas cadencias. El imperialismo cultural desea lo contrario, por eso necesitamos muchas voces. Porque una sola voz nos mata a las dos.

No quiero hablar por ti sino contigo. Pero si no aprendo tus modos y tu los mios la conversación es sólo aparente. Y la apariencia se levanta como una barrera sín sentido entre las dos. Sin sentido y sin sentimiento. Por eso no me debes dejar que te dicte tu ser y no me dictes el mio. Porque entonces ya no dialogamos. El diálogo entre nosotras requiere dos voces y no una.

Tal vez un día jugaremos juntas y nos hablaremos no en una lengua universal sino que vos me hablarás mi voz y yo la tuya.

Preface

This paper is the result of our dialogue, of our thinking together about differences among women and how these differences are silenced. (Think, for example, of all the silences there are connected with the fact that this paper is in English—for that is a borrowed tongue for one of us.) In the process of our talking and writing together, we saw that the differences between us did not permit our speaking in one voice. For example, when we agreed we expressed the thought differently; there were some things that both of us thought were true but could not express as true of each of us; sometimes we could not say 'we'; and sometimes one of us could not express the thought in the first person singular, and to express it in the third person would be to present an outsider's and not an insider's perspective. Thus the use of two voices is central both to the process of constructing this paper and to the substance of it. We are both the authors of this paper and not just sections of it but we write together without presupposing unity of expression or of experience. So when we speak in unison it means just that—there are two voices and not just one.

I. INTRODUCTION

(In the voice of a white/Anglo woman who has been teaching and writing about feminist theory)

Feminism is, among other things, a response to the fact that women either have been left out of, or included in demeaning and disfiguring ways in what has been an almost exclusively male account of the world. And so while part of what feminists want and demand for women is the right to move and to act in accordance with our own wills and not against them, another part is the desire and insistence that we give our *own* accounts of these movements and actions. For it matters to us what is said about us, who says it, and to whom it is said: having the opportunity to talk about one's life, to give an account of it, to interpret it, is integral to leading that life rather than being led through it; hence our distrust of the male monopoly over accounts of women's lives. To put the same point slightly differently, part of human life, human living, is talking about it, and we can be sure that being silenced in one's own account of one's life is a kind of amputation that signals oppression. Another reason for not divorcing life from the telling of it or talking about it is that as humans our experiences are deeply influenced by what is said about them, by ourselves or powerful (as opposed to significant) others. Indeed, the phenomenon of internalized oppression is only possible because this is so: one experiences her life in terms of the impoverished and degrading concepts others have found it convenient to use to describe her. We can't separate lives from the accounts given of them; the articulation of our experience is part of our experience.

    Sometimes feminists have made even stronger claims about the importance

of speaking about our own lives and the destructiveness of others presuming to speak about us or for us. First of all, the claim has been made that on the whole men's accounts of women's lives have been at best false, a function of ignorance; and at worst malicious lies, a function of a knowledgeable desire to exploit and oppress. Since it matters to us that falsehood and lies not be told about us, we demand, of those who have been responsible for those falsehoods and lies, or those who continue to transmit them, not just that we speak but that they learn to be able to hear us. It has also been claimed that talking about one's life, telling one's story, in the company of those doing the same (as in consciousness-raising sessions), is constitutive of feminist method.[1]

And so the demand that the woman's voice be heard and attended to has been made for a variety of reasons: not just so as to greatly increase the chances that true accounts of women's lives will be given, but also because the articulation of experience (in myriad ways) is among the hallmarks of a self-determining individual or community. There are not just epistemological, but moral and political reasons for demanding that the woman's voice be heard, after centuries of androcentric din.

But what more exactly is the feminist demand that the woman's voice be heard? There are several crucial notes to make about it. First of all, the demand grows out of a complaint, and in order to understand the scope and focus of the demand we have to look at the scope and focus of the complaint. The complaint does not specify *which* women have been silenced, and in one way this is appropriate to the conditions it is a complaint about: virtually no women have had a voice, whatever their race, class, ethnicity, religion, sexual alliance, whatever place and period in history they lived. And if it is as women that women have been silenced, then of course the demand must be that women as women have a voice. But in another way the complaint is very misleading, insofar as it suggests that it is women as women who have been silenced, and that whether a woman is rich or poor, Black, brown or white, etc. is irrelevant to what it means for her to be a woman. For the demand thus simply made ignores at least two related points: (1) it is only possible for a woman who does not feel highly vulnerable with respect to other parts of her identity, e.g. race, class, ethnicity, religion, sexual alliance, etc., to conceive of her voice simply or essentially as a 'woman's voice'; (2) just because not all women are equally vulnerable with respect to race, class, etc., some women's voices are more likely to be heard than others by those who have heretofore been giving—or silencing—the accounts of women's lives. For all these reasons, the women's voices most likely to come forth and the women's voices most likely to be heard are, in the US anyway, those of white, middle-class, heterosexual Christian (or anyway not self-identified non-Christian) women. Indeed, many Hispanas, Black women, Jewish women—to name a few groups—have felt it an invitation

[1] For a recent example, see Mackinnon (1982).

to silence rather than speech to be requested—if they are requested at all—
to speak about being 'women' (with the plain wrapper—as if there were one)
in distinction from speaking about being Hispana, Black, Jewish, working-class,
etc., women.

The demand that the 'woman's voice' be heard, and the search for the 'woman's voice' as central to feminist methodology, reflects nascent feminist theory.
It reflects nascent empirical theory insofar as it presupposes that the silencing
of women is systematic, shows up in regular, patterned ways, and that there
are discoverable causes of this widespread observable phenomenon; the demand
reflects nascent political theory insofar as it presupposes that the silencing of
women reveals a systematic pattern of power and authority; and it reflects nascent
moral theory insofar as it presupposes that the silencing is unjust and that there
are particular ways of remedying this injustice. Indeed, whatever else we know
feminism to include—e.g. concrete direct political action—theorizing is integral to it: theories about the nature of oppression, the causes of it, the relation
of the oppression of women to other forms of oppression. And certainly the
concept of the woman's voice is itself a theoretical concept, in the sense that
it presupposes a theory according to which our identities as human beings are
actually compound identities, a kind of fusion or confusion of our otherwise
separate identities as women or men, as Black or brown or white, etc. That is
no less a theoretical stance than Plato's division of the person into soul and
body or Aristotle's parcelling of the soul into various functions.

The demand that the 'woman's voice' be heard also invites some further
directions in the exploration of women's lives and discourages or excludes others. For reasons mentioned above, systematic, sustained reflection on being a
woman—the kind of contemplation that 'doing theory' requires—is most likely
to be done by women who vis-à-vis other women enjoy a certain amount of
political, social and economic privilege because of their skin color, class membership, ethnic identity. There is a relationship between the content of our
contemplation and the fact that we have the time to engage in it at some
length—otherwise we shall have to say that it is a mere accident of history that
white middle-class women in the United States have in the main developed
'feminist theory' (as opposed to 'Black feminist theory', 'Chicana feminist theory',
etc.) and that so much of the theory has failed to be relevant to the lives of
women who are not white or middle class. Feminist theory—of all kinds—is
to be based on, or anyway touch base with, the variety of real life stories women
provide about themselves. But in fact, because, among other things, of the
structural political and social and economic inequalities among women, the tail
has been wagging the dog: feminist theory has not for the most part arisen out
of a medley of women's voices; instead, the theory has arisen out of the voices,
the experiences, of a fairly small handful of women, and if other women's voices
do not sing in harmony with the theory, they aren't counted as women's voices—
rather, they are the voices of the woman as Hispana, Black, Jew, etc. There
is another sense in which the tail is wagging the dog, too: it is presumed to be

the case that those who do the theory know more about those who are theorized than vice versa: hence it ought to be the case that if it is white/Anglo women who write for and about all other women, then white/Anglo women must know more about all other women than other women know about them. But in fact just in order to survive, brown and Black women have to know a lot more about white/Anglo women—not through the sustained contemplation theory requires, but through the sharp observation stark exigency demands.

(*In an Hispana voice*)

I think it necessary to explain why in so many cases when women of color appear in front of white/Anglo women to talk about feminism and women of color, we mainly raise a complaint: the complaint of exclusion, of silencing, of being included in a universe we have not chosen. We usually raise the complaint with a certain amount of disguised or undisguised anger. I can only attempt to explain this phenomenon from a Hispanic viewpoint and a fairly narrow one at that: the viewpoint of an Argentinian woman who has lived in the US for 16 yr, who has attempted to come to terms with the devaluation of things Hispanic and Hispanic people in 'America' and who is most familiar with Hispano life in the Southwest of the US. I am quite unfamiliar with daily Hispano life in the urban centers, though not with some of the themes and some of the salient experiences of urban Hispano life.

When I say 'we',[2] I am referring to Hispanas. I am accustomed to use the 'we' in this way. I am also pained by the tenuousness of this 'we' given that I am not a native of the US. Through the years I have come to be recognized and I have come to recognize myself more and more firmly as part of this 'we'. I also have a profound yearning for this firmness since I am a displaced person and I am conscious of not being of and I am unwilling to make myself of—even if this were possible—the white/Anglo community.

When I say 'you' I mean not the non-Hispanic but the white/Anglo women that I address. 'We' and 'you' do not capture my relation to other non-white women. The complexity of that relation is not addressed here, but it is vivid to me as I write down my thoughts on the subject at hand.

I see two related reasons for our complaint–full discourse with white/Anglo women. Both of these reasons plague our world, they contaminate it through and through. It takes some hardening of oneself, some self-acceptance of our own anger to face them, for to face them is to decide that maybe we can change our situation in self-constructive ways and we know fully well that the possi-

---

[2] I must note that when I think this 'we', I think it in Spanish—and in Spanish this 'we' is gendered, 'nosotras'. I also use 'nosotros' lovingly and with ease and in it I include all members of 'La raza cosmica' (Spanish-speaking people of the Americas, la gente de colores: people of many colors). In the US, I use 'we' contextually with varying degrees of discomfort: 'we' in the house, 'we' in the department, 'we' in the classroom, 'we' in the meeting. The discomfort springs from the sense of community in the 'we' and the varying degrees of lack of community in the context in which the 'we' is used.

bilities are minimal. We know that we cannot rest from facing these reasons, that the tenderness towards others in us undermines our possibilities, that we have to fight our own niceness because it clouds our minds and hearts. Yet we know that a thoroughgoing hardening would dehumanize us. So, we have to walk through our days in a peculiarly fragile psychic state, one that we have to struggle to maintain, one that we do not often succeed in maintaining.

We and you do not talk the same language. When we talk to you we use your language: the language of your experience and of your theories. We try to use it to communicate our world of experience. But since your language and your theories are inadequate in expressing our experiences, we only succeed in communicating our experience of exclusion. We cannot talk to you in our language because you do not understand it. So the brute facts that we understand your language and that the place where most theorizing about women is taking place is your place, both combine to require that we either use your language and distort our experience not just in the speaking about it, but in the living of it, or that we remain silent. Complaining about exclusion is a way of remaining silent.

You are ill at ease in our world. You are ill at ease in our world in a very different way than we are ill at ease in yours. You are not of our world and again, you are not of our world in a very different way than we are not of yours. In the intimacy of a personal relationship we appear to you many times to be wholly there, to have broken through or to have dissipated the barriers that separate us because you are Anglo and we are raza. When we let go of the psychic state that I referred to above in the direction of sympathy, we appear to ourselves equally whole in your presence but our intimacy is thoroughly incomplete. When we are in your world many times you remake us in your own image, although sometimes you clearly and explicitly acknowledge that we are not wholly there in our being with you. When we are in your world we ourselves feel the discomfort of having our own being Hispanas disfigured or not understood. And yet, we have had to be in your world and learn its ways. We have to participate in it, make a living in it, live in it, be mistreated in it, be ignored in it, and rarely, be appreciated in it. In learning to do these things or in learning to suffer them or in learning to enjoy what is to be enjoyed or in learning to understand your conception of us, we have had to learn your culture and thus your language and self-conceptions. But there is nothing that necessitates that you understand our world: understand, that is, not as an observer understands things, but as a participant, as someone who has a stake in them understands them. So your being ill at ease in our world lacks the features of our being ill at ease in yours precisely because you can leave and you can always tell yourselves that you will be soon out of there and because the wholeness of your selves is never touched by us, we have no tendency to remake you in our image.

But you theorize about women and we are women, so you understand yourselves to be theorizing about us and we understand you to be theorizing about

us. Yet none of the feminist theories developed so far seem to me to help Hispanas in the articulation of our experience. We have a sense that in using them we are distorting our experiences. Most Hispanas cannot even understand the language used in these theories—and only in some cases the reason is that the Hispana cannot understand English. We do not recognize ourselves in these theories. They create in us a schizophrenic split between our concern for ourselves as women and ourselves as Hispanas, one that we do not feel otherwise. Thus they seem to us to force us to assimilate to some version of Anglo culture, however revised that version may be. They seem to ask that we leave our communities or that we become alienated so completely in them that we feel hollow. When we see that you feel alienated in your own communities, this confuses us because we think that maybe every feminist has to suffer this alienation. But we see that recognition of your alienation leads many of you to be empowered into the remaking of your culture, while we are paralyzed into a state of displacement with no place to go.

So I think that we need to think carefully about the relation between the articulation of our own experience, the interpretation of our own experience, and theory making by us and other non-Hispanic women about themselves and other 'women'.

The only motive that makes sense to me for your joining us in this investigation is the motive of friendship, out of friendship. A non-imperialist feminism requires that you make a real space for our articulating, interpreting, theorizing and reflecting about the connections among them—a real space must be a non-coerced space—and/or that you follow us into our world out of friendship. I see the 'out of friendship' as the only sensical motivation for this following because the task at hand for you is one of extraordinary difficulty. It requires that you be willing to devote a great part of your life to it and that you be willing to suffer alienation and self-disruption. Self-interest has been proposed as a possible motive for entering this task. But self-interest does not seem to me to be a realistic motive, since whatever the benefits you may accrue from such a journey, they cannot be concrete enough for you at this time and they may not be worth your while. I do not think that you have any obligation to understand us. You do have an obligation to abandon your imperialism, your universal claims, your reduction of us to your selves simply because they seriously harm us.

I think that the fact that we are so ill at ease with your theorizing in the ways indicated above does indicate that there is something wrong with these theories. But what is it that is wrong? Is it simply that the theories are flawed if meant to be universal but accurate so long as they are confined to your particular group(s)? Is it that the theories are not really flawed but need to be translated? Can they be translated? Is it something about the process of theorizing that is flawed? How do the two reasons for our complaint–full discourse affect the validity of your theories? Where do *we* begin? To what extent are our experience and its articulation affected by our being a colonized people, and thus by your culture, theories and conceptions? Should we theorize in community and thus

as part of community life and outside the academy and other intellectual circles? What is the point of making theory? Is theory making a good thing for us to do at this time? When are we making theory and when are we just articulating and/or interpreting our experiences?

II. SOME QUESTIONABLE ASSUMPTIONS ABOUT FEMINIST THEORIZING

(Unproblematically in María's & Vicky's voice)

Feminist theories aren't just about what happens to the female population in any given society or across all societies; they are about the meaning of those experiences in the lives of women. They are about beings who give their own accounts of what is happening to them or of what they are doing, who have culturally constructed ways of reflecting on their lives. But how can the theorizer get at the meaning of those experiences? What should the relation be between a woman's own account of her experiences and the theorizer's account of it?

Let us describe two different ways of arriving at an account of another woman's experience. It is one thing for both me and you to observe you and come up with our different accounts of what you are doing; it is quite another for me to observe myself and others much like me culturally and in other ways and to develop an account of myself and then use that account to give an account of you. In the first case you are the 'insider' and I am the 'outsider'. When the outsider makes clear that she is an outsider and that this is an outsider's account of your behavior, there is a touch of honesty about what she is doing. Most of the time the 'interpretation by an outsider' is left understood and most of the time the distance of outsidedness is understood to mark objectivity in the interpretation. But why is the outsider as an outsider interpreting your behavior? Is she doing it so that you can understand how she sees you? Is she doing it so that other outsiders will understand how you *are*? Is she doing it so that *you* will understand how you are? It would seem that if the outsider wants you to understand how she sees you and you have given your account of how you see yourself to her, there is a possibility of genuine dialogue between the two. It also seems that the lack of reciprocity could bar genuine dialogue. For why should you engage in such a one-sided dialogue? As soon as we ask this question, a host of other conditions for the possibility of a genuine dialogue between us arise: conditions having to do with your position relative to me in the various social, political and economic structures in which we might come across each other or in which you may run face to face with my account of you and my use of your account of yourself. Is this kind of dialogue necessary for me to get at the meaning of your experiences? That is, is this kind of dialogue necessary for feminist theorizing that is not seriously flawed?

Obviously the most dangerous of the understanding of what I—an outsider— am doing in giving an account of your experience is the one that describes what

I'm doing as giving an account of who and how you are whether it be given to you or to other outsiders. Why should you or anyone else believe me; that is why should you or anyone else believe that you are as I say you are? Could I be right? What conditions would have to obtain for my being right? That many women are put in the position of not knowing whether or not to believe outsiders' accounts of their experiences is clear. The pressures to believe these accounts are enormous even when the woman in question does not see herself in the account. She is thus led to doubt her own judgment and to doubt all interpretation of her experience. This leads her to experience her life differently. Since the consequences of outsiders' accounts can be so significant, it is crucial that we reflect on whether or not this type of account can ever be right and if so, under what conditions.

The last point leads us to the second way of arriving at an account of another woman's experience, viz. the case in which I observe myself and others like me culturally and in other ways and use that account to give an account of you. In doing this, I remake you in my own image. Feminist theorizing approaches this remaking insofar as it depends on the concept of women as women. For it has not arrived at this concept as a consequence of dialogue with many women who are culturally different, or by any other kind of investigation of cultural differences which may include different conceptions of what it is to be a woman; it has simply presupposed this concept.

Our suggestion in this paper, and at this time it is no more than a suggestion, is that only when genuine and reciprocal dialogue takes place between 'outsiders' and 'insiders' can we trust the outsider's account. At first sight it may appear that the insider/outsider distinction disappears in the dialogue, but it is important to notice that all that happens is that we are now both outsider and insider with respect to each other. The dialogue puts us both in position to give a better account of each other's and our own experience. Here we should again note that white/Anglo women are much less prepared for this dialogue with women of color than women of color are for dialogue with them in that women of color have had to learn white/Anglo ways, self-conceptions, and conceptions of them.

But both the possibility and the desirability of this dialogue are very much in question. We need to think about the possible motivations for engaging in this dialogue, whether doing theory jointly would be a good thing, in what ways and for whom, and whether doing theory is in itself a good thing at this time for women of color or white/Anglo women. In motivating the last question let us remember the hierarchical distinctions between theorizers and those theorized about and between theorizers and doers. These distinctions are endorsed by the same views and institutions which endorse and support hierarchical distinctions between men/women, master race/inferior race, intellectuals/manual workers. Of what use is the activity of theorizing to those of us who are women of color engaged day in and day out in the task of empowering women and men of color face to face with them? Should we be articulating and interpreting their experience for them with the aid of theories? Whose theories?

III. WAYS OF TALKING OR BEING TALKED
ABOUT THAT ARE HELPFUL, ILLUMINATING,
EMPOWERING, RESPECTFUL

(Unproblematically in María's & Vicky's voice)

Feminists have been quite diligent about pointing out the ways in which empirical, philosophical and moral theories have been androcentric. They have thought it crucial to ask, with respect to such theories: who makes them? for whom do they make them? about what or whom are the theories? why? how are theories tested? what are the criteria for such tests and where did the criteria come from? Without posing such questions and trying to answer them, we'd never have been able to begin to mount evidence for our claims that particular theories are androcentric, sexist, biased, paternalistic, etc. Certain philosophers have become fond of—indeed, have made their careers on—pointing out that characterizing a statement as true or false is only one of many ways possible of characterizing it; it might also be, oh, rude, funny, disarming, etc.; it may be intended to soothe or to hurt; or it may have the effect, intended or not, of soothing or hurting. Similarly, theories appear to be the kinds of things that are true or false; but they also are the kinds of things that can be, e.g. useless, arrogant, disrespectful, ignorant, ethnocentric, imperialistic. The immediate point is that feminist theory is no less immune to such characterizations than, say, Plato's political theory, or Freud's theory of female psychosexual development. Of course this is not to say that if feminist theory manages to be respectful or helpful it will follow that it must be true. But if, say, an empirical theory is purported to be about 'women' and in fact is only about certain women, it is certainly false, probably ethnocentric, and of dubious usefulness except to those whose position in the world it strengthens (and theories, as we know, don't have to be true in order to be used to strengthen people's positions in the world).

Many reasons can be and have been given for the production of accounts of people's lives that plainly have nothing to do with illuminating those lives for the benefit of those living them. It is likely that both the method of investigation and the content of many accounts would be different if illuminating the lives of the people the accounts are about were the aim of the studies. Though we cannot say ahead of time how feminist theory-making would be different if all (or many more) of those people it is meant to be about were more intimately part of the theory-making process, we do suggest some specific ways being talked about can be helpful:

(1) The theory or account can be helpful if it enables one to see how parts of one's life fit together, for example, to see connection among parts of one's life one hasn't seen before. No account can do this if it doesn't get the parts right to begin with, and this cannot happen if the concepts used to describe a life are utterly foreign.

(2) A useful theory will help one locate oneself concretely in the world, rather

than add to the mystification of the world and one's location in it. New concepts may be of significance here, but they will not be useful if there is no way they can be translated into already existing concepts. Suppose a theory locates you in the home, because you are a woman, but you know full well that is not where you spend most of your time? Or suppose you can't locate yourself easily in any particular class as defined by some version of marxist theory?

(3) A theory or account not only ought to accurately locate one in the world but also enable one to think about the extent to which one is responsible or not for being in that location. Otherwise, for those whose location is as oppressed peoples, it usually occurs that the oppressed have no way to see themselves as in any way self-determining, as having any sense of being worthwhile or having grounds for pride, and paradoxically at the same time feeling at fault for the position they are in. A useful theory will help people sort out just what is and is not due to themselves and their own activities as opposed to those who have power over them.

It may seem odd to make these criteria of a useful theory, if the usefulness is not to be at odds with the issue of the truth of the theory: for the focus on feeling worthwhile or having pride seems to rule out the possibility that the truth might just be that such-and-such a group of people has been under the control of others for centuries and that the only explanation of that is that they are worthless and weak people, and will never be able to change that. Feminist theorizing seems implicitly if not explicitly committed to the moral view that women *are* worthwhile beings, and the metaphysical theory that we are beings capable of bringing about a change in our situations. Does this mean feminist theory is 'biased'? Not any more than any other theory, e.g. psychoanalytic theory. What is odd here is not the feminist presupposition that women are worthwhile but rather that feminist theory (and other theory) often has the effect of empowering one group and demoralizing another.

Aspects of feminist theory are as unabashedly value-laden as other political and moral theories. It is not just an examination of women's positions, for it includes, indeed begins with, moral and political judgements about the injustice (or, where relevant, justice) of them. This means that there are implicit or explicit judgements also about what kind of changes constitute a better or worse situation for women.

(4) In this connection a theory that is useful will provide criteria for change and make suggestions for modes of resistance that don't merely reflect the situation and values of the theorizer. A theory that is respectful of those about whom it is a theory will not assume that changes that are perceived as making life better for some women are changes that will make, and will be perceived as making, life better for other women. This is NOT to say that if some women do not find a situation oppressive, other women ought never to suggest to the contrary that there might be very good reasons to think that the situation nevertheless *is* oppressive. But it is to say that, e.g. the prescription that life for women will be better when we're in the workforce rather than at home, when we are completely free of religious beliefs with patriarchal origins, when we live in complete separation from men, etc., are seen as slaps in the face to

women whose life would be better if they could spend more time at home, whose identity is inseparable from their religious beliefs and cultural practices (which is not to say those beliefs and practices are to remain completely un-criticized and unchanged), who have ties to men—whether erotic or not—such that to have them severed in the name of some vision of what is 'better' is, at that time and for those women, absurd. Our visions of what is better are always informed by our perception of what is bad about our present situation. Surely we've learned enough from the history of clumsy missionaries, and the white suffragists of the 19th century (who couldn't imagine why Black women 'couldn't see' how crucial getting the vote for 'women' was) to know that we can clobber people to destruction with our visions, our versions, of what is better. BUT: this does not mean women are not to offer supportive and tentative criticism of one another. But there is a very important difference between (a) developing ideas together, in a 'pre-theoretical' stage, engaged as equals in joint enquiry, and (b) one group developing, on the basis of their own experience, a set of criteria for good change for women—and then reluctantly making revisions in the criteria at the insistence of women to whom such criteria seem ethnocentric and arrogant. The deck is stacked when one group takes it upon itself to develop the theory and then have others criticize it. Categories are quick to congeal, and the experiences of women whose lives do not fit the categories will appear as anomalous when in fact the theory should have grown out of them as much as others from the beginning. This, of course, is why any organization or con-ference having to do with 'women'—with no qualification—that seriously does not want to be 'solipsistic' will from the beginning be multi-cultural or state the appropriate qualifications. How we think and what we think about does depend in large part on who is there—not to mention who is expected or encouraged to speak. (Recall the boys in the *Symposium* sending the flute girls out.) Conversations and criticism take place in particular circumstances. Turf matters. So does the fact of who if anyone already has set up the terms of the conversations.

(5) Theory cannot be useful to anyone interested in resistance and change unless there is reason to believe that knowing what a theory means and believing it to be true have some connection to resistance and change. As we make theory and offer it up to others, what do we assume is the connection between theory and consciousness? Do we expect others to read theory, understand it, believe it, and have their consciousnesses and lives thereby transformed? If we really want theory to make a difference to people's lives, how ought we to present it? Do we think people come to consciousness by reading? only by reading? Speaking to people through theory (orally or in writing) is a *very* specific context-dependent activity. That is, theory-makers and their methods and concepts constitute a community of people and of shared meanings. Their language can be just as opaque and foreign to those not in the community as a foreign tongue or dialect.[3] Why do we engage in *this* activity and what effect do we think it ought to have? As Helen Longino has asked: 'Is "doing theory" just a bonding

[3] See Bernstein (1972). Bernstein would probably, and we think wrongly, insist that theoretical

ritual for academic or educationally privileged feminists/women?' Again, whom does our theory-making serve?

IV. SOME SUGGESTIONS ABOUT HOW TO DO THEORY THAT IS NOT IMPERIALISTIC, ETHNOCENTRIC, DISRESPECTFUL

(Problematically in the voice of a woman of color)

What are the things we need to know about others, and about ourselves, in order to speak intelligently, intelligibly, sensitively, and helpfully about their lives? We can show respect, or lack of it, in writing theoretically about others no less than in talking directly with them. This is not to say that here we have a well-worked out concept of respect, but only to suggest that together all of us consider what it would mean to theorize in a respectful way.

When we speak, write, and publish our theories, to whom do we think we are accountable? Are the concerns we have in being accountable to 'the profession' at odds with the concerns we have in being accountable to those about whom we theorize? Do commitments to 'the profession', method, getting something published, getting tenure, lead us to talk and act in ways at odds with what we ourselves (let alone others) would regard as ordinary, decent behavior? To what extent do we presuppose that really understanding another person or culture requires our behaving in ways that are disrespectful, even violent? That is, to what extent do we presuppose that getting and/or publishing the requisite information requires or may require disregarding the wishes of others, lying to them, wresting information from them against their wills? Why and how do we think theorizing about others provides *understanding* of them? Is there any sense in which theorizing about others is a short-cut to understanding them?

Finally, if we think doing theory is an important activity, and we think that some conditions lead to better theorizing than others, what are we going to do about creating those conditions? If we think it not just desirable but necessary for women of different racial and ethnic identities to create feminist theory jointly, how shall that be arranged for? It may be the case that at this particular point we ought not even try to do that—that feminist theory by and for Hispanas needs to be done separately from feminist theory by and for Black women, white women, etc. But it must be recognized that white/Anglo women have more power and privilege than Hispanas, Black women, etc., and at the very least they can use such advantage to provide space and time for other women to speak (with the above caveats about implicit restrictions on what counts as 'the woman's voice'). And once again it is important to remember that the power of white/Anglo women vis-à-vis Hispanas and Black women is in inverse proportion to their working knowledge of each other.

---

terms and statements have meanings *not* 'tied to a local relationship and to a local social structure', unlike the vocabulary of, e.g. working-class children.

This asymmetry is a crucial fact about the background of possible relationships between white women and women of color, whether as political coworkers, professional colleagues, or friends.

If white/Anglo women and women of color are to do theory jointly, in helpful, respectful, illuminating and empowering ways, the task ahead of white/Anglo women because of this asymmetry, is a very hard task. The task is a very complex one. In part, to make an analogy, the task can be compared to learning a text without the aid of teachers. We all know the lack of contact felt when we want to discuss a particular issue that requires knowledge of a text with someone who does not know the text at all. Or the discomfort and impatience that arise in us when we are discussing an issue that presupposes a text and someone walks into the conversation who does not know the text. That person is either left out or will impose herself on us and either try to engage in the discussion or try to change the subject. Women of color are put in these situations by white/Anglo women and men constantly. Now imagine yourself simply left out but wanting to do theory with us. The first thing to recognize and accept is that you disturb our own dialogues by putting yourself in the left-out position and not leaving us in some meaningful sense to ourselves.

You must also recognize and accept that you must learn the text. But the text is an extraordinarily complex one: viz. our many different cultures. You are asking us to make ourselves more vulnerable to you than we already are before we have any reason to trust that you will not take advantage of this vulnerability. So you need to learn to become unintrusive, unimportant, patient to the point of tears, while at the same time open to learning any possible lessons. You will also have to come to terms with the sense of alienation, of not belonging, of having your world thoroughly disrupted, having it criticized and scrutinized from the point of view of those who have been harmed by it, having important concepts central to it dismissed, being viewed with mistrust, being seen as of no consequence except as an object of mistrust.

Why would any white/Anglo woman engage in this task? Out of self-interest? What in engaging in this task would be, not just in her interest, but perceived as such by her before the task is completed or well underway? Why should we want you to come into our world out of self-interest? Two points need to be made here. The task as described could be entered into with the intention of finding out as much as possible about us so as to better dominate us. The person engaged in this task would act as a spy. The motivation is not unfamiliar to us. We have heard it said that now that Third World countries are more powerful as a bloc, westerners need to learn more about them, that it is in their self-interest to do so. Obviously there is no reason why people of color should welcome white/Anglo women into their world for the carrying out of this intention. It is also obvious that white/Anglo feminists should not engage in this task under this description since the task under this description would not lead to joint theorizing of the desired sort: respectful, illuminating, helpful and empowering. It would be helpful and empowering only in a one-sided way.

Self-interest is also mentioned as a possible motive in another way. White/ Anglo women sometimes say that the task of understanding women of color

would entail self-growth or self-expansion. If the task is conceived as described here, then one should doubt that growth or expansion will be the result. The severe self-disruption that the task entails should place a doubt in anyone who takes the task seriously about her possibilities of coming out of the task whole, with a self that is not as fragile as the selves of those who have been the victims of racism. But also, why should women of color embrace white/Anglo women's self-betterment without reciprocity? At this time women of color cannot afford this generous affirmation of white/Anglo women.

Another possible motive for engaging in this task is the motive of duty, 'out of obligation', because white/Anglos have done people of color wrong. Here again two considerations: coming into Hispano, Black, Native American worlds out of obligation puts white/Anglos in a morally self-righteous position that is inappropriate. You are active, we are passive. We become the vehicles of your own redemption. Secondly, we couldn't want you to come into our worlds 'out of obligation'. That is like wanting someone to make love to you out of obligation. So, whether or not you have an obligation to do this (and we would deny that you do), or whether this task could even be done out of obligation, this is an inappropriate motive.

Out of obligation you should stay out of our way, respect us and our distance, and forego the use of whatever power you have over us—for example, the power to use your language in our meetings, the power to overwhelm us with your education, the power to intrude in our communities in order to research us and to record the supposed dying of our cultures, the power to engrain in us a sense that we are members of dying cultures and are doomed to assimilate, the power to keep us in a defensive posture with respect to our own cultures.

So the motive of friendship remains as both the only appropriate and understandable motive for white/Anglo feminists engaging in the task as described above. If you enter the task out of friendship with us, then you will be moved to attain the appropriate reciprocity of care for your and our wellbeing as whole beings, you will have a stake in us and in our world, you will be moved to satisfy the need for reciprocity of understanding that will enable you to follow us in our experiences as we are able to follow you in yours.

We are not suggesting that if the learning of the text is to be done out of friendship, you must enter into a friendship with a whole community and for the purpose of making theory. In order to understand what it is that we are suggesting, it is important to remember that during the description of her experience of exclusion, the Hispana voice said that Hispanas experience the intimacy of friendship with white/Anglo women friends as thoroughly incomplete. It is not until this fact is acknowledged by our white/Anglo women friends and felt as a profound lack in our experience of each other that white/Anglo women can begin to see us. Seeing us in our communities will make clear and concrete to you how incomplete we really are in our relationships with you. It is this beginning that forms the proper background for the yearning to understand the text of our cultures that can lead to joint theory-making.

Thus, the suggestion made here is that if white/Anglo women are to understand our voices, they must understand our communities and us in them. Again,

this is not to suggest that you set out to make friends with our communities, though you may become friends with some of the members, nor is it to suggest that you should try to befriend us for the purpose of making theory with us. The latter would be a perversion of friendship. Rather, from within friendship you may be moved by friendship to undergo the very difficult task of understanding the text of our cultures by understanding our lives in our communities. This learning calls for circumspection, for questioning of yourselves and your roles in your own culture. It necessitates a striving to understand while in the comfortable position of not having an official calling card (as 'scientific' observers of our communities have); it demands recognition that you do not have the authority of knowledge; it requires coming to the task without ready-made theories to frame our lives. This learning is then extremely hard because it requires openness (including openness to severe criticism of the white/Anglo world), sensitivity, concentration, self-questioning, circumspection. It should be clear that it does not consist in a passive immersion in our cultures, but in a striving to understand what it is that our voices are saying. Only then can we engage in a mutual dialogue that does not reduce each one of us to instances of the abstraction called 'woman'.

REFERENCES

Bernstein, Basil. 1972. Social class, language and socialization. In Giglioli, Pier Paolo, ed., *Language and Social Context*, pp. 157–178. Penguin, Harmondsworth, Middlesex.

Mackinnon, Catherine. 1982. Feminism, marxism, method, and the State: an agenda for theory. *Signs* 7 (3): 515–544.

PLATO, IRONY AND EQUALITY

Janet Farrell Smith

INTRODUCTION

'Sex equality', as we understand the contemporary term, is not the focus of Plato's arguments in Book V of the the *Republic*. Plato did, however, advance the thesis that the differences which did exist between the sexes were not sufficient to bar women of guardian caliber from equal training with men, so that the best talent could be selected for philosophic leadership. In *Republic* V Plato gives at least three arguments on the nature of sex differences in social context. When reconstructed, these arguments can be seen to be closely related to contemporary scientific interpretations of the data on sex differences. These interpretations challenge inferences to a generalized sex difference in human nature, where these inferences are based on statistical differences in performance between the sexes.

Plato's irony signals his awareness of the ridicule and discomfort likely to be elicited by his proposals. Because Plato was well aware of the radical nature of his proposals about women, he couched his arguments in an ironic frame, utilizing a style which has caused continuing misinterpretation. I discuss sources of these misunderstandings and attempt to clarify them in Part I of this essay. Part II reconstructs what can be called Plato's 'burden of proof' argument in favor of equal education for women. Part III analyses the crucial 'argument from individual variation', which is related to current psychology in Part IV. Part V shows how Plato, in an ironic turn, argues, contrary to the popular assumption of the time that it is 'unnatural' to educate women equally with men, that it is rather 'unnatural' to fail to do so.

I

Several factors have continued to obscure Plato's intent in presenting the claim for equal training for guardian women. The first is the tendency to read Plato with the cultural assumptions and terminology of a later historical period. The second is Plato's genuine ambivalence about women. The third is Plato's ironic and literary style in presenting his philosophical views.

Was Plato a feminist?

If we ask the question 'Was Plato a feminist?' or 'Was Plato in favor of sex equality?' we are sure to find evidence in the Platonic corpus to justify both positive and negative answers to these questions. This is partly because Plato's issues concerned neither the questions of contemporary feminism nor the liberal ideal of equality between the sexes. Sex equality in the fullest sense today includes the eradication of sex discrimination both in economic and educational opportunity and also in attitudes which are derogatory or devaluing of women and men. On most current definitions feminism asserts that women are objectified or made into 'the other', in Simone de Beauvoir's phrase. Feminism involves self-consciously adopting the viewpoints and interests of women to overcome objectification and subordination of women. Plato did not focus on the elimination of sex discrimination throughout his ideal state. Nor did he himself escape the objectifying of women. It is doubtful that he even conceived of either criteria for sex equality or feminism.

On the other hand, Plato was concerned with justice in an organic and functionalist sense. In elaborating the psychic and social structure of justice in the ideal state of the Republic, he explicitly argues against sex discrimination in education for guardian women. He also argues for giving qualified persons full opportunity for guardian training regardless of whether they are male or female. It must be noted that these arguments do not stand alone, but are made in the service of Plato's larger aim, which is to arrange hierarchy, social power, and control, so that 'the best' rules over the worst, with reason, according to nature. These hierarchic, aristocratic premises are inconsistent with most of the ideals which motivate sex equality or feminism in the post-Enlightenment era. Plato disdained democratic egalitarianism and accepted the principle that the greatest (moral) talent should correlate with the highest social status. Plato did not use terms such as 'equality', 'fairness', 'equality of opportunity', and of course, 'feminism'. As long as we frame his questions in these terms the debate over his position on women will be confused and unending.

Despite these cultural and political differences, Plato was the first Western philosopher to work out a philosophical thesis which takes a central place in many contemporary investigations in feminist theory. He recognized that cultural, social and political relations play a major role in forming what is commonly regarded as 'natural' in sex roles and familial behavior. Although contemporary theorists may not agree with Plato's purpose and conclusions, they may find some reasoning in his arguments which anticipates current scientific inquiry. For Plato did scrutinize the question of what is 'natural' in sex-related and familial structure more carefully than Aristotle, who simply took female subordination as a fact of nature.[1] Plato's scrutiny amounted to more than utopian

[1] Aristotle simply assumes in the *Politics* (1252a 30) that the social dominance of male over female is a 'natural' dominance or rulership, like that of master over slave, father over child. I take Plato as questioning the connection between 'natural' and social dominance. For treatment of Aristotle on this question see Okin (1979: Ch. 4). For a detailed examination of Aristotle's

tinkering with family structure. He saw the family and woman's role as intimately connected with property relations within the economic form of justice.

'Except for the fact that women are weaker'

Plato was genuinely ambivalent about women. He makes seriously miso-
gynistic and derogatory comments about women within the same dialogue in
which he argues that (some) women should be educated 'the same' as men.
These attitudes have been extensively documented.[2] While these attitudes may
indicate that Plato's views on women are 'an enigma' (Okin, 1979: 14) or 'inconsistent',[3] they are perhaps no more so than the presence of attitudinal sexism
in those who argue for equality between the sexes, or of anti-semitism or racism
in those who argue against minority or racial discrimination. This observation
does not, of course, justify holding such attitudinal prejudice.

Another curious factor in Plato's arguments concerning equal training for
women guardians is his insistent qualification of every positive thesis: 'Except
for the fact that women are weaker'. If 'weaker' is taken to mean 'generally
inferior' including inferior intellectual ability, then the thesis that women
should be equally educated falls prey to a series of *reductios*. Some commentators have indeed taken Plato in this manner. Strauss and Bloom regard Book
V as a comedy, with the consequence that Plato's arguments on human nature
there are neither serious investigations nor serious proposals for women's entry
into philosophic rulership. Whether the comedic interpretation shows an insistence on logical consistency or a predilection to take an interpretation least
sympathetic to women, there remains a problem for a consistent portrayal of
Plato as a serious advocate of equal training for women.[4]

There is, however, a way out of this dilemma. Rather than regarding the
qualification as undermining all Plato's arguments, on the one hand, or indicating his merely playful toying with the notion of women's education, on the
other, we could take the 'weaker' qualification as merely implying that women
should be excused from certain activities. But these activities, primarily concerning warfare, do not affect their ability to participate fully in political leadership. For example, in gymnastics, women might not be expected to perform
at the same level as men did. In physical combat, or 'guarding', women might
not be called to the same duties as men might:

> 'So women must share in war and in all the guarding of the city, and that shall
> be their only work. But in these same things lighter parts will be given to women
> than men because of the weakness of their sex.' (Rep 457a)

---

arguments on how these are assimilated to the 'natural' relations within the soul, see Spelman
(1983).

[2] See, e.g. Okin (1979: Ch. 1), Annas (1976: 307–321) stresses Plato's partronizing treatment
of women. Spelman, in her 'Metaphysics and Misogyny', ties Plato's misogyny to his dualistic
metaphysics.

[3] For an analysis of their positions see Allen (1975: 131). Also Lange (1979).

[4] Pierce (1973: 1–11). Also see Okin (1979: Appendix to Ch. 2). Both present counterarguments
and textual evidence against the Bloom-Strauss interpretation.

Reference to the 'lighter parts' of guarding may indicate lighter physical exertion in keeping with certain physical differences between the sexes. But these physical differences and their implied differential military functions do not disturb Plato's basic thesis—namely, that women should be trained equally with men, and that women and men alike should on the basis of individual talent rise to the position of leadership to which they are best suited.

Plato's insistence that 'women are weaker' must be seen in the context of his time and culture, i.e. a society called to defend itself against invasion. In addition, on the Athenian model of strength and physical excellence, handed down in the Western tradition of olympic sport, women's capacities did indicate a lesser degree of performance and achievement. But this fact does not imply that certain women, e.g. Olympic Javelin champion Kathy Schmidt, cannot excel beyond the capacities of the average man. Indeed, Plato himself makes this observation for other activities. So, given Plato's own arguments, it might initially seem odd that he should repeat the qualification where it might not be relevant. Yet, keeping in mind that Plato and his fellow Athenians had little opportunity to observe the women's athletic achievement, his qualification may indicate only relative ignorance within the cultural realities of his time. On other models of excellence of physical strength, for example, in sports or activities featuring stamina, endurance, agility, and coordination, in which women are 'strong' rather than 'weak', women should achieve as well as or better than men. But Plato might not have adequately incorporated even his own observation that Spartan and Sarmation women had aggressive and warlike natures.[5]

Irony, laughter and truth

Plato's 'three waves', leading to the establishment of the ideal state, are the equal training of guardian women, the abolition of the private family and its property, and finally, the institution of philosophic wisdom as 'king' or ruler of the state. If we regard the *Republic* as an integrated dramatic presentation, then Plato's heightened awareness of the ridicule each 'wave' might bring leads him to present it in a specialized manner. It is helpful to keep in mind that Book VI, following the radical proposals on women and the family, presents the even more radical views on the nature of the good.

Plato is a master stylist. He wields his powers of dramatic expression, wit, and, most of all, irony for a strategic purpose, when he presents material which he fears may be taken lightly or misunderstood. He often gives radical or dangerous material an ironic frame, a mode of presentation which both emphasizes and mitigates his point to those enveloped in shadows. While writing simultaneously on levels which may be only dimly grasped by someone who

---

[5] See Okin (p. 69) [*Laws*, 806b]. Annas, in her *Philosophy* (p. 309) article, takes the passage at 455b in the *Republic* as evidence that Plato considers women both mentally and physically inferior to men. I think this is a misinterpretation. Plato merely distinguishes here what he means by a 'natural gift', e.g. rapid and inventive learning. It is not until the next speech at 455c 7–8 that he introduces differential performance of the sexes. See section below on 'Argument from individual variation'.

catches only part of his point, he recognizes that what he says may be taken as a joke, provoking laughter. Yet his ironic recognition of this signifies that he is well aware of the difference between presenting a joke and presenting something which may be taken as a joke. At the beginning of his discussion of equal training for guardian women he remarks:

> 'He is a vain fool who thinks anything ridiculous but what is evil.' (452d)[6]

Bloom (1968: 382) takes the discussion of nakedness to imply the impossibility of training women and men equally (because, presumably, of licentiousness).[7] However, Plato is not talking about physical stripping alone, but using the Athenian custom of exercising naked as an ironic metaphor for stripping to reveal the truth.

> 'It was better to strip than to hide all such things; and soon the seemingly funny to the eyes melted away before that which was revealed in the light of reason to be the best.' (Rep 452d) [Rouse translation]

Plato also uses the occasion to remark that at one time the Greeks also thought it 'ridiculous' and 'comedic' to exercise naked when the Cretans originated the custom. Plato is also well aware of the fact that what seems 'natural' depends on what is 'customary', as John Stuart Mill remarked in his *Subjection of Women*.[8] He is also well aware of the ridicule that might follow his implicit thesis in Book V, that 'female nature is in fact what different societies have made of it'. (Okin, 1979: 69). He completes his ironic frame around the discussion of the 'first wave' with the warning on ignorance and ridicule:

> 'And the man who laughs at naked women, exercising for the greatest good, plucks an unripe fruit of wisdom from his laughter. He apparently does not know what he laughs at or what he is doing. For . . . the useful is beautiful and the harmful is ugly.' (Rep 457b)

II

The 'Burden of proof' argument

Starting with the premise that 'each single person must do his own business according to nature', (Rep 454a), Socrates takes up Glaucon's challenge of self-contradiction. If there is a putative difference between the natures of the sexes, then how can we say that men and women should do the same work?

---

[6] All translations, unless otherwise noted, are from Rouse (1956).
[7] Bloom (1968: 382). See Okin's discussion, p. 306.
[8] See (1970: 153).

'We agreed, you know, that a different nature ought to practice a different work, and that man and woman have different natures; now we say that these different natures must do the same work. Is that the accusation against us?'

The problem has to do with the oversimplification on 'same' and 'different' natures which have led into 'eristic wrangling'. Socrates' response further refines Plato's views on the nature of a person. If we inquire into the nature of the same vs different we find that (1) the nature of a thing is not absolute but qualified relevant to its calling or function. ['We were thinking of only that kind of sameness or difference which had to do with their actual callings'. 454c.] (2) Only differences relevant to actual callings are properly used to assign social functions to persons' natures. (3) Procreative differences between the sexes alone are not relevant to the actual callings (Cf. civic responsibility) under consideration.[9] (4) Hence, if procreative differences in function are the only differences between male and female, these are not sufficient to deny equal training to women of guardian potential.

Now, the last point concludes with the conditional proposition that *if* the only differences between male and female consist in procreative function, then these differences are not relevant. Does Plato concede a *prima facie* plausibility to the supposition that they are the only differences when he next casts the burden of proof on he who would 'say the opposite to tell us just which art or practice for which the nature of woman and man is not the same but different?' (455a).

I do not think that Plato does concede *prima facie* plausibility to a supposition of minimal procreative differences between the sexes. Rather, he takes a position in which a neutral or open scientific question on the differences between the sexes yields to a social and moral imperative. The evidence on sex differences is not all in. If there is a lack of definitive evidence, why suppose unequal status or training is preferable to equal training? Give the benefit of the open question to those who might excel under the more generous proposal of equal education. The burden of proof lies with those who would deny equal status.

In Plato's terms the reason why this argument stands is left implicit and unstated. It is that the basis (education) for the selection process for 'the best' philosophical rulers should be cast as widely as possible. The moral and social imperative is aristocratic, hierarchical and elitist. Plato wants the society structured so that it is more likely than not that the most talented and naturally gifted be prepared to rule. Hence, he claims that the burden of proof is on those who would deny equal training.

The argument as interpreted here states that the basis of sex differences relevant to civic leadership is an open question, emphasizing the fact that there is no evidence that sex differences do affect civic practice. Yet it infers on

[9] By 'procreative differences' Plato appears to refer simply to the minimal reproductive function. ('The male begets and the female bears' 454e.) In other words he is not referring to what we understand as 'biological factors', which include genetic, hormonal, genital and secondary sex differences, but merely to differences in biological reproductive activity.

separate grounds that the practice which extends the more generous social policy is preferable to one which does not. A similar type of argument arises for racial differences. In the absence of definitive evidence on innate racial differences, the burden of proof lies with those who would deny equal education. It should be noted, however, that most contemporary advocates of racial equality and sex equality argue that even if biological differences do exist, these differences are not grounds for denying social equality in a democratic state.

Contemporary social psychology of sex characteristics does in fact consider most sex differences an open question. In their definitive *Psychology of Sex Differences*, Maccoby and Jacklin (1974) cite such characteristics as women's fear, timidity, competitiveness, dominance and activity level, nurturance and 'maternal' behavior, as 'Open questions: too little evidence or findings ambiguous'. Even their summary of 'Sex differences that are fairly well-established', e.g. girls excel in verbal ability, boys in visual-spatial ability, faces challenge both from competing interpretations and new data (Maccoby and Jacklin, 1974: 352).

Given a lack of definitive evidence for sex differences relevant to education, what is the basis for social policy concerning it? Plato's case is instructive, for he, facing this lack of definitive evidence, appeals to a set of normative (moral and political) assumptions. In Plato's case, these assumptions amount to a principle for selecting the 'best' for a moral aristocracy, which would lead in the social hierarchy. Plato's basic premise, however, that in the absence of scientific evidence, social and moral assumptions account for political structuring of sex roles, can be extrapolated to contemporary democratic and egalitarian arguments.[10] Plato would not have agreed with the democratic aim of many of these arguments. Nor do many contemporaries committed to democratic aims agree with his political assumptions. Yet his philosophical moves illustrate similar transitions—in his case, openly stated and justified—in the face of open or disputed questions on sex differences.

III

The argument from individual variation

In the previous argument Plato throws the burden of proof on those who would deny equal training to women *if* sex differences amount merely to procreative differences in function. In the next stage of his presentation he himself

---

[10] While the political assumptions are quite different, and he is dealing with an IQ question, not sex differences, Green makes a related point in his criticism of the objectivity of studies by Jensen and Herrnstein:

'The distribution of IQ scores, and their alleged and partial correlation with occupational rank, is no guide at all to the amount of underlying intellectual talent that is potentially available to us.' (Green, 1976: 142).

takes up the question, what, relevant to the practice of civic leadership, is the 'nature' of differences between the sexes? He argues for a conclusion which anticipates the findings of contemporary psychology, that there exists greater variation *among* individuals within one sex group than *between* the two sex groupings, male vs female.

Plato begins with the general query: what civic practice is there 'for which the nature of woman and the nature of man is not the same but different?' A subsidiary purpose is to show the dubious interlocutor 'that there is no practice peculiar to women in the management of a city'. The argument is premised on the thesis that those who have the same nature should perform the same functions and those who have different natures should perform different functions.

Plato's argument requires a distinction which would resolve an ambiguity on the 'nature' of a person. Plato failed to draw this distinction as sharply as he could, causing confusion. It is doubtful whether his arguments are valid without it. The 'nature' of a person could be interpreted as

(a) What a person *actually* does

or

(b) What a person is *capable* of doing (or has a natural gift to do).

This distinction, between performance and capability in the 'nature' of persons, turns out to be critical in interpreting what I call Plato's 'argument from individual variation'. In the following reconstruction, I first give an interpretation of each step of Plato's argument. The relevant passage from the text follows.

(1) First, Plato defines by example what it means to have a 'natural gift' to do something. He seems to mean what we might call 'individual aptitude' or 'individual innate talent', e.g. for rapid or inventive learning, or ability to coordinate mental-physical functioning. In illustrating 'natural gift', he refers to capacity (in sense (b) above), not performance (though, of course, the former could be made evident by the latter).

> '[We mean by] having or not having a natural gift for anything—that one learned easily, the other with difficulty? One after short learning was very inventive in what he learnt, the other after long learning and practice could not even recall what he had learnt?' (455b)

(2) In the second step of the argument Plato moves to what can only be interpreted as performance on the part of groups, not innate natural talents of individuals. He must be talking about what could be called today mean or average performance, (appealing to sense (a) above). The claim is: in average (mean) performance the male sex group excels the female sex group in all activities in the above respects.

> 'Do you know anything at all practiced among mankind in which all these respects the male sex is not far better than the female? Or should we make a long story

of it—take weaving, tending of cakes and boiling pots, in which women think
themselves somebody and would be most laughed at if beaten? You are right,
he said, That one sex is much better than the other in almost everything.'

The third step asserts:

(3) However, despite the differential in group performance, many individual
women excel many individual men in many things. Glaucon says:

> 'Many women, it is true, are better than many men in many things, but generally
> it is as you say.' (455d)

Next, Socrates draws the pivotal and crucial inference on which the argument
turns.

(4) The 'natures' or individual talents and aptitudes are distributed in individuals in both sex groupings.

(5) Hence, from (4), woman can participate in all practices according to her
'nature'.

(6) Therefore, no civic practice is justifiably assigned to woman (or man) on
the basis of membership in a sex group.

'Natures' in steps (4) and (5) draws on sense (b) above as what a person is
capable of doing. The text states:

> 'Therefore, my friend, there is no practice of a city's governors which belongs
> to woman because she is woman, or to a man because he is man; but the natures
> are scattered alike among both sexes; and woman participates according to nature
> in all practices, and man in all, but in all of them woman is weaker than man.'
> (455e)

In the remainder of the argument Plato elaborates the character of individual
variation, reinforcing (4) and (5) above, and moves to his positive conclusion.

(7) Among women, individual variation in aptitude and talent ranges across
all activities relevant to social roles in the ideal society, e.g. from medical,
athletic, fighting, to philosophical talent.

> 'We shall say that one woman is athletic or warlike, and another is unwarlike
> and unathletic? Indeed.
> Shall we not say the same of philosophy and misosophy, that one loves wisdom
> and one hates it? One has high spirit and one has no spirit? That is so also.
> Then there may be a woman fit to be a guardian, although another is not; for
> such was the nature we chose for our guardian men also?
> Yes it was.'

(8) Individuals of the 'same nature' ((b) above) appropriate for civic leadership
(guardian status) are found in both sex groupings, male and female.

> 'Then both woman and man have the same nature fit for guarding the city, only
> one is weaker and one is stronger.'

The final conclusion:

(9) Civic leadership and social functions (social roles relevant to occupations) must therefore be assigned to [individual members of] both sexes, appropriate to the aptitudes ('natures' in the sense (b) above) of each. Those 'akin by nature' who have the same aptitudes should associate and receive the same training and education.

> 'Such women, then must be chosen for such men, to live with them and to guard with them, since they are fit for it and akin to them by nature.
> Certainly.
> Practice and calling must be assigned to both the same for the same natures.'

Some comments on the soundness of the above argument: First, Plato could be accused of equivocation on 'same nature' between step (2) and step (3), if we did not take him as making the distinction between performance and capacity (see (a) and (b) above). In addition, if 'natural gift or capacity' is defined only in terms of what an individual actually does (and hence 'can' do), Plato can also be accused of circularity. But since he makes explicit (*Republic* II, 369d) an assumption of individual innate talent he cannot be accused of circularity here.[11] That is, of course, a separate question from the empirical validity of his assumption of innate individual capacities or his claim in step (3), that individual women excel individual men in many things. The claim in step (3) can be demonstrated empirically in contemporary psychological data. But it is questionable whether there can be solid 'proof' of innate capacities.

It is reasonable to extend to Plato the distinction between 'nature' as innate capacity or educable talent and 'nature' as group performance. For he began the discussion with a determination to unravel the semantic tangle of 'same' vs 'different' natures. The 'ideal' state of the Republic is founded on a faith that innate human capacities can be socialized to higher moral ends, by joining 'intellectual wisdom with political power.' (Rep 473d)[12]

Finally, the qualification repeatedly inserted on the 'weaker' capabilities of females is relatively harmless if taken to mean 'physically weaker with respect to combat'. If this is not the likely interpretation and Plato means to assert a general inferiority of women in all physical-mental capacities, then he has indeed produced a series of *reductio ad absurdam* arguments. But this is unlikely. His seriousness in eliciting 'the best' from the population overrides prejudice on sex or class differentials. Although definitive textual evidence cannot be given for the 'physically weaker' interpretation, the additional point of joining women and men of the 'same nature' supports the abolition of private families and private property in the guardian class. This latter purpose is tied

---

[11] 'We are not born all exactly alike but different in nature, for all sorts of different jobs.' (Rep II 369d).

[12] This is the 'greatest wave', the third and final of the 'three waves' which will bring about the ideal society. It is 'certainly not small or easy, but it is possible', as, presumably, the other waves are.

in explicitly with his eagerness to avoid oligarchy and class interest over inherited property. (See Book VIII.)[13]

Julia Annas in her article 'Plato's Republic and feminism', interprets Plato's
argument here somewhat differently. She takes as Plato's leading query: 'Is
there no practice peculiar to women in the management of a city?' and interprets
Plato's point that 'men can do better than women' as 'men would do better
than women' (Annas, 1976: 309).[14] Then, she concludes, 'Now it is hardly a
feminist argument to claim that women do not have a special sphere because
men can outdo them at everything.' (p. 309). In contrast to Annas' interpretation, I take the claim that men 'can do better than women' as dealing with
group averages. It implies neither that 'men *would* do better' under different
conditions nor that individual women are not capable of doing better than
individual men. Annas' point that Plato is not making a feminist argument is
well taken. But Plato would also argue that men ('just because they are men')
do not have a special sphere or social role. Neither sex has a special sphere,
practice or calling because individual variability exceeds any differential in
average (sex) group performance.

IV

Findings in contemporary psychology

Plato's argument from individual variation finds support in the data of contemporary psychology, particularly in the critical step (3) asserting that individual women excel individual men in many things. This claim (3), combined
with claim (7) on the wide variability of female aptitude and achievement (which
ranges from musical talent to aggression in fighting), asserts that individual
variability among one sex (women) is of greater magnitude than the differences
in observed 'natures' between the sexes. Let us make this claim more precise:

> 'The difference between the means of male vs female groups on behavior, x, is
> less than the range of variation existing within one group for that behavior, x.'

This claim has been found to hold for the differences between verbal and spatial
ability, which might be taken to be the least susceptible to cultural and social
variation. The difference between the highest and the lowest scoring female,
for example, has been found to be greater than the differences between the
average female and the average male scorer. When psychologists, in other

[13] See also Lange (1979) who supports this view with her analysis that 'Plato has attempted to
remove the contradiction between public and private life for the guardians by raising familial
impulses from the private to the public sphere, where their effect is to promote unity in the state,
rather than disunity.' (p.11).

[14] The illicit transition depends on an inference from Plato's descriptive and declarative claim
that (as a group) 'man is better than woman' or 'man can [in sense (a) above] do better' to the
prescriptive and counterfactual claim that 'men would do better than women [in cake baking]'.
The latter is nowhere said or implied at Republic 457a.

words, speak of one sex outperforming the other, they are speaking of averages, not individuals (Maccoby and Jacklin, 1974: Ch. I).

Furthermore, even given statistically significant differences between the sexes on, say, verbal or spatial ability, these differences are never more than 0.25–0.50 standard deviation. It is questionable whether these differences constitute a practically significant difference. In her *Sex-Related Cognitive Differences* Julia Sherman remarks:

'Besides the *statistical* significance of a finding one may be concerned with its *practical* significance. Many apparently demonstrated sex-related differences are so small that they are of essentially no practical importance.' (Sherman, 1978: 23).

Concerning data which show that girls exceed boys in verbal ability, Sherman remarks, 'the demonstrated differences are so small as to be trivial' (Sherman, 1978: 38).

'While females scored significantly higher than males, the amount of the variance accounted for by sex (omega squared) did not even reach 1 per cent.' (Sherman, 1978: 43).

Evidence in psychology is continually challenged by new data. The result is that the so-called 'well established' differences found today may be outdated tomorrow. In 1974, Maccoby and Jacklin's 'fairly well established' results on verbal differences, though conceded to be small, were widely accepted. In 1978, Sherman considered these to be 'challenged and questioned' by current data (Sherman, 1978: 38–44).

In addition, verbal ability, as well as spatial ability, may be class and culture-bound. Cultural and social variation inhibit generalizations about sex-differences. E.g.

'Greater variability occurs across social class in maternal behavior with daughters [than with sons]. Upper middle class mothers have greater faith in their ability to affect their daughter's destinies, and spend more time talking to and entertaining them.' (Williams, 1977: 129).[15]

On the superior male performance on spatial ability, cultural factors are possible, but highly disputed. E.g. this is said about Eskimos:

'The lack of sex-difference in Eskimos has been variously attributed to the permissiveness of Eskimo childrearing, the relative emancipation of Eskimo women, the unique visual features of the Arctical environment, and/or an isolated gene pool among Eskimos.' (Lambert, 1978: 112).[16]

[15] Williams (1977: 129). Study is: Rothbart (1971: 113–120).
[16] Cited by Lambert. Studies are: Berry (1966); Kagan and Kogan (1970).

Another factor in tests showing sex differences may have to do, not with the specific aptitudes, but with the connection between certain testing conditions and performance. Boys and girls, for example, were tested for spatial ability under usual conditions and under 'empathy condition', (empathy is a stereotypically female trait).

> 'Males did better than females under the usual conditions and females did better than males under the empathy condition.' (Sherman, 1978: 144)[17]

These tests indicate that social conditions and background of performance may have a greater role than has been realized. Conclusions about 'well-established' sex differences, founded unwittingly on cultural background factors rather than intrinsic differences, must be re-examined.

These considerations show, not that the data themselves are intrinsically unreliable, but that it is questionable what they mean. What may be interpreted as 'innate' or intrinsic biological differences between the sexes may, on another model of interpretation, be taken as indicating differences in social and cultural factors in male-female socialization in a given society. But Helen Lambert claims that it may be an 'unrealistic goal', especially in the case of higher mental functions, to expect a precise separation of 'the biological bases . . . which are instrinsic in origin and those which are not' (Lambert, 1978: 105).

The few attempts to correlate cross-cultural sex differences with social factors, such as food accumulation and stratification, have not been consistent. Lambert remarks:

> 'Even if they had, this would not prove that intrinsic factors do not affect spatial ability, but only that the sum of the interaction between instrinsic and extrinsic factors varies with culture and geography.' (Lambert, 1978: 113).

Thus, questioning of the magnitude and relevance of observable sex difference as opposed to individual performance and capacity is typical of contemporary science, as it is of Plato's arguments on the 'nature' of sex differences. The within-sex variability of maternal behavior toward daughters indicates still a further factor which is ultimately Plato's concern: education and training (socialization). In Plato's most elite class grouping, the guardian children's training does not take the sex of the child into account, (except for the 'weaker' qualification). This point suggests Plato's theoretical position on psychic capacities in relation to social structure.

Plato's philosophical psychology is based within a functionalist framework. The individual's characteristics are those which make him or her best suited for a certain practice, i.e. a function in society. Correspondingly, the appropriate function for an individual in society is that which he or she is, by nature (individual innate aptitude), best suited to do. This position is not, as it may

---

[17] Study is: Naditch (1976).

sound, circular. Rather, Plato's position is that what a person is, is constituted, in part by social processes.

Although he did not make the following distinctions in precisely the same way, we can clarify Plato's intent by separating:

(a) Individual innate talents or capacities.
(b) Psychic traits.
(c) Behaviors.
(d) Social roles.

An (a) individual talent ('nature' in the sense of capacity), is a given, presumably from birth. Plato does not take a definitive position on whether it is inheritable or not, though he argues for social mobility on the basis that a 'gold' child could be born to 'brass' parents. He has argued, on the present interpretation, that because of (a), individual characteristics are subject to a broad *principle of individual variation*. Such variation is greater than any group of differences between the sexes in observed traits, (b), or behaviors, (c). Hence, Plato argues, social roles (what he would think of as functions) are not justifiably assigned on the basis of membership in a sex group, because individual natures, (a), could lead to traits, (b), and behaviors, (c), which are appropriate to certain social roles, (d), *if training and education appropriate* to (d) are given.

Plato's point can be put as follows: Traits and behaviors are educable. They can be shaped by socialization processes which take individual talents into account. They are not simply 'givens' apart from social processes. Hence, there is a centrality of education in the *Republic* as a whole. It is a mistake to attribute entrance into Plato's aristocracy to 'merit' and 'qualification'. For these, as he emphasizes repeatedly, are results of a process of training individuals' capacities. Yet Plato's individual is not totally malleable. He assumes a 'nature' from birth, perhaps somewhat like the 'readiness to learn' hypothesis in contemporary psychology.

Plato's arrangements for family structure and child-rearing must be mentioned as supporting factors for his thesis on equal training for women guardians. The entire community is 'the family'. 'Marriages' in the form of ritualized matings appear to be spontaneous but are actually arranged by a 'lawgiver' who selects partners who are 'as nearly as possible of the same nature'. [Rep 458d] Part of the purpose appears to be to avoid the disorder of ill-matched unions. [458e] The important aim is to mate the 'best' men with the 'best' women so as to produce a sterling 'herd' of guardians. If Plato's eugenic intentions are taken seriously, then, presumably, there would eventually be effects in the aptitudes of individual children produced. It is difficult to estimate these effects. From the standpoint of contemporary values concerning freedom of choice, Plato's eugenic program appears coercive and especially objectifying of women who were supposed to be freely available to the 'best' warriors.

Communal childrearing, carried out by male and female caretakers [Rep 460b], makes an 'easy job' of motherhood for the female guardians. 'Sleepless nights and other troubles will be left for nurses' and the guardian women will

be left free for civic activities. It is worth pointing out here that Plato's sex-blind specialization of function in professional childrearing might affect the formation of traits and behaviors associated with the child's female or male character structure. In societies where women mother, according to Nancy Chodorow in *Reproduction of Mothering*, female character structure is passed down from mothers (or other female caretakers) to daughters by a complex set of psychological and social relations. Chodorow claims that character structure would develop differently in female and male children if women and men were equally involved in caretaking of infants and young children. Plato did not explicitly anticipate such a situation. But his rearrangement of the social function of parenting does imply at least an absence of certain developmental factors such as maternal influence, which play a strong role in socialization of young children.

If certain 'predisposing factors' (Lambert, 1978: 113), factors such as verbal precocity in infant girls 'bend the twig' in a certain direction, then it is socio-cultural factors which shape the extent and the direction of the growth (Sherman, 1978: 174).[18] In Alexander Pope's words:

> 'Tis education forms the common mind;
> Just as the twig is bent, the tree's inclined.'

On this analogy, if cultural factors were to change, then the growth might alter and the twig might bend the branch in a different direction.

Sherman points out that in certain cultures biological factors might lead to the development of male vs female differences which for other cultures would no longer be 'maximally functional'. E.g. the attraction of animal attacks by menstruating women perhaps bars women from hunting in primitive societies. But what is functional in one society may be non-functional or even deleterious in another societal structure. What these cultures regard as 'natural' may vary with their needs, constraints and customs regarding the functions of individuals vs the functions of sex groupings. Something like this point is concluded by Plato in his third argument on what is 'natural' vs 'unnatural' in the education of males and females in his *Republic*. I turn now to his final argument on the nature of sex-differences in education.

---

[18] Sherman refers to the 'trivial and fragile nature of sex related differences in cognition and the flimsy quality of the theories of biological influence' (p. 172) in her conclusion to her detailed review of the evidence. Further,

> 'The bent twig hypothesis suggests that verbal skill may be sex preferred for more females than males. . . . Visual spatial skills have been sex-typed male; they have been part of the historic male role which has commonly involved tasks ranging far from home. As such, visual spatial skills have been thought to be 'naturally' acquired. However, these skills are probably maximally acquired only by males participating in relevant activities sex-typed male (and by those females who in one way or another manage to acquire the relevant experiences). Thus, without awareness, and because of the historic, cultural reasons based in biology, the male subculture has incuded activities which develop spatial skill (e.g. construction toys).' (p. 173).

V

The argument on what is 'Natural' vs 'Unnatural'

What is 'natural', in Plato's terms, is 'according to nature' (*kata physin*). What is 'unnatural' is 'contrary to nature' (*para physin*). What is most interesting about all these points in favor of educating women to guardian status is that Plato wants to conclude ultimately that it is 'natural', whereas the previous and traditional practice of not so educating women is 'unnatural'. Hence, discrimination against women gifted enough for guardianship is 'unnatural'.

> 'Practice and calling must be assigned to both sexes, the same for the same natures?
> Just the same.
> So we have come round to where we began, and we agree that is not against nature to assign music and gymnastic to the wives of the guardians.
> By all means.
> Then our law was not impossible, not only like a pious dream; the law we laid down was natural.
> But rather, it seems, what happens now, the other way of doing things, is unnatural.' (Rep 456c)

The reasoning appears to draw on the previous argument on the 'nature' of individual talent and the principle that persons ought to do what they are 'best suited' to do by nature. If each person and part of society (and each part of the soul) performs the function they are best suited for by nature, then we have a balanced and harmonious society (and person). Plato's conclusion, that education regardless of sex is 'natural', fits with and is partially derived from his definition of justice in Book IV, which immediately precedes his discussion of women and family structure in Book V.

> 'To make health is to settle the parts of the body so as to rule or to be ruled together, *according to nature*; To make disease is to settle that this part rules and that is ruled by another contrary to nature.
> It is.
> On the other hand, . . . to implant justice is to settle the parts of the soul so as to rule and be ruled together *according to nature*; to implant injustice is to settle things so that one part rules and one part is ruled by another *contrary to nature*.' (Rep 445a, my emphasis)

Also, the guardians require a special 'nature' and training:

> 'It needs more leisure than all the others, and more practice and further more skill and care. Does it also need a *nature* fitted for this pursuit? Of course.' (Rep 375a)

From this definition of justice and the claim that the guardians possess a certain 'nature' which is found in women as well as men, it follows that exclusion of women from guardian education is both *unjust and unnatural*. Inclusion of women is therefore both *just and natural*.

In this last argument Plato politicizes what is 'natural'. Against the Aristotelian claim that it is 'natural' that women be ruled by men, Plato puts the more radical claim that it is 'unnatural' that power be distributed in a way that prohibits women from attaining the social function (role) or leadership for which they may be suited. In Aristotle's view, the relation between the male and female is a union 'not of deliberate purpose', but a union of 'natural ruler and subject', (*Politics* 1252a 30). In Plato's view, 'natural leadership' must not slip by unexamined.

Plato, however, does not implicitly state that his proposals for women are just. Nor does he state that lack of equal education for women is unjust. So the above inference, that exclusion of gifted women from guardian education is unjust, needs further support.

We may distinguish three senses of 'natural' in the above argument. (1) A person's work in society is 'natural' in that it is suited to his or her individual nature; (2) when X is arranged 'according to nature', X functions well; (3) a law or practice arranged 'according to nature', is one that functions well. The best functioning society is one which is arranged according to nature so that the best rules. (3) is the social application of the more general (2) (which may apply to the soul or to society). It follows that when a society has laws or practices which bar persons from functions for which their nature (1) best suits them, such practices are 'unnatural' in sense (3). They fail to be arranged 'according to nature'. Plato develops the connection between (1) and (2)–(3) in the definition of justice: the best functioning society—i.e. the *just* society—is one which is arranged on a principle of specialization in accordance with individual natures, so that each part does its own function, namely, that for which it is best suited (Rep 433a).

Perhaps what is required here is a principle of maximal functioning to supplement Plato's principle of specialization of functioning. Justice requires not only that each part do its *own* work, but that *all* parts function according to their proper natures, and not lie dormant and unawakened. If the force of 'each' is taken to include 'all', then the criterion is met. At Republic 433a justice is defined:

> 'Every single person ought to engage in that social function [literally: that function which concerns the polis] for which their own nature is best fitted.' (Vlastos, 1971: 73).[19]

On the other hand, the active prohibition of some thing or person from functioning according to its nature runs counter to the requirement that the ideal

---

[19] Vlastos (1971: 72) points out that the principle—to do one's own—rests on an assumption of human interdependence.

society be structured along lines beneficial to the state. What fails stands in the way of such benefit, falls short of justice and in that sense is unjust. Plato explicitly concludes that education of women is both 'possible' and 'the best way' [Rep 456a]. Then, because there is 'nothing better for the state than the generation of the best leaders out of the best men and women' [Rep 457a], education of women is both possible and beneficial.

Given the close connections between Plato's arguments on the 'nature' of persons in Book V and his preceding definitions of justice, it seems misleading to claim that the 'sole ground' for his proposals is 'their usefulness to the state' (Annas, 1976: 312–313). Rather, the implication is that practices such as education of women fit into a conception of justice which is worthy for its own sake, in which one part rules according to nature. The value of justice, under this conception, is that it is a good in itself (Irwin, 1977: 213). But this does not preclude that it could have beneficial consequences in addition, as Plato points out.

Plato can be criticized for (1) objectifying women from a masculine viewpoint, e.g. in his frequent references to guardian women as 'wives of guardians'; (2) failing to take account of the sex of guardian children, e.g. of the fact that incoming female children might already have certain traits which would make the results of equal education be unequal for boys and girls (Martin, 1982); (3) imposing a masculine education on female guardians to such an extent that women lose their sense of identity as women (Elshtain, 1981: 37–38).

In response, Plato deserves criticisms on (1). But on (2) one wonders whether 'the same' education could be overinterpreted. Granted, socialized females and males, already possessed of a gender identity, will respond differently to the same curriculum. Yet 'the same' curriculum need not imply identical programs and methods, as Plato has already indicated in his (physically) 'weaker' qualification for the exercises for guardians. He remarks, in Book VII, that children should be taught, not by compulsory methods, but 'by a kind of a game, and then you will be able to see more clearly the natural bent of each' [Rep 537b]. Such methods could allow for developmental sex differences, e.g. that girls mature faster verbally and physically (contrary to Plato) than boys. Although misogyny and objectification remain in Plato's account, his educational program gives some principles for removing them. Plato's censors could be updated so that they would extract submissive wives from children's tales and feature strong women-gods. On (3), Plato's war-readiness training appears masculinized. Yet a careful reading of Plato shows that he considers the training in music and poetry equally important, to a degree that might make some contemporary men balk at being feminized. There is no evidence that gender-identity would disappear in the Republic, although there is indication that the concept of gender and its specific form of gender might be modified for the guardians. It is precisely this aspect of Plato's ideal state which illustrates how radical it actually is.

In concluding, I would like to emphasize the connection between what I have taken to be Plato's analytic probing of the 'nature' of sex differences and his radical assertion that, ideally, society would be arranged to elicit the best

from individuals regardless of gender. He claims that the latter is 'natural', whereas societal arrangements which preserve traditional gender-roles and division of labor are 'unnatural' if they fail to allow women civic leadership. As mentioned in the introduction, this last claim has more than a touch of irony. Plato surely recognizes that shifts in gender structure are deviations and commonly held to be 'unnatural'. Yet, when subjected to analytic scrutiny, the traditional sex-role divisions of labor are not based on the 'nature' of actual individuals but on another set of social and political imperatives.

Plato, it might be said, draws out the best *of* women (as individuals), rather than the best *from* women (as a group). This is a defect of his 'equality' of education. It is only 'equal' for a select set of guardian women. While there is strong basis for this criticism if Plato's discussion of his aristocracy is taken solely as a proposal for a social structure, I wish to suggest an alternate, less literal reading of Plato. In his dialogue *The Republic*, Plato continually shifts between and intertwines moral and social levels. The 'ideal state' presents the analogue to the soul, 'writ large' on the scale of society. In the ideal state, moral ends always inform social organization. What Plato says about the guardians is a metaphor for 'the best' in society as well as the soul. It is in the true interests of all that women contribute the best they have to offer, because whatever is beneficial to the ideal state is beneficial to all within it. In Book VII Plato follows his discussion of the cave with a description of the final stages of education in dialectic. In an indication of Plato's seriousness, Socrates admonishes Glaucon:

> 'And do not forget the women, Glaucon. They may be rulers too. Do not suppose that what I have said [on education into dialectic] was meant only for men; women too, as are born among us with natures sufficiently capable.' (Rep 540c)

Plato's reminder may be taken as an affirmation that women as well as men can live the philosophic life—in Plato's political analogy, become guardians. Such a life, which Plato has described in Book VII, is one of contemplation and practical action in pursuit of wisdom.[20]

REFERENCES

Allen, Christine. 1975. Plato on women. *Feminist Studies* 11(2/3): 131–138.
Annas, Julia. 1976. Plato's Republic and feminism. *Philosophy* 51: 307–321.
Berry, J. W. 1966. Temne and Eskimo perceptual skills. *Int. J. Psychology* 1.
Bloom, Allan. 1968. Interpretive essay. In *The Republic of Plato*. Basic Books, New York.

[20] For support during the research and writing of this essay I am grateful to the Smith College Mellon Project on Women and Social Change. My thanks to Dr Carla Golden (Psychology, Smith College), who gave technical advice and to the referees of *Hypatia* for helpful suggestions.

Chodorow, Nancy. 1978. *The Reproduction of Mothering*. University of California Press, Los Angeles.

Elshtain, Jean B. 1981. *Public Man, Private Woman*. Princeton University Press, Princeton, NJ.

Green, Philip. 1976. IQ and the future of equality. *Dissent* 409–424.

Irwin, Terence. 1977. *Plato's Moral Theory*. Clarendon Press, Oxford.

Kagan, J. and N. Kogan. 1970. Individual variation in cognitive processes. In Mussen, P. H., ed., *Carmichael's Manual of Child Psychology*. John Wiley, New York.

Lambert, Helen. 1978. Biology and equality: a perspective on sex differences. *Signs* 4(1): 97–117.

Lange, Lynda. 1979. The function of equal education in Plato's Republic and laws. In Clark, L. and L. Lange eds, *The Sexism of Social and Political Theory*. University of Toronto Press, Toronto.

Maccoby, E. and C. Jacklin. 1974. *The Psychology of Sex Differences*. Stanford University Press, Stanford.

Martin, Jane. 1982. Sex equality and education in Plato's Just State. In Mary Vetterling-Braggin, ed., *'Femininity,' 'Masculinity,' and 'Androgyny'*. Littlefield, Adams, New Jersey.

Mill, J. S. and Harriet Taylor. 1970. *Essays on Sex Equality*, Rossi, A., ed. University of Chicago Press, Chicago.

Naditch, S. F. 1976. Sex Differences in Field Dependence. American Psychological Association, Washington D.C.

Okin, Susan. 1979. *Women in Western Political Thought*. Princeton University Press, Princeton, NJ.

Pierce, Christine. 1973. Equality: Republic V. *The Monist* **LVII** (January: 1–11.

Rossi, Alice, ed. 1970. *Essays in Sex Equality*, by J. S. Mill and H. Taylor. University of Chicago Press, Chicago.

Rothbart, M. K. 1971. Birth order and mother-child interaction in an achievement situation. *J. Personality Soc. Psychology* 17: 113–120.

Rouse, W. H. D. 1956. *Great Dialogues of Plato*. New American Library, New York.

Sherman, Julia. 1978. *Sex-Related Cognitive Differences*. Charles Thomas, Springfield, Illinois.

Spelman, Elizabeth. 1983. Aristotle and the politicalization of the soul. In Harding, S. and Merill Hintikka, eds, *Discovering Reality*. D. Reidel, Dordrecht-Holland.

Vlastos, Gregory. 1971. Justice and happiness in the Republic. In *Plato II*, Vlastos, G., ed. University of Notre Dame Press, Indiana.

Williams, J. H. 1977. *Psychology of Women: Behavior in a Bisocial Context*. W. W. Norton, New York.

HOW ORDINARY (SEXIST) DISCOURSE RESISTS RADICAL (FEMINIST) CRITIQUE

Terry R. Winant

How is sexism in language to be understood? How ought we to go about eliminating it? In this essay, I explore in detail the workings of a particular piece of sexist communication. By way of this case study, I provide reason to believe that any adequate account of sexist discourse will require more than a semantics for sexist utterances, gestures and images. This is to say, we must go beyond the study of the meanings intrinsic to instances of sexist discourse, and begin to investigate the background beliefs and presuppositions which make such discourse intelligible. If we are to learn how to recognize and cope with sexist discourse, we will need to address the pragmatics of sexism.[1]

Recent work in the philosophy of language takes pragmatics seriously. This is to say that the study of discourse as part of the world of tools and goals, means and ends, has been recognized as an inescapable part of the study of language. There is no way to figure out how language works without taking into account the diverse ways in which it can function as means to certain ends, and there is no way to describe and explain in this diversity without learning how to discover the interests and goals of linguistic agents in terms of the situation of the agent in a world comprised of—among other things—discourse. Included among these other things are not only the conflicting interests of other agents, but also the agent's own conflicts of interest.

Once disinterestedness is understood to be a dangerous oversimplification (more dangerous even than context-free-ness), the philosophy of language can take an important political turn: pragmatic analysis becomes a tool not only for revealing the implicit presuppositions of a linguistic practice, but also for intervening in the process whereby the discursive situation circumscribes these

---

[1] By 'we', I mean 'we feminists'. But this will produce difficulties to which the reader should be alerted: ordinary language (in this case, ordinary English) is 'our' language in the sense that we have been raised with it (or have learned it as a second language) and we both can and do find it intelligible. But insofar as it systematically misrepresents us, so that we are not willing to own up to it, there is a sense in which it is not 'ours'.

presuppositions. The result is that pragmatic analysis can hope not only to figure out how specific bits of discourse reflect the specifics of the world in which they are situated, it can also aim to figure out how the bits of discourse help to generate the specifics of the world. Only an analysis which makes implicit presuppositions explicit and which shows the mechanism whereby they are (even only partially) generated as implicit presuppositions, will permit some sort of intervention in this mechanism.

Thus, a theory of the political critique of language involves both of these claims:

— An analysis that makes implicit presuppositions explicit in order to display the mechanism whereby they are generated can permit intervention in the mechanism of their generation.

— An account of this 'intervening' must be given in terms of the context-of-interest of the discourse in which the presuppositions are embedded.

Most of my essay is taken up with a case study of the sort of pragmatic analysis such a critique requires.[2]

In Part I, I introduce an argument designed to support a feminist political response to the publicity surrounding the movie, *Bloodline*—publicity which many feminists found offensive.[3] I then carry out a speech-act analysis of the *Bloodline* publicity. By a 'speech-act analysis' I mean the study of a particular piece of discourse understood as a human accomplishment. Such study is inspired by the work of J. L. Austin (Austin, 1962).[4] This sort of analysis treats the ad as a bit of ordinary discourse, i.e. as an act of communication. Part II of my paper uses the speech-act analysis to show the ad reflects a sexist background belief. It produces three claims:

(1) The ambiguity of the ad comes from flouting a rule about what is 'in' and what is 'out' of a picture.

(2) The proposition 'sex is violence' operates as background belief the denial of which would make the ad ineffectual as an ad.

(3) There must be some sort of rule about depicting actions, in accordance with which it's a woman whose picture is shown in the *Bloodline* ad.

---

[2] A version of some of my work on the *Bloodline* ad appeared under the title 'Decoding the Grammar of the Image' in the Winter 1982 issue of Madison, Wisconsin's feminist magazine, *Bread & Roses* (Winant, 1982).

[3] It's not my purpose in this paper to take sides in the feminist debate about pornography. The sort of analysis I'm attempting may or may not have consequences for that debate, but is of importance mostly for the feminist treatment of ordinary discursive abuse: we need to learn to analyse and criticize effectively the texts and images of our ordinary day-to-day lives, and the great majority of these are not pornographic.

[4] Austin observed that some deeds are done with words (He called words so used 'performative utterances' (Austin, 1970).) From this point of view, it is possible to ask what sort of activity human beings are engaged in, who participate in the discourse of which the *Bloodline* ad is an element. For an introductory handbook on the application of speech-act analysis to a very wide variety of texts, see Robert Fogelin's informal logic textbook, *Understanding Arguments*.

Part III of my paper provides an analysis of the distribution of power among the participants in the communication effected by the ad, thus showing how the ad helps generate the sexist background belief. It produces these results:

(1) An account of the devalorization of the feminist's judgment that violence isn't sexy.
(2) An account of the discounting of her finding the ad repulsive.
(3) An account of the resulting incapacity effectively to express her opposition to the ad.

Part IV of the paper attempts to explain why the sort of analysis I provide here was not readily available to feminists who needed it at the time of the movie's release. My explanation addresses the following question: what makes it so difficult to learn to recognize and handle sexism's appearance in ordinary discourse? I try to show how the violence perpetrated against us as women is compounded, at the level of communication, with a draining off of our capacity for critical analysis.[5] Thus, whenever these capacities are most relevant the communicative context will be one in which they are compromised.

I

The case I study arose in summer 1979, when a major movie, *Sidney Sheldon's Bloodline*, was publicized by means of billboards and newspaper ads showing a woman in a state one might equally well describe as ecstasy of sex or as terror of murder.

A feminist organization, Women Against Violence Against Women, complained to Paramount Pictures. Demonstrations were organized. Feminists wanted to get rid of this publicity and to extract from the motion picture industry a statement of policy aimed at avoiding publicity of this sort in the future. Such ads, WAVAW claimed, epitomize the sort of 'media images of women' that capitalize on the victimization of women in our sexist society.

Both strategically and theoretically, I support WAVAW's position on the *Bloodline* ad. But I do not believe that WAVAW's defense of the position was adequate. WAVAW needed—but failed to supply—an argument based on an interest-based, pragmatic analysis of the ad.

Instead, WAVAW allowed its position to rest on three observations:

— Such advertising assumes that violence is sexy.
— Such advertising is violent: it is an image of a victim as victim.
— Such advertising is deceptive: it portrays a terrible thing as if it were a fine thing.

---

[5] It will become clear that critical analysis at the level of communication is what's 'drained off', on my account: because our capacity to do the *pragmatic* analysis is compromised, we find the sexism of ordinary communication difficult to recognize and confront. Of course I do not mean to claim that the violence we experience as the target of sexist abuse is somehow drained off.

THE LINE BETWEEN LOVE AND DEATH IS THE BLOODLINE.

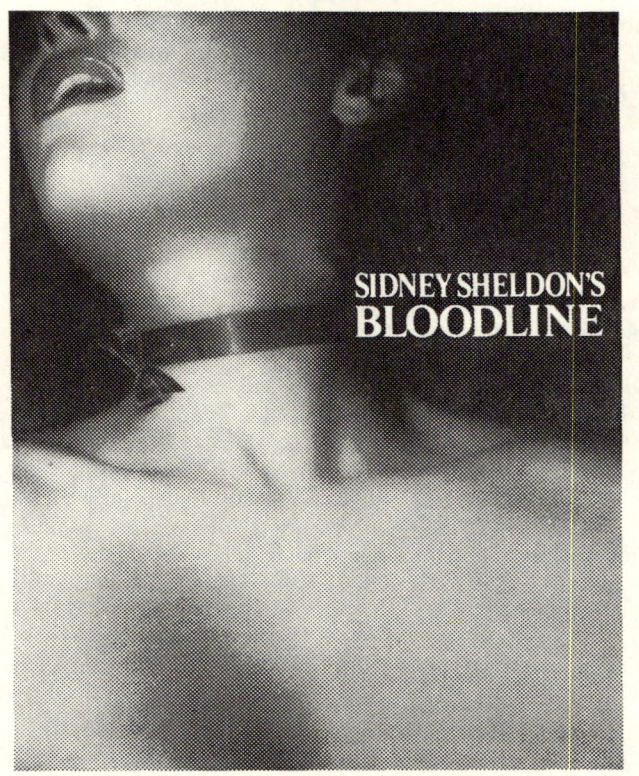

SIDNEY SHELDON'S
BLOODLINE

AUDREY HEPBURN	BEN GAZZARA	JAMES MASON	MICHELLE PHILLIPS	OMAR SHARIF

To oppose the ad on this basis is to sidestep what ought to be the main target of analysis and criticism: the mechanism that generates ideological legitimacy for the victimization of women as objects of sexual violence.

On my account, the argument WAVAW needed turns on a pragmatic analysis of the ad. This is to say, we (and WAVAW) ought to treat the ad as a sexist communicative act, and aim for a precise answer to the following question:

What makes this communicative act a *sexist* communicative act?

Here is the argument I believe WAVAW needed:

(1) The *Bloodline* ad, considered as a communicative act, is ambiguous between sex and violence.

(2) While an explicit identification of sex with violence would be overtly repulsive, the ad, by implicitly identifying them, deprives its audience of the opportunity to assess the truth of the claim 'sex is violence'.

(3) The intelligibility of the ad (together with its effectiveness as an advertisement) depends on its audience's readiness to identify sex with violence.

(4) Only in a society in which the perpetration of violence on one's sex partners is second nature would there be such a readiness to identify sex with violence.

(5) Only the explicit calling of our attention to this identification can, by providing the opportunity to assign a truth value, dislodge violent sex from its position as 'second nature', and thus allow its repulsiveness to play a leading role in its elimination.

From this it follows both that

(6) Paramount Pictures' *Bloodline* publicity depends for its effectiveness on this fact about our society: it's a matter of course that sex involves violence,

and that

(7) The *Bloodline* publicity helps sustain the position of sexual violence as 'a matter of course in our sexist society'.

Two separate sorts of analyses are required to support this argument. The speech-act analysis I provide in Part II supports the argument to the first part of the conclusion; it shows how the *Bloodline* ad reflects society's legitimation of violence against women. (Lines 1, 2, 4 and 6.) The remainder of the argument (Lines 3, 5 and 7) shows how the ad contributes to the production of such violence. It demands an inquiry into what power is conferred (and on whom) in the observance, exploitation, and manipulation of the rules governing communicative acts such as this ad. The analysis I give in Part III supports the argument to the second conclusion; it demonstrates that the ad helps create the legitimation of violence against women in a sexist society.

Notice that the argument I am offering emphasizes the ambiguity of the image rather than its violence, and that it turns on the difference between

implicit and explicit expression rather than on deception. These are among the argument's strengths, since, as I shall show, they ensure that the argument is not subject to refutation on the grounds that—in the sexist society in which we live—sex is, as a matter of fact, often violent, and violence is, as a matter of fact, often sexy.

II

My immediate aim is to discover the rules governing the use of the *Bloodline* ad as an act of communication. I try to find out how the ad works by adapting some methods from speech-act analysis to the 'speech' situation of a movie ad. Thus, I begin by imagining that the ad is an effective ad. On this assumption, I look for the mechanism that would make it effective. Since I'm dealing with publicity for a movie, to be an effective ad just is to help get people to see the movie. In a standard movie-publicity context, the viewer of the ad is a pro-spective moviegoer. In a standard context for such advertisements, the viewer is competent to make sense of the ad.[6] For the *Bloodline* ad to work as an ad, it must be intelligible to the great mass of moviegoers.

In a standard context, then, how does the ad appear? What does it seem to be from the point of view of a prospective moviegoer? The *Bloodline* ad appears to be a captioned photograph. In fact, it's a little more complicated than this. Although the photo is in Black & White, it has superimposed on it a picture of a red ribbon. The caption is partially superimposed on the photo, so that it seems to become a part of the photo itself. (I will say more below about the caption.)

Considered simply as a photograph, the *Bloodline* ad is ambiguous. Judging from the woman's facial expression, one might say this is a picture of someone in a great deal of pain—or in cosmic orgasm. The neck is at a very odd angle, as if to complement the extraordinary face. One might take it to have been pushed back and to the side by an assailant, absent from the photo (because— and this is a result of geometrical optics and the laws of perspective—such an assailant would have to be located 'behind the camera'). Or perhaps the woman has thrown her head back and tensed her neck muscles in sexual excitement (and it is her lover the viewer is to imagine in the place of the camera). There is a dark stripe across the woman's neck; one might take it to be a bloody gash, but it is a ribbon.

The ribbon is important. Suppose at first glance I were to take the photo in its violent reading as a woman being tortured. I would then anticipate that a close look at the photo would bear out this interpretation, and perhaps fill in more detail. But instead, a closer look would reveal the ribbon as other than

---

[6] The advertiser is also standardly aware of the viewer's competence as a viewer. For a discussion of what makes a speech situation 'standard', and of how to analyse speech acts by contrasting their standard functions with their actual accomplishments, see Grice (1975).

a wound, my expectations would be dashed, and the photograph would resolve itself into a photo of a woman in a state of sexual excitement.

Indeed, were things to reach this point I would do well, I believe, to ask myself how come I misread the photo; how come I mistook sex for violence. I should then, perhaps, even come to think that the subtlety of the photo was its having only this ribbon to decide which of the two readings is correct. Maybe this subtlety would then seem to be just what it takes to trick me into recognizing that—whatever I may do or say openly—I, too am among those capable of mistaking sex for violence.[7] But this is not yet an accurate account of how the ad works.

The ad, remember, is a *captioned* photo. It is captioned in two ways. The main caption is, 'The line between love and death is the bloodline'. In addition, the words 'Sidney Sheldon's BLOODLINE' occur on the photograph itself, with the word 'BLOODLINE' located so as to make it into a continuation of the ribbon. So the ribbon and the caption BLOODLINE are not two items but one, and this item is not genuinely either in the picture or out of it. Super-imposed on the photo, it maintains the photo's ambiguity. For while the ribbon would resolve the photo into its sexual interpretation, the word 'BLOODLINE' bears out a violent interpretation. No closer look at the ad will decide between them. The viewer is not to blame for the apparent misreading of the photo; the caption is. Moreover, the main caption reinforces this. It is less a caption for the photo than for the item superimposed on the photo, since it mentions the stripe (which is the bloodline) and so confirms the viewer in her incapacity to settle on one of the two interpretations of the image.

The central points here are that the ambiguity is in the ad rather than con-tributed by the viewer, and that the capacity of the ad to be intrinsically am-biguous is a function of the relationship between the photograph and its caption—in particular of the presence of material that is neither photograph nor caption, but transitional between the two. If the ad is a communicative act, its context turns out to be not a standard movie-publicity context after all: the ambiguity is produced as a 'special effect' of flouting a rule which governs such contexts, at least when they involve the use of photographic images.[8] The rule is, 'respect the distinction between the photograph (a fat, paper thing made by a certain chemical process) and the photograph's subject-matter!'

Now rules of this sort are often broken in ways that are not offensive, and this rule has no special status. In the *Bloodline* ad, however, the special effect produced by breaking this rule is not inoffensive. It tricks the viewer into

---

[7] I suspect that this is what the advertising experts at Paramount had in mind. And I suspect this is an account of the ad which Paramount Pictures would welcome. After all, it describes the ad as provocative, and thus goes at least part way towards explaining why it would be an effective lure into the movie houses.

[8] It will be objected that such flouting is totally normal in movie-publicity contexts. Indeed, it is normal to exploit the conventions of standard communicative contexts and thus to seduce (rather than persuade) people to flock to the movie houses. Here, however, I am making use of a technical sense of 'standard context': if one states (or portrays) one thing in order to communicate another, the context is not a standard one.

taking the blame for her inability to decide between the sexual reading and the violent reading of the ad. She does not suspect that a rule has been broken, and so takes the ribbon to be a part of the photo's subject-matter (a part which she tellingly took for a bloody gash) while taking the word 'BLOODLINE' to be a part of the caption. As long as she supposes the rule to be in force, i.e. as long as she takes this context to be a standard context, she will not see the word 'BLOODLINE' to be part of the ambiguous image, and will blame herself for the misinterpretation. As I will argue, such misplacing of blame—and not the mere flouting of the rules—is what turns out to be offensive.

Having rejected the account according to which the viewer contributes the ambiguity, I seem to have produced a riddle: if the ad is genuinely intrinsically ambiguous, how can the viewer make sense of it all? How come it doesn't wobble back and forth or shimmer the way an optical illusion does? How come the viewer is not simply confused by it, as one typically is by ambiguity that goes unresolved?

Where there is nothing at all to select one reading over the other, stability can be attained, and confusion forestalled, by conflating the two. I believe that there are several ways to show that the *Bloodline* ad does indeed conflate sex with violence. Such conflation would make the expectation that there be a resolution in favor of one or the other into a mistaken expectation.[9] One way to show that there is such a conflation is to consider the ad as offering an argument to the conclusion that we (the ad's viewers) ought to go to see the movie. The caption superimposed on the photo tells us the movie's title: *Bloodline*. It's reasonable to suppose that a movie with this title is about the bloodline (whatever that might be). So, if we're interested in the bloodline, we ought to go see the movie. Yet the main caption tells us that the line between love and death is the bloodline. Are we interested in the line between love and death? (If so, we ought to go see the movie.) Now, if love and death are to have a line drawn between them, it must be that they have a range of borderline cases between them. Among the rules of communication is 'Be sympathetic!' The viewer thus standardly grants the missing premise, and everything proceeds as though there were no disagreement as to the existence of a range of borderline cases in which love passes over into death. In such borderline cases the sexual love and the violent death would be conflated. (On the off chance that the viewer is less than sympathetic, the ad portrays a borderline case in point, using the photographic special effects described above to keep the image on the borderline.)

A second way to show that the ad conflates sex with violence is to notice that my story about a viewer whose expectations were dashed is inaccurate in a way I have yet to mention. The initial reading of the ad as purely violent doesn't actually occur. Rather, the initial reading makes the image out to be an erotic gory image. That's all. The viewer may be angered, or otherwise aroused, but the image is familiar and the viewer is not surprised by it. The image is genu-

[9] It is also the 'identification of sex with violence' that WAVAW has made such an issue of.

inely ambiguous, and it would be unstable were it not for the viewer's readiness to contribute the required conflation of the sexual with the violent reading. This conflation is so familiar, though, that the ad needn't even give the viewer a clue, and can nonetheless count on the viewer's contribution of exactly the right equation. Indeed, the ad can even seem to contest the equation of sex and violence, and still not lose (but rather reinforce) the background belief in their identity.

It is not only with violence, but with violence perpetrated against women that sex is identified: the erotic gory image is an image of a woman, and needs to be. Had the image been of a human being, but not obviously of a woman (or a man) the viewer would still take it to be of a woman.[10] What accounts for the fact that this image has to be an image of a woman? If this is a fact about the way images work in communication, then there must be some sort of rule governing communication by pictures, which rule restricts the gender of a human being pictured as victim of sex/violence. I want to formulate a rule of the sort that could do this, in order to show how such a rule might work.[11] I think that such a rule must accomplish what grammatical inflection accomplishes for spoken language: it indicates the 'grammatical roles' of various discursive elements by means of their placement in the discourse, just as in English, say, word order indicates the grammatical roles of various linguistic elements.

A rule I suggest might be at work here is an analogue of the English grammar rule, 'When the subject is the receiver of the action, the verb is in the passive voice, and the doer of the action may occur in a prepositional phrase beginning with "by", or may be left out'. While voice is marked by an inflection of the verb, it expresses a relation between the subject and the predicate of a sentence.

But a sentence is also, in its context, deployed in one or another speech act. Something about the relation between the subject and the speech act is indicated in the distinction among 1st, 2nd and 3rd persons. Passive impersonal constructions are often 3rd-person constructions, e.g. 'The dog's been fed'. Stating this sentence would be a speech act performed between two people; the dog is an absent object referred to in the 3rd person. Unless the context supplies another likely candidate, an interlocutor who wonders who fed the dog is likely to suppose it to have been the speaker. (The interlocutor is not out of bounds even in suspecting that the speaker is attempting to shirk the responsibility—why else use the impersonal construction?)

Pulling these remarks about grammar back to the *Bloodline* ad, my invented rule governing the images of actions is: 'When the subject is the receiver of the action, the image is grammatically passive and the doer of the action may be altogether absent'. The ad shows someone on the receiving end of a sexual/

---

[10] It could not be an image of a man and still work as publicity for a major Hollywood movie, for the suggestion of homosexuality would be too strong. Here 'too strong' just means strong enough to be distracting. The fact that it would be this strong is a symptom, I believe, of the way that sexism and heterosexism are linked together and reinforce one another.

[11] I don't claim to have found exactly this rule at work in the social world; the empirical investigation of gender grammar is not part of my project her. All I claim is that a rule of a certain kind would explain this bit of gender differentiation. All I do is suggest a candidate for such a rule.

violent action. The perpetrator of this action is not shown in, but absent from, the image.

To label the image grammatically passive does not say very much unless we also notice its use in a communicative act. In this case, the image is deployed in advertising the movie. Both the advertiser and the potential customer must be parties to the communication the ad effects. It is a significant feature of the *Bloodline* ad (and perhaps of discursive abuse generally) that the ad's subject is not among parties to the communicative act. The victim is shown in the image, but absent from the speech situation in which the image is effective.[12] In fact, the *Bloodline* ad is 'grammatically 3rd-person'. But how is this effected? My proposal is this: the gender of the picture's subject makes the image 3rd-person.

What I am suggesting is that in our society's dominant discourse (a discourse within which our socialization was accomplished and which we must continue to use, even as it marginalizes us and we attempt to break away from it) a grammatically passive image of a woman is a 3rd-person 'impersonal' image. Were this the case, it would explain why a viewer who wonders who the agent is most likely will suppose that the agent is the only person whose absence from the picture is at all salient: whoever is located 'behind the camera'. On this account, the agent of the sexual/violent act would be someone whose point of view is identical to that of the viewer herself: this would help explain the provocativeness of this image.

If I'm anywhere near right about the 'grammar' of the 3rd-person passive image, then the *Bloodline* ad is a good example of how ordinary discourse is sexist in a way that pragmatic analysis can help display. The analysis of the ad also shows how the readiness to buy the claim that sex is violence is a reflection not simply of our society's readiness to perpetrate sexual violence, but rather of its readiness to perpetrate violence on women as such. Taken together with the doctoring of the image which manipulates the viewer into blaming herself for its ambiguity, the grammatical analysis begins to make explicit the mechanisms of the 'blame the victim' phenomenon.

So far, my speech-act analysis has shown how the *Bloodline* ad reflects the background belief that sex is violence. By making the assumption that the context is a standard one, I have been able to compare the actual workings of this image with the conventions governing communication generally. The comparison shows that the ambiguity arises from the flouting of a communicative convention which may be formulated as follows: 'In using images, respect the distinction between what is 'in' and what is 'out' of the picture!' This tacit rule

---

[12] I don't want to claim that those who are drawn to this movie by the ad are never themselves the victims of sexual violence. And certainly, I don't want to claim that the victims of sexual violence cannot find this ad intelligible. Either of these claims would, I believe, commit me to the (false, I believe) view that women are not part of the audience of this ad. I do want to claim, however, that for any woman the price of entry into this communicative situation is the denial of her victimization. Insofar as we refuse to deny that we are victims of sexual violence we find that the discourse within which this image is intelligible is not our discourse, but that of a misogynist culture we intend to overthrow.

is among the presuppositions which make ordinary communicative acts intelligible. Its violation shows that the ambiguity is in the ad; it's not the viewer's contribution.

By describing two ways in which the intrinsic ambiguity may be read, I have shown the role of the conflation of sex with violence in the mechanism which makes the *Bloodline* ad intelligible. It plays the role of a background belief. I have argued that the tacit conventions presupposed by this image must include a rule restricting the gender of the image. I have provided a rule of the appropriate sort, suggested by an analogue in ordinary English. I have also shown how the presuppositions that render the image intelligible reflect the familiar pattern known as 'blame the victim'.

III

Having looked at how ordinary (sexist) discourse might be the means whereby the *Bloodline* ad reflects the perpetration of violence against women in our society, it behooves me to look at how the *Bloodline* ad helps to produce the perpetration of violence against women. Still considering the ad as an act of communication, I want to ask just how the ad helps limit communication to ordinary (sexist) discourse, and just what power relations are created by this limitation.

I said above that the ad's effectiveness depends on the background belief that sex is violence. Here I want to go further, and point out that this particular mechanism for communication actually amounts to a limitation on communication: I mean that were communication fully possible within ordinary discourse, there could be no communicative acts depending on such a background belief. I do not want to argue that no background beliefs whatsoever could be presupposed, but rather that the belief that sex is violence is typical of a sort of background belief that could not be presupposed.

This is so because in an unrestricted communicative situation everyone would share whatever background beliefs could be presupposed. Those of us who are the victims of sexual violence cannot share the belief that sex is violence. To the extent that we behave as though we did share this belief, e.g. we don't find the *Bloodline* ad unintelligible, we either reject our interest in our sexuality or we mistake our own interest for that of the perpetrator of sexual violence.[13] To the extent that ordinary discourse presupposes background beliefs held by the perpetrators but not by the victims of violence (and more generally, of exploitation and oppression), ordinary discourse limits the possibilities for communication.

This sort of limitation may be characterized as the absence from the ad's context of any opportunity to call the presupposition into question. It is a feature

---

[13] Catherine MacKinnon's work is relevant here (1982).

of background beliefs that they are too obvious to need discussion. In the context of the *Bloodline* ad, the feminist who claims that violence isn't sexy, or that sex needn't be violent, is guilty of a *non sequitur*. Her judgment is irrelevant because the opportunity to pass judgment is absent.

It will be objected that this absence is not really produced by the ad, but rather is a simple lapse, a sin of omission, as it were. This would be mistaken. For if it were merely a lapse, the ad would differ somehow from the communicative act one would perform were one actively engaged in making the feminist's judgment irrelevant. But it doesn't. To see that this is so, notice that in order to render her judgment irrelevant it's necessary to deprive her of the opportunity to judge. This in turn requires that the proposition 'sex is violent' not occur explicitly, even in order to be affirmed: any communicative act explicitly affirming it counts as an opportunity for its denial. Indeed, the *Bloodline* ad is typical of the sort of communicative act that effectively deprives some members of a speech community of an occasion for contesting a judgment passed by others and in respect of which they cannot help but behave.

Now, recall that the proposition 'sex is violence' is kept merely implicit (and thus made to work as a background belief) by a mechanism involving the flouting of a rule about how photographs picture their subject-matter (see above). As it turns out, the opportunity of which the viewer is deprived is not only the opportunity to deny that sex is violence, but also the opportunity to find the erotic gory image to be a repulsive image. The communicative special effects of the ad include stabilization of the image's ambiguity by means of displacement onto the viewer of the blame for the image's intrinsic ambiguity (see above). Thus, the viewer has only herself to blame if she finds the image repulsive. Moreover, should her emotional response be other than repulsion, the object of her feelings will not be the ad.

The *Bloodline* ad exemplifies how the constitution of ordinary discourse limits the range of our emotional response, for it is our being repulsed by the ad itself which would lead us to interrogate its conflation of sex with violence. This interrogation does not lead quickly and easily to the simple denial of the proposition that sex is violence. Rather, it leads to a difficult project—the uncovering of the historical and cultural locus of sexual violence: when and where, and how and why is sex violent or violence sexy? This is work feminists need to undertake. But these questions are hard to confront without oversimplification. What such difficulties show is that the tendency to oversimplistic treatment of these questions is itself a sexist tendency.

The speech act analysis of the *Bloodline* ad reveals that the ambiguity of the image is stabilized by the flouting of a rule governing communication. In so doing it displaces blame for the ambiguity into the viewer. The discourse thus reflects the familiar pattern known as 'blame the victim'. Considered as limiting communicative acts, however, flouting this rule also helps create that pattern. As long as the viewer suspects no flouting of the rules, she will not see the ribbon as part of the caption, but rather as part of an ambiguous image. The image's failure to resolve itself one way or the other will be blamed on the

viewer: she can make the image settle down only by 'overcoming' her repulsion and conflating violence with sex. This amounts to looking at the image from the point of view of the perpetrator of sexual violence (who ostensibly doesn't find the erotic gory image repulsive).

This shift of point of view is a consequence of presupposing the rule the ad flouts, namely: the rule that demands a sharp distinction between what is 'in' and what is 'out' of the picture. Because the rule is partly constitutive of the discourse, the viewer fails to make this shift only at the expense of her place in the discursive community. If she does not make this shift the ad will seem unintelligible to her, and she will seem naïve.

Let me emphasize again that it is not as though all flouting of rules governing communication, or even of this rule about what is in and what is out of the picture, count as sexist (or otherwise offensive) limiting of communication. Rather, the flouting of this rule in this way—forcing the viewer to either sacrifice her place in the discourse or else make a self-compromising shift of viewpoint within it—is a particular type of manipulation of the discourse: it distorts critical capacities to the detriment of the victims of sexist violence. This is so because the victim needs to recognize that her victimization is unbearable if she is ever to oppose it effectively, and the image is doctored in such as way as to constrain her options: she must either withdraw from an unintelligible object as though it were of no concern to her, or else 'overcome' the repulsion which might have led her to the sorely needed recognition of her victimization. What is missing from this communicative context is the opportunity explicitly to recognize the image as doctored. The absence of this opportunity is a *sexist* feature of ordinary discourse. Hence, to open up such an option we need feminist analysis of ordinary discourse.

In order to change an unbearable situation, one needs not only to recognize it as unbearable but also to recognize some alternative as genuinely possible.

I suggested in Part II that something like a grammar rule is at work in the *Bloodline* ad, somehow making the image 'grammatically' 3rd-person passive (its subject is elsewhere, and so it is an object of—not a participant in—the communicative act), and setting up in the viewer an expectation that the doer of the action, absent from the photo, is located 'behind the camera'. This relation between the pictured woman and the communicative act in which she is pictured, together with the expectation it sets up, reflects a fact about our sexist society: women are the victims of sexual/violent acts, and this is a matter of course. Now I want to go further, and suggest that in a non-sexist discourse, such a grammar rule could have no place. I do not mean that there could be no inflections (or their syntactical equivalents), nor do I mean that there could be no distinctions of grammatical person or even of grammatical gender. Rather, I mean that a rule that uses the *gender* of the picture's subject as a device for marking the 3rd-person passive is typically a grammar rule that restricts women's possibilities. As such it would have no place in a non-sexist discourse.

This is so because a discourse that depends on the gender of the picture's subject as a marker of the grammatical person and voice is not merely a limited discourse, but a discourse limited to the detriment of women: whenever our

subject-matter would straightforwardly use a gender, voice, and person other than those the rule prescribes, we are forced to devise a paraphrastic form (actually, to devise the pictorial equivalent of a paraphrastic form). A male subject in an impersonal transitive construction becomes difficult; implicit responsibility is almost impossible to attribute to a female photographer. 'Paraphrases' are not always available, and even when they are, they sap the strength of the communication that uses them.

Perhaps this limitation may more easily be seen as the banal acceptance of the fact that it is a woman who is pictured as an object of sex/violence in the *Bloodline* ad. The erotic gory image is banally accepted not so much because erotic gore is banal as because readily available alternative images are, so to say, ungrammatical. Erotic gory images thus become banal and acceptable. This is why an effective opposition to them (and to the *Bloodline* ad in particular) requires an effective critique of the grammar of the image.

My aim in this part of my essay has been to extend the pragmatic analysis of the ad, making it into an interest-based analysis of the distribution of power in its communicative context. By means of this extended analysis, I have been arguing that the *Bloodline* ad not only reflects, but also helps to generate the (sexist) background belief that sex is violent, and violence sexy.

The conflation of sex with violence forces us to choose between communicative power and sexual self-interest. The conflation appears, not as an opportunity to make such a choice, but as the rendering irrelevant of our claim to a sexually self-interested response. In this way, the conflation of sex with violence produces an imbalance in the distribution of communicative power. The result is a devalorization of the feminist's judgment that violence is not sexy. This effects an imposition on the victims of sexual violence of the viewpoint of the perpetrator. The imposition appears as the rendering invalid of sexually self-interested emotional response. The internalization of such discounting of emotional responses helps generate disenfranchisement. The gender-determinations of imagery force a choice between ready communication and a self-interested emotional response. It appears, not as an opportunity to make such a choice, but as a tendency to accept ordinary discursive abuse. In this way, the genderization of imagery contributes to the imbalance in the distribution of discursive power.

IV

It remains for me to explain why arguments such as mine (in Part I above) are scarce, even in recent feminist work on sexism in language. Obviously, I want to do this by way of an appeal to some of the results of the foregoing analysis of the pragmatics of the sexist image. Not so obviously, I want to appeal to exactly the same results in explaining the argument's scarcity as I did in clarifying the claim that the *Bloodline* ad epitomizes the genre of media images that capitalize on the victimization of women.

Even if it should turn out that my analysis of the *Bloodline* ad is inadequate,

and even if the difficulties in generalizing from it to other apparently sexist images are insurmountable, my analysis is nonetheless revealing in its way of operating on two levels. Its description of the ad's sexism is at one and the same time a description of the ad's resistance to feminist critique.

When we attempt to express our opposition with a slogan like 'Violence against women is not sexy' we are tolerated fairly well within the dominant (sexist) discourse: for it is ordinarily expected that feminists would say such a thing (but it is only a matter of opinion); and feminists are not generally supposed to be all that numerous; and it is ordinarily assumed that most people feel this ad is indeed sexy, and are fascinated by this image, and will pay money to see the movie. If we allow ourselves to express our disgust openly, we risk ridicule. When we call attention to the vulnerability and the objectification of the woman as she is pictured in the ad we should not be surprised by the response, which will be expressed explicitly as the ordinary belief that if this is an effective way for Paramount Pictures to advertise their product then we have no right to try to stop it. In short, as long as feminist opposition to the ad is focused solely on the level of the ad's sexist content, it falls prey to the efficiency of the ad itself: our opposition works out to be evidence of the power of this erotic gory image, and makes the image all the more provocative.

No amount of pointing to the violence and deception of the ad can disarm the ad.

Instead, we must work at the level of the discourse within which the ad does its communicating. We must point to the presuppositions for its effectiveness, and thereby explain how the image works: We need to expose its ambiguity and its implicit dependence on our internalization of sexism as 'second nature'. For while the ad itself resists our attack, the discourse making such an ad possible may be shown to fall short of a discourse in which communication both by and concerning women would be fully possible.

Here is how I want to explain the seeming scarcity of arguments like the one I offer above. Our first feminist reaction to the ad is to oppose it as one instance of a sexist advertising practice offensive to women, and (since we want to do one thing at a time) to point to its flagrantly sexist portrayal of a woman. These activities, though strategically necessary, do not go far enough. While their public impact is minimal, they also heighten the confusion and ambiguity that the ad turns on. One aspect of the confusion is the ad's power to close off avenues for deeper investigation of the ad's sexism. Focused on the deception and violence of the ad but ill-equipped, at the time, to broach the broader issue of how the sexism of the discourse becomes a part of the mechanism for the sexism of the individual act, WAVAW had noticed and protested the ambiguity but had not gone on to study it.

This amounts to saying that, as feminists, we've been used. The strategy we need to follow has, as its first stages, gestures that serve the purposes of the advertiser. This is cause for concern, but not for alarm. It is also the hint that begins to clarify WAVAW's description of such ads as 'capitalizing' on the victimization of women. For what is truly remarkable is the efficiency with which

the ad exploits our discovery that we are oppressed by it: instantly we feminists ourselves become a part of the mechanism on which the ad relies.[14]

REFERENCES

Austin, J. L. 1962. *How to do Things with Words*. Harvard University Press, Cambridge, Massachussetts.

Austin, J. L. 1970. Performative utterances. In Urmson, J. O. and G. J. Warnock, ed., *Philosophical Papers*, 2nd ed. The Clarendon Press, Oxford.

Grice, H. P. 1975. Logic and conversation. In Davidson D., and G. Harman, ed., *The Logic of Grammar*. Dickenson Publishing, Encino, California.

MacKinnon, Catherine. 1982. Feminism, marxism, method, and the state: an agenda for theory. *Signs* 7: 515–544.

Winant, T. R. 1982. Decoding the grammar of the image. *Bread & Roses: A Women's Journal of Issues and the Arts* 3: 14–19. Madison, Wisconsin.

[14] A version of this paper was read at the Spring, 1981, meeting of the Midwestern Society for Women in Philosophy, at Minneapolis, Minnesota.

I am indebted to many feminist and philosophical friends and colleagues for helpful discussion, comments, and criticism. I want especially to acknowledge the help of Louise Sherley, Harriette Andreadis, Azizah al-Hibri, Naomi Scheman, Margie Kelly, and a number of anonymous reviewers. My thanks to the Women's Forum at California State University, Northridge, where this work began. Time to edit the paper was provided by an Andrew Mellon Post-Doctoral Fellowship at the University of Pittsburgh.

RE-FUSING
NATURE/NURTURE

Nancy Tuana

Dichotomy—from the Greek, a cutting in two. A division into two mutually exclusive classes having contradictory marks. One such dichotomy which I believe to be at the heart of a world view which is both oppressive to women and racist is the dichotomy between nature and nurture. In this paper, I will argue that this distinction is metaphysically linked to a cluster of dichotomies: sex/gender, female/male, essence/accident. I will begin by discussing some historical examples of the ways in which the nature/nurture dichotomy was employed to support biological determinism. I then attempt to uncover the metaphysical presuppositions underlying traditional versions of this dichotomy. At this point it becomes possible to illustrate the crucial relationship between the nature/nurture dichotomy and the sex/gender dichotomy. I then turn to alternative interpretations of the nature/nurture dichotomy, arguing that any interpretation which treats nature and nurture as dichotomous is an incorrect and, in our history, pernicious representation of the world. In the process of rejecting such interpretations an alternative view will unfold, a view which re-fuses this division.

THE TRADITION: SOCIAL ABUSES OF THE
NATURE/NURTURE DICHOTOMY TO
SUPPORT BIOLOGICAL DETERMINISM

According to the tradition, all characteristics of human beings (and other living things) are seen as a function of either nature or nurture. This dichotomy is at the root of numerous other dichotomies: biology/culture, innate/learned, inherent/acquired, genetic/environmental. The nature/nurture dichotomy has been part of the grounding of a variety of theories of biological determinism; that is, biology (nature) necessarily determines individual characteristics and thus sets the limits of possible behavior, such characteristics being seen as inherited, as inborn. In addition, perceived variations between groups (races, sexes, the insane, criminals, etc.) are interpreted as the result of biological, inherited, differences. This line of reasoning is extended to social structures

arguing that particular social structures had their origins in the facts of biology, and were thus a reflection of biology.

Theories involving the thesis of biological determinism have had a long history. I will highlight a few examples of this history. Prior to Darwin's theory of evolution, justification for biological determinism came from two different schools of thought: monogenism—origin from one source, and polygenism—from many sources. Monogenists argued that humans originated from the creation of Eve and Adam. Current races were then seen as products of degeneration from the perfection of that initial creation. It was believed that the races had degenerated to different degrees—the darker the color of one's skin, the higher the rate of degeneration. Defenders of this view include Etienne Serres (1960). Polygenists believed that the races were separate species descending from different origins. Certain races (it is easy to guess which) were then seen as naturally inferior to others. Supporters of polygeny included the philosopher David Hume (1965) and the famous naturalist Louis Agassiz (1850).

By the late 19th century through the early 20th century, more sophisticated versions of biological determinism were developed which were based upon evolutionary theory. It was held in the late 19th century that facial configuration, and in particular skull size, were indicators of an individual's evolutionary developmental level. One of the most famous proponents of this view is the clinical surgeon Paul Broca (1861). Those groups of people with smaller skulls were believed to be at a lower stage of evolution. Furthermore, intelligence was seen by such determinists as correlated with such evolutionary stages. That is, those races with smaller skulls would be of lower intelligence because their brains would not be as highly evolved. Louis Pierre Gratiolet (1856) argued that the skull sutures of black babies closed earlier than those of white babies, and closed from front to back rather than the back to front closure hypostasized for white babies, thus accounting for smaller brain size, especially of the frontal regions, and thereby entailing lower intellectual abilities. Within races there was an additional correlation between brain size and intelligence. Women, having smaller craniums, were seen as biologically inferior to the men of their races, though perhaps equal or superior to the men of less evolved races.

Another postevolutionary form of biological determinism was based upon the theory of recapitulation—the repetition of evolutionary stages in the growth of an animal.[1] Inferior groups were seen by such theorists as having a lower maturation level; that is, they were seen as being more childlike and thus less evolved. Proponents of the recapitulationist version of biological determinism included the anthropologist D. G. Brinton (1890) and the paleonthologist E. D. Cope (1887). The theory of recapitulation was replaced in the 1920s by the theory of neoteny which supported completely opposite views concerning evolution. According to the theory of neoteny, the more advanced species would have a *slower* maturation rate such that the features of youth would be retained

---

[1] Recapitulation theorists saw, e.g. the gill slits of human embryos as representing an adult ancestral form, in this case a fish, and the temporary tail as representing a reptilian ancestor.

in the adult. In this case, unlike recapitulation, it was a mark of an advanced race to retain childlike physical traits. The work of Louis Bolk provides an example of this position (1929). The history of science here takes an interesting twist, for instead of using the evidence amassed during the reign of recapitulation to demonstrate the childlikeness of blacks and other races, and women, to now conclude to the superiority of these groups, scientists ignored such data and occupied themselves with demonstrating the childlike characteristics of white males.

Such postevolutionary theories were versions of what we now call Social Darwinism. According to social darwinism, it is natural for the more fit to dominate the less fit. This idea represents a corruption of Darwin's thesis of natural selection into this naïve notion of the survival of the fittest. Inequalities in ability and in moral sensitivity were viewed as natural. By 'natural' the Social Darwinists meant 'inherited' and 'unchangeable', and (tacitly) good. Because they believed that differences in individual abilities were inevitable and natural, they inferred that social hierarchies would also be inevitable and natural (Spencer, 1969). Such a theory thus provided justification for the domination of some races over others, of some classes over others, and of men over women. In this way one could account for social inequalities while maintaining the justice of present social institutions—they were a result of natural inequalities, not social conditions.[2]

With the discovery and development of genetic theory, there were corresponding attempts to explain such inferiorities genetically. Thus came the eugenic movement which had as its purpose the prevention of the degeneration of the race. This theory was based on the claim that intelligence and various other characteristics were determined by one's genes and were thus hereditary. Proponents of eugenics insisted that the less intelligent were producing more children than the more intelligent, and that, without intervention, the world would be populated with people of lower intelligence. They thus held that failure to intervene would lead to the degeneration of the human race. Employing this theory, a movement developed to eliminate or reduce undesired traits from the population by restricting birth rates for 'lower' races by legislating marriage prohibitions, instituting immigration restrictions, and, in the extreme cases, through forced sterilization. At the same time people of 'good stock' were encouraged to have more children. The movement thus embraced the two-part plan of negative and positive eugenics.[3]

With the discovery of sex hormones in the early 20th century, another justification of biological determinism was developed. It was believed that the formation and function of such hormones was sex-specific with females producing only estrogens and males producing only androgens. It was argued that differences in female and male abilities, roles, and interests could be explained by such hormonal differences. It was, of course, later discovered that both

---

[2] For a good history of Social Darwinism in America see Hofstadter (1955).
[3] Representatives of the eugenics movement include: Davenport (1911), Stokes (1917) and Woods (1913).

sexes produce both hormones, and this particular version of biological determinism had to be modified. Current versions of this theory refer to relative
proportions of female and male hormones in the individual to account for differences in female and male abilities, roles, and interests. Such a theory is
exemplified by Tiger and Fox (1971) who argue that differences in roles and
social status of women and men can be accounted for by different levels of
aggressiveness: women are less aggressive than men because of lower levels of
testosterone which, they hold, correlates positively with aggression.[4] Another
contemporary version of biological determinism is developed by Jensen (1969,
1972, 1973). He argues that critical differences in hormonal levels between
women and men result in differences in brain functions which lead naturally
and unavoidably to male dominance. In addition he sees biological determinism
resulting in economic and scholastic achievement differences between the
races. Herrnstein offers a parallel analysis with the intention of proving that
class differences are based on intelligence, which is in turn genetically based.
Here's an example of the genre:

> 'The privileged classes of the past were probably not much superior biologically
> to the downtrodden, which is why revolution had a fair chance of success—by
> removing artificial barriers between classes, society has encouraged the creation
> of biological barriers. When people can take their natural level in society, the
> upper classes will, by definition, have greater capacity than the lower.' (Herrn-
> stein, 1972: 221).

We have gone beyond measuring skull sizes, but not very far beyond. One
response to such theories would be a critical analysis of their experimental and
statistical techniques.[5] But my response is not to critique such particulars, but
rather to question their entire metaphysical basis. I shall attempt to argue that
the nature/nurture dichotomy inherent in such accounts goes against contemporary biological theory and is metaphysically unsound.

THE NATURE OF THE DICHOTOMY—THE TRADITIONAL VIEW

In speaking of the traditional nature/nurture dichotomy, I am referring to a
viewpoint which has held sway over recorded Western philosophical thought
from its inception until the late 19th century, and continues to influence contemporary philosophical thought. Until the last century this dichotomy was
part of the Western conceptual framework, influencing both the sciences and
the humanities. Although I shall argue that this dichotomy is no longer an
accepted part of the Western scientific worldview, versions of it continue to
be part of the layperson's worldview.

---

[4] See also: Tiger (1970) and Goldberg (1973).
[5] Examples of such studies include: Reed (1978), Chase (1977) and Gould (1981).

Aristotle's writings offer a paradigm example of this viewpoint. After arguing for clear physical differences between the sexes in *De Generatione Animalium* (1912) he insists upon corresponding psychological differences between women's and men's natures in *Historia Animalium* (1910).

> 'In all genera in which the distinction of male and female is found, Nature makes a similar differentation in the mental characteristics of the two sexes . . . the nature of man is the most rounded off and complete, and consequently in man the qualities or capacities above referred to are found in their perfection. Hence woman is more compassionate than man, more easily moved to tears, at the same time is more jealous, more querulous, more apt to scold and to strike. She is, furthermore, more prone to despondency and less hopeful than the man, more void of shame or self-respect, more false of speech, more deceptive, and of more retentive memory. She is also more wakeful, more shrinking, more difficult to rouse to action, and requires a smaller quantity of nutriment.' (Aristotle, 1910: Book IX, Ch. 1, 608a, 22–608b, 20).

This viewpoint is retained with surprisingly little variation in much of the history of philosophy. Similar passages can be found in the writings of St Augustine, St Thomas Aquinas, Spinoza, Rousseau, Kant, Hegel, Kierkegaard, Schopenhauer, and Nietzsche, to name a few.[6]

The dichotomous nature of the traditional nature/nurture distinction is disclosed by an examination of the characteristics customarily attributed to each division. According to this view, those characteristics seen as being due to nature are static. That is, they are properties that a being has from birth to death. Further, such properties are unchangeable as long as the species survives. Such traits are accepted as being governed by natural laws not within human control. Hence, if a property is seen as being due to nature, it is believed to be impossible to do anything to change that property in any given individual or living species. To this extent human nature is determined and not subject to the will.

Individual characteristics due to nurture, on the other hand, are viewed as changeable and (to some extent) within human control. Such properties are accepted as being due to the particular environment in which one lives. Not only may such qualities change with a change in environment, but to the extent that we can alter environments, we can cause alterations in such properties. Hence we have innate or inherent qualities with which we are born (which the modern traditionalists will say are genetically determined) which are immutable, and we have learned or acquired characteristics which are mutable.[7]

To illustrate this dichotomy, consider hair color versus preference for hair

[6] A good discussion of such viewpoints can be found in Gould (1976). For selections from such philosophers see Osborne (1979).

[7] This dichotomy is well illustrated in Plato's *Republic* (1971). Although he claims that women's nature is different and inferior to men's he argues for the education of women on the ground that doing so will enable them to acquire such talents as they are suited for by their nature and thereby enable them to become better citizens

style. What color one's hair is at birth is seen as due to nature. That is, it is determined by the particular genetic coding the individual inherits. If one's inherited chromosome contains two genes for black hair, then regardless of the genes for hair color in the second chromosome, that individual will have black hair, since genes for black hair are dominant. Black hair is thus seen as innate for that individual.

On the other hand, preference for hair style is seen as culturally acquired. There are cultures in which girls and women prefer longer hair styles and boys and men prefer shorter hair styles. In other cultures both groups prefer longer styles, and in yet others preference is not divided along girl/woman, boy/man lines. Being due to cultural influences, which are in part within human control, such a preference would also be seen as alterable by human action. A change in culture or in individual values could bring about a change in such a preference. An individual is not born with such a preference, or even a disposition to such a preference, but rather acquires it through the learning of and adoption of cultural values specific to this characteristic.

There is a second distinction interwoven here: the distinction between essential and accidental properties. Essential properties are those that are necessary and sufficient for being a particular thing, say a human. The set of essential properties for a class will be those which are universal and unique to it. A change in essential properties would change the fundamental nature of the individual because they are that which makes a thing what it is. Accidental properties, on the other hand, are those which are neither necessary nor sufficient to the identity of the object. Such qualities can be changed with no corresponding change in the fundamental nature of the object. For example, being a mammal is said to be an essential property of humans; one cannot be human and not be a mammal. But whether one is born in Asia or South America is an accidental characteristic, and not part of the essential nature of that individual.

The essential/accidental dichotomy neatly parallels and supports the nature/nurture dichotomy. Essential properties, because they constitute the fundamental nature of human beings, cannot be acquired. Thus, by definition, from the moment of conception the individual must possess its essential (natural) properties. Hence, they must be inherent properties, ones which the individual is born with and which cannot therefore be changed. This is an outline of the metaphysical base which make possible scientific and philosophical theories of the nature of human nature.

In addition, the nature/nurture dichotomy contains an implicit valuation. Innate properties, as we have just seen, are natural properties—'natural' frequently connoting 'best' or 'right'. For the last few centuries, natural properties were accepted as proceeding from natural laws. Such laws were seen as governing the function and purpose of all things in the universe. This view often involved the belief in a creator, a god, who designed its creation with a particular end in mind, and in creating, set up such laws to insure this ordering. Each thing was held to have an essential nature, a nature and function governed by

natural laws. Trying to go against these laws was seen as being immoral.[8] A natural property or function would then be seen not only as an inherent property, but also as a *desirable* property. Such a perspective will be recognized as being at the heart of Christianity.

The traditional view concerning intercourse well illustrates this equation of natural with inherent and desirable. It was held that the only natural function of intercourse was reproduction. Individuals would inherently have both the ability and the desire to engage in intercourse for the purpose of reproduction. But because reproduction was seen as the *only* function of intercourse, it was argued that to have or desire intercourse for reasons other than reproduction was unnatural, was in violation of natural laws. Since using something for other than its natural function was accepted as being immoral, sexual acts for any reason other than reproduction were viewed as immoral (Aquinas, 1956).

Western notions of nature are strongly influenced by this religious worldview. Something which is seen as being due to biology is seen as part of 'the way things were meant to be'. Thus any divergence from what is seen as natural is viewed as, at best, an unfortunate deviance, at worst, immoral. Many have rejected large parts of this worldview. It requires not only the existence of a god, but also an equation of physical regularities with morality, and there are many who are not willing to accept these conditions. However, similar evaluations of nature continue due to three mistaken beliefs people commonly hold about the nature of human evolution. One of these is the view that evolution is always evolution to a higher, better species. Another is that the evolutionary process has a limit; that is, it is evolution to a 'perfect' species—it has a purpose and an end-point at which it will culminate. The third is that the human species is no longer evolving for it has already reached its end-point. Despite the incorrectness of all of these views, many people hold them and use them to explain the value they place on 'natural' properties. A corollary to this view is that any attempt to modify such qualities goes contrary to nature and will either fail or will lead to a deterioration of the human species. Hence the equation of 'natural' with 'best'. So we have not just a dichotomy, but a dichotomy which contains an evaluative distinction.[9]

THE RELATION BETWEEN NATURE/NURTURE
AND SEX/GENDER

There is another distinction which is intimately related to the nature/nurture dichotomy—the sex/gender dichotomy. It is important to realize that the sex/gender dichotomy presupposes the nature/nurture dichotomy. It is only when one believes that some properties are innate and others are acquired or ac-

---

[8] The most famous illustration of this view can be found in the writings of St Thomas Aquinas. See, in particular, his *Summa Theologiae*, (1969).

[9] Contemporary examples of the traditional dichotomy abound in such works as: Goldberg (1973), Tiger and Fox (1971), Tiger (1970) and Storr (1968).

quirable, that the possibility of the sex (innate properties)/gender (acquired properties) dichotomy can arise. In the well known text *Sex, Gender and Society* Ann Oakley delineates the sex/gender distinction in the following way:

> ' "Sex" is a word that refers to the biological differences between male and female: the visible difference in genitalia, the related difference in procreative function. "Gender" however is a matter of culture: it refers to the social classification into "masculine" and "feminine" . . . *the constancy of sex must be admitted, but so also must the variability of gender*'. (Oakley, 1972: 16; my emphasis).

The sex/gender dichotomy is more specific than the nature/nurture dichotomy. It is designed to distinguish the properties definitive of being a woman or a man from properties associated with being feminine or masculine. Only factors that are seen as being unique to one sex or the other: hormonal levels, genitals, work preferences, etc., are of interest. This dichotomy does not deal with characteristics shared by the sexes—how one absorbs oxygen into the blood stream, enjoyment of discordant music, etc. Sex then refers to essential, inherited, properties unique to women or to men, giving us the notion of woman's nature or man's nature. Gender, on the other hand, refers to accidental, acquired properties that constitute being feminine or being masculine. Once the distinction is made, a series of questions arise to which many researchers, both feminist and nonfeminist, have devoted much energy attempting to answer.

> ' . . . we can further ask how sex differences came about. Are biological or social forces to account for them? If biological, exactly what takes place? If social, what contributions do cultured, parental socialization practices, and social attitudes make to sex-role differentiation? If both biological and social forces are at work, how can we describe the interaction leading from a simple sex differentiation (like men having beards and women not) to sex-role differentiation (like men working outside the home and women inside)?' (Brooks-Gunn and Schempp Matthews, 1979: 4).

It should thus be clear that the dichotomy between sex and gender rests on the nature/nurture dichotomy. Although the latter is a necessary precondition for making a dichotomy between sex and gender, it is not sufficient. The sex/gender dichotomy requires, in addition that there be at least two sexes. The nature/nurture dichotomy does not of itself require the existence of more than one sex, nor does it restrict the number of sexes to only two. Thus to presume, as one does in employing the current sex/gender dichotomy, that there are two and only two sexes involves the adoption of this additional postulate.[10] Thus, the currently invoked sex/gender dichotomy cuts two ways: first, nature/nur-

---

[10] The sex/gender dichotomy does not in itself require that there be two and only two sexes. It is compatible with any number of sexes more than one. However, I am here discussing the relationship between the nature/nurture dichotomy and the *currently accepted* sex/gender dichotomy, which does in fact presuppose two and only two sexes.

ture, and second, women/men. By combining these two, one is able to think about differences in the traits of women and men, and to wonder of them whether they are due to inborn biological differences or are due to differences in the upbringing of girls and boys. Hence, the question as to whether a property such as biceps muscle development is due to innate factors or is a result of upbringing differences between women and men rests on the nature/nurture dichotomy and also presupposes two sexes. The nature/nurture dichotomy is thus a necessary but not sufficient basis for deriving this sex/gender dichotomy. Schematically illustrated:

$$\text{nature/nurture} + \text{two sexes} = \text{sex/gender}.$$

Given the nature/nurture metaphysic, in order to pick out a kind such as female, one must identify essential and thus inherent properties definitive of this class—sex. Other properties that may be correlated with that class are then accidental—gender. Only after one has made the sex/gender dichotomy does it make sense to inquire as to which traits possessed uniquely by women and uniquely by men are due to nature (sex) and which are due to nurture (gender). Allegedly biological based sex differences which have received considerable attention in recent years include aggression, IQ levels, and brain lateralization.[11]

Because the question as to which traits of women and men are due to sex versus gender presupposes two dichotomies: nature/nurture and women/men, it is possible to adopt one of two attitudes toward it. First, one can accept the sex/gender distinction and then attempt to answer this question. On the adoption of this attitude, there are three possible positions one can take: (1) that there are significant biological differences between women and men which biologically dispose them to different activities and interests; (2) biological differences between women and men are insignificant, the major differences being due to environmental factors which are, in principle, alterable; (3) it is not at the present time possible to determine which of the differentiating traits of women and men are due to nature and which are due to nurture. The first of these positions is a hereditarian position involving the beliefs that women and men have unchangeable differences, that to attempt to modify them is either impossible or wrong, and that we must work for a society in which these differences are reinforced and respected. Hence, woman's and man's natures require different social roles.[12] The second position is an environmentalist position commonly held by feminists and social scientists.[13] Proponents of this position deny that there are any biological differences between women and

---

[11] For agression see Goldberg (1973), Tiger (1970) and Storr (1968); for IQ levels see Ann Arbor Science for the People Editorial Collective (1977).

[12] Goldberg (1973) offers an excellent example of such a position.

[13] See Gove and Carpenter (1982). In their introduction, they state that ' . . . in sociology, many introductory sociology textbooks include the following theses—any consideration of biological factors believed to be innate to the human species is completely irrelevant in understanding the nature of human behaviour and society. All differences between cultures are attributable to sociological factors, etc. . . . a consensus exists that the human self is exclusively sexually determined' (p. 4).

men significant enough to dispose them to certain social roles. They hold rather that it is environment which determines behavior. Changes in behavior can then in principle be brought about through modifying environment. The third position holds that due to the complexity of human nature it is not now possible to determine empirically whether a trait is biologically or socially determined. The dichotomy between nature and nurture is not viewed as false, but rather epistemologically irrelevant at the present time.

> 'What does it mean to say that biological factors are more "basic" or unchangeable than cultural ones? Such statements can only take on meaning if there is a clear way of distinguishing biological inputs from cultural ones in the life of a person or of a social structure. Given our current state of knowledge about the role of hormones in human behavior, we are simply not at the stage where such mechanisms can be specified with any degree of certainty' (Weitz, 1977: 55).

Given such an attitude, it is further claimed that justice requires provision of as much freedom as possible which will minimize the coercive effects of socialization without going against biology.

There is a second attitude one can adopt toward this question. *One can reject the presuppositions which generate the question,* that is, reject the nature/ nurture dichotomy, and in so doing undercut the entire debate. Most participants in the debate, feminists and nonfeminists alike, take for granted not only that the nature/nurture distinction is metaphysically acceptable, but also that the positing of two and only two sexes is ontologically correct. I hold that both of these assumptions must be critically examined. Although I believe that a strong critique of the women/men dichotomy is tied to my analysis of the nature/nurture distinction, I will limit myself in this paper to the nature/nurture dichotomy.[14]

AN ALLEGED REJECTION OF THE NATURE/NURTURE DICHOTOMY

One attempt to undercut the nature/nurture dichotomy, which I will demonstrate to be unsuccessful, has been to reject the above characterization on the ground that the effects of biology and of environment cannot be simply separated off in the way that such an analysis desires. That is, to make a dichotomy between innate factors and environmentally determined traits, and to then attempt to assign all traits to one or the other of these divisions is incorrect because the influences of biology and of the environment are not exerted upon different parts of the organism, but effect, in different ways, the development of the same traits. This then is one interpretation of the biological concept of epigenesis—the concept that an organism develops by the new appearance of structures and functions through the interaction of gene and

---

[14] See Dworkin (1976) for an attack on the position of two and only two sexes.

surrounding conditions. This view was developed in opposition to the hypothesis that an organism develops by unfolding the growth of entities already present at its conception—the thesis of preformation. Waddington (1957, 1961) is a major proponent of epigenetic theory, a theory which is now widely accepted as correct. Upon the interpretation of epigenetic theory now under consideration, one could argue that there are genetic factors and environmental factors for each trait. Therefore traits due to nature and traits due to nurture cannot be isolated, because any trait's presence is due to both. Each trait is thus the result of an interweaving of genetic and environmental factors. On the basis of such an account, one could attempt to ascribe a certain percentage of a trait of an individual to nature, and another percent to nurture. Since environmental factors can change, and all traits are due to part to the environment, such an account would reject the view that certain traits are static and unchanging. In the same way it would deny that certain properties are essential to the nature of species or a sex, although it would acknowledge that some traits are much less variable than others. The question has thus changed from 'Which traits are due to innate factors and which are due to environmental factors?' to 'To what extent is the trait in question due to innate factors and to what extent is it due to environmental factors?'

The rejection of the traditional view under discussion can perhaps be better understood with the help of a metaphor—what I will call a fabric metaphor. See the vertical threads in a fabric, the warp, as representing genetic factors, and the horizontal threads, the woof, as representing environmental factors. The fabric and its particular shape is then produced from the tension of the two. Thus for any characteristic, there will be genetic factors and environmental factors combining to produce that trait. The genetic factors, like the warp, once set are static and unchanging. However, just as you would not have fabric without some intertwining of two sets of threads, you cannot have a trait without the intertwining of genetic and environmental factors. So although genetic factors are static, there will not be static traits. The particular qualities of the warp (the size and tension, etc.) limit the possible shapes, and other qualities, of the fabric—but not uniquely. The actual shape of the fabric will also depend on the horizontal threads which are woven in. Since those threads can be varied, the shape of the fabric can be changed. According to this interpretation, although genetic factors determine in the sense of limiting the possibilities for certain traits, they do not do so uniquely. Since environmental factors are involved in the development of any trait, and since such factors can be altered, the actual manifestation of a trait can vary to the extent that the genetic factors underdetermine that trait. As the shape of the fabric is produced by the number and strength of individual threads, so too the traits of an individual are caused by the joint forces of nature and nurture in their various proportions.

I think that this alternative interpretation of the relationship between nature and nurture is an advance over the traditional viewpoint insofar as it recognizes that traits of organisms result from the joint operation of genes and environment. Nevertheless, this interpretation is not a radical departure from the traditional nature/nurture dichotomy. On this interpretation, the relationship

between nature and nurture is seen as additive, that is, biological factors plus environmental factors add together to produce a given trait. On this model, one still continues to view nature as a distinct and separate (although perhaps not empirically separable) *mechanism* from the *mechanism* of nurture. So although the thesis, accepted by the traditional view, that an individual possesses a set of innate, unchanging traits and then acquires an additional group of traits is rejected, this alternative interpretation persists in holding the view that elements of traits have *dichotomously different developmental origins*. The dichotomy still holds, it now cuts across developmental origins. Not only does the alternative interpretation continue to treat genetic mechanisms as innate, it persists in equating innateness with fixity. To the extent to which a trait is innate, it is also fixed. Nature is still being seen as static, nurture as variable. The warp is static, only the woof can be altered. The genetic factors are still unchanging. They delimit a set of possibilities, and that set is static. Given that all traits have some environmental components, such a theorist will not hold that there are traits which are *totally* unchanging. However, the notion of fixity is not completely rejected but rather replaced with a degree notion. The degree of fixity then will be a function of the percentage of genetic mechanisms at play in the development of a trait. Crudely put, a trait which was a result of 80 per cent genetics and 20 per cent environment would be much less subject to change than one in which these percentages were reversed. In the following section I will argue that such a mechanistic mode of the relationship between genes and environment is unacceptable and must be replaced with a model which treats the relationship as a *dynamic interaction*. One important consequence of the latter model will be a refusal to treat nature and nurture as dichotomous.[15]

[15] Herrnstein (1972) offers a good example of this type of interpretation of epigenesis. His claim that intelligence is 85 per cent inherited is interpreted as meaning that one's intelligence is largely predetermined at birth. Although he explicitly denies holding an additive model of nature/nurture (p. 175), his conclusions in the final chapter belie this denial. In discussing a society in which environmental influences upon intelligence (10 percent according to Herrnstein) are removed, he states that ' . . . as everyone approaches the optimal environment, only their genes distinguish them. The total amount of intellectual variation would be reduced to the extent that environmental factors had been causing it, *but what remains would be stubbornly intractable*' (p. 198, my emphasis). He argues that the minimization of environmental factors will result in a caste society where one's status is based upon inherited differences. 'Actual social mobility is blocked by innate human differences after the social and legal impediments are removed' (p. 202). 'The theme that runs throughout is that mobility flows along the channels cut by the occupational requirements for IQ (among other personal traits), which in turn, flows largely via the germ plasm. Moreover, to restate the point of this corollary, as the contribution of fundamentally irrelevant factors like family connections, inherited wealth, race, and religion diminish, the inherent factors, like occupational demands for inborn capacity, will take on increasing importance' (p. 208). 'This points to a future in which social classes not only continue but become ever more solidly built on inborn differences . . . in Aldous Huxley's *Brave New World*, it was malevolent or misguided science that created the "alphas", "gammas" and the other distinct types of people. But nature itself is more likely to do the job or something similar . . . ' (pp. 214–215). Herrnstein insists that in such circumstances the human society would ' . . . approach a virtual caste system, with families sustaining their position on the social ladder from generation to generation as parents and children grow more nearly alike in their essential features' (p. 220). It should be clear from such quotes that Herrnstein's position still involves a notion of innateness which is tied to genetic mechanisms as static and unchanging.

FUSING NATURE/NURTURE

In order to understand the relationship of gene and environment it is necessary to rethink the traditional notion of innateness. The second account was correct in insisting that both genes and environment are factors in the development of any trait. However, this account continues to be grounded on an unacceptable notion of innateness which perpetuates a misunderstanding of the gene-environment relationship. Indeed, I shall argue that a more radical interpretation of epigenesis is required for a complete understanding of this relationship.

The notion of innateness working in both the traditional view and the alternate interpretation is that of developmental fixity. That is, certain aspects of the organism—traits on the traditional view and developmental mechanisms on the alternative interpretation—are independent of environmental influence. Because of this, I contend that neither position fully supports epigenetic theory, since both continue to hold that individuals unfold structures or actualize potentials present at conception and thereby are versions of a preformation thesis. The notion of innateness involved in both views still means that organisms must, on the traditional account, develop certain characteristics regardless of the environment, or, on the alternative interpretation, organisms have a potential only for a certain range of responses to environmental factors. Notice that on the alternative interpretation of nature/nurture, the primary difference is that talk of innate traits becomes talk of potential for a set range of responses. On both accounts there is a 'natural' or 'true' state of genotype—they still have a notion of human nature. They both then involve a notion of essential properties—a particular set of properties or potential which all individuals of a group necessarily have and which they will continue to possess as long as they remain members of that group.

Evolutionary theory entails a rejection of any account based on an essentialist metaphysic because organisms which evolve will have no eternal, immutable essences. Both the traditional view and the alternative interpretation are based on an incorrect understanding of the relation of gene, environment, and organism, and fail to correctly understand the interactive view of development prevalent amongst biologists.[16] They fail to acknowledge that all observable features of an individual (phenotype) result from the genetic makeup of the individual (genotype) *interacting with* the environment in which the genotype develops. This interaction must be seen as dynamic and nonlinear. Contrary to previous theories genotype does not determine a set of characteristics or potentials (a human nature), but specifies *patterns of reaction of a developing organism to the environment it encounters*. There is no set of outcomes of this development that is more 'natural'. Organisms with a particular genotype may

---

[16] I especially recommend the writings of Lewontin (1974) which well illustrate such an interactive view. Also see the work of Weiss. I found the essay 'The living system: determinism stratified' (1969) particularly helpful.

grow tall in one environment and short in another, while those with another genotype respond in the opposite way to the same two environments.

Treating 'innate' as 'fixed' or 'unchangeable' obscures the developmental process just described. This process is the development of new structures and patterns from the results of the interaction of previously existing structures and patterns both *within* the organism and its internal environment, and *between* the organism and its external environment. At every stage of development, new patterns emerge from such interactions. The interactions from which an organism develops are *not* between what is inherited and the environment— the traditional model. The interactions are between the *whole* organism and the environment, and *the organism is different at each stage of its development*. To see nature and nurture as dichotomous is a way of cutting up the world which does not permit an understanding of this process. The two are not separate and discrete factors or mechanisms, but rather are names of abstractions from a process in which each change affects the entire organism. In order to fully understand such interactions we must reject a mechanistic model of such relations, with its linear, additive view of the relationship, and replace it with a process metaphysics.

A process metaphysics replaces the notion of unchanging substances affecting one another by external contacts (billiard balls colliding), with activity (force, energy) interacting with other activity. No organism then is fixed, but is in a continual process of change. Further, causal interactions between activities inevitably change the previous structure of each activity. On a mechanistic view, the objects are not internally changed by their relations with other objects. Instead organisms maintain their essential character throughout history. On a process view, the notion of essential characteristics persisting in a continually changing organism would be incoherent. We have, on the mechanistic model, a billiard ball model of the universe with objects bouncing off one another, but maintaining their natures. On the process model we have an electron cloud model of the universe, with electron clouds interacting with electron clouds, the interaction itself being another bundle of energy.[17] On the process view, such permanence as there is is the result of the continued maintenance of patterns of activity by those activities.[18]

It should now be clear that the fabric metaphor will not accurately portray what is actually going on in the developmental process. This model does serve to emphasize the mutual intertwining of genes and environment, but models it in such a way that each remains a separate mechanism unaffected by the process of their intertwining. The threads of the warp are separate and discrete from those of the woof, a model which precludes the possibility of a dynamic interaction. The alternative interpretation introduced in the preceding section

[17] I realize that this illustration may be too compressed to be of much use to the reader. Books written for nonscientists which more fully explain this idea are: Baker (1970), Burnett (1957) and Gamow (1957).

[18] Those interested in examining an attempt to fully develop a process metaphysic should see Whitehead (1954).

involves a mechanistic view which treats genetic mechanisms as maintaining their essence throughout their contacts with the environment. This model of separate genetic and environmental mechanisms is not adequate to the actual dynamic gene, environment, organism interaction. It should now be clear why it is misleading to ascribe a certain percentage of a trait of an individual to the operation of genes and another percentage to the operation of the environment. Given the actual nature of the interaction, this relationship cannot be treated as additive. One cannot parse out the contributions of genes, of the developmental environment, of culture, etc., and sum the results. To do so restricts the range of relationships possible and leads one to adopt a simplistic nature/nurture dichotomous thinking.

To support a process interpretation of epigenesis does not mean that no distinctions can or should be made. But it is important to recognize that such distinctions will not create dichotomies. A sense of 'inherited' can even be retained, as long as it is divorced from a notion of fixity and combined with the acknowledgement of the complexity of the developmental interaction. 'Inherited' would then mean that one can, with some reliability, predict the distribution of some trait in an offspring population from their knowledge of the distribution of that trait in the parent population and of mating patterns therein. To say this, though, is not to give an explanation of the nature of the developmental processes involved, nor the extent to which they are subject to change with changes in the environment. We could thus only talk of a trait as inherited relative to a particular environment. To do so however is no indication as to that trait's heritability in alternate environments. Such a notion of heritability applies only to the set of environments in which the determination was made and cannot be extrapolated to other environments—a fallacy frequently found in the literature. Furthermore, the heritability of a trait has no correlation with its changeability. To conclude as did Herrnstein that the heritability of IQ is 85 per cent does not license an inference that this trait is, for the most part static. Such a notion of 'inherited' does not involve the traditional view of separate and separable causes. We must be careful not to confuse a type of explanation (genetic) with the set of factors which act as causes in such an explanation. On this account a genetic explanation would include environmental causes, developmental causes, and etc., as well as genes.

A process interpretation of epigenetic theory entails a rejection of any view which treats nature and nurture as dichotomous. The ability to offer the above type of genetic explanation does not license a biological determinism. In fact, on the above account, the theory of biological determinism *makes no sense*. Biology here would mean epigenesis in the above sense which is incompatible with determinism in the sense of static, unchanging traits or potentials. In a parallel fashion one could choose to stress the necessary effects of environment in development if that is the variable of interest in one's study. But again doing so does not prove that all traits are acquired. *The point is that such categories themselves stem from an inadequate metaphysical viewpoint.*

We must develop frameworks which will enable us to see biological and

cultural adaptation as interdependent processes. Cultural innovations may have biological consequences which in turn may have cultural consequences, and so on. Dinnerstein (1976) offers an example which illustrates this interdependence when she discusses Washburn's (1960) account of evolution. She is concerned to emphasize not that this account is correct in each detail, but rather that it contains such a notion of the interaction of genetic and cultural factors.

Washburn's account is the following: limited bipedalism in our ancestors freed their hands for tool use, namely the use of sticks and stones. The advantage given by tools led to further bipedalism, which in turn allowed for more efficient tool use. Greater use of tools for fighting, seizing, and pulling—actions once the functions of incisors—allowed for changes in skull and teeth structure. Bipedalism selected for an upright skeletal structure, resulting in a modification of the pelvic size, namely, it became smaller. A smaller pelvic size required delivery of fetuses at earlier stages of development when skull sizes are small enough to pass through the canal. This meant that babies would be less developed at the time of birth and would thus need a longer maturation period. These changes required a change in the social organization which would allow for a longer parenting period. And so on.

A simpler example of this interdependence is the following. An improvement in medical technology and health care will result in more individuals surviving to reproduce. Those with characteristics which would have resulted in their early death, now not only reproduce, but also continue to exist after reproduction. In this way there will be a change in the gene frequencies in the population, since those with disabilities which would have resulted in an early death now survive to reproduce. This will result in a demographic change, that is, there will be more disabled people. A cultural response to such a change might be then made in terms of special housing, transportation, etc. And so on.

THE CONSEQUENCES FOR CONTEMPORARY DISPUTES OF THE RE-FUSING OF NATURE/NURTURE

In this section I will briefly discuss a few of the practical implications of the theory developed in this paper. I will concentrate first upon its import for political theories concerning social change, and then consider the impact of this analysis upon the sex/gender dichotomy.

The adoption of a process interpretation of the interaction between organism and environment will involve an undercutting of the nature/nurture dichotomy, along with its attendant essentialist view of human nature. That is, the thesis that human beings have inevitable, unchanging properties must be abandoned. Political, social, economic, etc., theories which are founded on such theses must in turn be abandoned. In other words, theories which employ a notion

of an essential human nature as an axiom from which they derive the remainder of the theory, an axiom without which the theory could not work, must be rejected as grounded upon an incoherent notion, and thus themselves incoherent. For example those people who advocate social changes have found it necessary to debunk versions of biological determinism which defended the status quo via such a notion of human nature. This usually meant laboriously illustrating errors in experimental methods or describing faulty assumptions of the experiments employed by the determinists to defend their interpretation of human nature. The argument I have advanced makes all such effort unnecessary by rejecting the nature/nurture dichotomy presupposed by the experiments under attack. The theory I have advanced entails not only a rejection of any such version of biological determinism, but also entails a rejection of the opposite extreme of environmental determinism. That is, theories which treat individuals exclusively as the results of stimulations and reinforcements must also be rejected. Given an interactionist account, such positions will be rejected not as incorrect, but as meaningless. Thus both naïve sociobiologies and naïve learning theories are rendered incoherent.

I see yet another implication for some social and political theorists. Efforts to formulate an ideal end for social action—the ideal society—are brought into serious question by this re-fusing of nature/nurture. Those, whether feminist or nonfeminist, who envision the ideal society and do so in terms of an essential human nature which is to be suppressed or fulfilled (depending on their view of the nature of human nature) are basing their vision on a nonexistent foundation. Given an interactionist view, there is no such thing as correct evolution. That is, there is not just one path or one best path of evolution, but numerous possibilities. Such postulations of the ideal society would require either that the path of evolution is singular, or that humans are no longer evolving—both of which are false. But it is however quite possible to envision societies better in certain respects than our own, and doing so is very important for effective social action. It must be remembered however that envisioning societies better than our own can only be effectively done by appreciating fully present historical conditions, 'biological' and 'cultural'. Although the notion of an ideal society must be rejected, we can and should continue to image societies better than the present one.

Another dichotomy which a process interpretation calls into question is that of sex/gender. As I demonstrated earlier, this dichotomy is founded upon a dichotomy between nature and nurture; thus refusing the latter will require a rethinking of the former. The sex/gender dichotomy merely repeats the same debate about determinism, now focusing instead on differences between women and men. Participants continue to debate the extent to which certain traits of women and men are due to their biology and thus cannot be changed.[19] The

---

[19] Such views are ubiquitous in the literature. As just one example consider the following set of quotes from Gillie (1976). 'The differences in intellectual ability between the sexes have been explained by some as being caused by heredity and by others as being caused by environment.' 'In Western society, the popular view seems to be that differences in gender roles reflect innate

important point is that feminists who participate in this debate are, *in the very act of participation*, buying into the same metaphysical presuppositions as those who use a determinist position to defend racism, sexism, or classism. My claim is, then, that feminists must see that they are accepting a worldview which is at heart incoherent.[20]

I want to emphasize, as I did in discussing the nature/nurture dichotomy, that to reject the sex/gender dichotomy does not mean that no distinctions can or should be made. It is only to deny that such distinctions are, so to speak, carved into our genes. *Distinctions can be made, but they will be time, situation, and value relative.* What will be a good distinction is then decided by whether or not it is useful to make such a distinction at that particular time in that particular situation. Such distinctions will not report 'biological facts'.

To clarify this point, let me suggest an example of such a sex/gender distinction which seems valuable to make in the Western culture at the present time, although it may not be valuable in other cultures, or at other times. Given that the incidence of rape is much higher for women than for men in our present culture, and given differences in training in self-defense and muscle development, it is appropriate to develop self-defense classes designed for women. However, the determination of the various forms of sex/gender distinction which are useful in our culture is a complex and controversial issue and thus further development along these lines must be subject for future papers.

While a relative sex/gender distinction may be useful in some ways, it is even more critical that we uncover the pernicious effects when such a distinction is absolutized. The result is that women and men are constricted in roles that limit their development as humans. Refusing any essential/accidental dimension to the sex/gender distinction means rethinking this distinction in all its appearances, holding each of them up to critical scrutiny, and exorcising those that cannot stand up under examination. This appears to be the larger task which stands before us.

---

and inevitable differences between the sexes.' 'This belief that masculine and feminine gender roles are innate stems from an unquestioning acceptance of the way in which our society is organized'. 'It appears to be fear of the consequences of success, rather than innate preference or limited ability, that drives women to seek jobs in traditional roles'. 'The strength of purely biological influences on the roles of men and women in society is difficult to estimate. At present time there are still so many social and legal ways in which women are repressed that biology is of secondary importance. It is possible that the social roles of men and women are influenced by differences in sex hormones in their bodies that make men more competitive and women relatively passive. But as long as women are legally and socially restricted it is impossible to attempt to evaluate the importance of any biological influences apart from the basic fact that only women can bear children and breast-feed them.' 'The major causes of the different roles of men and women in our society have in reality nothing directly to do with biology or genetics but are almost wholly social and economic.' 'Our lives are built on an assumption that men and women are innately different and that labor should be divided in a prescribed way between the sexes.' 'Change is possible: there is nothing biologically inevitable about the present roles and status of men and women' (pp. 90–97).

[20] Such an analysis of the sex/gender dichotomy points out yet another assumption we are tricked into accepting. Although it has not been my focus in this paper, it should be noted that my analysis also undercuts the claim that there are two and only two sexes because this claim is based on an essentialist interpretation of biology. It involves the view that being human means being either female or male—that this is an essential property of human. In that this women/men dichotomy is based on an essentialist position, it too must be rejected.

REFERENCES

Agassiz, Louis. 1850. The diversity of origin of the human races. *Christian Examiner* **49**: 110–145.

Ann Harbor Science for the People Editorial Collective. 1977. *Biology as a Social Weapon*. Burgess, Minneapolis.

Aquinas, St Thomas. 1956. *On the Truth of the Catholic Faith, Summa Contra Gentiles*. Book Three: Providence, Part II (translated by Vernon Bourke). Doubleday, New York.

Aquinas, St Thomas. 1969. *Summa Theologiae*. Gilby, Thomas, ed. Image Books, New York.

Aristotle. 1910. *Historia Animalium*. Book IX, Ch. 1. In Smith and Ross, eds, *The Works of Aristotle*, Vol. VI (translated by D'Arcy Wentworth Thompson). Oxford/Clarendon Press.

Aristotle. 1912. *De Generatione Animalium*. Book I, Ch. 2. In Smith and Ross, eds, *The Works of Aristotle*, Vol. V (translated by Arthur Platt). Oxford/Clarendon Press.

Baker, Adolph. 1970. *Modern Physics and AntiPhysics*. Addison-Wesley, Mass.

Bolk, Louis. 1929. Origin of racial characteristics in man. *Am. J. phys. Anthrop.* **13**: 1–28.

Brinton, D. G. 1890. *Races and Peoples*. N. D. C. Hodges, New York.

Broca, Paul. 1861. Sur le volume et la forme du cerveau suivant les individus et suivant les races. *Bull. Soc. Anthrop. Paris* **2**: 139–207, 301–321, 441–446.

Brooks-Gunn, Jeanne and Wendy Schempp Matthews. 1979. *He and She: How Children Develop Their Sex-Role Identity*. Prentice-Hall, New Jersey.

Burnett, Lincoln. 1957. *The Universe and Dr. Einstein*. Bantam Press, New York.

Chase, Allan. 1977. *The Legacy of Malthus: The Social Costs of the New Scientific Racism*. Alfred A. Knopf, New York.

Cope, E. D. 1887. *The Origin of the Fittest*. Macmillan, New York.

Davenport, Charles, B. 1911. *Heredity in Relation to Eugenics*. Henry Holt, New York.

Dinnerstein, Dorothy. 1976. *The Mermaid and the Minotaur: Sexual Arrangements and Human Malaise*. Harper and Row, New York.

Dworkin, Andrea. 1976. *Our Blood: Prophecies and Discourses on Sexual Politics*. Harper and Row, New York.

Gamow, George. 1957. *Mr. Thomkins in Quantum Land*. Cambridge University Press, London.

Gillie, Oliver. 1976. *Who Do You Think You Are? Man or Superman: The Genetic Controversy*. Hart-Davis, MacGibbon, London.

Goldberg, Steven. 1973. *The Inevitability of Patriarchy*. William Morrow, New York.

Gould, Carol. 1976. The woman question: the philosophy of liberation and the liberation of philosophy. In Gould, Carol and Marx Wartofsky, eds, *Women and Philosophy: Toward a Theory of Liberation*. Capricorn Books, New York.

Gould, Stephen, J. 1981. *The Mismeasure of Man*. W. W. Norton, New York.

Gove, Walter and G. Russell Carpenter. 1982. *The Fundamental Connection Between Nature and Nurture*. Lexington Books, Massachussets.

Gratiolet, Louis Pierre. 1956. Mémoire sur le développement de la forme du crâne de l'homme, et sur quelques variations qu'on observe dans la marche de l'ossification de ses sutures. *C. r. hebd. Séanc. Acad. Sci., Paris*. **43**: 428–431.

Herrnstein, Richard. 1972. *I. Q. in the Meritocracy*. Little, Brown and Co., Boston.

Hofstadter, Richard. 1955. *Social Darwinism in American Thought*. Beacon Press, Boston.

Hume, David. 1965. *A Treatise of Human Nature*. Book I, Part III, Ch. xiii. Selby-Bigge, ed. Clarendon Press, Oxford.

Jensen, Arthur R. 1969. *Environment, Heredity, and Intelligence.* In Reprint series, No. 2. *Harvard Educational Rev.* Cambridge.

Jensen, Arthur R. 1972. *Genetics and Education.* Harper and Row, New York.

Jensen, Arthur R. 1973. *Educability and Group Differences.* Harper and Row, New York.

Lewontin, Richard. 1974. *The Genetic Basis of Evolutionary Change.* Columbia University Press, New York.

Oakley, Ann. 1972. *Sex, Gender and Society.* Temple Smith, London.

Osborne, Martha Lee. 1979. *Women in Western Thought.* Random House, New York.

Plato. 1971. *Plato: The Collected Dialogues.* Hamilton and Cairns, eds. Princeton University Press, New Jersey.

Reed, Evelyn. 1978. *Sexism and Science.* Pathfinder Press, New York.

Serres, Etienne. 1960. Principles d'embroyogénie, de zoogénie et de teratogénie. *Mém. Acad. Sci.* **25**: 1–943.

Spencer, Herbert. 1969. *The Man versus the State. With Four Essays on Politics and Society.* Donald Macrae, ed. Penguin Books, Baltimore.

Stokes, W. E. D. 1917. *The Right to be Well-Born.* C. J. O'Brien, New York.

Storr, Anthony. 1968. *Human Aggression.* Atheneum, New York.

Tiger, Lionel. 1970. *Men in Groups.* Vintage, New York.

Tiger, Lionel and Robin Fox. 1971. *The Imperial Animal.* Holt, Rinehart and Winston, New York.

Waddington, C. H. 1957. *The Strategy of the Genes.* Allen and Unwin, London.

Waddington, C. H. 1961. *The Nature of Life.* Allen and Unwin, London.

Washburn, Sherwood. 1960. Tools and human evolution. *Scient. Am.*

Weiss, Paul A. 1969. The living system: determinism stratified. In Koestler and Smythies, eds. *Beyond Reductionism: New Perspectives in the Life Sciences.* Hutchinson, London.

Weitz, Shirley. 1977. *Sex Roles: Biological, Psychological, and Social Foundations.* Oxford University Press, New York.

Whitehead, A. N. 1954. *Adventures of Ideas.* MacMillan, New York.

Woods, Frederick Adams. 1913. *The Influence of Monarchs.* MacMillan, New York.

MASCULINITY AS IDEOLOGY IN POLITICAL THEORY
HOBBESIAN MAN CONSIDERED[1]

Christine Di Stefano

'He that is to govern a whole nation, must read in himself, not this or that particular man; but mankind; which, though it be hard to do, harder than to learn any language or science; yet when I shall have set down my own reading orderly and perspicuously, the pains left another, will be only to consider, if he also find not the same in himself.'

Thomas Hobbes, Introduction to *Leviathan*

It is no secret that Western political thought is overwhelmingly male-dominated. Less obvious and more interesting, however, are the wide-ranging dimensions and implications of this phenomenon which, over the last decade, have received increasing critical attention from feminists. What are we to make of this diverse collective expression of male hegemony in Western culture's various attempts to establish the possibilities, limits and contours of political life? How much of this tradition is potentially useful to feminist visions and critiques of political arrangements? How much of it is deeply flawed and hence, practically irretrievable? To what extent does the critical excavation and perusal of the male monopoly in Western political theory illuminate deeply entrenched and inherited features of contemporary political discourse?

These sorts of questions have both motivated and been generated by several recent feminist reappraisals of Western political theory.[2] In other fields as well,

[1] This paper is a revised version of a chapter from my doctoral dissertation, Masculinity as ideology in political theory, unpublished, University of Massachussets, Amherst, (1983). Special thanks are due to Jean Elshtain and Sara Lennox for their generous support and criticism of that work.
[2] Okin's *Women in Western Political Thought* (1979) and Elshtain's *Public Man, Private Woman: Women in Social and Political Thought* (1981) come to mind as significant recent efforts to interpret political theory from feminist vantage points. O'Brien's *The Politics of Reproduction* (1981) is especially instructive on the centrality of reproductive issues to other classic concerns of political theory. The pathbreaking nature of O'Brien's work consists in her insistence on taking seriously some of the most basic and gender differentiated aspects of life experience surrounding biological and social reproduction which are then elaborated and transposed in various political theory texts in distinctively male-based ways. For helpful documentation and analysis of sexism in Western philosophy and political thought, see the following: Clarke and Lange (1980); Mahowald (1978); Osborne (1979).

most especially psychology, feminists have been re-thinking the significance of gender differences, while criticizing the unequivocal valorization of male experience at the expense of female (Chodorow, 1979; Dinnerstein, 1976; Gilligan, 1982; Miller, 1976; Ruddick, 1980). Such work has contributed to our critical understanding of the ways in which 'human' standards of identity, behavior and development have reproduced (unwittingly and deliberately) Everyman standards that denigrate and deny female experiences.[3] Simone de Beauvoir's earlier claim that 'Representation of the world, like the world itself, is the work of men; they describe it from their own point of view, which they confuse with absolute truth', has received extensive substantiation (de Beauvoir, 1952: 161).[4]

Her insight may also be extended to the terrain of the sociology of knowledge. For those feminists who argue that knowledge is materially situated in particular ways of life (Flax, 1980; Hartsock, 1983), the issue of the generic dimensions of knowledge becomes especially salient. As Jane Flax (1980) has argued: 'Knowledge is the product of human beings, for whom knowing is only one form of activity. The history and life situation of the knower cannot be completely different in kind from the form and content of the knowledge that this subject produces' (Flax, 1980: 21).

Self-knowledge and social knowledge intersect in the full-bodied understanding of our female particularity in a gendered and male dominated world.[5] It is this knowledge which keeps us simultaneously grounded and intellectually honest, better able to understand our own partial, yet radically underrepresented, portion of the human condition.

We have reached that point in the development of feminist consciousness, practice and theory where it makes sense and becomes possible to explore the notion that male hegemony in political theory inhabits and structures that body of knowledge in a multiplicity of complex and significant ways. The simultaneous appreciation of male dominance, gender differences, and the material rootedness of knowledge lends itself to a new and exciting critical interpretive focus in political theory. This focus enables the identification of masculinity as an ideological structure with specific cognitive and perceptual tendencies which reflect and reproduce the special interests of men as men. I would suggest that this ideological form may be usefully thought of as a 'deep structure'. By 'deep structure' is meant that masculinity is an ideology comprised of systematically interrelated elements which do not necessarily manifest themselves at the surface of theoretical discourse in direct or transparent ways, although they do exert a powerful influence on it. Identifying such an ideological structure, or subtext, requires an interpretive method akin to that used in psychoanalytic

[3] For a philosophical treatment of the legal dimensions of this issue, particularly as they relate to liberal conceptions of equality, see Wolgast (1980).

[4] Much of the work of contemporary French feminists relates to this issue as well. See the following anthologies: Eisenstein and Jardine (1980); Marks and de Courtivron (1980).

[5] 'Gendered' and 'male-dominated' are logically and descriptively distinct categories. Gender, universal in nearly all known human cultures, with tremendous cross-cultural variation in meaning, does not automatically entail male domination and female subordination to men. For a helpful anthropological exploration of this important distinction, see Sanday (1981).

explanations of symptoms and outward behaviour, which reconstruct the hidden systems of meaning and logic embedded and presupposed, usually in opaque form, in their visible and outer manifestations.[6]

While this deep structure of masculinity ramifies on women in directly perceptible ways and is an essential part of the sexist depiction of women in Western political thought, it also informs other topics of political interest which are not usually associated with specifically feminist concerns.[7] Hence, a focus on masculinity as deep ideological structure might be capable of promoting a broader understanding of the links between issues and concepts of perennial interest in political theory and those of feminists, thus expanding the potential of feminist theorizing in two ways. On the one hand, a specifically feminist reconstruction of political theory is made more likely. On the other, critical feminist appraisals of Western political thought might have an import that extended beyond the limited interests of political theorists.

What do we find if we look at political theory with the notion of masculinity as deep ideological structure in mind? What follows is a critical account of selected aspects of the thought of Thomas Hobbes which was gleaned and developed by means of this interpretive scheme. As I will seek to demonstrate, previously hidden and less salient aspects of this theory emerge with new clarity, while some of the apparently contradictory features of Hobbes's work are explicated and resolved into a more coherent pattern when he is read as a masculine thinker. My aim is to provide an analysis that is capable of highlighting a relatively unexamined dimension of political theory: masculinity as an ideological form constituted in terms of gendered experiences and interests, which embodies a gender-based logic, epistemology, ontology and intellectual style.

Why do we continue to read Hobbes today? What makes him an important thinker for our time? MacPherson (1962) has argued that Hobbes provides the first and freshest portrait of bourgeois, propertarian man. Others see his principles actively at work in contemporary American politics, which preserve and perpetuate Hobbesian notions of ruthless individualism, transactional relations between individuals and among interest groups, a civil authority whose sole function is that of policeman, and a view of politics as nothing but conflict-management (Coleman, 1977). For some, Hobbes is the crucial connecting link between the political thought of the Renaissance and that of modern liberal democracy (Jacobson, 1978; Hirschman, 1977). MacPherson (1962) has also suggested that we are drawn to Hobbes because his state of nature lurks in the horrifying scenario of nuclear war and its socio-political aftermath.

I would add yet another: Hobbes's thought reflects and perpetuates a distinctively masculinist orientation to the realm of politics that continues to be

[6] Flax's notion (1980) of 'the unconscious of political theory' gets at a similar structural image.

[7] See, for example, O'Brien's fascinating discussion (1981) of the problem of succession and regeneration of political authority, which she links up with gender differentiated experinces of time and the male denial of the maternal role in generational continuity. For a related psychoanalytic argument on the patriarchal and masculinist foundations of the modern Western state, see Breger (1981).

male-dominated and governed by masculinist presumptions in our time. To the extent that this masculinist orientation dovetails with other aspects of Hobbes's contemporary relevance, feminist criticisms of his thought promise to illuminate Hobbesian features of contemporary social life in politically helpful ways.

Hobbes is most famous, of course, for his *Leviathan*, the grand masterwork in which he sought to provide a comprehensive scientific theory of civil society for a radically changing time. He is probably best known for his notorious yet compelling description of the state of nature, in which life is grimly portrayed as a war of all against all, where insecurity and fear are the primary constants. Hobbes's effort was to deduce a theory of legitimate, uncontested and stable civil authority from what he saw as the dismal facts of the human condition. In doing so, he rejected both divine right and majority choice theories of authority, arguing instead for a secular political authority capable of withstanding the vagaries of competing and always private interests. The legitimacy of Hobbes's sovereign authority was based on the quasi-democratic hypothetical consent of all rational and right-thinking individuals who, according to Hobbes, would freely agree to such authority on the basis of their rational recognition of their desires for life and security. This initially democratic basis of civil authority could not, however, be renegotiated, since men's (and Hobbes did mean 'men') unruly passions were untrustworthy. Hence, Hobbes's civil authority is fully sovereign and self-generating over time. It must be, since it rules over an unsteadily harnessed state of nature.[8]

Although Hobbes entreats his readers to reflect on their own patterns of motivation and behavior as a test and confirmation of his theory of human nature,[9] he probably didn't expect women to take him up on his offer. Within the context of Hobbes's time, in which most women were illiterate and lacking in political power (Laslett, 1965), such a proposition would have made little sense. Today, however, in keeping with the spirit of Hobbes's maxim that we 'read mankind in ourselves', such a task is an important part of the effort to come to critical terms with the Hobbesian vision of a political order built on the foundation of 'human' passions and requirements.[10]

---

[8] While Hobbes's theory of sovereign rule did not specifically exclude female authority, this says more about his theory of legitimate authority, succession and obedience to the authority than indicating any particular generosity towards women as citizens and rulers. Hobbes's deliberate underdescription of the sovereign leaves the questions of gender quite open logically. But this must be understood as a side effect of his attempt to sever the issue of legitimate authority from the personal characteristics of the sovereign.

[9] '. . . whosoever looketh into himself, and considereth what he doth, when he does *think, opine, reason, hope, fear*, &c. and upon what grounds; he shall thereby read and know, what are the thoughts and passions of all other men upon the like occasions.' Thomas Hobbes (1651a: 6).

[10] Not only was Hobbes writing for a male audience, he was also writing from a male point of view. Consider his definition of the family as 'a *father*, with his sons and servants, grown into a civil person by virtue of his paternal jurisdiction'. (Hobbes, 1651b: 219). Female servants notwithstanding, where have the daughters and wives gone? Women join the ranks with cattle and children as those possessions which men in the state of nature stand to lose in those inevitable skirmishes with other men. (Hobbes, 1651a: 81). These and other examples leave little doubt that Hobbes's 'man' is male. The issue, of course, is not whether Hobbes meant to include or exclude women in his studies of human nature and civic life. Conceivably, a *pro forma* inclusion of women would not automatically close the search for masculinist idealogy in his work. Conversely, the

The account which follows relies extensively on and presumes the reader's familiarity with psychoanalytic theory and the more recent feminist applications of post-Freudian theory (Benjamin, 1980; Chodorow, 1979; Dinnerstein, 1976; Flax, 1980; Keller, 1978). The works of Nancy Chodorow (1979) and Dorothy Dinnerstein (1976) figure prominently in this account, which utilizes in particular their vivid descriptions of the pre-Oedipal dynamics of mother-child interaction, separation-individuation, and the early stages of identity formation. This account is also indebted to Mary O'Brien's (1981) notion of gender-differentiated reproductive experience. In both frameworks, mothers occupy privileged positions within vital arenas of human experience. Also in both, maternity threatens males in identifiable ways. The denial of and attempt to appropriate such threats become, in turn, constitutive features of distinctly patterned ways of interpreting and acting in the world which may be called 'masculine'.[11] Thus, patriarchy may be understood as men's attempts to overthrow female control over reproduction, while masculinity embodies a fundamental turn away from the mother. In both scenarios, maternal power is denied even as it poses the ultimate threat. Its denial, in fact, serves to make it even more threatening.

An important feature of masculine development, well worth noting for the analysis to follow, is the *negative* articulation of masculine selfhood in relation to the pre-posited maternal presence. It would seem that there are significant links between masculinity as an achieved and precarious identity, and negatively conceived feminity as represented by the mother. The horror of identification with the feminine, the strictness with which masculinity is defined and established in relation to feminity, suggest an intimate pairing of rigidity and vulnerability.[12] Because the defining parameters of masculinity are so strictly set, they are all the more susceptible to identity-threatening phenomena. The flip side of masculine ego 'strength' is a brittle rigidity, the diminished ability to accomodate a shifting and unpredictable environment inhabited by independent fellow creatures and an enigmatic nature.

A specifiably masculine outlook and sense of identity can be roughly sum-

---

exclusion of women does not automatically imply the presence of masculinist ideology. However, the evidence for an unreflectively assumed male subject certainly invites further exploration.

[11] 'Masculinity' is being used here in the historically and culturally specific sense of the outcome of a process of identity formation and acquisition undergone by males and secured within a relational and symbolic social context that includes all or most of the following factors: primary care of infants and children provided by a single female mother and/or groups of females; general lack of intimate contact betwen fathers and young offspring; a social structure organized in terms of a sexual division of labor, male dominance in certain key sectors, and highly articulated cultural expressions of gender differences and male superiority. See the following anthropological works for helpful discussions of masculinity in this sense: Sagan (1974); Sanday (1981); Whiting and Child (1953). These studies seem to indicate that female dominated child-rearing and a masculinity at least partially constituted in terms of the need to dominate women are coterminous. While these findings cannot provide final causal explanations for male dominance, they do substantiate the argument that female mothering and masculinity as a defensive identity with overdetermined needs to control women are connected in some important way.

[12] In cultures that put a high value on sex differences which are hierarchically related in favour of men, the boy exhibiting effeminate behavior learns quickly and painfully that 'sissiness' is a big no-no. The taboo against effeminate boys suggests a powerful brand of horror at the mixing or confusion of cherished and vulnerable categories.

marized in the following way:[13] heading the list is a vigorous brand of dualistic thinking, a persistent and systematic amplification of the primal Self-Other oppositional dynamic and the creation of dichotomously structured polarities by which to describe and evaluate the events, objects and processes of the natural and social worlds (Hartsock, 1983; Keller, 1978; Benjamin, 1980). The need for singular identity and certainty with respect to one's own identity and that of other 'objects' in the environment, a concomitant of which is panic in the face of threats to such certainty, is another perceptual tendency which may be associated with masculinity. The denial of relatedness would be a feature of masculine identity as well. We can also anticipate a repudiation of natural contingency, including those limits imposed by the body and the natural surround (Dinnerstein, 1976). This will be especially important in connection with the subsequent discussion of Hobbes's heroism. Because of the tendencies towards a radical individualism built into the masculine differentiation process, we might also search for various versions of a solitary subject immersed in a hostile and dangerous world. In Hobbes's case, as we will see, this will apply to his state of nature, his actual political environment, and to his interpretation of his intellectual environment. Autonomy is also likely to figure as a prominent theme and ideal within a masculine frame. Significantly, it is one of the key concepts of liberal political theory. Finally, we can expect to find versions of knowledge-through-opposition, -tension, and -conflict, an antagonistic and distanced relation between the subject and object of knowledge, which recapitulates the earlier experience of identity through opposition and negation (Keller, 1978).[14]

Hobbes's famous state of nature in *Leviathan* is an imaginary zone which represents an intermediary state of reconstruction from the building blocks of human nature, the passions, to the completed architecture of civil society. What we find in this account is a vital concern with the survival of a self conceived in masculine terms. Hobbes's prior discussion of the passions and his portrayal of man as a kind of desiring machine have already set the stage for an essentially atomistic account of the human subject.[15]

While Hobbes's description of human nature is quite pessimistic, it is important to bear in mind that his catalogue of the passions contains a balanced

[13] This summary should be understood as a necessarily simplified ideal-type scheme which is in no way capable of capturing the dynamic experience and expression of gender identity. Let me also stress that I am not arguing that all men think alike or that all men think in identifiably masculine ways. To say that gender is necessarily constitutive of identity, that it is an unavoidable ground of thought and experience, is not to say that it determines personality or intellectual creations in some simplistic or linear fashion.

[14] The awareness of masculinity as a specifiable standpoint has been brought about by the work of countless women. I have tried to acknowledge sources for the discussion of masculinity in this paper even as a full accounting seems an impossible task. So many ideas have become an established part of feminist discourse, while many similar ideas have been articulated by different women in the context of different inquiries. For example, Flax (1980) has also commented on the missing mother syndrome in Hobbes's state of nature, while Hartsock (1983) has identified many of the same features of masculine thinking which are treated here.

[15] For helpful discussions of Hobbes's method, see Oakeshott (n.d.: vii–xvi; 1962: 248–300); MacIntyre (1971: 130–140).

itemization of qualities which we would label as 'good' in the sense of being conducive to sociability. Courage, benevolence, magnanimity, good nature (good will) and even kindness find their way into the account of the passions which Hobbes set forth in *Leviathan*.[16] While life in the state of nature may be 'nasty, mean, brutish, and short', human beings are by no means all nasty. Unfortunately, the nasties, however few, set the pace for everyone else in a zero sum game where every winner implies a loser. Hobbes's point is not that human beings are especially evil or deliberately anti-social. It is rather, that we inevitably get into each other's way. As appetitive machines that engage in the incessant pursuit of pleasure and avoidance of pain, we cannot help bumping into each other and impeding the motion of others.

For our purposes, the noteworthy aspect of Hobbes's chronicle of the passions is that it presents and requires a view of desire and motivation that is strictly self-originating and self-contained within the bounds of a clearly delineated ego. Objects of desire derive only from individual will. Commonality of desire— for example, the universal fear and avoidance of death—figures only as the sum total of individual desires bound in external allegiance to a shared object.

What is markedly absent here is the notion of types of desire constituted socially or intersubjectively. Objects of desire for Hobbes can only pertain to individual yearnings for satisfaction. And those of us who might invoke persuasion, as a counter-example to Hobbes's ultra-individualized conception of desire, which might open the way towards a recognition of intersubjectively secured values and desires, will have to contend with the Hobbesian retort that persuasion, after all, is nothing but the displacement of one will by another. Hobbes's egoism 'is only the individuality of a creature shut up, without hope of immediate release, within the world of his own imagination. Man is, by nature, the victim of solipsism; he is an *individuae substantia* distinguished by incommunicability' (Oakeshott, n.d.: liv). What communication there is takes place as a result of agreement on the definition of terms. Hence, Hobbes's nominalist epistemology and his egoism are fundamentally connected.

Hobbes's thoroughly inviolable ego is perpetually threatened by the fear and distinct possibility of untimely dissolution—namely, death at the hands of some other similarly constructed ego. This bleak and stark picture of social life in the state of nature provides the components for Hobbes's depiction of a civil order which is either governed by the strong hand of authority (an inviolable ego in the ultimate sense) or reduced to a state of internal and violent dissension (a sure sign of the ultimate demise and 'death' of civil authority). In *The Citizen*, which was Hobbes's early draft of the later *Leviathan*, he puts the choice between the state of nature and civil society as he conceived it in these terms:

[16] Given the close and often verbatim overlap between Hobbes's discussion of the passions in *On Man* and *Leviathan*, it is interesting to note that he obviously chose to eliminate compassion from the *Leviathan* version of human passions. He may well have had his reasons for keeping it out. Perhaps the human capacity for compassion undercut the political message he was trying to convey. We might also note that compassion flies in the face of an atomistic conception of man, which is a major cornerstone of his theory.

'Out of this state (of civil society), every man hath such a right to all, as yet he can enjoy nothing; in it, each one securely enjoys his limited right. Out of it, any man may rightly spoil or kill another; in it, none but one. Out of it, we are protected by our own forces; in it, by the power of all. Out of it, no man is sure of the fruit of his labors; in it, all men are. Lastly, out of it, there is a domain of passions, war, fear, poverty, slovenliness, solitude, barbarism, ignorance, cruelty; in it the domain of reason, peace, security, riches, decency, society, elegancy, science, and benevolence' (Hobbes, 1651b: 222).

For obvious reasons, Hobbes believes he has made us an offer that we can't refuse.

Norman Jacobson (1978) has suggested that 'We still read *Leviathan* after three centuries . . . because we have all experienced the threat to the self implicit in the dread of personal annihilation' (Jacobson, 1978: 59). His insight into Hobbes's psychological appeal could be further refined by asking whether this threat is not also significantly tinged with a specifically masculine sense of selfhood. It is plausible to suggest that what we find in Hobbes's account of human nature and political order is a vital concern with the survival of a self conceived in masculine terms. The strict differentiation of self from others, identity conceived in exclusionary terms, and perceived threats to an ego thus conceived which will be minimally displaced and maximally dissolved by an invader, all recapitulate issues which are materially grounded in the experiential process of securing a masculine identity by means of struggle against a female maternal presence. The masculine dimension of Hobbes's atomistic egoism is powerfully underscored in his state of nature, which is effectively built on the foundation of denied maternity.

In *The Citizen*, where Hobbes first elaborated in a systematic fashion those aspects of the state of nature which would make his prescriptions for civil society in *Leviathan* so welcome and reasonable, he asks us to 'consider men as if but even now sprung out of the earth, and suddenly, like mushrooms, come to full maturity, without all kind of engagement with each other' (Hobbes, 1651b: 205). Although he did not specifically repeat this imaginative directive in *Leviathan*, the mushroom metaphor[17] holds important clues concerning Hobbes's style of thinking on human nature in the later work. The image of mushrooms, I would argue, provided a tangible and vivid means for Hobbes to work through his abstract and general discussion of human nature. As a latent image in *Leviathan*, it provides an indispensable means of access to the gender-specific symbolic and emotional substructure of his state of nature.[18]

The mushroom is a charming and ingenious metaphorical choice; it works in

[17] Strictly speaking, this is a simile rather than a metaphor. Nonetheless, I would argue that mushrooms work as metaphorical image in this context. If 'the essence of metaphor is understanding and experiencing one thing in terms of another', then surely the metaphorical cast of Hobbes's phrasing will be granted (Lakoff and Johnson, 1980).

[18] Given the close overlap between the state of nature sections in *The Citizen* and *Leviathan*, I think it is fair to argue that the mushroom metaphor survives in *Leviathan* and provides important clues to the style and train of Hobbes's thoughts on the state of nature.

ways that 'cabbages' or 'maple trees' would not, conveying a host of images that are worth extracting for perusal. Mushrooms do seem to spring up overnight; they grow rapidly in the wild and require no special tending. Hobbes uses his state of nature construct to eliminate factors such as socialization, education, and other means of 'cultivating' human beings, removing those secondary features of human motivation and behaviour which might be mistakenly attributed to first nature. His insistence that 'nature has made man unfit for society' requires a careful distinguishing of learned behaviors appropriate to peaceful social life from innate disposition. Another feature of mushrooms is that they grow in clusters; hence, Hobbes is able to slip in a picture of human beings in close proximity to each other. The image of crowded mushrooms, as opposed to that of solitary and stately trees, reminds us that humans will inevitably confront each other in disputes over goods that are limited, since genuine security and gain require the accumulation of a relative surplus. Man in the state of nature may be a radical individual, but like the mushroom, he is not solitary. Finally, mushrooms reproduce quietly and apparently asexually; spores are scattered by the wind and land haphazardly, sprouting when moisture and temperature conditions are right. This feature of the metaphorical image allows us to accept that much more quietly one of the most incredible and problematic features of Hobbes's state of nature. And it is this: that men are not born of, much less nurtured by, women, or anyone else for that matter.[19]

In the process of extracting an abstract man for rational perusal, Hobbes has also expunged human reproduction and early nurturance, two of the most basic and typically female-identified features of distinctively human life, from his account of basic human nature. Such a strategy ensures that he can present a thoroughly atomistic subject, one whose individual rights, sparsely conceived, clearly precede any obligation to belong to civil society. With the help of the mushroom metaphor, Hobbes's atomism affirms the self-sufficiency of gender-specific man alone in the crowded midst of other men.

The mushroom imagery, in its unmistakable denial of human sexuality, reproduction and maternal nurturance, makes that much more plausible a central tenet of Hobbes's theory of civil authority, obligations and rights. As Charles Taylor (1979) argues, the doctrine of the primacy of rights relies on an atomistic conception of the individual in the sense of affirming 'the self-sufficiency of man alone' (Taylor, 1979: 41). Self-sufficiency here refers not to the ability to survive alone in the wilderness, but rather, to the notion that characteristically human capacities need no particular social life forms in which to develop. In the state of nature scene being considered here, which we might subtitle the Case of the Missing Mother, the issue is not whether infants would survive

---

[19] The point here is not whether Hobbes's state of nature is realistic. No state of nature is going to be realistic if, by 'realistic', we mean conforming to the standards and contours of life as we know and cherish it. State of nature constructs are intended to make us more self-conscious about the unreflectively accepted particularities of our life-forms. They could not do this if they simply reproduced social organization. But we do need to ask, what is the *point* of including and excluding particular features of social life? Is our understanding of the human condition enhanced or handicapped by the simplifications and fantasies of the theorist?

untended in the wild. Hobbes made it clear to his critics that he never intended self-sufficiency in this sense either.[20] The issue concerns instead the ways in which early maternal and parental care provide a social, intersubjective context for the development of particular capacities in children—emotive, social and cognitive capacities—which are presupposed to some extent in Hobbes's state of nature being, who is capable of implementing compacts and contracts as well as of deducing the dictates of right reason from his natural circumstances. Hobbes's metaphor, of course, aims at avoiding any such discussion of the etiology of capacities such as these. In providing us with fully sprung and atomistically conceived men and tracing out their hypothetical social exchanges prior to civil order, Hobbes can keep his schedule of human rights to a bare minimum: the right to life, maximum pleasure so long as it does not interfere with the pleasure of others, and maximum freedom from pain. Social obligation is presented as a purely pragmatic affair, external to the identities of the participants. Social obligation is derived from sparsely conceived natural right and hence, is secondary to it.

Hobbes's denial of the mother, with its unmistakable ramifications on his portrayal of atomistic identity and contractual social intercourse, is also refracted in his theory of legitimate authority and required obedience to that authority. As the inaugurator of a liberal tradition which deauthorized individuals in the name of the abstract individual (Bronstein, 1980), breaking the more traditional associations between authority, persons and their special (divinely ordained) attributes, Hobbes presented a radically new, and, to many, disturbing interpretation of authority as simultaneously arbitrary and absolute. It was arbitrary in the sense that the question of who might be invested with sovereign civil authority was effectively inconsequential for Hobbes. What ultimately mattered was that a strong, central and uncontested form of authority be identifiably located in some one person or executive body and that the problem of succession be abstractly settled ahead of its required implementation.

Hobbes's deauthorization of authority, whereby authority is legitimate and must be obeyed simply by virtue of the fact that it is the authority, rests squarely on a prior deauthorization of the mother. The connecting link is the depersonalization of authority (Bronstein, 1980). Maternal authority embodies a view of authority to which Hobbes's scheme is thoroughly opposed. Not only is maternal authority indelibly personal and organically based, it also stands in a

---

[20] Hobbes anticipated objections to his formulations of state of nature life and specifically addressed the social needs of infants. It may be found in the famous section from *The Citizen* entitled 'Of the state of men without civil society' (p. 110), in the edition cited here: 'Therefore I must more plainly say, that it is true indeed, that to man by nature, or as man, that is, as soon as he is born, solitude is an enemy; for infants have need of others to help them live. . . . Wherefore I deny not that men (even nature compelling) desire to come together. . . . (However) it is one thing to desire, another to be in capacity fit for what we desire.' Because of Hobbes's individually and solipsistically cast notion of desire, howeveer, this response does not meet the objection addressed here, namely, that the care of infants and children invokes the question of intersubjectively constituted and secured capacities which, while eminently 'natural', require particular social contexts in which to emerge and flourish.

complex relation to its subjects, one that cannot be characterized in the simple linear terms of commandments and prescriptions with merely behavioral consequences. Parental authority is at least partially introjected. For this reason, our relation to it cannot be cast in simple contractarian terms, despite Hobbe's efforts to do this.[21] That Hobbes attempted to do precisely that suggests that he understood the significant difficulties that parental authority posed for his theory of civil authority and civic obligation. Hobbes treats the relation between parent and child and sovereign and subject in the same essential way: the terms of allegiance and obedience are strictly external to the pre-constituted identities of the participants.

The Leviathan is effectively comprised of a body politic of orphans who have reared themselves, whose desires are situated within and reflect nothing but independently generated movement. Disagreements are likely to erupt and, because there are no conceivable means for adjudicating rationally between competing and always private desires, there must be a locus of authority which can pronounce on such disputes. Such pronouncements must be obeyed, not because they might be wise or in our or someone else's best interests, but simply because they reflect the voice of sovereign authority. The prime directive, after all, is peace; and justice refers only to a correspondence to the written law. Our relation to sovereign authority, like our relations to fellow human beings, takes place within a behavioral panorama peopled by strictly differentiated, masculinized, unmothered individuals whose highest civic achievement is mutual accommodation.

We should also take note of the congruence between Hobbes's masculinist depiction of human identity and the social relations it entails, and his nominalism. Knowledge, like desire and identity, is hermetically privatized; whatever communication takes place can only proceed by way of formal agreement on the meaning of terms 'by exact definition first snuffed and purged from ambiguity . . . ' (Hobbes, 1651a: 30).

In Hobbes's version of the ideal civil society, the atomistic individuals of the state of nature remain essentially unchanged except for their mutually contracted allegiance to a single civil authority brought about by the collective sum of their individual fears of injury, loss of property and untimely death. State of nature man is simply transplanted from one environment to another. Death, that most radical equalizer in the state of nature, is transposed into the singular power to punish by the sovereign authority. And fear, which in the state of nature kept men at odds with each other, becomes the social gluten of the civil order. In sum, Hobbes's civil society has no transformative effect on its body politic. His 'grand artifice' consists of a recombination, clever but not especially creative, of the given elements of the state of nature. These essential elements are natural human beings conceived along masculine lines. This masculine tenor

---

[21] Hobbes does argue that we are indebted to our parents for our physical survival as youngsters. This, however, is fashioned in contract-like terms: 'the preserved oweth all to the preserver'. Biological parenthood is fairly inconsequential for Hobbes. Whoever rears the child is entitled to absolute obedience in exchange for parental provisions for physical survival.

may be found initially in Hobbes's conception of a clearly unified and discrete ego, one that is unassailable except in combative terms, approachable only on the terms of contracted and nominalist exchanges. We can also discern masculinity at work in the fantasy pattern which underlies his state of nature: men magically sprung like mushrooms, unmothered and unfathered. While such a fantasy deals a blow to parenthood in general and the organic notion of generational continuity through time (O'Brien, 1981), it strikes especially hard at the maternal contribution, whose denial is uniquely remarkable and difficult to implement, since it is so biologically and socially apparent.

An important link in the chain of explanation connecting masculinity with the denial of maternity is provided by psychoanalytic observations on the acquisition of masculinity within the context of female-dominated childrearing (Chodorow, 1979; Dinnerstein, 1976; Sagan, 1974; Whiting and Child, 1953). The boy child coming of age in a sexually inegalitarian society is eventually forced to demonstrate his masculinity in overdetermined ways which include the denial of an earlier identity secured within the female maternal sphere. At the personal level, this is likely to include the denial of the power and formative influence of one's mother. Such a denial would also involve the repudiation of the introjected mother within oneself. If this is achieved at the individual level of personal identity, extending it to a generalized view of humanity and the civil order is a small step. We cannot be sure that this characterization of masculinity and denied maternity correctly or adequately captures the origins and development of Hobbes's thought.[22] On firmer ground, however, we can more comfortably reflect on the ways in which Hobbes's thought may have resonated with just such a set of meanings in the minds of subsequent readers. It is reasonable to suggest that part of the undeniable power and appeal of Hobbes's analysis may be traced to this masculine dimension of his theory.

Hobbes's work also merits scrutiny at the level of style and what Sheldon Wolin has termed its 'informing intention' (Wolin, 1970: 4). While intention and style invariably affect the substance of thought, in Hobbes's case especially they have a direct bearing on our consideration of the masculinist stamp of his work.

In terms of the often strained relation between his 'walk' and his 'talk', between his avowed philosophy of 'right method' and his actual implementation of that method, Hobbes is a fascinating patchwork of contrasts. His sceptical and nominalist epistemology coexists with a genuine respect for the lessons of experience. Another significant contrast may be located between Hobbes's own prescription for 'right method'—a plodding, methodical and rational arrangement of basic definitions and propositions—and the sheer power of his prose, which is characterized by an imaginative, flamboyant and persuasive style. Notwithstanding his protests against the improper use of poetic and rhetorical flourishes in a philosophic and scientific enterprise that ought to be soberly dedicated to the careful study of causes and their consequences. Hobbes himself

---

[22] See Stone (1979) for a discussion of family history which suggests indirectly that Hobbes's life-span may have been situated in the midst of an emerging affective and nuclear family structure.

was often a dazzling rhetorician and highly adept at flourishing potent metaphors to convince readers of his right thinking.

Hobbes's avowed epistemological scepticism, which is rescued from a solipsistic stance by his faith in shared common sense experience, contrasts sharply with his argumentative mode, which seeks to demonstrate the air-tight logic and common-sense truth of his arguments. Consider this choice excerpt:

> 'It may seem strange to some man, that has not well weighed these things; that nature should thus dissociate, and render men apt to invade, and to destroy one another; and he may therefore, not trusting to this inference, made from the passions, desire perhaps to have the same confirmed by experience. Let him therefore consider with myself, when taking a journey, he arms himself, and seeks to go well accompanied; when going to sleep, he locks his doors; when even in his house, he locks his chests; and this when he knows there be laws, and public officers, armed, to revenge all injuries shall be done him; what opinion he has of his fellow-subjects, when he rides armed; of his fellow citizens, when he locks his doors; and of his children and servants, when he locks his chests. Does he not there as much accuse mankind by his actions, as I do by my words?' (Hobbes, 1651a: 82–83).

One of his intellectual biographers, Miriam Reik (1977), has this observation to offer on the tone of Hobbes's method and mode of presentation:

> '(O)ne of the most prominent characteristics of Hobbes's philosophic impulse (is) the drive toward discovering and building on the simplest, most basic elements of reality, and reasoning about them with such force and directness that his explanations seem to become almost intellectually *coercive*.' (Reik, 1977: 71).

A fruitful means of exploring and accounting for this series of interesting incongruities in Hobbes's work is provided by Sheldon Wolin's thesis (1970) that Hobbes cast himself in the role of epic-theorist. In the following discussion, Wolin's thesis will be surveyed with a view towards establishing some of the connections between masculinity and the epic heroism which characterizes Hobbes's work.

Wolin (1970) argues that Hobbes had epical intentions in writing *Leviathan*, intentions that he shares with Plato, Machiavelli, Hegel and Marx, whose collective great works comprise an epic tradition in Western political theory:

> 'The phrase "epic tradition" refers to a type of political theory which is inspired mainly by the hope of achieving a great and memorable deed through the medium of thought. Other aims that it may have, such as contributing to the existing state of knowledge, formulating a system of logically consistent propositions, or establishing a set of hypotheses for scientific investigation, are distinctly secondary.' (Wolin, 1970: 4).

Political theories of the epic mold are intended by their authors as forms of action, where the written work itself is the deed, a thought-deed that will

hopefully be translated into reality. But if it is not to be actualized, the residual hope is that the thought, like the preserved chronicles of long dead heroes, will endure through time. Theories cast in the epic mold reveal 'an attempt to compel admiration and awe for the magnitude of the achievement' (Wolin, 1970: 5). As such, the epic theorist casts himself in the role of epic hero. His aim extends beyond the relatively humble one of logical persuasion to that of astonishing his audience by a remarkable thought-deed.

Like the hero of epic poetry, the heroic theorist is a single individual figure whose exploits surpass those of other men and whose talents and strengths are specifically human.[23] Just as divine intervention cannot make the hero (although it may aid him) so too the epic theorist performs his intellectual feats through the evident use of his unique and natural brain power and imagination (Wolin, 1970). Finally, the hero of epic poetry and the heroic political theorist share another significant trait: their achievements are bound up with the stuff of manhood. Bowra's account of heroic poetry (1966) is especially provocative for what it suggests about the links between epic heroism, masculinity, and Hobbes's individualism:

> 'Heroes are the champions of man's ambition to pass beyond the oppressive limits of human frailty to a fuller and more vivid life, *to win as far as possible a self-sufficient manhood*, which refuses to admit that anything is too difficult for it and is content even in failing, provided that it has made every effort of which it is capable.' (Bowra, 1966: 4; my emphasis).

The theme of self-sufficiency recapitulates one of the most distinctive psychological features of masculinity. To the extent that masculine identity is bound up with a repudiation of the mother, vigorous self-sufficiency emerges as a kind of defensive reaction-formation against memories of dependence and the early symbiotic relation. Hobbes's atomistic individualism also invokes this image of self-sufficiency, as we have seen, which is strengthened by the effective displacement of mothers from the state of nature. We encounter it in yet another form in the figure of the heroic subject.

The epic hero achieves immortality by surpassing the standards of achievement set by others. Thus, competition is an essential feature of epic heroism. It is this competitive and individualistic quality of action—competition directed at the select few who have set the highest intellectual standards—which marks the style of Hobbes's approach to his work. As Wolin (1970) documents, Hobbes never argued with any but the most prominent and formidable recognized intellects: among them, Aristotle and the best mathematicians of his time. Furthermore, these disputes were cast by Hobbes into some of the most vivid combative terminology that has ever been written, as this excerpt from his *Autobiography* (1679) reveals plainly:

---

[23] Bowra argues for the individualism of the hero and for the epic stress on his uniquely human and secular capacities. (See Bowra 1966: Ch. I and III; 1945: especially Ch. I.)

'. . . I brought out another little book on Principles. . . . Here my victory
was acknowledged by all. In other fields my opponents were doing their best
to hide their grievous wounds. Their spirits were flagging and I pressed home
the assault on my flagging foes, and scaled to topmost pinnacles of geometry . . . Wallis enters the fray against me, and in the eyes of the algebraists and
theologians I am worsted. And now the whole host of Wallisians, confident of
victory, was let out of their camp. But when I saw them deploying on treacherous
ground, encumbered with roots thick-set, troublesome and tenacious, I resolved
on fight, and in one moment scattered, slaughtered, routed countless foes.'
(Hobbes, 1679: 30; also cited in Wolin, 1970).

We also find a relevant complaint inscribed in Hobbes's criticism of too much
attention and respect directed towards the thinkers of old: 'competition of
praise, inclineth to a reverence of antiquity. For men contend with the living;
not with the dead; to these ascribing more than due, that they may obscure
the glory of the other' (Hobbes, 1651a: 64). Hobbes wanted to shine forth in
his day and after, unimpeded by the ghosts of the past who attracted attention
to themselves and therefore detracted from the attention that he sought. As
would-be epic theorist, Hobbes himself is in the midst of the competitions for
power, gain and glory which he depicted so vividly.

Leviathan opens with the image of Hobbes as a Ulysses figure carefully
maneuvering between the Scylla and Charybdis of liberty and authority: 'For
in a way beset with those that contend, on the one side for too great liberty,
and on the other side for too much authority, 'tis hard to pass between the
points of both unwounded' (Hobbes, 1651a: 2). We should bear in mind that
Hobbes's characterization of his enterprise here is not entirely fanciful. Many
were the unlucky victims of the raging political disputes of his time. And Hobbes
himself was lucky to have survived the political upheavals of seventeenth-
century England.[24] However, his sense of risk here goes beyond the arena of
immediate political intrigue to that of intellectual combat and risk as well, as
he reveals so engagingly in the *Autobiography*. Heroic honor is predicated on
the pursuit of risk (Bowra, 1945: 10). And the ultimate risk is loss of life, to
which most heroes inevitably succumb, often prematurely, always bravely and
gloriously, if sometimes from the view of hindsight, foolishly. The casting of
heroic honor in these terms, labelled by Marina Warner as 'our necrophiliac
culture's ideology of heroism,' (Warner, 1981: 272) has tended to exclude females who, as the anthropological record suggests, have been less willing to
risk their lives in ultimate confrontations.[25] This is not to say that women have
been historically unwilling to risk their lives. Certainly, women have risked
and courted death on behalf of their children. But this is better understood as
a kind of last-ditch effort. The willingness to risk life would seem to be less a

[24] Hobbes's remarkable longevity is one notable biographical feature which distinguishes him
from the hero who must usually die prematurely.
[25] See Sanday (1981: 210–211): 'If there is a basic difference between the sexes, other than the
differences associated with reproductivity, it is that women as a group have not willingly faced
death in violent conflict.'

constitutive feature of femininity and more an instrumental means of preserving life.

The strong connections between heroism, masculinity and the willingness to risk life are unmistakable.[26] These connections are further strengthened if we stop to ponder the gender-specific dimensions of the heroic quest for immortality. As Mary O'Brien (1981) has argued, men's alienated relationship to reproduction, manifested most clearly in the uncertainties of paternity, is carried over into their conceptions of time. 'Men have always sought principles of continuity outside of natural continuity' (O'Brien, 1981: 33). Among the many cultural forms of temporal continuity instituted by men, within which we may include patrilineal descent and the regenerative succession of political authority embodied in the state (O'Brien, 1981), immortality is especially noteworthy. It defies the biological pronouncements of death, decay and ultimate defeat, provides a tangible sense of generational continuity over time for the male 'family' of heroes and their admirers, and, above all, assures men of an uncontested role in their 'reproduction' through time. Like Hobbes's state of nature man, the immortal hero is self-made and lives in a motherless world.

Hobbes's portrayal of the state of nature, a frightening and awesome spectacle, serves to dramatically enhance the heroic-masculinist dimension of his work. As Wolin tells us:

'Epic heroes move in a world of dark and occult forces; they encounter great perils and horrors, sometimes at the hands of nature, sometimes by the machinations of malevolent powers; they are constantly in the midst of violent death and widespread destruction; and yet by a superhuman effort, which stretches the human will to its limits, they succeed nonetheless.' (Wolin, 1970: 20).

'Violent death' and 'widespread destruction' appropriately describe both the England of the Civil Wars as well as Hobbes's state of nature. His theoretical feat was to rescue us from an existence that would otherwise be 'nasty, mean, brutish and short.' This salvation is made possible by the theorist-hero's courage in exploring that dark and dangerous terrain of the state of nature and human nature, which he makes available for all to see in its full horror.

Along with his courage, Hobbes wields a remarkable weapon which, like the requisite special weapon of the epic hero, is both the instrument and emblem of his power. Hobbes's special power is knowledge; and his weapon, writes Wolin, is 'right method':

'Rational method is not a weapon easily fashioned or easily mastered, especially in political matters. The prolonged preparation, constant practice, and pure

[26] Warner's discussion (1981) of Joan of Arc's fate at the hands of a 'masculine lexicon of heroic meaning' supports the argument that heroism is distinctively masculine. (See Warner, 1981: 3–10.) This suggests that female heroes, rather than being simply 'hidden from history', need to be rescued, revived and recreated by means of reinterpretation rather than simple excavation. Female heroes are probably not so much hidden as automatically excluded by definition from cultural chronicles because their activities cannot be captured or framed within the existing lexicon of heroic meaning.

dedication which it demands are analogous to the long apprenticeship and severe trials which a knight had to undergo before he was declared fit for chivalric tests.' (Wolin, 1970: 22).

It is Hobbes's *heroic* use of a deductive method cast in a sober, plodding and hyper-rational terminology which helps to account for the incongruity between his avowed philosophy of method and his actual implementation of it. Under such circumstances, Hobbes-as-heroic-theorist and Hobbes-as-scientific-philosopher are bound to be caught in a paradoxical relationship to each other. When Hobbes's political geometry is employed in a battleground environment, incongruous, as well as exciting, things are bound to happen. This is the stuff of Hobbes's achievement. If he had been more consistent, enacting his method to the letter of the law, we would not continue to read him and to be provoked by his analysis of the requirements of and limited possibilities for civil society.

Like the curiously strained yet compelling notion of 'the war to end all wars', Hobbes's heroic enterprise is paradoxically aimed at eliminating future heroes by creating a civil order in which heroism would have no legitimate space. Strictly bound in allegiance to a central and absolute ruler, citizens of his Leviathan would be effectively stripped of heroic motivation. Hobbes's aim was to create the risk-free society. Heroism is necessarily sacrificed to long range peace and stability. And the choice as Hobbes presents it is overwhelmingly tempting. Hobbes's all-or-nothing choice, between a chaotic and violent state of nature or a predictable civil ler, points to a solution which conveniently leaves Hobbes as the last hero. The heroic dismantling of the requisite conditions for heroism is an altogether remarkable feat (Wolin, 1970), one from which Hobbes could hope to derive uncontested future praise, admiration and immortality.

Hobbes's political theory has been subjected to a number of criticisms, many of which center directly on his treatment of human nature and argue that he failed to provide a convincing account of generalized humanity. This failure becomes all the more dramatic when Hobbes is read as a masculine thinker. Masculinity inhabits his work throughout a remarkably broad range of levels, from his unself-conscious adoption of a male standpoint in his prose, to his depiction of a motherless state of nature, to his atomistic portrayal of the human subject in that state and in civil society, to his heroic conception of his own work. The substance and style of Hobbes's work, which significantly includes a specific notion of the human subject in various capacities—state of nature man, civil subject, and heroic intellectual—betrays a specifically masculine cast, one that necessarily ignores and debases the female presence in and contribution to social life. As such, Hobbes's political theory is distinctively flawed in newly apparent ways which are both disturbing and instructive.

The most significant finding involves the denial of the maternal contribution. This denial, as I have tried to show, is logically central to and required by Hobbes's atomistic account of human nature, social interaction, and civic life. In other words, the denial of the mother here is not an incidental feature of Hobbes's theory; it saturates his analysis throughout. From a feminist stand-

point (Hartsock, 1983; Smith, 1979), we are forced to conclude that the substance and structure of Hobbes's thought is fundamentally flawed.

The heroic dimensions of Hobbes's style also point convincingly in the direction of masculinity. Hobbes's sense of himself as a heroic intellectual actor and his depiction of nature have quite a bit in common. Significantly, the threat of personal annihilation in the state of nature and the promise of its elimination in civil society share with the heroic conception of risk a highly individualized and masculinized sense of selfhood. A self conceived along such lines is simultaneously vulnerable to attack and capable of heroic feats in a dangerous world. Hobbes's feat was to cast himself as the last hero by proposing a solution to a predicament that was more masculine than human in tenor. The external and inviolable authority of the sovereign would replace the social anarchy of a world populated by motherless self-sprung men.

A portion of Hobbes's genius thus might be said to include the unwitting exploration of a masculine politics, one that is premised on a distinctly gendered and distorted sense of identity. It is a negative politics that is grim and instrumentally limited in its abilities to transform the human condition. Hobbes's abstract man is a creature who is self-possessed and radically solitary in a crowded and inhospitable world, whose relations with others are unavoidably contractual and whose freedom consists in the absence of impediments to the attainment of privately generated and understood desires. Abstract man thus bears the tell-tale signs of a masculinity *in extremis:* identity through opposition, denial of reciprocity, repudiation of the mother in oneself, a constitutional inability/refusal to recognize what might be termed dialectical connectedness. Hobbes's genius and courage was to face the momentous and uncomfortable truth of this masculine revelation. His failure was the inability to recognize it as a half-truth.

REFERENCES

Benjamin, Jessica. 1980. The bonds of love: rational violence and erotic domination. *Feminist Studies* **6** (1): 144–174.

Bowra, C. M. 1945. *From Virgil to Milton.* MacMillan, London.

Bowra, C. M. 1966. *Heroic Poetry.* St Martin's Press, New York.

Breger, Louis. 1981. *Freud's Unfinished Journey: Conventional and Critical Perspectives in Psychoanalytic Theory.* Routledge and Kegan Paul, London and Boston.

Bronstein, Zelda. 1980. Psychoanalysis without the father. *Humanities in Society* **3** (2): 199–212.

Chodorow, Nancy. 1979. *The Reproduction of Mothering: Psychoanalysis and the Sociology of Gender.* University of California Press, Berkeley and Los Angeles.

Clarke, Lorenne and Lynda Lange, eds. 1980. *The Sexism of Social and Political Theory: Women and Reproduction from Plato to Nietzsche.* University of Toronto Press, Toronto.

Coleman, Frank M. 1977. *Hobbes and America: Exploring the Constitutional Foundations.* University of Toronto Press, Toronto.

de Beauvoir, Simone. 1952. *The Second Sex*. Random House (Vintage Books), New York (1974).

Dinnerstein, Dorothy. 1976. *The Mermaid and the Minotaur: Sexual Arrangements and Human Malaise*. Harper and Row, New York.

Eisenstein, Hester and Alice Jardine, eds. 1980. *The Future of Difference*. G. K. Hall, Boston.

Elshtain, Jean Bethke. 1981. *Public Man, Private Woman: Women in Social and Political Thought*. Princeton University Press, Princeton.

Flax, Jane. 1980. Mother-daughter relationships: psychodynamics, politics and philosophy. In Eisenstein, Hester and Alice Jardine, eds, *The Future of Difference*, pp. 20–41. G. K. Hall, Boston.

Gilligan, Carol. 1982. *In a Different Voice: Psychological Theory and Women's Development*. Harvard University Press, Cambridge.

Hartsock, Nancy. 1983. The feminist standpoint: developing the ground for a specifically feminist historical materialism. Forthcoming in Harding, Sandra and Merrill Hintikka, eds, *Discovering Reality: Feminist Perspectives on Epistemology, Metaphysics, Methodology and the Philosophy of Science*. Reidel, Dordrecht.

Hirschman, Albert O. 1977. *The Passions and the Interests: Political Arguments for Capitalism Before Its Triumph*. Princeton University Press, Princeton.

Hobbes, Thomas. 1651a. *Leviathan*. Michael Oakeshott, ed. Basil Blackwell, Oxford (n.d.).

Hobbes, Thomas. 1651b. *The Citizen: Philosophical Rudiments Concerning Government and Society*. Bernard Gert, ed. *Man and Citizen: Thomas Hobbes's De Homine and De Cive*. Doubleday, Garden City (1972).

Hobbes, Thomas. 1679. *Autobiography*. B. Farrington, trans. *The Rationalist Annual for 1958*, pp. 22–31.

Jacobson, Norman. 1978. *Pride and Solace: The Functions and Limits of Political Theory*. University of California Press, Berkeley.

Keller, Evelyn. 1978. Gender and science. *Psychoanalysis and Contemporary Thought* **1** (3): 409–433.

Lakoff, George and Mark Johnson. 1980. *Metaphors We Live By*. The University of Chicago Press, Chicago and London.

Laslett, Peter. 1965. *The World We Have Lost: England Before the Industrial Age*. Charles Scribner's Sons, New York (1973).

MacIntyre, Alasdaire. 1971. *A Short History of Ethics*. Macmillan, New York.

Macpherson, C. B. 1962. *The Political Theory of Possessive Individualism: Hobbes to Locke*. Oxford University Press, Oxford.

Mahowald, Mary. 1978. *Philosophy of Woman: Classical to Current Concepts*. Hackett, Indianapolis.

Marks, Elaine and Isabelle de Courtivron, eds. 1980. *New French Feminisms*. University of Massachussets Press, Amherst.

Miller, Jean Baker. 1976. *Towards a New Psychology of Women*. Beacon Press, Boston.

Oakeshott, Michael. n.d. Introduction to *Leviathan*, pp. vii–vxi. Basil Blackwell, Oxford.

Oakeshott, Michael. 1962. The moral life in the writings of Thomas Hobbes. In *Rationalism in Politics*, pp. 248–300. Methuen, London and New York.

O'Brien, Mary. 1981. *The Politics of Reproduction*. Routledge and Kegan Paul, London and Boston.

Okin, Susan Moller. 1979. *Women in Western Political Thought*. Princeton University Press, Princeton.

Osborne, Martha Lee, ed. 1979. *Woman in Western Thought*. Random House, New York.

Reik, Miriam. 1977. *The Golden Lands of Thomas Hobbes*. Wayne State University Press, Detroit.

Ruddick, Sara. 1980. Maternal thinking. *Feminist Studies* **6** (2): 342–367.

Sagan, Eli. 1974. *Cannibalism: Human Aggression and Cultural Form.* Harper and Row, New York.

Sanday, Peggy Reeves. 1981. *Female Power and Male Dominance: On the Origins of Sexual Inequality.* Cambridge University Press, Cambridge.

Smith, Dorothy. 1979. A Sociology for Women. In Sherman, Julian and Evelyn Torton Beck, eds, *The Prism of Sex: Essays in the Sociology of Knowledge.* University of Wisconsin Press, Madison.

Stone, Lawrence. 1979. *The Family, Sex and Marriage in England 1500–1800.* Harper and Row, New York (abridged edition).

Taylor, Charles. 1979. Atomism. In Kontos, Alkis ed. *Powers, Possessions and Freedom: Essays in Honor of C. B. MacPherson.* University of Toronto Press, Toronto.

Warner, Marina. 1981. *Joan of Arc: The Image of Female Heroism.* Random House (Vintage Books), New York (1982).

Whiting, John and Irving Child. 1953. *Child Training and Personality: A Cross-Cultural Study.* Yale University Press, New Haven.

Wolgast, Elizabeth. 1980. *Equality and the Rights of Women.* Cornell University Press, Ithaca and London.

Wolin, Sheldon. 1970. *Hobbes and the Epic Tradition of Political Theory.* University of California Press, Los Angeles.

Part II

Affections of Feminism

Introduction
Ruth M. Schwartz

In this part, which presents selections from the second issue of *Hypatia*, Caroline Whitbeck describes a feminist viewpoint as one that "aims to provide concepts and models that make possible the articulation of women's experience and women's practices." The elucidation of such a viewpoint serves a dual purpose. First, a feminist viewpoint aims to give women's experience equal validity with men's. Doing so involves the examination of women's experiences and issues traditionally ignored or devalued in philosophy. In the course of examining women's experiences it was discovered that traditional methodologies and perspectives were inadequate for rendering satisfactory explanations of that experience. Thus traditional methodologies and concepts drew a picture of reality that was fundamentally inadequate because women did not fit in or were distorted by them.

For such reasons, feminism grew into an approach in philosophy, i.e., a methodology and perspective (or set of methodologies and perspectives) that will provide an adequate account of women's experience. Hence the second purpose of the feminist viewpoint became ridding philosophy of ties to concepts of gender, in order to develop a picture of reality that accounts for women as well as men. Although within feminist philosophy there are differing aims and viewpoints (some aim at creations of a gynocentric reality, others at an androgenous one; some aim at elucidating and eliminating male bias in traditional systems and theories, others at using traditional methods of analysis in varying degrees to explore women's experience), the feminist perspective furthers philosophy as a whole insofar as it contributes not only to its scope but also to the ultimate creation of gender-free conceptions of reality.

The development of feminist perspective and methodology has coincided with and contributed to other changes in philosophy. In particular, changes in the focus of ethics have shifted studies from metaethics to an increasing concern,

first with normative ethics, then with questions of applied ethics. Feminist emphasis on the connection between theory and practice, the personal and the political, and feminist focus on the examination of all the complexities of single problems rather than predefined specific concepts are particularly suited to questions of applied ethics and their relation to gender. It is around a group of problems in applied ethics that the second issue of *Hypatia* was organized.

Sandra Lee Bartky and Eva Feder Kittay focus on problems concerning sexuality. Kittay examines the notion of a "correct" sexuality for women, within the context of society's power relations between the sexes. She criticizes Freud for his biological determinism and for assuming a self/other dichotomy that views male features as positives and women's as defects. For these reasons Freud failed to see that penis envy, "the conceptual linchpin of his theory of female sexuality," has no force outside the conditions of male dominance, and he failed to develop a needed theory of womb envy. The envies of both sexes must be analyzed in the context of the social conditions that give rise to them in order to develop an adequate understanding of sexual development and the ways in which it contributes to the subordination of women.

Bartky addresses the moral dilemma of the individual whose masochistic sexual desires oppose her principles. She criticizes liberal defenses that one ought not to feel shame at such desire, on the grounds that sadomasochism constitutes "erotization of relations of domination" and is thus opposed to feminism by helping to perpetuate that domination. Rejecting the claims of "sexual voluntarism" that sexual desire can be altered in all cases, she finds the moral dilemma of desire versus principle an individually insoluble one. Using a phenomenological analysis of an individual's shame at such unalterable desires, she finds it to be a justified response to a real inner division. Obligation to alter desire in such cases rests not only with the individual but also with the group. Thus she calls for the development of an adequate theory of sexual development and an effective praxis concerning issues of personal transformation in response.

Mary E. Hawkesworth defends affirmative action, which she construes not as a policy of compensatory justice designed to remedy the results of "blind social processes" through the overriding of individual rights but as grounded in principles of distributive justice that address current biases in criteria of excellence and merit. She traces the debate over affirmative action to conflicting conceptions of individual identity: a Hobbesian concept of "atomistic individualism" is presupposed by opponents of affirmative action, while proponents accept a notion of "socialized individualism." She criticizes "atomistic individualism" for its failure to address social and cultural influences on individual identity and for self-contradiction in its conception of individual freedom, both of which lead to blindness, to manifestations of sexual and racial bias, and to ensuing restrictions on the freedom of the disadvantaged.

Margaret A. Simons examines similarly conflicting conceptions of individual identity that exist within feminism and create conflicting moral views on motherhood. She provides a critical analysis of the individualist feminist tradition dating back to Beauvoir, which expresses a negative view of motherhood, and a "romantic tradition," which emphasizes the nurturing values of motherhood.

Neither tradition is able to account for the full range of women's experience, and Simons proposes an integrationist position that affirms the values of autonomy and of nurturing as parts of women's identity. She asserts that all can be pursued, both by women who choose motherhood and by women who choose not to be mothers. While women ought to claim as much of their identity as they can, few women experience motherhood as a real choice, and moral obligations will depend upon and, by implication, include striving for changes that would allow women further opportunities for the expression of that identity.

Gillian Michell focuses on the question of whether women's frequent distortions of truth ("telling it slant") are morally excusable. She analyzes these distortions as violations of Grice's rules for rational conversation. Yet they are needed to achieve maximally effective information exchange, the purpose of Grice's rules, in mixed-sex conversation predicated upon conditions of male dominance. While "telling it slant" promotes conversational effectiveness, it also helps perpetuate the situation that makes such distortions necessary by not pointing out the limitations of male-defined reality. Michell concludes by saying that "this dilemma complicates [women's] moral choices about truth telling," which may require more courage than had been thought.

Whitbeck sketches a distinctively feminist erotics. She criticizes traditional accounts of erotics for taking as central that desire is desire for an opposite and a self/other–male/female dichotomy that makes the idea of knowing one's beloved contradictory. She proposes a different characterization of eros as a "transforming contact with an other that brings one to a turning point . . . or takes one out of one's limited self." Knowing and seeing oneself in an other analogous to oneself is a common vehicle for transformation in such erotic relationships. This erotics, which is developed through analysis of particular ingredients in women's relationships, is based on a gender-free ontology and includes in its scope intimate relationships that are not sexual (such as the mother-child relationship). Whitbeck echoes Bartky's theme in her emphasis on issues of practice as well as theory in personal transformation, outlining an erotics that is not merely a new understanding of an erotic engagement but a "fundamentally different engagement," thus contributing, like the other authors in this part, to the development of a gender-free ethics for actual modes of human interaction.

FEMININE MASOCHISM AND THE POLITICS OF PERSONAL TRANSFORMATION

Sandra Lee Bartky

To be at once a sexual being and a moral agent can be troublesome indeed: no wonder some philosophers have wished that we could be rid of sexuality altogether. What to do, for example, when the structure of desire is at war with one's principles? This is a difficult question for any person of conscience but it has a particular poignancy for feminists. A prime theoretical contribution of the contemporary feminist analysis of women's oppression can be captured in the slogan 'the personal is political.' What this means is that the subordination of women by men is pervasive, that it orders the relationship of the sexes in every area of life, that a sexual politics of domination is as much in evidence in the private spheres of the family, ordinary social life and sexuality as in the traditionally public spheres of government and the economy. The belief that the things we do in the bosom of the family or in bed are either 'natural' or else a function of the personal idiosyncrasies of private individuals is held to be an 'ideological curtain that conceals the reality of women's systematic oppression.' (Jaggar, 1983: 122). For the feminist, two things follow upon the discovery that sexuality does indeed belong to the sphere of the political. The first is that whatever pertains to sexuality—not only actual sexual behavior, but sexual desire and sexual fantasy too—will have to be understood in relation to a larger system of subordination; the second, that the deformed sexuality of patriarchal culture must be moved from the hidden domain of 'private life' into an arena for struggle, where a 'politically correct' sexuality of mutual respect will contend with an 'incorrect' sexuality of domination and submission.

A number of questions present themselves at once. What is a politically correct sexuality, anyhow? What forms should the struggle for such a sexuality assume? Is it possible for individuals to prefigure more liberated forms of sexuality in their own lives now, in a society still marked by the subordination of women in every domain? Finally, the question with which we began, the moral worry about what to do when conscience and sexual desire come into conflict, will look like this when seen through the lens of feminism: what to do when

one's own sexuality is 'politically incorrect,' when desire is wildly at variance with feminist principles? I turn to this question first.

I. THE STORY OF P.

If any form of sexuality has a *prima facie* claim to be regarded as politically incorrect, it would surely be sadomasochism. I define sadomasochism as any sexual practice that involves the eroticization of relations of domination and submission. Consider the case of P., a feminist, who has masochistic fantasies. If P. were prepared to share her secret life with us, this is what she might say:

> 'For as long as I can remember (from around age six . . .), my sexual fantasies have involved painful exposure, embarassment, humiliation, mutilation, domination by Gestapo-like characters.' (*Ms.*, July/August 1982: 35).

P. regarded her fantasies as unnatural and perverse until she discovered that of all women who have sexual fantasies, 25 per cent have fantasies of rape. (Marcus, 1981: 46).[1] Indeed, much material which is often arousing to women, material not normally regarded as perverse, is thematically similar to P.'s fantasies. Many women of her mother's generation were thrilled when the masterful Rhett Butler overpowered the struggling Scarlett O'Hara and swept her triumphantly upstairs in an act of marital rape; 'treating 'em rough' has enhanced the sex appeal of many a male film star ever since.[2] The feminine taste for fantasies of victimization is assumed on virtually every page of the large pulp literature produced specifically for women. Confession magazines, Harlequin Romances and that genre of historical romance known in the publishing trade as the 'bodice ripper' have sales now numbering in the billions, and they can be bought in most drugstores and supermarkets across the land. The heroes of these tales turn out to be nice guys in the end, but only in the end; before that they dominate and humiliate the heroines in small 'Gestapo-like' ways. In the Harlequin romance *Moth to the Flame* (she the moth, he the flame), the hero, Santino, 'whose mouth, despite its sensual curve looked as if it had never uttered the word "compromise" in its life,' insults the heroine, Juliet, mocks her, kidnaps her, steals her clothes, imprisons her in his seaside mansion in Sicily and threatens repeatedly to rape her (Craven, 1979: 33). Ginny, the heroine of *Sweet Savage Love* is 'almost raped, then almost seduced, then deflowered—half by rape and half by seduction, then alternately raped and

---

[1] Needless to say, the having of a fantasy, every detail of which the woman orchestrates herself is not like a desire for actual rape. The pervasive fear of rape hangs like a blight over the lives of many women, where it may severely restrict spontaneity and freedom of movement. Even if a woman escapes impregnation, venereal disease or grave bodily injury during a rape, the psychological consequences to her may be devastating. The aftermath of rape, only recently documented by feminist scholars, may include nightmares, excessive fearfulness, phobic behavior, loss of sexual desire and the erosion of intimate relationships. None of this is part of the typical 'rape fantasy'.

[2] A recent history of women in Hollywood film sets out at some length the increasingly brutal treatment of women in the movies, movies made by men to be sure but patronized and enjoyed by large numbers of women. See Molly Haskell (1974).

seduced'—all by this Steve, who is by turns her assailant and lover (Faust, 1980: 147).[3] The purity and constancy of women like Juliet and Ginny finally restrain the brutality of their lovers and all ends happily in marriage, but one cannot escape the suspicion that the ruthlessness of these men constitutes a good part of their sex appeal. When at last brutality recedes and the couple is reconciled, the fantasy ends; *the story is over.*[4]

It might be ventured that standard heterosexual desire in women has often a masochistic dimension, though such desires would fall out far lower on a continuum of masochistic desire than P.'s fantasies or the average Harlequin Romance. Essential to masochism is the eroticization of domination. Now women are regularly attracted by power, its possession and exercise. Male power manifests itself variously as physical prowess, muscular strength, intellectual brilliance, worldly position or the kind of money that buys respect. One or another of these kinds of power may become erotically charged for a woman depending on her values, her history or her personal idiosyncrasies. In a sexually inegalitarian society, these manifestations of male power are precisely the instruments by which men are able to accomplish the subordination of women. Hence, insofar as male power is eroticized, male dominance itself becomes erotically charged.

One might object that there is nothing masochistic in the female attraction to power at all, that because the possession of power is a source of status for men, a woman who can attach herself to a powerful man will thereby enhance her own status. But this implies that the woman attracted by the athlete is aware only that his muscular prowess can protect her or gain him the esteem of his fellows, not that he can use it to restrain her if he wants or that the student who idolizes her professor is unaware that he can use his stinging wit as much to put her down as to overawe his classes. I suggest instead that there is contained in the very apprehension of power the recognition that it can overwhelm and subdue as well as protect and impress. Power can raise me from my lowly status and exalt me; it is also that *before which I tremble.*

P. is deeply ashamed of her fantasies. Shame, according to John Deigh, is typically expressed in acts of concealment; it is a reaction to the threat of demeaning treatment one would invite in appearing to be a person of lesser worth (Deigh, 1983). P. would be mortified if her fantasies were somehow to be made public. But she suffers a continuing loss of esteem in her *own* eyes as well. While one of Schlafly's lieutenants might be embarassed by such fantasies, too, P.'s psychic distress is palpable, for she feels obliged to play out in the theatre of her mind acts of brutality which are not only abhorrent to her but which, as a political activist, she is absolutely committed to eradicating. She experiences her own sexuality as doubly humiliating: not only does the

---

[3] 'Sweet Savagery girls cede a great deal of the responsibility to the heroes, saying no until virile and sometimes vicious men force them to say yes. Much of the time the relationship between heroines and heroes is that of master and slave, teacher and pupil, leader and the led. The heroines achieve autonomy only to relinquish it in marriage.' (Faust, 1980: 156).

[4] For a penetrating analysis of the modern, Harlequin-type romance, see Ann Barr Snitow (1979).

content of her fantasies concern humiliation but the very having of such fantasies, given her politics, is humiliating as well. Two courses of action seem open to someone in P.'s predicament: she can either get rid of her shame and keep her desire or else get rid of her desire. I shall discuss each of these alternatives in turn.

II. SADOMASOCHISM AND
SEXUAL FREEDOM

Sadomasochism has been roundly denounced in feminist writing, in particular the sadism increasingly evident in much male-oriented pornography (Lederer, 1980). Feminists have argued that sadomasochism is one inevitable expression of a women-hating culture. It powerfully reinforces male dominance and female subordination because, by linking these phenomena to our deepest sexual desires—desires defined by an ideologically tainted psychology as instinctual—it makes them appear natural. To participate willingly in this mode of sexuality is thus to collude in women's subordination. No wonder, then, that the emergence of *Samois* has shocked and offended many in the feminist community. *Samois* is an organization of and for sadomasochistic women which describes itself both as 'lesbian' and 'feminist.'

In several recent publications, members of *Samois* have tried to justify their sexual tastes against the standard feminist condemnation. Women like P. are urged to set aside shame, to accept their fantasies fully, to welcome the sexual satisfaction such fantasies provide and even, in controlled situations, to act them out. Most manifestations of sexuality are warped anyhow, they argue, so why the particular scorn heaped upon sadomasochism? Why are the acts of sadomasochistic women—'negotiated mutual pleasure'—in which no one is *really* hurt worse than e.g. conventional heterosexuality where the structure of desire in effect ties a woman erotically to her oppressor? (Schrim, 1979: 24). The critics of sadomasochism conflate fantasy and reality: representations of violent acts should not be regarded with the same loathing as the acts themselves. Sadomasochism is ritual or theatre in which the goings-on are entirely under the control of the actors; the participants are no more likely to want to engage in *real* acts of domination or submission than are the less sexually adventurous. Further, sadomasochism is liberatory in that it challenges the sexual norms of the bourgeois family, norms still rooted to a degree in an older, more repressive sexual ethic whereby sexual acts are justified only in the service of reproduction. Sadomasochism is the 'quintessence of non-reproductive sex . . . '; its devotees have a 'passion for making use of the entire body, every nerve fiber and every wayward thought.' (Califia, 1981: 32). Some members of *Samois* claim that there are values inherent in the sadomasochistic encounter itself, for example in the heightened trust the submissive member of a pair practising bondage must have in the dominant member. An unusual attentiveness and sensitivity to the partner are required of one who has permission to inflict pain (' . . . good tops are the most compassionate and sensitive beings on earth') while overt physical

aggression 'can function to keep a relationship clean', i.e. free of festering guilt and psychological manipulation (Equinox, 1981: 36; Farr, 1981: 187).

Finally, sadomasochism is defended on general grounds of sexual freedom. Here, three arguments are brought forward. First, since sex is a basic human need and the right to seek sexual satisfaction is a basic human right it follows that sexual freedom, in and of itself, is an intrinsic good provided of course that the sexual activity in question is consensual. Second, the feminist condemnation of sadomasochism is said to be sexually repressive, perpetuating shame and secrecy in sexual matters and discouraging sexual experimentation and the exploration of unfamiliar terrain. Third, anything less than a total commitment to sexual freedom is said to endanger the future of the women's movement by giving ground to the newly militant Right. In the wake of its crusade against pornography, so say the women of *Samois*, the contemporary women's movement has abandoned its earlier commitment to sexual freedom and taken up positions that are clearly reactionary. Gayle Rubin, feminist anthropologist and leading *Samois* theorist, is highly critical of a recent resolution of the *National Organization for Women* which denies that sadomasochism, cross-generational sex, pornography and public sex—unlike gay and lesbian sexuality—are issues of sexual or affectional preference which merit its support. For Rubin, this puts NOW on record as opposing sexual freedom and the civil rights of sexual nonconformists. But, she argues, sexual freedom is inextricable from political freedom. The rejection of persecuted and stigmatized erotic minorities plays into the hands of the conservative Right, which has been extraordinarily successful of late in tapping 'pools of erotophobia in its accession to state power', power it uses, in turn, to consolidate its hold over many other kinds of erotic activity (Rubin, 1981: 211, 193).

How convincing is *Samois*' defense of sadomasochism? There is, first of all, some question whether the arguments they adduce are mutually consistent. It seems odd to insist that sadomasochistic practises are isolated and compartmentalized rituals which do not resonate with the rest of one's life activity and at the same time to claim that they can enhance the quality of ongoing real relationships, e.g. in the development of trust or the 'clean' acting out of aggression. The claim that sadomasochism creates unique opportunities for the building of trust, while true in some sense, strikes me as peculiar. If someone— the 'bottom'—allows herself to be tied helplessly to the bedpost, she must of course trust the one doing the tying up—the 'top'—not to ignore whatever limits have been agreed upon in advance. If the bottom already knows her top and has reason to believe in her trustworthiness, how can this trust have come about except in the ordinary ways in which we all develop trust in intimate relationships? But if top and bottom are not well acquainted and the activity in question caps a chance meeting in a bar, the awarding of trust in such circumstances is an act of utter foolhardiness. Further, there is little consolation in the observation that sadomasochistic sexuality is no worse than the usual forms of sexuality under patriarchy. If true, this claim does not establish the allowability of sadomasochism at all but only highlights once more the thoroughgoing corruption of much of what we do and the urgent need for a radical

revision of erotic life. Nor can sadomasochistic sexuality be justified solely on the grounds that it is frequently non-procreative or that it violates the norms of the bourgeois family. As there are morally reprehensible practices, e.g. necrophilia, which shock respectable people too and are non-procreative into the bargain it seems clear that the permissibility of sadomasochism must be established on some other foundation.[5]

I agree entirely with Gayle Rubin's demand that feminists defend sexual freedom, most tested in the case of sexual minorities, against a newly militant Right. But a political movement may defend some type of erotic activity against prudery or political conservatism without implying in any way that the activity in question is mandated by or even consistent with its own principles. Prostitution is a case in point. There are reasons, in my view, why feminists ought to support the decriminalization of prostitution. If prostitution were legalized, prostitutes would no longer be subject to police or Mafia shakedowns or to the harassment of fines and imprisonment nor would they need the protection of pimps who often brutalize them. However none of this implies approval of prostitution as an institution or an abandonment of the feminist vision of a society without prostitutes.

The most convincing defense of sadomasochism, no doubt, is the claim that since sexual satisfaction is an intrinsic good, we are free to engage in any sexual activities whatsoever, provided of course that these activities involve neither force nor fraud. But this is essentially a *liberal* response to a *radical* critique of sexuality and, as such, it fails entirely to engage this critique. As noted earlier, one of the major achievements of contemporary feminist theory is the recognition that male supremacy is perpetuated not only openly, through male domination of the major societal institutions but more covertly, through the manipulation of desire. Moreover, desires may be produced and managed in ways which involve neither force nor fraud nor the violation of anyone's legal rights. Elsewhere none other than Gayle Rubin herself has described the 'sex-gender system,' that complex process whereby bi-sexual infants are transformed into male and female gender personalities, the one destined to command, the other to obey:

> 'While particular socio-sexual systems vary, each one is specific and individuals within it will have to conform to a finite set of possibilities. Each new generation must learn and become its sexual destiny, each person must be encoded with its appropriate status within the system.' (Rubin, 1975: 161).

From this perspective, the imposition of masculinity and femininity may be regarded as a process of organizing and shaping desire. The truly 'feminine' woman, then, will have 'appropriate' sexual desires for men but she will wish to shape herself, physically and in other ways, into a woman men will desire. Thus, she will aspire to a life-plan proper for a member of her sex, to a certain

---

[5] For another analysis of *Samois'* position and an attack on lesbian sadomasochism, see Sarah Lucia Hoagland (1982). See also, Bat ami, Bar-On (1982).

ideal configuration of the body and to an appropriate style of self-presentation. The idea that sexual desire is a kind of bondage is very ancient; the notion takes on new meaning in the context of a radical feminist critique of male supremacy.

The 'perverse' behavior defended by Rubin and the other members of *Samois* is clearly not identical to 'ordinary' feminine masochism, to that masochism so characteristic of women that it has been regarded by all psychoanalysts and many feminists as one of the typical marks of femininity in this culture.[6] But it is not so very different either. The 'normal' and the 'perverse' have in common the sexualization of domination and submission, albeit to different degrees. Feminine masochism, like femininity in general, is an economical way of embedding women in patriarchy through the mechanism of desire and while the eroticization of relations of domination may not lie at the heart of the system of male supremacy, it surely perpetuates it. The precise mechanisms at work in the sexualization of domination are unclear and it would be difficult to show in every case a connection between a particular sexual act or sexual fantasy and the oppression of women in general. While it would be absurd to claim that women accept less pay than men because it is sexually exciting to earn 59¢ for every dollar a man earns, it would be equally naive to insist that there is no relationship whatever between erotic domination and sexual subordination. Surely women's acceptance of domination by men cannot be entirely independent of the fact that for many women, *dominance in men is exciting.*

The right, staunchly defended by liberals, to desire what and whom we please and, under certain circumstances, to act on our desire, is not at issue here; the point is that women would be better off if we learned when to refrain from the exercise of this right. A thorough overhaul of desire is clearly on the feminist agenda: the fantasy that we are overwhelmed by Rhett Butler should be traded in for one in which we seize state power and re-educate him.

P. has no choice, then, exept to reject the counsel of *Samois*, i.e. that unashamed, she make space in her psyche for the free and full enjoyment of every desire. *Samois* in effect advises P. to ignore in her own life a general principle to which, as a feminist, she is committed and which she is therefore bound to represent to all other women: the principle that we struggle to decolonize our sexuality by removing from our minds the internalized forms of oppression that make us easier to control.

In their enthusiasm for sexual variation, liberals ignore the extent to which a person may experience her own sexuality as arbitrary, hateful and alien to the rest of her personality. Each of us is in pursuit of an inner integration and unity, a sense that the various aspects of the self form a harmonious whole. But when the parts of the self are at war with one another, a person may be said to suffer from self-estrangement. That part of P. which is compelled to

---

[6] 'I believe that freedom for women must begin in the repudiation of our own masochism . . . I believe that ridding ourselves of our own deeply entrenched masochism, which takes so many tortured forms, is the first priority; it is the first deadly blow that we can strike against systematized male dominance.' (Dworkin, 1981: 111).

produce sexually charged scenarios of humiliation is radically at odds with the P. who devotes much of her life to the struggle against oppression. Now perfect consistency is demanded of no one and our little inconsistencies may even lend us charm. But it is no small thing when the form of desire is disavowed by the personality as a whole. The liberal is right to defend the value of sexual satisfaction, but the struggle to achieve an integrated personality has value too and the liberal position does not speak to those situations in which the price of sexual satisfaction is the perpetuation of self-estrangement.

Phenomenologists have argued that affectivity has a cognitive dimension, that emotions offer a certain access to the world. P.'s shame, then, is the reflection in affectivity of a recognition that there are within her deep and real divisions. Insofar as these divisions cannot be reconciled—the one representing stubborn desire, the other a passionate political commitment—there is a sense in which P. is entitled to her shame. Now this is *not* to say that P. *ought* to feel shame: profound existential contradictions are not uncommon and our response to them may vary. But it seems equally mistaken to claim that P. ought not to feel what she feels. Her desires are not worthy of her, after all, nor is it clear that she is a mere helpless victim of patriarchal conditioning, unable to take any responsibility at all for her wishes and fantasies.

It is often the case that the less unwanted desires are acknowledged as belonging to the self and the more they are isolated and compartmentalized, the more psychic distress is minimized. The more extreme the self-estrangement, in other words, the less intense the psychic discomfort. P.'s shame and distress may well be a sign that she is *not* reconciled to her lack of inner harmony and integration and that she clings to the hope that the divisions within her personality will still somehow be reconciled.

III. THE STRANGEST ALCHEMY:
PAIN INTO PLEASURE

If P. is not well-advised just to keep her desires, getting rid of them seems to be the obvious alternative. Now it seems reasonable to assume that an unwelcome thought, e.g. an obsession, might be banished more easily from the mind if one could learn how it got there in the first place. What, then, are the causes of masochism? Two difficulties present themselves at the outset.

First, writers in the psychoanalytic tradition have used the term 'masochism' to refer to anything from the self-chosen martyrdom of a Simone Weil to the bizarre rituals of the leather fetishist, from the hysteric who uses an illness to manipulate those around her to the cabinet minister who pays a prostitute to whip him. Second, even a cursory review of the psychological literature turns up a bewildering array of theories. For the sake of simplicity, let us restrict our investigation to behavior with some directly sexual cast and to theories of masochism which focus on feminine masochism in particular.

Freud and the early psychoanalysts never doubted that the female nature

was inherently masochistic.[7] They believed masochism in women to be largely instinctual in origin, i.e. the consequence of a certain channeling of libido away from its earlier 'active-sadistic' clitoral 'cathexis' to a 'passive-masochistic' investment in the vagina. What does this mean? A 'narcissistic wound' is suffered by the girl when she discovers the 'inferiority' of her own organ; this causes her to turn away in disappointment from her 'immature' clitoral investment and from active self-stimulation of her own body. She then begins to anticipate fulfillment first from the father, then, much later, from his representative. Since the potential of the vagina for sexual pleasure is awakened only by penetration, the psychosexually mature woman, fit for heterosexual intercourse and hence for the reproduction of the species must wait to be chosen and then 'taken' by the male. The repression of clitoral sexuality is necessary if this is to happen (Freud, 1933).

The eminent Freudian, Helen Deutsch, believed that since menstruation, defloration and childbirth—the principal events in the sexual lives of women—are painful, feminine masochism is functionally necessary for the preservation of the species (Deutsch, 1944). Marie Bonaparte believed that the idea of intercourse causes the girl to fear attack to the inside of her body; only the transformation from the active-sadistic to the passive-masochistic libido can allow a woman to accept the 'continual laceration of sexual intercourse.'[8] Sandor Rado, another Freudian, believed that the extreme mental pain suffered by the girl when she discovers her 'castration' excites her sexually; hereafter she can only attain sexual satisfaction through suffering (Belote, 1976: 337). This seems counter-intuitive: why should the trauma of an imagined castration be sexually exciting? In a later and more convincing attempt to account for the eroticization of suffering Rado tries to show how some pains can become pleasures: the pain the masochist seeks is expiation, the pleasure the license purchased by pain to gratify forbidden desires (Rado, 1956). The idea that sexual guilt is the key to an understanding of masochism is a common thread that connects a variety of theories of masochism and appears to be favored by the very few feminists who have had something to say on the topic. Women are taught to be more inhibited and guilty about their sexual desires than are men; hence the greater proneness of women to masochism. Rape and bondage fantasies, in particular, are said to allow a woman to imagine herself engaged in wicked, but intensely pleasurable activities without any connivance on her part whatsoever; pleasure, so to speak, must be inflicted upon her (Marcus, 1981).

Adolf Grunberger believes that women have a guilty fantasy of stealing the penis: 'Women pretend to offer themselves entirely, in place of the stolen penis proposing that the partner do to her body, to her ego, to herself, what she had in fantasy done to his penis.'[9] Here the principal mechanism at work seems not so much the need to expiate the sin of sexual desire, but the displacement

---

[7] This receives confirmation from a contemporary feminist psychologist: ' . . . masochistic and hysterical behavior is so similar to the concept of "femininity" that the three are not clearly distinguishable.' (Belote, 1976: 347).

[8] Quoted in Janine Chasseguet-Smirgel (1981: 29).

[9] Quoted in Chasseguet-Smirgel, *op. cit.*, p. 131.

of aggression: Hostility aimed at first outward toward another, gets turned round upon the self. Social constraints, fear of punishment or else guilt in the face of one's own anger (especially when the parents are its object) make it unsafe to vent aggressive feelings against anyone but oneself. Theodore Reik, in particular, is associated with the view that masochism in both sexes is frustrated sadism. Since our system of social conventions allows men more freedom to vent their anger no wonder that the masochistic disposition is observed more frequently in the female (Reik, 1962: 217).[10]

The same phenomenon—feminine masochism—is ascribed by Melanie Klein to infantile hatred for the mother and by Helle Thorning, a contemporary feminist psychologist, to desire to merge with the mother. According to Klein, when the little girl finds that the mother cannot satisfy all her desires, she turns away from the 'bad' maternal breast—symbol of libidinal frustration—and seeks a 'good object'—the father—who will furnish her with the 'object-oriented and narcissistic satisfactions she lacks.'[11] Her second object, the father, will be idealized in proportion to the child's disappointment in her first object—the mother. Because of this, the girl will have to repress and, in psychoanalytic jargon, 'countercathect' the aggression which exists in her relation to the father: the anal-sadistic desire for the penis is thus changed into the typical passive-masochistic posture of the 'feminine' woman. A number of themes are brought together in this account: penis envy; incestuous fantasy; the helplessness and dependency of the child and the inhibition of infantile aggression. Thorning starts from the same premise, i.e. the child's total dependency upon the maternal care-giver. But for her, feminine masochism, female passivity and the fear of independent action in general represent an incomplete individuation from the mother, the failure to achieve an independent identity. The fantasy of total powerlessness is really an attempt to achieve oneness once more with the omnipotent caretaker of early childhood (Thorning, 1981: 3–6).[12] This sampling of psychoanalytic theories of masochism should not obscure the fact that there are non-psychoanalytic theories as well. Georges Bataille has produced a neo-Hegelian theory of erotic violation while Sartre and Simone de Beauvoir believe that masochism is a self-deceived futile effort to turn oneself into an object for another in order to escape the 'anguish' of freedom and the frightening evanescence of consciousness (Bataille, 1962; Sartre, 1956: 361–430).

What is P. to make of this chaos of theories? Indeed, what are we to make of it? Which account best explains that perverse alchemy at the heart of masochism—the transformation of pain into pleasure? Is it possible that the variety of things that go by the name of masochism are really multiple effects of multiple causes and that each theory captures something of what went on sometime, somewhere, in the psychosexual development of someone? To whom ought P. to turn for advice? What Sartre tells us in regard to the choice of a moral

---

[10] Even Freud recognizes this (see Chasseguet-Smirgel, *op. cit.*, p. 13).

[11] Quoted in Chasseguet-Smirgel, *op. cit.*, p. 97.

[12] For a more complex development of a similar theory see Jessica Benjamin (1980: 144–174). Thorning and Benjamin make use of Chodorow's theory of the development of male and female gender-personality. See Nancy Chodorow (1978).

authority is true of the choice of a psychotherapeutic 'expert' as well, namely, that the decision to whom to turn for advice is already a decision about what sort of advice we are prepared to take.

Determined to bring her desires into line with her ideology, let us suppose that P. embarks upon a course of traditional psychotherapy, and let us further suppose that her psychotherapy is unsuccessful. As part of her political education, P. is now exposed to a radical critique of psychotherapy: psychotherapy is sexist; it is authoritarian and hierarchical; it is mired in the values of bourgeois society. P. now resolves to consult a 'politically correct' therapist, indeed, a feminist therapist. In order to bring our discussion forward, let us suppose that this second attempt is unsuccessful too, for in spite of its popularity there is evidence that therapy fails as often as it succeeds, whatever the theoretical orientation of the therapist (Eysenck, 1952).[13]

P. is finding it no simple thing to change her desires. Ought she to try again? In a society with little cohesiveness and less confidence in its own survival, an obsessional preoccupation with self has come to replace more social needs and interests. For many people, there is no higher obligation than to the self—to get it 'centered', to realize its 'potentialities,' to clear out its 'hangups'—and little to life apart from a self-absorbed trek through the fads, cults and therapies of our time. But how compatible is such a surrender to the 'new narcissism' (the old 'bourgeois individualism') with a serious commitment to radical reform? Few but the relatively privileged can afford psychotherapy anyhow and the search for what may well be an unrealizable ideal of mental health can absorb much of a person's time, energy and money. It is not at all clear that the politically correct course of action for P. is to continue in this way whatever the cost; perhaps she is better advised to direct her resources back toward the Movement. She is, after all, not psychologically disabled; within the oppressive realities of the contemporary world, her life is richer and more effective than the lives of many other people and she is reconciled to her life—in every respect but one.

IV. PARADISE LOST AND NOT REGAINED: THE FAILURE OF A POLITICS OF PERSONAL TRANSFORMATION

The view is widespread among radical feminists, especially among certain lesbian separatists, that female sexuality is malleable and diffuse and that a woman can, if she chooses, alter the structure of her desire. Here then is a new source of moral instruction for P., a source at the opposite pole from *Samois:* without the help of any paid professional—for no such help is really needed, P. is now to pull herself up by her own psychological bootstraps.

The idea that we can alter our entire range of sexual feelings I shall call 'sexual voluntarism'. Sexual voluntarism has two sources: the first, the fact that

---

[13] For further discussion of this topic, see A. J. Fix and E. Haffke (1976).

for many women, thoroughgoing and unforeseen personal changes, including the rejection of heterosexuality for lesbian sexuality have often accompanied the development of a feminist politics; the second a theory of sexuality that relies heavily on Skinnerian-style behaviorism. While it is a fact that many women (and even some men) have been able to effect profound personal transformations under the influence of feminist ideas, a theory of sexuality I believe to be both false and politically divisive has taken this fact as evidence for the practicability of a willed transformation of self.

For the sexual voluntarist, individuals are thought to be blank tablets on which the culture inscribes certain patterns of behavior. Sexual norms are embedded in a variety of cultural forms, among them 'common sense,' religion, the family, books, magazines, television, films and popular music. Individuals are 'positively reinforced,' i.e. rewarded, when they model their behavior on the images and activities held out to them as normal and desirable, 'negatively reinforced', i.e. punished, when their modelling behavior is done incorrectly or not done at all.

> 'If we come to view male-dominated heterosexuality as the only healthy form of sex, it is because we are bombarded with that model for our sexual fantasies long before we experience sex itself. Sexual images of conquest and submission pervade our imagination from an early age and determine how we will later look upon and experience sex.' (Phelps, 1979: 22).

The masters of patriarchal society make sure that the models set before us incorporate their needs and preferences: all other possibilities become unspeakable or obscene. Thus, the pervasiveness of propaganda for heterosexuality, for female passivity and male sexual aggressivity are responsible not only for ordinary heterosexuality but for sadomasochism as well. Sadomasochists reveal to the world, albeit in an exaggerated form, the inner nature of heterosexuality and they are stigmatized by the larger society precisely because they tear the veil from what patriarchal respectability would like to hide (Hoagland, 1982). Sadomasochism is

> 'a conditioned response to the sexual imagery that barrages women in this society . . . it is not surprising that women respond physically and emotionally to sadomasochistic images. Whether a woman identifies with the dominant or submissive figure in the fantasy, she is still responding to a model of sexual interaction that has been drummed into us throughout our lives.' (Nichols et al., 1982: 139).[14]

The language of these passages is graphic and leaves little doubt as to the theory of sexuality, which is being put forward. Models of sexual relationship 'bombard'

---

[14] Many feminists in the anti-pornography movement believe that men in particular will want to imitate the images of sexual behavior with which they are now being bombarded; this accounts

us; they are 'drummed' into our heads: the ideological apparatus of patriarchal society is said to condition the very structure of desire itself.

What is valuable in this view is the idea that sexuality is *socially constructed*. But are the voluntarists right about the *mode* of its construction? And those patterns of desire which may have been present in a person's psyche from the virtual dawn of consciousness: are voluntarists perhaps too sanguine about the prospects of radically altering these patterns in adult life? (See Section V, below). Writing in *Signs*, Ethel Spector Person denies the ability of theories like this to account for sexual deviance, why it is, for example, that fully 10 per cent of the American population is said to be exclusively homosexual, in spite of incessant bombardment by propaganda for heterosexuality (Person, 1980). Quite early in life, many people discover unusual sexual predilections which have been 'modelled' for them by no one. 'I thought I was the only one,' such people say, when they 'come out,' enter psychoanalysis or write their memoirs. Furthermore, deviance rarely goes unpunished: punishments may range from a purely private embarassment before the spectacle of one's own fantasy life to electric shock, the stake or the concentration camp. Indeed, the history of sexual deviance, insofar as this history is known at all, is the history of the failure of massive negative reinforcement to establish an absolute hegemony of the 'normal'.

One can deviate from a feminist standard of sexual behavior as well as from the obligatory heterosexuality of the larger society. Given their theoretical commitments, feminist sexual voluntarists are unable to regard departure from feminist sexual norms as due to anything but a low level of political understanding on the one hand, or to weakness of will on the other or, of course, to a little of both.[15] They reason that if our sexuality is in fact a product of social conditioning, then we can become to ourselves our own social conditioners and programmers, substituting a feminist input for a patriarchal one. Failure to do this is made out to fear, or insufficient determination, or not trying hard enough, i.e. to some form of *akrasia* or else to an inability to comprehend the extent to which certain patterns of sexual behavior, for example, sadomasochism or heterosexuality support the patriarchal order. The feminist analysis of sexuality has, quite correctly, been a major theoretical achievement of the Second Wave; crucial to this analysis is an understanding of the extent to which our sexuality has been colonized. Hence the refusal or inability of a woman to bring her sexuality into conformity is a serious matter indeed and may tend, in the eyes

---

for the urgency of their attack on male-orientated violent pornography. See Laura Lederer (1980), esp. Ann Jones (1980: 179, 183); Diana E. H. Russell (1980: 236).

[15] The literature of lesbian separatism, in particular, is replete with examples of sexual voluntarism: ' "Do what feels good. Sex is groovy. Gay is just as good as straight. I don't care what you do in bed, so you shouldn't care what I do in bed." This argument assumes that Lesbians have the same lifestyle and sexuality as straight women. But we don't—straight women choose to love and fuck men. Lesbians have commitments to women. Lesbians are not born. We have made a conscious choice to be Lesbians. We have rejected all that is traditional and accepted, and committed ourselves to a lifestyle that everybody . . . criticizes.' Barbara Solomon (1975: 40). For further examples, see pp. 18, 36, 70.

of many, to diminish her other contributions to the women's movement, whatever they may be. This kind of thinking has led to painful divisions within the radical women's movement. The accused, guilt-ridden heterosexuals or closeted masochists stand charged with lack of resolve, inconsistency or even collusion with the enemy, while their accusers adopt postures of condescension or self-righteousness.

'Any woman can'—such is the motto of voluntarism. Armed with an adequate feminist critique of sexuality and sufficient will-power, any women should be able to alter the pattern of her desires. While the feminist theory needed for this venture is known to be the product of collective effort and while groups of women—even, in the case of lesbian separatism, organized communities of women—may be waiting to welcome the reformed pervert, the process of transformation is seen, nonetheless, as something a woman must accomplish *alone*. How can it be otherwise, given the fact that no tendency within the contemporary women's liberation movement has developed a genuinely collective *praxis* which would make it possible for women like P. to bring their desires into line with their principles? (I shall return to this point later.) A pervasive and characteristic feature of bourgeois ideology has here been introduced into feminist theory, namely, the idea that the victims, the colonized, are responsible for their own colonization and that they can change the circumstances of their lives by altering their consciousness. Of course no larger social transformation can occur unless individuals change as well, but the tendency I am criticizing places the burden for effecting change squarely upon the individual, an idea quite at variance with radical feminist thinking generally.

One final point, before I turn to another mode of theorizing about sexuality—one not as subject to moralism and divisiveness. Those who claim that any woman can reprogram her consciousness if only she is sufficiently determined hold a shallow view of the nature of patriarchal oppression. Anything done can be undone, it is implied; nothing has been permanently damaged, nothing irretrievably lost. But this is tragically false. One of the evils of a system of oppression is that it may damage people in ways that *cannot* always be undone. Patriarchy invades the intimate recesses of personality where it may maim and cripple the spirit forever. No political movement, even a movement with a highly developed analysis of sexual oppression, can promise an end to sexual alienation or a cure for sexual dysfunction. Many human beings, P. among them, may have to live with a degree of psychic damage that can never be fully healed.

V. SEX-PRINTS, MICRODOTS AND THE STUBBORN PERSISTENCE OF THE PERVERSE

The difficulties individuals experience in trying to propel themselves, through 'will-power' or various therapies into more acceptable modes of sexual desire may be due to a connection between sexuality and personal identity too complex and obscure to be contained within the simple schemas of deter-

minism. Ethel Spector Person has suggested that the relationship between sexuality and identity is mediated not only by gender, but by what she calls the 'sex print'. The sex print is 'an individualized script that elicits erotic desire,' an 'individual's erotic signature,' (Person, 1980: 620). Because it is experienced not as chosen but as revealed, an individual script is normally felt to be deeply rooted, 'deriving from one's nature,' unchanging and unique, somewhat like a fingerprint. Person does not claim that one's sex print is absolutely irreversible, only relatively so, in part because the learning of a sex-print is so connected to the process of identity formation. 'To the degree that an individual utilizes sexuality (for pleasure, for adaptation, as the resolution of unconscious conflict) . . . one's sexual "nature" will be experienced as more or less central to personality.' (p. 620). In other words, what I take to be my 'self' is constituted in large measure by certain patterns of response—to the events that befall me, to other people, even to inanimate nature. Thus, if someone asks me what I am like and I describe myself as aggressive, or ambitious or fun-loving, I am naming certain modes of adaptation that capture *who I am*. Since sexuality is a major mode of response—a way of inhabiting the body as well as entering into relationships with others—patterns of sexual response may well be central to the structure of a person's identity.

Person suspects some factors that may be involved in psychosexual development. Following Chodorow, she grants that the larger observed differences between male and female sex-prints may be due to the differing outcomes of virtually universal female mothering for boy and girl children. Repression and fixation play a role too as does the general structure of the family in modern patriarchal society and one's own family romance in particular. 'Direct cultural proscriptions' (including that ideological conditioning discussed in Section IV) have some influence, too, though 'such strictures are not usually decisive in psychological life.' (p. 625). The fact that sexual excitement is so often tied to ideas of domination and submission may be due to the fact that sensual feeling develops in the helpless child, dependent not only for gratification but for its very survival on powerful adults (p. 627).

The psychoanalyst Robert Stoller characterizes the individualized sexual script not as a 'sex print' but as a 'microdot', a highly compressed and encoded system of information out of which can be read—by one who knows how to read it—the history of a person's psychic life. Stoller regards as central a person's sexual scenario the history of her infantile sexual traumas and her concomitant feelings of rage and hatred. Of the various modes of adaptation and response that get inscribed in the sex-print or microdot

'. . . it is hostility—the desire, overt or hidden, to harm another person—that generates and enhances sexual exitement . . . The exact details of the script underlying the excitement are meant to reproduce and repair the precise traumas and frustrations—debasements—of childhood . . . ' (Stoller, 1979: 6, 13).

Theories of the microdot and sex-print provide an alternative to the Skinnerian-style behaviorism of some radical feminists. While they remain within the

psychoanalytic mode, these formulations nonetheless avoid the arbitrariness and excessive speculation so characteristic of earlier psychoanalytic theories. More general than the earlier theories, they are, in a sense, less informative but their weakness in this regard may turn out to be an advantage. One suspects that many classical psychoanalytic theories (including some I examined earlier) are based on little more than an extrapolation from the analysis of a very few patients. Theories of this sort may well be subsumable under the more general formulations put forward by Person and Stoller, for the tales of psychosexual development told by these older theories may represent nothing more than the analyst's reading of the microdots of a limited range of patients.

There exists a substantial theoretical literature on the subject of human psychosexual development. Taken as a whole, this literature is confusing and often contradictory. While highly provocative and at times extraordinarily illuminating, much of it is methodologically suspect, lacks an adequate empirical foundation and is often grounded in systems of ideas, e.g. Freudian psychology, which continue to generate enormous controversy. While some factors involved in the genesis of a sexual script have surely been identified, albeit in a very general way, Ethel Spector Person can still judge, correctly, I think, that 'the mechanism of sex-printing is obscure' and that the connection between the learning of a sexual scenario and the process of identity formation remains mysterious (p. 621).

Whatever the precise mechanisms involved in the formation of a sex print, it seems clear to me that each of us has one and that feminist theorists have focussed far too much on the larger and more general features of a scenario such as a person's sexual orientation and too little on its 'details'. Does a person favor promiscuity or monogamy, for example, sex with 'irrelevant' fantasies or sex without them, sex with partners of her own or of another race? People with the 'wrong' kind of sexual orientation suffer a special victimization in our society; nevertheless, less dramatic features of the sex-print may be quite as saturated with meaning and just as revelatory of the basic outlines of a personality: the fact, for example, that Portnoy desires only Gentile women is not less important in understanding *who he is* than the fact that he desires women.

Stoller has written that the history of a person's psychic life lies hidden in their sexual script. This history and the meanings which compose it can sometimes be read out of someone's scenario but often as not, it is shrouded in mystery—as P., to her sorrow, has already learned. Portnoy's attraction to Gentile women, is it a manifestation of Jewish self-hatred? Or a feeble attempt to deceive the superego about the real object of desire, his mother—a Jewish woman? Or, by picking women with whom he has little in common, is Portnoy acting on a masochistic need to be forever unhappy in love? The pattern of Portnoy's desire may reflect a mode of adaptation to the conflict and pain of early life, to a buried suffering Portnoy can neither recover nor surmount.

Sexual desire may seize and hold the mind with the force of an obsession, even while we remain ignorant of its origin and meaning. Arbitrary and imperious, desire repels not only rational attempts to explain it but all too often the efforts of rational individuals to resist it. At the level of theory the lack of

an adequate account of the mechanisms involved in sex-printing (and hence of sado-masochism) is a failure of *science*; at the level of personal experience, the opacity of human sexual desire represents a failure of *self-knowledge*.

VI. INSTEAD OF A CONCLUSION

P. will search the foregoing discussion in vain for practical moral advice. The way out of her predicament seemed to be the abandonment either of her shame or of her desire. But I have suggested that there is a sense in which she is 'entitled' to her shame, insofar as shame is a wholly understandable response to behavior which is seriously at variance with principles. In addition, I have argued that not every kind of sexual behavior, even behavior that involves consenting adults or is played out in the private theatre of the imagination is compatible with feminist principles, a feminist analysis of sexuality or a feminist vision of social transformation. To this extent, I declare the incompatibility of a classical liberal position on sexual freedom with my own understanding of feminism.

P.'s other alternative, getting rid of her desire, is a good and sensible project if she can manage it, but it turns out to be so difficult in the doing that to preach to her a feminist code of sexual correctness in the confident anticipation that she will succeed would be a futility—and a cruelty. Since many women (perhaps even most women) are in P.'s shoes, such a code would divide women within the movement and alienate those outside of it. 'Twix't the conception and creation,' writes the poet, 'falls the shadow.' Between the conception of a sexuality in harmony with feminism and the creation of a feminist standard of political correctness in sexual matters, fall not one but two shadows: the first, the lack of an adequate theory of sexuality, the second the lack of an effective *praxis* around issues of personal transformation. The second need not wait upon the emergence of the first, for to take seriously the principle of the inseparability of theory and practice is to see that a better theoretical understanding of the nature of sexual desire might well begin to emerge in the course of a serious and sustained attempt to alter it.

I am not suggesting that human sexuality is entirely enigmatic. Quite the contrary. There have been revolutionary advances in our knowledge of human sexual psychology over the last ninety years and the work of feminist theorists like Nancy Chodorow (1978), Ethel Person (1980) and Dorothy Dinnerstein (1976) promises to extend our understanding still further. Nor do I want to substitute a sexual determinism for sexual voluntarism. Some people try to reorganize their erotic lives and they succeed. Others, caught up in the excitement of a movement that calls for the radical transformation of every human institution, find that they have changed without even trying. But more often than not, sexuality is mysterious and opaque, seemingly unalterable because its meaning is inpenetrable. The significance of a particular form of desire as well as its persistence may lie in a developmental history only half-remembered or even repressed altogether. However embarassing from a feminist perspec-

tive, a tabooed desire may well play a crucial and necessary role in a person's psychic economy.

The order of the psyche, here and now, in a world of pain and oppression, is not identical to the ideal order of a feminist political vision. We can teach a woman how to plan a demonstration, how to run a mimeograph machine, or how to lobby. We can share what we have learned about starting up a Women's Studies Program or a battered women's shelter. But we cannot teach P. or the women of *Samois* or even ourselves how to de-colonize the imagination: this is what I meant earlier by the claim that the women's movement has an insufficiently developed praxis around issues of sexuality. The difficulties which stand in the way of the emergence of such a *praxis* are legion; another paper would be required to identify them and also to examine the circumstances in which many women and some men *have* been able to effect dramatic changes in their lives. But in my view, the prevalence in some feminist circles of the kind of thinking I call 'sexual voluntarism', with its simplistic formulas, moralism, intolerance and refusal to acknowledge the obsessional dimension of sexual desire is itself an obstacle to the emergence of an adequate praxis.

Those who find themselves in the unfortunate situation of P. are living out, in the form of existential unease, contradictions which are present in the larger society. I refer to the contradiction between our formal commitment to justice and equality on the one hand—a commitment that the women's movement is determined to force the larger society to honor—and the profoundly authoritarian character of our various systems of social relationships on the other. Those who have followed my 'Story of P.' will have to decide whether P. is in fact caught in an historical moment which we have not as yet surpassed or whether I have merely written a new apology for a very old hypocrisy.[16]

REFERENCES

Bataille, Georges. 1962. *Death and Sensuality*. Walker & Co., New York.
Bat Ami, Bar-On. 1982. Feminism and sadomasochism: Self-critical notes. In Linden, *et al.*, eds, *Against Sadomasochism: A Radical Feminist Analysis*. Frog-in-the-Well Press, E. Palo Alto, Calif.
Belote, Betsy. 1976. Masochistic syndrome, hysterical personality and the illusion of a healthy woman. In Cox, Sue, ed., *Female Psychology: The Emerging Self*. Science Research Associates, Chicago.

[16] An earlier version of this paper was first presented to the Society for Women in Philosophy, Midwest Division, at Indiana University, Bloomington, Indiana, October, 1982. A subsequent version was presented to the Society for the Philosophy of Love and Sex, meeting with the American Philosophical Association, Pacific Division, Oakland California, March, 1983. Many people in discussion at those meetings contributed incisive comments and criticisms. I would like to thank the following persons in particular for comments on earlier drafts of this paper: Alison Jaggar; Richard Wasserstrom; Rob Crawford; Joyce Trebilcot; Irving Thalberg; Isaac Balbus; Carole Isaacs; Martha Pintzuk; Julia LeSage; Alan Soble.

Benjamin, Jessica. 1980. The bonds of love: Rational violence and erotic domination. *Feminist Studies* 6(1): 144–174.
Butler, Judy. 1982. Lesbian S & M: The politics of disillusion. In Linden *et al.*, eds, *Against Sadomasochism: A Radical Feminist Analysis*. Frog-in-the-Well Press, E. Palo Alto, Calif.
Califia, Pat. 1981. Feminism and sadomasochism. *Heresies* **12**: 30–34
Chasseguet-Smirgel, Janine. 1981. *Female Sexuality, New Psychoanalytic Views*. Virago Press. London.
Chodorow, Nancy. 1978. *The Reproduction of Mothering: Psychoanalysis and the Sociology of Gender*. University of California Press, Berkeley, Calif.
Craven, Sara. 1979. *Moth to the Flame*. Harlequin Books, Toronto.
Deigh, John. 1983. Shame and self-esteem: A critique. *Ethics* **93** (Jan): 225–245.
Deutsch, Helene. 1930. Significance of masochism in the mental life of women. *Int J. Psychoanal.* **11**: 48–60.
Deutsch, Helene. 1944. *Psychology of Women*, Vol. 1. Grune and Stratton, New York.
Dinnerstein, Dorothy. 1976. *The Mermaid and the Minotaur*. Harper and Row, New York.
Dworkin, Andrea. 1976. *Our Blood: Prophecies and Discourses on Sexual Politics*. Perigee Books, New York.
English, Deirdre, Amber Hollibaugh and Gayle Rubin. 1981. Talking Sex. *Socialist Rev.* **58** (July–August): 43–62.
Equinox, Martha. 1981. If I ask you to tie me up, will you still want to love me? In Samois, ed., *Coming to Power*. Samois, Berkeley, Calif.
Farr, Susan. 1981. The art of discipline: Creating erotic dramas of play and power. In Samois, ed., *Coming to Power*. Samois, Berkeley, Calif.
Faust, Beatrice. 1980. *Women, Sex and Pornography*. MacMillan, New York.
Fix, A. J. and E. A. Haffke. 1976. *Basic Psychological Therapies: Comparative Effectiveness*. Human Sciences Press, New York.
Freud, Sigmund. 1925. Some psychological consequences of the anatomical distinction between the sexes. *Int. J. Psychoanal.* **8** (1927): 133–142.
Freud, Sigmund. 1931. Female Sexuality. *Int J. Psycholanal.* **13** (1932): 281–297.
Freud, Sigmund. 1933. The psychology of women, Chapter XXIII, *New Introductory Lectures on Psycho-Analysis*. Hogarth Press, London.
Haskell, Molly. 1974. *From Reverence to Rape*. Penguin Books, New York.
Hoagland, Sarah Lucia. 1982. Sadism, masochism and lesbian-feminism. In Linden *et al.*, eds., *Against Sadomasochism: A Radical Feminist Analysis*. Frog-in-the-Well Press, E. Palo Alto, Calif.
Jaggar, Alison. 1983. *Feminist Politics and Human Nature*. Rowman and Allanheld, Totowa, N.J.
Jones, Ann. 1980. A little knowledge. In Lederer, Laura, ed., *Take Back the Night, Women on Pornography*. William Morrow, New York.
Lederer, Laura. ed. 1980. *Take Back the Night, Women on Pornography*. William Morrow, New York.
LeSage, Julia. 1981. Women and pornography. *Jump Cut* **36**: 46–47, 60.
Linden, Robin Ruth, Darlene R. Pagano, Diana E. H. Russell and Susan Leigh Star, eds. 1982. *Against Sadomasochism: A Radical Feminist Analysis*. Frog-in-the-Well Press, E. Palo Alto, Calif.
Marcus, Maria. 1981. *A Taste for Pain, On Masochism and Female Sexuality*. St Martin's Press, New York.
Myron, Nancy and Charlotte Bunch. 1975. *Lesbianism and the Women's Movement*. Diana Press, Baltimore, MD.
Nichols, Jeanette, Darlene Pagano and Margaret Rossoff. 1982. Is sadomasochism feminist? A critique of the Samois position. In Linden *et al.*, eds, *Against Sadomasochism: A Radical Feminist Analysis*. Frog-in-the-Well Press, E. Palo Alto, Calif.

Person, Ethel Spector. 1980. Sexuality as the mainstay of identity: psychoanalytic per-
    spectives. *Signs* **5** (4) (Summer): 605–630.
Phelps, Linda. 1979. Female sexual alienation. In Freeman, J. ed., *Women: A Feminist
    Perspective*, 2nd Edn. Mayfield, Palo Alto, CA.
Rado, Sandor. 1956. *Psychoanalysis of Behavior*. Grune and Stratton, New York.
Reik, Theodore. 1962. *Masochism in Sex and Society*. Grove Press, New York
Rubin, Gayle. 1975. The traffic in women. In Reiter, Rayna, ed., *Toward an Anthro-
    pology of Women*. Monthly Review Press, New York.
Rubin, Gayle. 1981. The leather menace: Comments on politics and S/M. In *Coming
    to Power*. Samois, Berkeley, Calif.
Russell, Diana E. H. 1980. Pornography and violence, what does the new research say?
    In Lederer, ed., *Take Back the Night, Women on Pornography*. William Morrow,
    New York.
Samois, ed. 1979. *What Color is Your Handkerchief? A Lesbian S/M Sexuality Reader*.
    Samois, Berkeley, Calif.
Samois, ed. 1981. *Coming to Power, Writings and Graphics on Lesbian S/M*. Samois,
    Berkeley, Calif.
Sartre, Jean-Paul. 1956. Concrete relations with others, Part Three, Chap. 3, *Being
    and Nothingness*. Philosophical Library, New York.
Schrim, Janet. 1979. A proud and emotional statement. *What Color is Your Handker-
    chief?* Samois, Berkeley, Calif.
Snitow, Ann Barr. 1979. Mass market romance: Pornography for women is different.
    Radical History Rev. **20** (Spring–Summer): 141–161.
Solomon, Barbara. 1975. Taking the bullshit by the horns. In Myron, Nancy and Char-
    lotte Bunch, eds, *Lesbianism and the Women's Movement*, pp. 39–47. Diana
    Press, Baltimore, MD.
Thorning, Helle. 1981. The mother-daughter relationship and sexual ambivalence. *Her-
    esies* **12**: 3–6.

THE AFFIRMATIVE ACTION DEBATE AND CONFLICTING CONCEPTIONS OF INDIVIDUALITY

Mary E. Hawkesworth

The debate over the legitimacy of Affirmative Action[1] and the related issues of preferential treatment[2] and reverse discrimination[3] has steadily intensified during the seventeen years since the program's inception. Arguments supporting and denouncing the government policy have been aired in scholarly journals, in court cases and in the chambers of the U.S. Congress. Proponents have attempted to justify this governmental program as a mechanism of compensatory justice affording individuals benefits to counterbalance burdens and injuries previously imposed, as an instrument of distributive justice intended to

This article was completed under the auspices of a grant from the Academic Excellence Commission of the University of Louisville.

[1] Title VII of the Civil Rights Act of 1964 and Executive Orders 11246 and 11375 constitute the foundation of the government's Affirmative Action program. In essence, the program requires that job opportunities be publicly advertised, that the criteria for hiring employees be related to job performance, that sex, race and ethnicity may not be used as criteria for employment unless it can be demonstrated that they are legitimate occupational requirements and that employers make a good faith effort to recruit qualified women and minority candidates. Although Title VII specifically prohibits the use of quotas and the lowering of standards in order to give preferential treatment to minority and women applicants, implementation efforts by the Office of Federal Contract Compliance (OFCC) within the Department of Labor have included the establishment of 'numerical objectives' for minority employment within a specified time frame.

[2] Preferential treatment refers to the policy of counting minority status or female sex as *additional* qualifications when considering applicants for employment, promotion or admission to higher education. Thus given two competent candidates for a job, one white male and one black male, the policy of preferential treatment would suggest that the black male has an additional qualification and therefore ought to be hired.

[3] Reverse discrimination is a label frequently given to the policy of preferential treatment. Although popularized in the course of the Bakke case, the phrase incorporates several contentious assumptions. For instance, the term 'reverse discrimination' implies that white males have rights to certain educational and employment opportunities which are being violated when women or minorities are admitted or hired. In a meritocratic, capitalist society, no particular individual ever

eliminate inequities in the distribution of income, power, education and other social benefits, and as a means to maximize social utility by reducing poverty and its attendant evils, producing a more efficient utilization of human resources and talents and providing needed services for the economically disadvantaged. Opponents have castigated the program for being overinclusive, i.e. providing compensation to individuals who have suffered no personal injury, underinclusive, i.e. failing to compensate victims of discrimination who are not members of targeted minority groups, and for sacrificing individual rights to an ill-conceived notion of social justice. These various moral arguments have in turn been related to constitutional issues in an effort to establish either the constitutional permissibility of Affirmative Action in terms of the state's compelling interest in social justice or the impermissibility of the program as a violation of the individual's right to the equal protection of the law.

In this paper I shall attempt to demonstrate that the intensity of this debate among scholars and jurists committed to constitutionalism, justice and the protection of individual rights is related to divergent assumptions about the fundamental nature of individuality. I shall argue that two different conceptions of individuality replete with presuppositions about the nature of individual identity and individual freedom, the relationship of the individual to other people, to social groups and to impersonal forces, underlie the arguments of proponents and opponents of Affirmative Action. I shall attempt to show that the proponents of Affirmative Action tacitly adopt a conception of 'socialized individualism' which emphasizes the impact of cultural norms and group practices upon the development of individual identity and the pervasive influence of internal as well as external obstacles to individual freedom; while opponents of Affirmative Action adopt a model of 'atomistic individualism' which assumes that identity is a matter of individual choice and will—unconstrained by racial, sexual or cultural experiences—and which posits a conception of freedom as simply the absence of external coercion. I shall further argue that the tacit acceptance of these divergent conceptions of individuality influences the very capacity to perceive the existence of discrimination in the contemporary United States and hence, affects the assessment of the need for a remedy and of the propriety of Affirmative Action as such a remedy. Finally having demonstrated the importance of these conceptions of individuality as a foundation for the moral and constitutional arguments concerning Affirmative Action and indeed, for the very perception of the existence of a problem of discrimination, I shall examine the theoretical adequacy of these two models of individuality in an effort to assess the merits of several arguments central to the Affirmative Action debate.

---

has a right to any job or university slot. Furthermore, using the term 'discrimination' to describe the case of white men who are no longer permitted to take advantage of opportunities created by racism and sexism, suggests that the current experience of white men is indistinguishable from the oppression experienced by women and minorities, a suggestion which could not be substantiated by any detailed analysis of these experiences. Despite the questionable implications of the phrase, 'reverse discrimination' is used in this article in order to accurately convey the views of those who use the label.

CONFLICTING CONCEPTIONS
OF INDIVIDUALITY

'Individualism' as a social doctrine asserts the moral primacy of the individual in society and recognizes the right of the individual to freedom and self-realization. Yet, what it means to be an individual, the processes by which individual identity is constituted, the nature of the individual's relation to other people and to social institutions, the scope and depth of self-realization, may be topics of debate among those equally committed to the protection of individualism.[4] Those who incorporate a conception of atomistic individualism within their work and those who adopt a conception of socialized individualism are equally committed to the protection and enhancement of individual freedom. They differ, however, in their understandings of the constitution of individual identity and the elements of individual liberty.

The atomistic conception posits the individual as radically independent, in the sense that the individual exists as a self-contained entity, impervious to history, culture or society, motivated solely by appetites or aversions which are subjectively determined and unalterable.[5] Individuals differ from one another both in the objects they desire and in the amount of effort which they expend to satisfy their desires. Although a scarce supply of most goods dictates that competition will characterize the relations among individuals and that the outcome of such competition will be zero-sum, all individuals are endowed with fairly equal capacities and as such, all have an equal opportunity to emerge victorious from the throes of competition. Given the assumption of fairly equal natural assets, differences in outcomes can be attributed solely to variations in individual effort. But because intensity of effort is a matter of individual choice and because an individual who chooses to work hard can hardly be faulted for achieving a great deal, the unequal outcome of the competitive process is morally justifiable. Success is a function of individual initiative and effort and is, consequently, deserved.[6]

The atomistic conception of the individual envisions self-realization as the satisfaction of subjectively determined desires. To achieve this goal individuals

[4] Ellen Wood argues in *Mind and Politics* (1972) that commitment to individualism as a social doctrine is compatible with two divergent interpretations of individuality which she dubs 'dialectical individualism' and 'metaphysical individualism'. While there are some similarities between my conceptions of socialized individualism and atomized individualism and Wood's two conceptions, I refrain from adopting her terminology for I doubt that the assumptions underlying the debate discussed in this paper reflect the depth of commitment to distinct worldviews which her analysis suggests. Operating solely within the confines of contemporary American culture, I wish to suggest simply that there exist at least two different ways of understanding what it means to be an individual and that these different understandings have social policy implications. For a comprehensive analysis of individualism, see Steven Lukes, *Individualism* (1973).

[5] A great deal has been written about the atomistic conception of the individual and its relation to liberal theory, for example, see C. B. Macpherson (1962). Roberto Unger (1975), Zillah Eisenstein (1981), Mark Weaver (1980) and Lukes, *op. cit.*

[6] For an analysis of the social and psychological consequences of the acceptance of these assumptions see, Michael Lewis (1978), and Richard Sennett and Jonathan Cobb (1972).

must devote their energies toward the achievement of success through competition. Precisely because scarcity and competition are accepted as given, obstacles to self-realization are defined solely in terms of external constraints intentionally imposed by other human beings. Thus the individual is free in the absence of the willful coercion of other persons. According to the perspective of atomistic individualism, human freedom is not incompatible with subjection to objective forces external to the individual as long as these objective forces are 'impersonal', such as the products of the market's 'Invisible Hand'. Although the market is acknowledged to be a stern task master, its functioning is deemed essential to the distribution of economic rewards on the basis of individual effort. Individuals are free to reap the rewards of their hard work, if and only if, the market distribution is safeguarded. Moreover, the only alternative to the market according to this view, is the arbitrary command of some self-serving decision-maker which would undermine the very possibility of freedom.

> 'Man in a complex society can have no choice between adjusting himself to what seems to be the blind forces of the social process and obeying the orders of a superior. So long as he knows only the hard discipline of the market, he may well think the direction by some other human brain preferable; but when he tries it, he soon discovers that the former still leaves him at least some choice, while the latter leaves him none and that it is better to have a choice between several unpleasant alternatives than being coerced into one.' (Hayek, 1948: 24).

When the options available to individuals are construed this narrowly, either subordination to the command of a fallible decision-maker or open competition with the prospect of unlimited success, it is clear that only the latter sustains a conception of meaningful freedom. Thus it is not surprising that the market is depicted as a precondition of freedom, 'so essential that it must not be sacrificed to the gratification of our sense of justice or of envy.' (Hayek, 1948: 24). Within the parameters of the atomistic conception then, the individual is 'self-made': identity is a function of individual desire, will and effort; freedom is simply the power to do or forbear according to one's subjectively determined appetites or aversions unconstrained by other human beings; and self-realization is nothing more than success in the competition for necessarily scarce goods. The individual alone is responsible for choices made, for effort invested and for the outcomes achieved, be they successes or failures. Impersonal forces mediate the competition among individuals but because they cannot be controlled by humans and because they affect all individuals in the same neutral way, they cannot be considered to be constraints upon individual freedom. Impersonal forces may establish the rules of the game but it is individual effort which determines the outcome.

The conception of socialized individuality is premised upon an image of society and culture as a 'complex web of values, norms, roles, relationships and customs which do not merely confront the individual as external barriers or

constraints but which are internalized by individuals' (Weaver, 1980: 197),[7] shaping their self-understanding, their interests and their desires. The individual's identity, expectations and aspirations are formed within the context of a host of intersubjective understandings incorporated in a language, a culture, and a particular history. Whether described as a process of socialization or enculturation, individuals are taught determinate ways of being human. Although individuals are not merely passive recipients of cultural norms, their options for response to existing patterns of interaction are circumscribed by the range of possibility incorporated in the existing cultural universe. Any individual may choose to perpetuate or repudiate dominant cultural values, but no individual can escape altogether the legacy of membership in a particular community within a particular nation at a particular point in history.

The conception of socialized individualism suggests that freedom involves a great deal more than absence of coercion. The individual's capacity to act freely, to choose certain options, to undertake particular risks may be undermined by the internalization of images, insults and stigmas associated with group membership. The inculcation of cultural, ethnic, racial, or sexual norms may constitute formidable internal obstacles to individual freedom. The very meaning of self-realization may be unduly constricted by the tacit incorporation of derogatory stereotypes within the individual's self-understanding.

In addition to recognizing that certain cultural values may limit the range of individual freedom, the conception of socialized individuality suggests that 'impersonal' or 'objective' forces may also constitute an enormous impediment to personal liberty. Rather than accepting that 'impersonal' forces such as market mechanisms are a necessary evil which people must accept if they desire any freedom whatsoever, the conception of socialized individualism admits the possibility that human agency may underlie 'objective' forces. The 'Invisible Hand' can be conceived as a cultural creation which serves the interests of some to the detriment of others. Once conceived as cultural constructs, market mechanisms too can be considered targets for political action. If particular human actions responsible for the 'blind forces of the social process' could be identified, then it is possible that the intended and unintended consequences of such behavior could be isolated and altered. The modification of individual action in order to eliminate deleterious social consequences could thereby enhance the prospects for individual freedom. The perspective of socialized individualism then acknowledges individual identity, as well as the conceptions of personal liberty and 'objective' forces, to be social products, shaped by the beliefs and values of the prevailing culture. While such cultural constructs circumscribe the possibilities for individual choice and action, they are not invariable; they can themselves become the target for systematic criticism and reform. Existing beliefs and values may narrow the range of choice available to individuals, but they cannot foreclose choice or change altogether.

---

[7] The conception of socialized individualism is developed in the works of a number of contemporary critical theorists. For an overview of this work, see Richard Bernstein (1976).

In the following sections of this paper, I shall attempt to demonstrate that various arguments against Affirmative Action incorporate the conception of atomistic individuality, while arguments in favor of this policy are informed by a conception of socialized individuality. I shall argue that these conflicting conceptions of individuality color not only the moral and constitutional arguments which opponents or proponents of Affirmative Action advance, but they also shape the most fundamental perception of the 'facts' of the case, that is, the perception of the existence of discrimination as a social problem in the late twentieth century United States.

ATOMISTIC INDIVIDUALISM AND THE
REJECTION OF AFFIRMATIVE ACTION

A recurrent theme among opponents of Affirmative Action is the denial that discrimination in hiring, wage scales, promotion and admissions currently exists in the United States.[8] While they acknowledge that 'Blacks as a group earned less than Whites as a group, and women as a group earned less than men as a group and both minorities and women were a smaller percentage of the academic and other professions than of the general population' (Sowell, 1977: 119), they deny that the explanation of these facts lies in employer/admissions officer's deliberate discrimination. They suggest that a combination of two factors, personal choices made by individuals of their own free will and objective forces over which discrete individuals have no control, provide a more adequate explanation of these phenomena. Arguing that the inference that gross racial/sex differentials in admissions, employment, pay, and promotion reflect a deliberate policy of exclusion cannot be validly drawn from 'superficial, raw and uninterpreted statistical data concerning the relative distribution of members of minorities and women' (Hook, 1977: 89), opponents of Affirmative Action suggest that the problem of underrepresentation does not reflect discrimination against qualified applicants, but rather reflects the fact that women and minorities lack the requisite qualifications and therefore fail to apply. The problem is primarily one of inadequate supply of qualified women and minority applicants, not one of demand hampered by willful discrimination (Lester, 1974). In its most extreme form this view claims that not only are there too few qualified women and minority applicants in general, but also that women and minority applicants who are hired in academia for example, are less qualified than their white male colleagues. 'Blacks or female academics have a Ph.D. less than half as often as the rest of the profession, publish less than half as many articles per person and specialize in the lowest paying fields—notably education, the social sciences and the humanities, with very few being trained in the natural sciences, medicine, law or other highly paid specialities. Thus even if no employer had

[8] Thomas Sowell (1977) and Sidney Hook (1977) base their arguments against Affirmative Action on this premise. These and a number of similar articles are included in *Reverse Discrimination* edited by B. R. Gross (1977).

a speck of prejudice, black and female academics would still have lower pay and promotion prospects' (Sowell, 1977: 119–120).[9] It is lack of qualifications which impair the employment potential of women and minorities, not discrimination.

Two themes are reiterated in explanations of the lack of qualifications among women and minorities: individual choice and objective forces. Empirical evidence is said to indicate that women and minority individuals freely choose career patterns which differ from those of white males and 'this crucial element of individual choice is routinely ignored in syllogistic arguments that go directly from statistical "underrepresentation" to "exclusion" or "discrimination" ' (Sowell, 1977: 129). A second approach to the explanation of lack of qualifications suggests that these deficiencies may stem from either the 'lack of equitable social, economic and educational stimuli or opportunities, for which the entire community must accept the blame' (Hook, 1977: 90)[10] or from the 'pervasive effect of social attitudes' concerning the proper role of women and minorities, both of which can be subsumed under the category of objective forces. But whether social attitudes or the absence of social, economic and educational opportunities is responsible for the dearth of qualified female and minority applicants, Affirmative Action is clearly a misguided and inappropriate remedy.

Affirmative Action is designed as a social policy to end intentional discrimination in admission, employment, pay, promotion, etc. Since any underrepresentation which currently exists can at best be described as the unintended consequence of social attitudes and is not related to any deliberate policies of discrimination, the disease and the cure are mismatched. The basic lack of correspondence between problem and solution stems from the failure to draw an important distinction between problems caused by deliberate individual actions, which are susceptible to solutions aimed at specific individuals and problems caused by impersonal/objective social forces for which no individual can justly be held accountable. Imbued with the perspective of atomistic individualism, critics of Affirmative Action argue that since the lack of requisite qualifications is the unfortunate consequence of pervasive social attitudes, it falls under the category of 'objective forces' which lie beyond the scope of

[9] In his article, Sowell does not actually include statistical tables to support this summary statement and one wonders what data he used. F. K. Barasch provides statistical evidence to support just the opposite claim about female academicians' publishing records and professional qualifications in HEW, The University and Women (Gross, 1977).

[10] In *Fair Game: Inequality and Affirmative Action* (1979), John Livingston cites several other factors which have been advanced to explain racial inequality: (1) genetic inferiority; (2) the 'recent' arrival of blacks in the U.S. and insufficient time for their full assimilation into the 'melting pot' of American culture; (3) the comparative youth of the black population—the median age of black Americans at the last census was 23 years, too young to have acquired the years of education and experience requisite to high level posts; and (4) the values of different ethnic groups which accord priority to the development of different aptitudes and consequently predispose individuals to choose different sorts of career goals (pp. 53–55). Except for the claim of genetic inferiority, all of these could be subsumed under the category of 'objective forces'; genetic inferiority would be rejected by those who accept an atomistic conception of the individual because it violates the fundamental assumption that all individuals have equal natural assets which is necessary to the justification of competition as a fair method of distribution.

political remedies. Solutions to problems rooted in impersonal social processes
are extraordinarily complex and elusive and unfortunately, political efforts to
implement them frequently degenerate into hapless social engineering which
strips individuals of their freedom and autonomy. If individual freedom is not
to be sacrificed, the most acceptable remedies for problems caused by objective
forces must be recognized to be time and education: with time and increasing
education, social attitudes can be expected to change. As attitudes change even
unintentional discrimination will be relegated to the museum of antique relics.
Education is a comprehensive remedy which can influence the values and choices
of the entire community. Furthermore, as the level of education of all community members is raised, the educational level and hence, the qualifications,
of women and minority group members will simultaneously be raised, thereby
eliminating the inadequate supply of qualified female and minority applicants.
Affirmative Action, on the other hand, is a thoroughly inappropriate remedy
for a problem caused by impersonal social forces for it arbitrarily imposes responsibility for a collective problem upon specific individuals; it requires preferential treatment for 'unqualified' women and minority group applicants and
consequently, it discriminates in reverse against the 'best qualified' candidates
who just happen to be non-minority men. Such reverse discrimination is all
the more intolerable because it is not the result of the market's 'Invisible Hand'
but the clear manifestation of government bureaucrats' attempts to impose their
vision of the good upon the society at large. The bureaucracy's usurpation of
the 'power of judge, jury, accuser and patron combined' (Todorovich [Todo-
rovich and Glickstein] 1977: 34) places universities and employers in the position of having to placate federal officials under penalty of loss of federal
contracts vital to their very survival. Thus bureaucratic whim becomes a ty-
rannical task master which strips would-be federal contractors of their autonomy
and their fidelity to standards of pure meritocratic excellence.

Having diagnosed the cause of underrepresentation as an insufficient supply
of qualified women and minority applicants, opponents of Affirmative Action
insist that Affirmative Action is synonymous with reverse discrimination: government policies necessitate the use of 'quotas', the hiring of less qualified
candidates, the obliteration of merit as a criterion of desert and consequently,
the sacrifice of creative, hardworking individuals. Since qualified women and
minority applicants are not available according to this analysis of the facts, it
follows that school administrators and employers must engage in all these abuses
in order to increase the number of women and blacks in their institutions as a
demonstration to the government of their 'good faith'. Giving less qualified
women and minority group members preference in admissions, hiring and promotion can only result in new forms of discrimination which will entail 'the
erosion of the principles of merit, scholarly quality and integrity . . . which is
not only unconstitutional, but immoral, for it makes a mockery of the principle
of desert which was the basis of denunciation of past discriminatory practices.'
(Hook, 1977: 90).

Opponents of Affirmative Action also argue that it is naive to believe that

reverse discrimination can remedy the current effects of past discrimination; on the contrary, they assert that it can only create further injustices:

> 'The belief that discrimination can be administered to the body politic in judicious doses in order to create non-discrimination is akin to the medical wisdom of curing an alcoholic with whiskey. Discrimination is addictive. Its use cannot be precisely controlled . . . (It is wrong) to imagine that one discrimination can compensate for another. Discrimination causes individuals to suffer. If they can be individually compensated, well and good. But compensating their grand-children at the cost of discriminating against someone else does not compensate them in the slightest. It does replace private discrimination (or at least supple-ment it) with public discrimination, sanctioned by the laws. It also sets up another imaginary debt for the social engineer, whose successors will one day have to compensate the grandchild of the one victimized today, at the expense of the one benefitted today' (Todorovich [Todorovich and Glickstein] 1977: 37–38).

These objections to reverse discrimination express the belief of many opponents of Affirmative Action that in the absence of deliberate discriminatory policies in the contemporary United States, the only possible moral justification for the government's policies is compensatory justice for groups. They suggest that 'the entire early federal Affirmative Action drive was motivated and stimulated by the history of three hundred years of injustice against blacks. Only after the argument for reparation to blacks had prevailed as the single determining factor of overriding importance in justifying a temporary preferential treatment for aggrieved groups were the programs for minorities implemented. Women were added later.' (Hook, 1977: 20). Yet this concept of compensatory justice to groups for past injustices suffered by them as groups is completely foreign to the notions of morality associated with atomistic individualism; not surprisingly then, opponents of reverse discrimination have little difficulty identifying suf-ficient deficiencies in the arguments for compensatory justice to sustain its rejection.

The assault on compensatory justice for groups frequently begins with a brief reference to Aristotle who originally formulated the concept of compensatory justice as a rectifying or reparatory transaction between one person and another. The goal of corrective justice was to impose a penalty upon the party who inflicted the injury and confer a corresponding benefit upon the injured indi-vidual in order to restore the kind of equality which existed prior to the injury. Aristotle envisioned a close correspondence or proportionality between the harm suffered and the compensation received. Contemporary proponents of compensatory justice stray markedly from Aristotle's ideals: they insist upon blanket preferential treatment for certain persons on the basis of race, sex or minority group membership even if those persons did not personally suffer past injustices. Thus, preferential treatment for groups as a social policy is noto-riously overinclusive. But it is simultaneously underinclusive, for, in providing compensation only for specific groups, it ignores the claims of other individuals

who have personally suffered injustice, yet who are not members of the groups targeted for compensation. Furthermore, reverse discrimination imposes the cost of compensation upon individuals who did not perpetrate the injustice and who cannot fairly be dubbed beneficiaries of the injustice since they neither sought the benefit nor the opportunity to reject it; in other words, reverse discrimination imposes the cost of compensation upon innocent parties. Thus reverse discrimination can be faulted as arbitrary both in the distribution of benefits to the disadvantaged and in the assignment of the costs of compensation (Blackstone, 1977). And such rampant arbitrariness seriously impairs its status as a persuasive moral argument or justification.

It is also said that compensatory justice for groups substitutes concern with 'abstract groups and their purported rights' for concern with the atomistic individual; as such, it violates that 'essence of liberalism which has always been concerned with the welfare, rights and responsibilities of individuals *qua* individuals, not the masses or classes or other such linguistic abstractions.' (Nisbet, 1977: 52). Those who accept the atomistic conception of the individual cannot make sense out of the claims that certain groups have inflicted, and continue to inflict, sufferings upon other groups and that individuals experience injury as members of a distinctive group and therefore deserve to receive compensation as members of the group. Focusing solely upon individuals who 'make themselves', they reject any notion of a legacy of group injury, just as they reject any notion of collective guilt on the part of the group which historically imposed the suffering. They argue instead that preferential treatment for specific groups violates the 'spirit of the laws, the Constitution and the Declaration of Independence which assert that governments are created to assure individuals (not groups) the retention of their inalienable natural rights, one of which is the pursuit of happiness.' (Todorovich [Todorovich and Glickstein] 1977: 38). To endorse a policy of preferential treatment for groups, would be to subordinate individual's rights to equal treatment to the broader social aim of making amends for a past injustice which they did not perpetrate, a policy which is clearly unconstitutional. According to the opponents of Affirmative Action, justice can require nothing more than the use of neutral principles, such as non-discrimination, in admissions and employment. Since deliberate discrimination is not a contemporary problem, the use of neutral principles will promote meritocratic decisions while simultaneously according justice to individuals regardless of the group to which they happen to belong. For it will allow each individual to 'make it' on his/her own.

Under the Equal Protection clause of the Fourteenth Amendment, the constitutional permissibility of differential treatment for different groups hinges upon the demonstration of relevant grounds for the difference in treatment. Moreover, in cases which involve a suspect classification such as race, the state must show not only that there are relevant grounds to sustain the use of the classification but that the state has a 'compelling interest' in achieving the ends which the classification was devised to facilitate and that no alternative, less harmful means are available to achieve the same end.

For those who accept a conception of atomistic individualism, compelling

state interest constitutes an exceptionally stringent standard which can legitimize overriding individual rights only in the most desperate circumstances, such as a war-time emergency.[11] Indeed, Chief Justice Burger argued in his dissent in *Dunn vs Blumstein* that no state law has ever 'satisfied this seemingly insurmountable standard.' (pp. 363–364). It is not surprising then that numerous Constitutional scholars, as well as Mr Justice Powell speaking for the Supreme Court majority in *Regents of the University of California vs Bakke*,[12] have argued that preferential treatment also fails to satisfy this insurmountable standard.

Mr Justice Powell acknowledged that in the past the Court had ordered extreme remedies involving preferential treatment and the use of quotas in cases in which there had been a judicial or administrative finding of intentional discrimination on the part of employers, unions or school authorities. However, in the case of the University of California Davis Medical School, he argued, 'there has been no determination by the legislature or a responsible administrative agency that the University engaged in a discriminatory practice requiring remedial efforts.' (Bakke, 1978: 4906). Moreover, underrepresentation could not be accepted as a demonstration of a policy of discrimination. The fact that in the two years prior to the establishment of a special admissions program for minorities and the economically disadvantaged, only two Blacks and one Mexican-American had been admitted to the medical school, while in the four years of program operation 26 Blacks, 33 Mexican-Americans and one American Indian had been admitted did not constitute proof that exclusion of minorities had been based upon racial grounds. On the contrary, Mr Justice Powell cited a study published in the *New England Journal of Medicine* which attributed the underrepresentation of blacks in medical schools to 'the small size of the national pool of qualified black applicants' and which endorsed pre-college remedial programs for blacks as an appropriate remedy (Bakke, 1978: 4907).[13] Given the Court's conviction that no intentional discrimination had occurred, Mr Justice Powell examined the claim that it was 'societal discrimination' which warranted a voluntary special admissions program for minority applicants. Rejecting 'societal discrimination' as 'an amorphous concept of injury that may be ageless in its reach into the past' (Bakke, 1978: 4906), Mr Justice Powell asserted that there is 'nothing in the Constitution [which] supports the notion that individuals may be asked to suffer otherwise impermissible burdens in order to enhance the societal standing of ethnic groups.' (*ibid:* 4904). In the absence of proof of intentional discrimination, 'it cannot be said that the government has any greater interest in helping one individual than in refraining from harming another.' (*ibid:* 4906–4907). Thus, Mr Justice Powell concluded that 'the

---

[11] *Korematsu vs United States* (323 U.S. 214, 1944) sustained a classification based upon race or ancestry using strict scrutiny due to a wartime emergency.

[12] *Regents of the University of California vs Bakke* (438 U.S. 265, 1978). The text of the Bakke decision which I have used in this analysis is that printed in *The United States Law Week*, 46 LW 4896 (June 27, 1978). The page references in the text refer to this copy of the decision.

[13] The study, authored by Sleeth and Mishell was published in the *New Eng. J. Med.* on November 24, 1977. The reference appears in footnote 47, p. 4907 of the Court decision.

purpose of helping certain groups whom the faculty of the Davis Medical School *perceived* as victims of "societal discrimination" does not justify a classification that imposes disadvantages upon persons like the respondent [Bakke] who bear no responsibility for whatever harm the beneficiaries of the special admissions program are *thought to have suffered* (*ibid*: 4907, emphasis added). Echoing the assumptions of atomistic individualism, Mr Justice Powell's decision insists that discrimination is not the problem, that the Davis preferential treatment policy is an inappropriate and unconstitutional remedy, and that discussions of 'societal discrimination' conjure images wholly at odds with the atomistic assessment of what it takes to succeed: individual will and initative. Thus, Mr Justice Powell concluded his decision with a reaffirmation of the atomistic principle that applicants should be treated as individuals in the admissions process. While race or sex might constitute factors important in consideration of particular individuals' merits, they ought not be given undue weight. In a 'nation of minorities' where the 'white majority itself is composed of various minority groups, most of which can lay claim to a history of prior discrimination at the hands of the state and private individuals' (*ibid*: 4903), it is the individual not the group, who should be given careful consideration. Race, ethnic background or sex should be considered on the same footing as other qualities such as 'exceptional personal talents, unique work or service experience, leadership potential, maturity, demonstrated compassion, a history of overcoming disadvantage, ability to communicate with the poor or other qualifications deemed important' (*ibid*: 4909) in any selection process. Open competition among talented and ambitious individuals ought not to be corrupted by the imposition of arbitrary standards by misguided administrators. No bureaucratic obstacles should be allowed to interfere with the free rein of individual will and initiative.[14]

SOCIALIZED INDIVIDUALISM AND THE JUSTIFICATION OF AFFIRMATIVE ACTION

Proponents of Affirmative Action often introduce their arguments with the assertion that 'racial, sexual and no doubt other forms of discrimination are not antique relics but are living patterns which continue to warp selection and ranking procedures.' (Beauchamp, 1977: 90). Rather than assuming that the United States represents a just and primarily nondiscriminatory society, they suggest that empirical evidence supports the belief that discrimination is currently widespread and that present discrimination differs from past discrimination only in the degree of subtlety and visibility. While this very subtlety

---

[14] It is interesting to note that it is not just scholars and jurists who believe that success depends solely upon individual will and effort. Survey research conducted by the National Opinion Research Center (NORC) indicates that as recently as 1977, 65% of the white individuals interviewed attributed economic disadvantage experienced by blacks to the moral failings of individual blacks: 'most blacks just don't have the motivation or will power to pull themselves up out of poverty'. For a review of NORC data, see Seymour Martin Lipset and William Schneider (1977).

makes present discrimination far more difficult 'to prove statistically', it renders the effects of discrimination no less pernicious. Acknowledging that statistics cannot provide decisive indicators of discrimination, proponents of Affirmative Action yet insist that the pervasiveness of statistical underrepresentation of women and minority groups in higher education, in higher paving employment and in positions of prestige and power is sufficient to establish a *prima facie* case of discrimination.[15] But proponents of Affirmative Action do not rest their arguments concerning the persistence of discrimination upon a demonstration of underrepresentation alone, for as their opponents have argued, any number of variables can be introduced to explain such underrepresentation. Instead, they emphasize 'underutilization' in an effort to explode the myth that the principle cause of underrepresentation is the inadequate supply of qualified women and minority applicants. 'Underutilization is defined as having fewer members of the group in the category actually employed than would reasonably be expected from their availability, e.g. in universities, from the percentage of available Ph.D's in a given field' (Goldman, 1977: 194). The phenomenon to be explained, then, is not the dearth of minority or female professionals *per se*, but the dearth of such professionals given the availability of a certain percentage of qualified minority and female candidates.[16] The pervasive underutilization of qualified women and minorities in the United States renders suspicious any explanation of the phenomenon which emphasizes personal choice. For it seems unlikely that individuals who have invested great effort to become qualified to apply for certain careers should suddenly choose not to pursue those professions.[17]

Having challenged the adequacy of 'personal choice' and 'lack-of-qualified applicant' explanations of underrepresentation, proponents of Affirmative Action also challenge the assumption that all individuals have an equal opportunity to compete for economic and educational benefits in the contemporary United States, and that the differential rewards simply reflect differences in effort. Proponents of Affirmative Action argue that 'background conditions, such as unequal treatment relating to occupational preparation and expectations in the course of childhood, upbringing and education, ego development, psychological counseling, technical and higher education, etc., which would make it more difficult for women and non-whites as a group than for white men as a group to succeed occupationally, are factors contributing to the denial of equal op-

[15] A series of court decisions concerning Title VII cases of the Civil Rights Act of 1964 have sustained the use of statistical evidence showing underrepresentation as sufficient to establish a *prima facie* case of discrimination: *United States vs Iron Workers Local 86*; *United States vs Hayes International Corp.*; *United States vs United Brotherhood of Carpenters and Joiners*.

[16] For an example of the use of underutilization to make a case for the existence of discrimination against women, see F. K. Barasch, HEW, The University and Women (Gross, 1977).

[17] Given the suspicious circumstances surrounding the causes of underutilization, both EEOC officials and the Courts have laid the burden of proof on non-discrimination upon employers: given a *prima facie* case of discrimination, it becomes the burden of the person or institution accused of discrimination to convince the court that minorities or women are underutilized for reasons other than discrimination. *United States vs Iron Workers Local 86*, 443 F. 2d. 544 (9th circuit, 1971), cert. denied, 404 U.S. 984, 92 S.Ct. 447, 30 L. 2d. 367 (1971).

portunity for occupational attainment.' (Held, 1975: 33). In short, they argue that racist and sexist biases which pervade American culture establish a system of differential rewards which benefit certain individuals but not on the basis of neutral criteria of talent and effort. On this view, one great benefit of Affirmative Action's insistence that group results be considered stems from its demand 'that whites recognize that their own advantages are, in significant measure, group benefits, rather than individual achievements and that their own success has been, in part, a matter of their own superior group opportunities, purchased at the expense of opportunities for non-whites' (Livingston, 1979: 182). Opportunities accrue not to atomistic individuals but to individuals as members of particular families, particular communities, particular ethnic, racial and sexual groups.

Articulating the premises of socialized individualism, proponents of Affirmative Action emphasize that individual identity as well as preparation for educational and economic opportunities ordinarily develop within the confines of family life. 'The self-concept, life-style and careers of parents have a tremendous impact upon their children. Such factors greatly influence the home environment and in turn play a significant role in shaping a child's interests and motivations. The financial, intellectual and social resources accumulated by parents play a large role in determining the opportunities their children get' (Katzner, 1982: 75). To the extent that diet, housing, medical care, intellectual stimulation, cultural enrichment, and family connections can enhance the individual's chances for success, mobility within the meritocracy is and will continue to be a function of luck in the birth lottery. Success will come more readily to the sons and daughters of the successful and disadvantage will remain a legacy to those born of the disadvantaged (Livingston, 1979: 120–128; Held, 1975: 33–34).

Proponents of Affirmative Action argue that racism and sexism may handicap minority and female applicants in a number of ways. Racist and sexist stereotypes may curb the expectations and aspirations of women and minorities. Disadvantaged backgrounds and inadequate education may make it more difficult for women and minorities to achieve particular goals than it is for a middle-class white male to achieve those same goals. But more importantly, when women, minorities and white males do achieve the same goals, racism and sexism may preclude recognition of the accomplishments as identical. The tendency to view women and minorities as less capable, less creative, less willing to work and less deserving of serious consideration and respect culminates in a refusal to acknowledge the merit of members of oppressed groups. Given identical qualifications or performance, psychologists have documented that 'there is a general tendency to give men more favorable evaluations than women' (Nieva and Gutek, 1980: 267–276) and to give whites more favorable evaluations than minorities. Moreover, 'there is psychological evidence to indicate that women and minority group members are systematically down-graded by school teachers (and graded higher when race or sex is unknown to the grader) . . . and that a woman's name on an assigned paper leads students to rate it lower than the same paper with a man's name on it' (Beauchamp, 1977:

110). Thus women and minorities experience a form of discrimination which is analytically distinct from the problems of underrepresentation and pay differentials (Hughes, 1975: 26). They are treated as beings less worthy of respect than the average white male, not because of any individual foible but simply because they are members of a particular group. The disrespect shown to women and minorities on the irrational basis of their sex, race or ethnicity highlights the fact that the competition for educational and economic opportunities is neither neutral nor fair, for women and minorities are judged by standards irrelevant to the competition (Livingston, 1979: 38). A tacit pro-white, pro-male bias in admissions and hiring procedures constitutes a form of discrimination which continues to harm women and minorities not because of their individual characteristics but because of their membership in particular groups. Thus, proponents of Affirmative Action, insist that:

'It is absurd to suppose that young blacks and women now of an age to apply for jobs have not been wronged. . . . It is only within the last 25 years (perhaps the last 10 years in the case of women) that it has become at all widely agreed in this country that blacks and women must be recognized as having, not merely this or that particular right normally recognized as belonging to white males, but all of the rights and respect which go with full membership in the community. Even young blacks and women have lived through down-grading for being black or female; they have not merely not been given that very equal chance at the benefits generated by what the community owns which is so firmly insisted on for white males, they have not until lately even been felt to have a right to it.' (Thompson, 1977: 36).

Discussions of continuing racist and sexist bias illuminate one other factor central to admissions and hiring procedures: neither the criteria employed nor the individuals employing them are neutral or 'impersonal'. It is not 'objective forces' which determine individual applicants' merit and prospects for success, but the decisions of fallible administrators. 'In the modern meritocracy, the process of selection is not made by nature or by Adam Smith's "Invisible Hand", but by admissions and personnel officers who apply cultural standards to applicants for admissions, appointment and promotion.' (Livingston, 1979: 132). Thus, it is not 'blind social processes' which Affirmative Action must remedy, but rather the particular decisions of concrete individuals who serve as gate-keepers to the positions of power and privilege in contemporary society.

Given their diagnosis of the problem as on-going discrimination in the form of anti-minority, anti-female bias, those who accept the socialized conception of individuality suggest that Affirmative Action is a fair and appropriate remedy. As a mechanism for the cultivation of a 'mature recognition of the talent of all persons in society' (Pottinger, 1977: 49), Affirmative Action does not jeopardize principles of merit or standards of excellence; it simply prohibits situations in which 'the only ones allowed to demonstrate their "merit" are white males' (Glickstein [Todorovich and Glickstein] 1977: 30). Through the establishment of fair hiring practices and competition open to public inspection, Affirmative

Action ensures that 'men . . . compete fairly on the basis of merit, not fraternity; on demonstrated capability, not assumed superiority' (Pottinger, 1971). By focusing attention on admitting, hiring and promoting members of particular target groups, Affirmative Action draws attention to both the consequences of historic racism and sexism and to the extent, the gravity and the immediacy of the injuries still sustained by minorities and women in the United States (Livingston, 1979: 32).

Recognition of the tenacity of the presumption of racial and sexual superiority and of the pervasive discrimination in the contemporary United States causes believers in socialized individualism to reject the claim that compensatory justice constitutes the only moral ground for the justification of social policies designed to ameliorate the conditions of women and minorities. They reject compensatory justice, in part, because it facilely perpetuates the myth that discrimination is a social atavism. Instead they insist that the appropriate moral justification for contemporary programs to eliminate current discrimination lies in arguments for distributive justice. Both Affirmative Action and the more stringent policy of preferential treatment can promote the redistribution of income, power and prestige, reduce the distributive inequities which plague the present racist and sexist society and thereby enhance the freedom and the possibility for self-realization of women and minority group members. Concern with distributive justice focuses attention upon the crucial role which higher education performs in certifying individuals for positions of power and prestige. Ending the exclusion of women and minorities from higher education can contribute to the creation of a society in which 'the power of the white middle-class male is broken . . . where those who are now the victims of the social order have their fair share of power.'[18] Affirmative Action and preferential treatment in admissions to higher education then is cast as one means by which to improve the employment prospects, income, status, security and chance for self-determination of women and minorities. Awareness of underutilization, of the truncated life prospects of women and minority group members who are qualified for but not employed in positions of power and prestige, however, cautions against too great a reliance upon Affirmative Action in educational opportunities as a remedy to racial and sexual discrimination. This awareness has culminated in the rejection of excessive reliance upon 'neutral' or 'colorblind' principles, such as 'non-discrimination' as inadequate to accomplish the goals of distributive justice. For non-discrimination alone can make no assault upon the 'standards of excellence' devised by white middle-class males as admission criteria which have not been proven to have any direct relation to an individual's performance in a professional capacity but which have worked admirably to screen out minority candidates.[19] Furthermore, implementation of the non-discrimination principle since 1964 has made virtually no impact upon

[18] Letter to the Editor, *New York Times* quoted in Nisbet, p. 52.
[19] For an example drawn from the medical profession, see Price *et al.* (1964). Price found no correlation between student grades in undergraduate or medical school and physician performance on Medical School faculties, as Board Certified Specialists or as urban or rural general practitioners.

the problem of underrepresentation. For that reason, many who hold the socialized conception of individuality have concluded that 'When society has committed past injustices or when historically disadvantaged groups exist side by side with more advantaged groups, it simply is not possible to achieve equality and fairness by applying neutral principles' (Glickstein [Todorovich and Glickstein] 1977: 29).

Arguments on the grounds of distributive justice, therefore, justify not only Affirmative Action but also preferential treatment, emphasizing that without such stringent measures little progress will be made toward the elimination of racial and sexual inequality. The conception of socialized individuality allows a construction of the case for the legitimacy of preferential treatment which simultaneously recognizes that such a policy will cause white males to lose certain advantages yet denies that the loss constitutes violation of individual rights. Socialized individualism suggests that the white men currently occupying favored positions in existing organizations have themselves been the beneficiaries of some preferential treatment: 'they are members of a group of persons who have been privileged in hiring and promotion in accordance with normal practices of long-standing, persons who have been offered better educational preparation than others of the same basic talents, persons whose egos have been strengthened more than members of other groups' (Held, 1975: 34). Because these white males did not deserve such preferential treatment, because they had no right to the advantages afforded by a racist and sexist society, no rights are being violated by the removal of those advantages. Policies to promote justice for the victims of injustice may require that white men lose their unwarranted privilege in society but they do not strip these individuals of legitimate rights.

Constitutional arguments concerning the permissibility of both Affirmative Action and preferential treatment have also articulated the assumptions incorporated in the socialized conception of individuality.[20] In their separate opinion, dissenting from the Court's decision to rule the Davis Special Admissions Program unconstitutional, Justices Brennan, White, Marshall and Blackmun insisted that 'a glance at our docket and at those of the lower courts will show that even today officially sanctioned discrimination is not a thing of the past' (Bakke, 1978: 4912). Indeed, they argued that 'the generation of minority students applying to Davis Medical School since it opened in 1968—most of whom were born before or about the time *Brown I* was decided—clearly have been the victims of discrimination' (*ibid:* 4923), a discrimination based solely on membership in particular racial and ethnic groups. Mr Justice Marshall added that 'It is unnecessary in twentieth century America to have individual Negroes

---

[20] Although I shall only discuss the views expressed by Justices Brennan, White, Marshall and Blackmun in their separate opinion, (concurring in the judgment that race can be used in admissions programs and dissenting to the Majority's decision to strike down the Davis special admissions policy), in the Bakke case, I believe that the assumptions of the socialized conception of individualism appear in a number of other Court decisions. See, for example, the Washington State Supreme Court decision in *Defunis vs Odegaard*, Justice Tobriner's dissent from the California Supreme Court ruling in *Bakke*, and *Brown vs Board of Education*.

demonstrate that they have been victims of racial discrimination, the racism of our society has been so pervasive that none, regardless of wealth or position, has managed to escape its impact.' (*ibid:* 4931). The Justices also argued that there was good reason to believe that the failure of certain racial minorities to satisfy entrance requirements is not a measure of their ultimate performance as doctors but a result of the lingering effects of past societal discrimination (*ibid:* 4918). Having argued that discrimination is an ongoing problem in the United States and that the exclusion of minorities from medical school was simply one manifestation of such discrimination, the Justices asserted that it is constitutionally permissible that Federal and State legislatures require that recipients of federal funds accord 'preferential consideration to disadvantaged members of racial minorities as part of a program designed to enable such individuals to surmount obstacles imposed by racial discrimination.' (*ibid:* 4912). Moreover, they insisted, that preferential treatment does not violate any fundamental rights, nor does it constitute a form of invidious discrimination against whites (*ibid:* 4919–4920). Finally, they urged that the commitment to neutral principles and to the concept of a 'colorblind' Constitution not be allowed to 'become myopia which masks the reality that many "created equal" have been treated within our lifetimes as inferior both by the law and by their fellow citizens' (*ibid:* 4912). Instead, they recommended the implementation of color conscious remedies both to prevent the perpetuation of discrimination and to undo the iniquitous effects of social injustice.

THE DISPUTE LAID BARE

To this point, I have attempted to demonstrate that the dispute over the legitimacy of Affirmative Action involves more than a simple disagreement over the utility of a particular social policy; it reflects fundamental differences in the understanding of the nature of individual identity and freedom. Indeed, I have suggested that these basic conceptions of individuality so structure the interpretation of contemporary social life that the very capacity to perceive the existence of discrimination turns on the tacit acceptance of the socialized conception of individuality. It is important to stress that these conceptions operate at the tacit level, that most people are unaware of the influence of these presuppositions upon their perceptions and analyses of contemporary events and that this lack of awareness places these fundamental assumptions beyond examination and critical scrutiny. Now, there is more at stake in the explication of these divergent conceptions of individuality than a mere plotting of the conceptual terrain. For when these tacit assumptions about the nature of individuality are made explicit and subjected to critical assessment, it becomes clear that both conceptions are not equally capable of providing an adequate account of the formation and development of individual identity.

The atomistic conception of individuality misconstrues the individual's relation to self, others, society and tradition. In assuming that individual desires are subjectively determined, the atomistic conception overlooks the extent to

which the individual's impressions, desires, sensations and aspirations are socially constructed, founded upon a host of intersubjective understandings incorporated in language, culture and tradition. The atomistic conception of the individual must deny the pervasive impact of history and culture upon the formation of individual identity if it is to retain its assumption concerning the radical independence of the individual and the primacy of choice and effort as determinants of individual success. Yet precisely this denial renders the atomistic ideal incapable of accounting for the ethno-cultural and historical diversity of individual personalities and self-understandings documented in anthropological and historical studies.[21] The atomistic conception is at a loss to explain the shared values and valuations characteristic of distinct peoples, whether they be tribes, clans, nations, ethnicities, races, religions or genders. Moreover, in treating individual passions, appetites and desires as permanently fixed, the atomistic conception denies the individual's capacity to reflect upon, criticize and alter both desires and the behavior which is informed by those desires. In short, it denies what many philosophers have considered the essence of moral freedom. While this denial sustains platitudes such as, 'You can't change human nature,' which serve to challenge the efficacy of any political action designed to achieve social justice, its determinist roots drastically constrict both the meaning of and the possibility for individual freedom.[22] The determinist underpinnings of the atomistic account of individual desire might well undermine the claim that choice and effort are the principle determinants of success. For a consistent determinism negates the possibility of choice and nullifies the effect of effort.

The atomistic conception of individuality is marred by its inability to provide an account of individual identity consistent with the empirical findings of anthropologists and historians and its theoretical foundations are endangered by the possibility of a logical contradiction. The prospects for future social policy founded upon atomistic assumptions are also problematic. For those who build their political prescriptions upon the atomistic conception of individuality advocate the use of neutral principles as the sole constitutional remedy for racial and sexual inequality. If underrepresentation, underutilization and the irrational disrespect for women and minority individuals persist, on this view, they must be discounted as the private preferences of particular individuals or as the consequence of the inexorable workings of impersonal forces, in both instances they are beyond the scope of a political remedy. The atomistic prescription urges resignation to injustice as an inevitable aspect of the human condition. In denying the existence of culturally shared values, it denies the possibility that systematic racism or sexism can cripple the life prospects of entire groups of individuals. It renders humanity helpless in the face of grave social evils. It is ironic that the atomistic conception which flaunts a boundless

---

[21] This point has been made by L. Dumont (1965, 1970). See also Lukes, pp. 146–157 (1973).

[22] Thomas Hobbes, one of the first theorists to develop the atomistic conception of the individual, recognized clearly the implications of his determinist assumptions for a conception of freedom, thus he rejected notions of free will as 'words without meaning, that is to say absurd.' (1958: 47).

confidence in the capacities of individuals to make anything of themselves as individuals simultaneously denies their capacity to achieve anything as a community.

It is time that the atomistic conception of the individual, replete with its empirical and theoretical defects and its overbearing pessimism concerning the possibility of collective choice and action be subjected to explicit criticism and public scrutiny. The implications which flow from the pervasive acceptance of the atomistic conception of individuality are manifest in the context of the Affirmative Action debate: the perpetuation of a systematic blindness to the pernicious consequences of racism and sexism, the toleration of racial and sexual inequality with an untroubled conscience, the denial of a wide range of opportunities to members of oppressed groups and the restriction of the sphere of freedom of the disadvantaged.[23] Such policies challenge the authenticity of our commitment to the principles of liberty, equality and justice. Such policies should not be accepted as the only feasible political possibilities. Rigorous examination of the theoretical presuppositions of various policy prescriptions may contribute to the reconstitution of the very conception of political possibility.

REFERENCES

Barasch, F. K. 1977. H. E. W., The University and women. In Gross, Barry R., ed. *Reverse Discrimination.* Prometheus Books, New York. Also published in *Dissent* (Summer, 1973).

Beauchamp, Tom L., ed. 1975. *Ethics and Public Policy.* Prentice-Hall, Englewood Cliffs, New Jersey.

Beauchamp, Tom L. 1977. The justification of reverse discrimination. In Blackstone, William T. and Robert D. Heslop, eds, *Social Justice and Preferential Treatment.* University of Georgia Press, Athens, Georgia.

Bernstein, Richard. 1976. *The Restructuring of Social and Political Theory.* Harcourt, Brace and Jovanovich, New York.

Blackstone, William T. 1977. Reverse discrimination and compensatory justice. In Blackstone, William T. and Robert D. Heslop, eds, *op. cit.*

Cohen, Marshall, Tomas Nagel and Thomas Scanlon, eds. 1976. *Equality and Preferential Treatment.* Princeton University Press, Princeton, New Jersey.

Dumont, L. 1965. The modern conception of the individual: notes on its genesis and that of concomitant institutions. *Contr. Indian Sociology* 8: 13–61.

Dumont, L. 1970. *Homo Hierarchicus: The Caste System and Its Implications* (trans. by Mark Sainsbury). Weidenfeld and Nicolson, London.

Dunn vs Blumstein. 1972. (405 U.S. 30).

Eisenstein, Zillah. 1981. *The Radical Future of Liberal Feminism.* Longman, New York.

Goldman, Alan H. 1976. Affirmative Action. In Cohen, Marshall, Thomas Nagel and Thomas Scanlon, eds, *op. cit.*

[23] Both John Livingston and Virginia Held have suggested that the perpetuation of racial and sexual inequality poses a threat to the legitimacy of the democratic order in the U.S. See Livingston, pp. 186–199 (1979) and Held, pp. 39–40 (1975).

Gross, Barry, ed. 1977. *Reverse Discrimination*. Prometheus, Buffalo, New York.

Hayek, F. A. 1948. *Individualism and Economic Order*. University of Chicago Press, Chicago, Illinois.

Held, Virginia. 1975. Reasonable progress and self-respect. In Beauchamp, Tom L., ed., *Ethics and Public Policy*. Prentice-Hall, Englewood Cliffs, New Jersey.

Hobbes, Thomas. 1958. *Leviathan*. Bobbs-Merrill, New York.

Hook, Sidney. 1977. The bias of anti-bias regulations. In Gross, Barry R., ed., *op. cit.* Also published in *Measure* 14 (October 1971).

Hughes, Graham. 1975. Reparations for Blacks. In Beauchamp, Tom L. ed. *op. cit.*

Katzner, Louis. 1982. Reverse discrimination. In Regan, Tom and Donald Van de Veer, eds, *And Justice For All*. Rowman and Littlefield, Totowa, New Jersey.

Korematsu vs United States. 1944. (323 U.S. 214).

Lester, Richard. 1974. *Anti-Bias Regulations of Universities: Faculty Problems and Their Solutions*. McGraw-Hill, New York.

Lewis, Michael. 1978. *The Culture of Inequality*. New American Library, New York.

Lipset, Seymour M. and William Schneider. 1977. An emerging national consensus. *New Republic* 177(16): 8–12 (October 15).

Livingston, John. 1979. *Fair Game: Inequality and Affirmative Action*. W. H. Freeman, San Francisco.

Lukes, Stephen. 1973. *Individualism*. Harper and Row, New York.

Macpherson, C. B. 1962. *The Political Theory of Possessive Individualism*. Clarendon Press, Oxford.

Nieva, Veronica and Barbara Gutek. 1980. Sex effects on evaluation. *Acad. Management Rev.* 5(2): 267–276.

Nisbet, Lee. 1977. Affirmative action—A liberal program? In Gross, Barry R. ed., *op. cit.*

Pottinger, J. Stanley. 1971. Come now, Professor Hook. *New York Times* CXXI: 29. (Saturday, December 18).

Pottinger, J. Stanley. 1972. The drive toward equality. In Gross, Barry R. ed., *op. cit.*

Price, Philip B., James N. Richards, Calvin W. Taylor and Tony L. Jacobsen. 1964. Measurement of physician performance. *J. Med. Educ.* 39: 203.

Regan, Tom and Donald Van de Veer, eds. 1982. *And Justice For All*. Rowman and Littlefield, Totowa, New Jersey.

Regents of the University of California vs Bakke. 1978. (438 U.S. 265; in *The United States Law Week* 46 LW 4896, June 27).

Sennett, Richard and Jonathan Cobb. 1972. *The Hidden Injuries of Class*. Alfred A. Knopf, New York.

Sleeth, Boyd C. and Robert Mishell. 1977. Black underrepresentation in United States Medical Schools. *New Engl. J. Med.* 297(21): 1146–1148 (November 24).

Sowell, Thomas. 1977. 'Affirmative Action' reconsidered. In Gross, Barry R., ed., *op. cit.* Also published in *The Public Interest* (Winter 1976).

Thompson, Judith Jarvis. 1977. Preferential hiring. In Cohen, Marshall, Thomas Nagel and Thomas Scanlon, eds, *op. cit.*

Todorovich, Miro M. and Howard Glickstein. 1977. Discrimination in Higher Education: a debate on faculty employment. In Gross, Barry R., ed., *op. cit.* Also published in *Civil Rights Digest* (Spring, 1975).

Unger, Roberto. 1975. *Knowledge and Politics*. Free Press, New York.

United States vs Iron Workers Local 86 443 F.2d 544 (9th Circuit, 1971). cert. denied. (404 U.S. 984).

Weaver, Mark. 1980. The concept of mind in political theory, Ph.D. Dissertation. University of Massachusetts, Amherst.

Wood, Ellen. 1972. *Mind and Politics*. University of Berkeley Press, Berkeley, California.

MOTHERHOOD, FEMINISM AND IDENTITY

Margaret A. Simons

Along with other members of 'the baby boom generation' who have reached their thirties, I have begun to hear my biological clock ticking away the remaining minutes of my life as a 'fertile' woman, a potential mother. For those women, who like me, felt themselves at twenty, drawn to the pursuit of a career which seemed to exclude motherhood, this can be a time of reflection on that earlier 'choice'. It's not an easy decision, I'm sure, for any of us, and is made especially difficult for those women whose tenuous hold on a middle-class identity has been seriously shaken by the current economic depression.

But I am talking about a choice. This, in itself, might strike some people as odd, since motherhood is very often experienced as a fact of life over which we have little control. Some indeed seem to feel we should not have any control in this matter, fearing that if we were actually given the choice, women would never have any more babies. One of my colleagues, an ardent male socialist, with a, perhaps not unexpectedly, conservative social philosophy, seems to hold this view. In response to my (somewhat hesitant) revelation that I seemed to be deciding not to have any children, he angrily replied that it was another instance of privileged feminists casting off their burdens onto the backs of the poor.

This strikes me as a strangely ahistorical response. For not since slavery have the policies of this country encouraged the poor, black, Native American, or Hispanic women of this country to bear children at all. The racist ideology that has too often defined those policies has, instead, been designed to discourage people of color from reproducing themselves. Programs of forced sterilization have threatened the survival of entire communities and made the struggle to give birth a social and political, as well as a personal and economic one, for many American women. Reproductive rights for these women has meant asserting their right to have children, as well as their right to decide not to.

But his remark reveals some of the complexities that surround motherhood as a moral issue. It can present a woman with one of the most profound decisions

I would like to thank the following persons for their encouragement and helpful discussions about motherhood: Azizah al-Hibri, Ann Ferguson, Maryellen MacGuigan, Cathy Surack, the members of the congregation of the Alton Illinois First Unitarian Church, the members of Metro-East NOW, my sister, Jacqueline Hill and my mother, Nina Simons.

of her life, requiring tremendous emotional as well as intellectual effort to resolve. Motherhood has thus become an apt candidate for philosophical inquiry. Its absence from the traditional philosophical literature is due, no doubt in large part, to the men who have claimed the discipline of philosophy as their own, to the exclusion of women. Male philosophers have lacked the experiential knowledge that poses motherhood as an issue and defines its content. At best (or rather, worst) they have shared in defining its context, which Adrienne Rich (1976) has called the oppressive 'institution' of motherhood.

My own interest is in providing a philosophical justification for the choice not to be a mother. For it's my belief that for feminism to be really 'pro-choice', a woman must be able to choose not to be a mother without losing her self-respect or identity as a woman.

I remember watching a television special on the efforts of women to become pregnant through fertility clinics. The interviewer asked some of the women why they were spending so much time and money trying to have a child. I'll never forget the response of one of them, as she first glanced shamefully across at her husband, and then answered that the future of her marriage depended on it, that her husband felt that without children there would be no family, no reason to stay married. At some basic emotional level, women's liberation from oppressive roles has had no effect at all, if a woman is thought to have no value outside of her role as wife-and-mother.

This husband's and my male colleague's response to the motherhood issue point out the necessity for men to explore the complexities of their own feelings about parenthood and their own need for children, and how it's related to their feelings about women, who they need in order to have children. They, like women, seem to be ambivalent: 'wanting an heir', resenting the power this gives women over them; or, thanks to the early pregnancies of a young nurturing wife-and-mother, being able to leave their own feelings unexamined, unacknowledged until late in their own middle age crisis (too late to have to change diapers). I have a suspicion that many men are being forced by their thirty-year-old career-women wives to become involved in this decision. If so, this gives them an opportunity which was available to few of their fathers. If that's the case, then parenthood should be a topic of philosophical interest and exploration for male as well as female philosophers of my generation.

That I feel the need to defend the choice not to be a mother also reflects an important historical development in feminism: the rebirth of mothering as a respectable feminist experience. In the 60s and 70s many feminists felt forced to defend their decision to have children, as though it were a sign of their lack of radical commitment to the feminist cause. Barbara Ehrenreich and Deirdre English in their 1978 book, *For Her Own Good,* describe feminism as having reached a theoretical impasse. As Betty Friedan correctly observes in *The Second Stage* (1982), many women both inside and outside the movement were alienated from what they saw as the feminist demand that they choose between their family and their individuality. They felt that equality could only be gained at the cost of their mothering; and, for many traditional women this price was too high.

Providing a feminist justification for the choice to become or not to become a mother necessitates finding a way out of this apparent impasse. To do that, let's start by examining some feminist conceptions of the problem and their proposed solutions.

FEMINISM VS MOTHERHOOD

Ehrenreich and English describe feminism as having reached an impasse. The romantic view of women, based on a recognition of womanly values and experience, had, in their view, been defeated. What had triumphed in its place was the Beauvoirian rationalist view, which they describe as 'masculinist' and selfish. This view glorifies individualists who are earnestly pursuing careers in the well established male way. It bases women's liberation on a principle of equality that treats persons as isolated competitive individuals. This totally ignores the predicament of children (those most unequal of people) and those who care for them who are not able to achieve the individualist ideal.

What Ehrenreich and English didn't anticipate in 1978 was the re-emergence of the romantic view brought in on the conservative political tide. Within feminist philosophy, this perspective is perhaps best represented by Mary Wolgast's *Equality and the Rights of Women* (1980). In this work, Wolgast argues that feminism must discard the principle of equality, in spite of its past effectiveness in gaining legal rights for women. Her reasoning echoes the perception of Ehrenreich and English that this approach is based on an atomistic individualism. It treats people as social isolates and is thus unable to deal with the realities of women's relationships to their children and families.

Her solution to this impasse does not move forward, however, as much as it harkens to the past; for she suggests founding women's rights on the principle of special rights due them as birth mothers. This solution confounded many of her feminist readers, who, like myself, were not birth mothers and would thus have been legally left out in the cold. Its benefits would have applied primarily to that limited, economically privileged segment of society able to support a full-time homemaker.

But her book does emphasize the reality that for at least some women, the traditional romantic view of womanhood, with its separate social spheres for men and women, provides an appreciation of the values and life missing from individualistic feminism.

A more important feminist work that sees feminism as facing an impasse, but has a broader, more popular basis for its conclusion, is *The Second Stage* by Betty Friedan. Friedan, an astute observer of American life, argues that the feminist movement, if it is to continue to thrive, must follow her lead out of the egoistic individualism. This is characteristic of the anti-family, anti-male, anti-life sentiment that characterized its first stage, according to Friedan. We must now inaugurate the second stage of the sex-role revolution in which women and men will, together, affirm the values of life, family and society that were, in our earlier anger, given short shrift.

There are some very serious problems to Friedan's solution: she misrepresents the early movement, ignoring its rich diversity and evidence of life-affirming, mother-affirming values in feminist theory and practice; thus she plays into the hands of conservative anti-feminists. Furthermore she encourages a distorted egoistic view of the movement's history. This view ignores the contribution of other feminists and thus discounts the real differences among women. By claiming that all women really want the love of a husband and a child, she implies that (a) lesbians and women who choose not to be mothers don't know what they want, i.e. are immature, suffer from 'false consciousness', lack fully developed self concepts, or moral sense and that (b) she does know what those women 'really' want, i.e. a man and child, an epistemologically questionable claim at best.

Discounting the experiences of women when those experiences differ from our own, as white feminists have done in regard to women of color, and now Friedan has done in regard to lesbians and women who choose not to be mothers, does not ultimately advance the feminist movement. Such actions, in excluding women or silencing them, cut off the source of feminism's strength and flexibility, and endanger its own future survival.

What is positive in Friedan's perspective is its effort to acknowledge the experiences of women who had previously felt denied and excluded by feminism because of its angry attack on the important values associated with motherhood in their lives. The theoretical fruitfulness which this step, moving beyond the impasse described by Ehrenreich and English, has for feminism, can be seen by applying it in an area unnoticed by Friedan because of her focus on conservative women, that of reproductive rights.

In the chapter on reproductive rights in her book, *Women, Race and Class*, Angela Davis provides an historical analysis of the unwillingness of most black and Hispanic women to identify with the movement to legalize abortion. Her analysis makes the point that giving birth, when a woman's community is threatened with extinction by a racist government, is an act fraught with political significance. Far from being meaningless or essentially oppressive, as the feminism of Simone de Beauvoir (1952), for example, would suggest, giving birth in this social, political context can be one of the most meaningful actions in the life of a woman who is denied most other meaningful opportunities.

Davis' analysis shows that the reluctance of black and Hispanic women to identify with feminism should be seen as an opportunity for the movement to engage in self-reflection, to re-examine its theoretical frameworks. It's no doubt evidence of the invisibility of women of color in white America in the 70s (as well as the relative youth of the feminist movement at that time) that this feminist reexamination of motherhood now in process did not begin until the resurgence by the New Right in 1980.

The growing feminist acknowledgment of the profound meaningfulness and positive values that can find an expression in motherhood is a positive development in feminism. It opens up the movement to an aspect of women's experience and to the presence of women themselves who were not given a voice in the early years of the movement.

The challenge that remains is to provide a theoretical integration of these new insights with the insights produced by the early movement and, from the perspective of my more immediate concern, to provide a justification for the decision not to have a child, which does not deny the validity of the opposite choice.

In order to do that, we'll have to reexamine the early movement, asking the following questions: Is the impasse described by Ehrenreich and English, and Friedan as absolute as they make it out to be? Or can, as I suspect, the history of the early movement provide a foundation for this new integrative solution, as well as evidence of the individualist feminism described by its critics?

HAS FEMINISM REACHED AN IMPASSE?

My own experience in a university based women's liberation movement from 1969 and early 70s was that practical activities such as cooperative day care centers designed to help mothers and their children existed side by side with efforts to open up career opportunities by combatting employment discrimination. Some feminists, of course, rejected the validity of any activities that supported women in what they considered to be the definitionally oppressive roles of wife and/or mother. But there have always been integrators who saw the relationship between activities such as work in a day care center, projects to combat violence against women, and legal efforts to end employment discrimination and secure health benefits for women.

Integrative theory has also always existed that has supported the equality of women and their rights as individuals, while respecting mothers and fighting for their right to make motherhood a positive, enriching experience rather than an alienating one. *Our Bodies, Our Selves* (1971) is such an example. Shirley Chisholm is an example of a feminist political leader who, although not herself a mother, fought for an integrative solution to racism, sexism and class oppression, fired by her profound belief that motherhood gives women a unique sense of social value that is desperately needed in public life.

Nor did we have to wait for Friedan's 1982 book, for an eloquent analysis and defense of mothering. We got that in Adrienne Rich's 1976 classic *Of Woman Born*, where she makes the tremendously clarifying distinction between the institution of motherhood, which has so often been oppressive, and the experience itself, which has so much capacity for beauty. For a deeper historical foundation, we could go all the way back to the eighteenth-century feminist Mary Wollstonecraft, who argued for equality and motherhood in practically the same breath.

But it takes a sympathetic observer to find this tradition in feminism. There's no denying the existence of a militant, angry feminist attack on women's traditional role. It certainly received much more press coverage than moderate feminism and even intimidated some moderate feminists from speaking out. Some feminist mothers, like Gabrielle Burton, author of the early book, *I'm Running away from Home, but I'm Not Allowed to Cross the Street* (1972) were

able to use the radical's fervor to aid them in self discovery, in breaking out of their shell, without feeling forced to throw out their family along with their oppressive place in it.

The hidden strength of this integrative response to feminism is reflected in the results of a university study discussed by Friedan (1982: 220–227). The researchers studied white middle-class mothers in central Michigan, expecting to find the group divided into those women who expressed primarily family centered values, and those who expressed individualist values. To their surprise, the findings revealed that most of the women expressed a combination of the two value systems, that they were not as opposed in practice, in the lives of these women, as the researchers had hypothesized they would be.

The emphasis on more-radical-than-thouism both within the feminist movement and in the media coverage of the movement may have masked the historical presence and contemporary endurance of integrative traditions in feminist theory and practice. But these traditions should provide encouragement that integrative solutions are part of the ongoing reality of feminism, rather than impossible or even unusual.

Now that we've located an historical foundation for an integrative feminist resolution of the apparent opposition between motherhood and feminism, the next step is to examine more closely the individualist feminist position in the light of the critical perspective provided by its opponents, which means going back to Simone de Beauvoir's classic work, *The Second Sex*, the major theoretical source for the radical feminist attack on motherhood and woman's traditional role.

BEAUVOIR'S PHILOSOPHY OF MOTHERHOOD

The French bourgeois society in which Simone de Beauvoir grew up was radically divided into male and female spheres, which presented almost insurmountable obstacles for a woman aspiring to a career. Her analysis of motherhood reflects this reality. In a concluding chapter of *The Second Sex* on the independent woman, Beauvoir remarks that: 'there is one feminine function that it is actually almost impossible to perform in complete liberty: that is maternity . . . [The independent woman] is forced to choose between sterility, which is often felt as a painful frustration, and burdens hardly compatible with a career.' (Beauvoir, 1952: 774).

The absence of women who successfully combined a professional career with motherhood and Beauvoir's own profound alienation from woman's traditional role of wife and mother can provide insight into her angry, ambivalent, but largely negative view of motherhood in *The Second Sex*.

The philosophical challenge that Beauvoir faced in her analysis was twofold. She had to provide a serious philosophical description and analysis of women's experience, which other, male, phenomenologists such as Jean-Paul Sartre, had failed to do. She also had to combat the conservative position exemplified

by Hegel's philosophy, that women's differences from men define/confine her to the limited sphere she then occupied.

Her response was to make some philosophical distinctions—between necessary and contingent aspects of human existence, for example. The effect of this distinction was to make sexual differentiation not definitional, or essential to our experience. It was an unfortunate tack to take since it both undercut her phenomenological commitment to describe experience without preconceptions, and left her own work describing women's experience without adequate philosophical foundation.

When she felt forced, in the context of a discussion of various male phenomenological analyses of biology, to see the phenomenon of reproduction as ontologically founded, she projected her own struggle against the oppressive institution of woman's traditional role onto her interpretation of biological reproduction. In this description in her chapter on the biological givens of experience, Beauvoir sees woman as engaged in a struggle to assert her individuality against the efforts of nature to enslave her to the species. Nature condemns woman to an animal-like maintenance of biological life and prevents her from engaging in the truly creative, human, transcendent work of producing culture for which nature rewards individual men.

She writes in a chapter on history that is much indebted to Hegel, that the male activity of warfare is superior to giving birth. For, in risking life for human ends, war creates human values which the mere reproduction of life does not. The values of women's traditional sphere are the creation of men anxious to justify woman's dependent, subordinate status. Women accept this role, because men have denied them any other alternatives, and because of an inauthentic desire to evade the anxieties of their own autonomy.

It's important to note here that Beauvoir, in fact, had experienced the desire for social identification and dependence as an inauthentic temptation to abdicate her responsibility for her own life by seeking to identify with and live her life through an Other. This problematic relationship with the Other is, of course, a major theme in Beauvoir's work.

Later in *The Second Sex*, in the chapter on motherhood, where her descriptions of women's lived experience come not from arguments with male philosophers, but from writings by women, her description of motherhood is much less negative. Beauvoir is there able to recognize that motherhood can be the source of authentic experience for women. For it confronts the mother with the profound human realities of identification and separation from another person and provides her with the opportunity to develop the authentic human value of generosity.

But these later insights on motherhood undoubtedly came to Beauvoir in the course of writing *The Second Sex*. They are not incorporated into the fundamental philosophical position defined in its opening chapters. This philosophical position does go beyond Sartre's radical individualism in acknowledging the interconnectedness of individual freedoms. Beauvoir defines a social ethic that condemns oppression and establishes generosity as a defining element in moral authenticity. But this acknowledgement of moral obligations between

individuals leaves unaddressed the moral values entailed, for example, by the nurturing of a helpless infant. Social identification and loving devotion are not positive values in Beauvoir's philosophy. They are, rather, evidence of an inauthentic evasion, the mystification of oppression, or an undeveloped, immature consciousness.

Beauvoir's mistake was in thinking that the desire to nurture another person, to accept a relationship of social identification and dependency was only a temptation, rather than the expression of a positive human value and activity. What she was unable to fully realize from her sociohistorical standpoint was the limitations of an ethos defined solely by the individual pursuit of transcendence over nature.

But now, for many American women who have sought their personal success in a society defined by individual mobility, the avoidance of personal commitment and social identity can seem, at thirty, just as immature and inauthentic as getting married and/or pregnant to avoid finishing one's thesis did some years earlier. The question is how feminism can integrate the changing values in women's lives as we strive to act in both the private and public spheres.

What we need, and Beauvoir wasn't able to provide for us, is a philosophical appreciation of the social values engaged by mothering as well as the value of individual autonomy. It's possible though, and important, for a feminist philosophy both to acknowledge the value of nurturant relationships between adults and to describe the unique relationship with our mothers. They are, after all, connected. We often emotionally reenact that first intimate relationship of our childhood in our adult relationships. But the fundamental significance of this relationship for moral philosophy has only recently begun to be explored philosophically, as for example in the work of Sara Ruddick (1982).

A FEMINIST MATERNAL ETHIC

Ruddick's objective in 'Maternal Thinking' is to define the moral structures of maternal thinking and the temptations and virtues conceived through the social practice of mothering. 'Interests in preservation, growth, and acceptability of the child govern maternal practices in general.' (Ruddick, 1972: 79). Each of these interests defines its own set of temptations and virtues. Her interest in preservation, for example, makes the mother liable to the temptations of fearfulness and excessive control, just as it defines the virtues of humility and resilient cheerfulness, according to Ruddick.

Ruddick implies that her description of maternal thinking is generally applicable to both men and women outside of biological or adoptive parenting practices (Ruddick, 1972: 89). But women who choose not to give birth appear as either disabled or moral failures in her analysis (Ruddick, 1972: 79 and 89). We must define a feminist maternal ethic that supports a woman's right not to have children. We must also recognize the problems and difficulties created by the institution of mothering that would lead some women to decide that they ought not to become mothers.

One such problem not fully discussed in Ruddick's article is child abuse. As Chinese mothers once bound their daughters feet, contemporary American mothers pass on to their daughters the physical and emotional abuse they suffered in childhood. No description of maternal thinking can be complete without a recognition of the rage and bitterness hidden in the heart of an abused child/mother. Carol Conger's courageous analysis of her child abuse in 'Child Abuse: A Lesbian Anarchist Perspective' (1983), suggests some of the short-comings of Ruddick's analysis and some possible directions for developing a more adequate feminist maternal ethic.

Ruddick describes the daily expression of the maternal virtue of cheerfulness as 'a matter-of-fact willingness to continue, to give birth and to accept having given birth, to welcome life despite its conditions.' (Ruddick, 1972: 81). Consider a possible effect of such a morality on a victim/survivor of child abuse. Such an attitude of cheerfulness might well seem utterly inauthentic, emotionally inconceivable. The imperative to be cheerful becomes, in fact, what Ruddick terms its degenerative form: denial. In the light of such a woman's experience, Ruddick's list of moral virtues evokes the very sentimentalized concept of motherhood that she wanted to avoid.

When cheerfulness is a moral virtue, furthermore, not being cheerful becomes another instance of a mother's failure, feeding into the patriarchal attack on mothers which both Adrienne Rich (1976) and Conger (1983) describe. One of the factors that lead to child abuse, according to Conger, is the 'rage and guilt at not being able to fulfill the romantic ideals of motherhood and childhood' (1983: 21).

The danger in defining idealized virtues as central to the maternal experience, as Ruddick has done, is that such an approach takes an emotionally privileged maternal practice as the norm. It can thus compound the suffering of women who are still striving to overcome the effects of their victimization. As Conger writes: 'The scars left on me will *always* impair my ability to love and respect myself and others' (1983: 21). In not evidencing a caring attitude towards the suffering of those women, such an ethic fails to reflect what must be a central value of feminist maternal ethic: a caring and nurturing of all women, along with their children.

Conger's analysis provides insight into an alternative conception of a feminist maternal ethic. Instead of accepting the maternal role, and defining its moral dimensions from within its present oppressive structures, her own work in 'reinventing child rearing' to eliminate the possibilities for abuse, involved radically transforming the entire institution of motherhood. Her radical approach involves bringing 'more women to mother children, trying to do away with acting out of the mother role/child role, teaching them to recognize and defend themselves against abuse, taking the issue out of the closet' (Conger, 1983: 20).

In order to encompass experiences as disparate as Ruddick's and Conger's, a feminist maternal ethic must be context dependent. We could thus recognize that the opportunities and obstacles present to mothers and their children differ radically. Rather than offering a set of ideals reflective of a given idealized

maternal practice, such an ethic could be based upon feelings of nurturance and compassion for others as well as the rights to be assertive and to pursue one's own goals. Since one can use such values not merely in relationships with one's own children, but in one's social life, the ethic would be applicable to non-mothers as well. Since some people, furthermore, are more successful at nurturing others than their own children, some women not only have a right not to mother but perhaps ought not to do so.

This framework for a feminist maternal ethic may enable us to proceed further in our project of integrating the apparently conflicting experiences of motherhood present in feminism. One starting point for this project might be a criticism of the individualist feminist tradition made by Ehrenreich and English (1978: 269–313). They charge that this tradition, which we've traced back to Beauvoir, is selfish and masculinist. This is a tough criticism for a 'career woman' to face, because there's more than a grain of truth in it. But a consideration of its implications can reveal much about the problems in defining a feminist analysis of mothering and maternal ethic.

FEMINISM AND SELFISHNESS

My own experience confirms the insight that being totally caught up with one's own self and one's success in a career insulates a person (traditionally, men) from another important aspect of human reality: the experience of true generosity and nurturing. I remember responding to a questionnaire a couple of years back about my anticipated future activities as a professor. At the time I couldn't imagine acting as a mentor for younger people in the field—'Who could I possibly help?' I remember asking myself, 'I'm the most junior member.'

The challenge for women who choose not to have children is in their temptation to evade relationships involving commitment and love. A career woman may fear, as Beauvoir described, that once she admits her vulnerabilities, she would be unable to stop from dumping her entire self onto the Other. We can see from this vantage point how Beauvoir felt this to be a temptation to abdicate the responsibility for one's own life. On the contrary, however, often only when a woman can admit her own feelings of vulnerability and dependency can she really accept herself, be receptive to other people, and be cognizant of their needs.

For those of us who are not mothers the challenge is to find other ways of expressing the social values that find their existential origins in the experience of motherhood. We can start by trying to understand the experience that was our daughterhood. This will help us come to terms with those feelings within ourselves which draw us into nurturing relationships. These are relationships in which we are genuinely concerned with the life and happiness of another person, in which competitiveness is not a defining feature, and in which we no longer fear our own individual obliteration in opening up to another person and giving of ourselves to them. For a career woman, it can mean learning to

help a younger colleague, for example, and to accept one's limitations without feeling threatened.

We can find opportunities for caring, nurturant relationships in many of our social relationships, with our clients, students, co-workers, friends, and family members. A career woman can feel a tremendous social responsibility to her aging parents or to young women in need of role models and mentors. Thus, claiming that a woman is selfish because she doesn't bear a child is a non sequitur: instead, one needs to look at all of her social relations to see whether she is practicing a maternal ethic.

The Second Sex reflects Beauvoir's profound concern for the fate of women, few of whom had access to the educational opportunities that enabled her to write so eloquently in defense of their liberation. A woman who is not a mother can devote herself, as Shirley Chisholm has done, for instance, to the struggle for social justice and opportunities for the children born of other women.

We should remember also that a feminist maternal ethic includes a recognition and affirmation of the rights to be assertive and to pursue one's own goals. It thus incorporates the values of individualist feminism, rather than rejecting them. The charge that pursuing one's individual goals is selfish can ignore the reality that respecting ourselves and our interests is part of a feminist maternal ethic. It is not something that society has made easy for any of us. It can also discourage women in nurturing roles from facing the moral challenges of self-affirmation. Indeed, learning how to be 'selfish' without feeling guilty can be as profound a challenge for a full-time nurturer, as learning to nurture can be for a woman used to the competitive environment of the public arena.

IS FEMINISM MASCULINIST?

This is a serious, troubling criticism, since it can imply that women who honestly prefer a career over motherhood are male-identified in that choice and especially in their rejection of women's traditional role. It thus raises important questions about who we are as women, who we will become as our roles change, and what will happen to our woman-identity in the process.

It would be hard to imagine anything more closely tied to a daughter's sense of being a woman than being a mother, since we get so much of our emotional concept of what a woman is by relating to real women, and, for most of us, the woman who was most present in our earliest, impressionable years was the woman (or women) who mothered us. But many career women, in fact, share the experience of having been treated in some respects as a son by their father. Our father often identified with us, giving us many of the pressures to achieve, if few of the privileges of freedom of movement that they would have given a son. My father was demanding and harshly critical of my performance at school, but wouldn't allow me to start the power mower or run the power saw. I could get hurt.

Beauvoir's father was much the same. I remember criticizing Beauvoir's perspective for being masculinist, in my dissertation on *The Second Sex* in

1976. And there is an element of truth in that criticism. She does accept what she terms masculine values, but not all of them. She only accepts those values of self assertion and individual achievement necessary for productive, creative work in the public sphere. She rejects those male values that denigrate women and consign them to a subordinate social sphere. She also criticizes male values that make relationships into battlegrounds.

Beauvoir's mother was a very traditional, religious woman, who identified with the role of a wife and mother. Beauvoir knew of few independent women in the professions, and none of them had children. Now more and more women, like me, have mothers who have also held full-time jobs. One result we might expect from this change is that women will increasingly come to experience a job or career as part of their identity as women rather than as something opposed to it, as Beauvoir did.

It's interesting to note, in this regard, that Beauvoir, in *The Second Sex*, does not disclaim her identity as a woman while accepting the male values of individual accomplishment. She just locates that identity elsewhere than in the values implicit in the role of wife-and-mother. She drew extensively on the work and insights of women writers who preceded her, such as Virginia Woolf, and acknowledged their insight into the tremendous difficulties and ambivalence experienced by women in trying to escape the confines of their traditional role. She thus identified with these women both as women and as writers, and she found confirmation of her own experiences in their writings.

Sexuality was another aspect of her experience that expressed her identity as a woman. One of the few instances in which she criticized men's values and experience in the name of woman's experience, comes in her description of sexuality. Woman has a more authentic erotic experience, she argues, than does man, who uses his aggressive posture to avoid seeing himself fully as flesh (1952: 450).

In a sense, her entire book, *The Second Sex*, is a reflection and analysis of her woman-identity; it is out of her experience that she feels so threatened by motherhood, so rejecting of the role that bourgeois society would force on her, a role that she saw as causing the death of her best friend Zaza. Those are a woman's experiences of oppression. I wonder now about the validity of charging Beauvoir with being masculinist. The connotations of the term are wholly negative in a feminist context. A simplistic charge, it ignores the importance of traditional 'masculine' values of economic, political, literary achievement in contemporary feminist practice.

We career women have unique experiences from which all women can learn. Career women extend the limitations of woman's traditional role, making inroads into male territory. Our challenge, like Beauvoir's is not to end up like men in the process. This means several things: First, one must make special efforts to tie into woman-identified activities. Secondly, heterosexual women need to overcome our alienation by the early lesbian-feminist definition of the woman-identified-woman and rediscover the pleasures and love of women friends.

Another difficult step is learning to be woman-identified in a male-dominated

career. This means learning loyalty to women who are trying to break into the field. It means trying to make it easier for them, those women who come after us, by forcing the criteria of excellence in our fields to accommodate themselves to women's lives. It means overcoming feelings of resentment and competitiveness against women colleagues in order not to force them to conform to the same alienating demands from the male status quo that we had to face. We must acknowledge and express our nurturing, maternal feelings. This will allow us to discover the power such feelings have to enable us to stand up for values which we may not find the strength to defend when it is only ourselves at stake.

Now that we've explored some of the problems in reconciling individualist feminism with those values and experiences that have identified women's traditional role, let's see if these explorations have suggested an alternative feminist position.

MOTHERHOOD AND HETEROSEXUALITY

The issue of a feminist analysis of motherhood is analogous in many ways to that of the other defining element in woman's traditional role: her heterosexual identification with a husband. Being attractive to a man has been seen, along with her desire to be a mother, as a defining element of a woman's female identity. A review of the problems raised in a feminist analysis of heterosexual marriage might thus provide some insight into the issue of motherhood.

The radical lesbian feminist redefinition of loving women as the only genuinely feminist expression of woman identity thus could provide a model for one alternative to the traditional identification of woman as mother. Analogous to the redefinition of woman's sexual love outside the context of heterosexual marriage would be a redefinition of the expression of women's nurturant love outside the context of motherhood. Such a view might argue, for example, that social activism nurturing and defending the lives of other women is more authentically feminist than the nurturing care of a child fathered by a man and destined to carry on a patriarchal heritage.

But this alternative shares with Beauvoir's rejection of motherhood the problematic claim that the redefined identity is superior—politically, in the case of the woman-identified-woman analogy and ethically, in the case of Beauvoir's analysis—to motherhood itself. We once again seem to be in the presence of an impasse. How can such positions be incorporated into a feminism which also recognizes an opposing view? For example, what if one believes that one's ethnic and racial heritage must be preserved for the future and that real social transformation must begin in the family where children, exposed to nurturing care by autonomous men and women, will create a future not defined by oppressive relations?

The context dependent character of the feminist maternal ethic provides a way out of this conceptual impasse by recognizing the real differences between women. Feminists espousing radically different views exist simultaneously,

each addressing important problems from equally valid, if different, perspectives. But, in working separately, they often remain ignorant of one another's interests. They thus fail to acknowledge those interests and even work against them. A racist white feminist, for example, could, if unchallenged, act on unacknowledged racist fears in working for birth control among poor women and women of color. A homophobic feminist could, if unchallenged, contribute to a resurgence of heterosexist oppression and violence against lesbians while alledgedly just building alliances with conservative women. Something like that has happened between some mothers and non-mothers.

If we are genuinely committed to combatting oppression in all its forms, and are willing to admit that the ever changing diversity of women's experiences prevents any one of us from ever reaching the definitive, absolute feminist position, then what we need is a method to maintain an openness of perspective. Inviting criticism is one such method which would seem to have application to the issue of motherhood, as well as that of heterosexuality.

The problem is that criticism can be seen—and be meant to be seen—as undermining the entire philosophical foundation of one's experience and identity, as radical lesbian feminism challenged women's participation in heterosexual relationships. But such criticism, especially that issued with the anger of long silenced frustration, provides us with the all too rare opportunity to learn about ourselves and, hopefully, to grow—as heterofeminists who have answered the radical lesbian challenge have discovered.

Of course, what one discovers are the limitations, the boundaries that define one's particular identity: that heterosexual marriage, for instance, does in fact require a woman to invest considerable emotional energy into a relationship with a man, energy which, in a lesbian relationship, would be given to a woman. Such a revelation, made possible by the radical lesbian criticism, can lead a heterosexual feminist to explore the emotional roots of her heterosexuality for the first time. This may lead to a new critical awareness and, eventually, to a more profound affirmation of herself and her own values.

Having one's assumptions called into question can thus be a valuable gift, especially for a philosopher. That seems to be the case here. Beauvoir radically called into question the philosophical foundations of woman's traditional role. In the dialectical process that followed, later feminists have responded to the gradual economic erosion of that role, by questioning the assumptions at the heart of Beauvoir's original criticism and defending the social values embedded in woman's mothering.

These criticisms, and our biological clocks, have, in turn, forced many women like myself to reconsider our previous rejection of motherhood and face the questions about our identity as women that such a reconsideration raises. 'Don't I really want children?' I felt forced to ask myself. 'Am I, in a prolonged adolescent rebellion against my parents, denying a need that is going to appear suddenly when I'm 45, and it's too late?'

My response to this challenge has been to formulate an alternative feminist analysis of motherhood that, hopefully, is appreciative of the social and individual value of motherhood while reflective of the validity of my own choice not

to become a mother. First, I define my position in juxtaposition to various other feminist perspectives, including Beauvoir's and the position on motherhood analogous to the radical lesbian analysis of heterosexuality. Then I briefly describe the features of my experience that support my position and conclude by suggesting some of the ethical challenges present in that experience.

FEMINIST ALTERNATIVES

One alternative to the feminist positions on motherhood described above could be based upon Adrienne Rich's (1976) distinction between the valuable experience of mothering and its oppressive institutionalized form. Such an alternative would be analogous to the efforts of heterosexual women to defend the experience of heterosexual love while attacking the oppressive institution of patriarchal marriage.

Both of these alternatives, in affirming the values implicit in women's lives, represent an advance upon Beauvoir's adoption of men's values and rejection and alienation from values engaged by women's traditional role.

I would suggest that we reject any feminist position that would try and limit any authentic alternatives of women by trying to find a new, fixed definition of woman's nature. Instead we should recognize that our sense of our woman-identity results from our experiences with the various women who have been important throughout our lives, especially the women who nurtured us in our childhood. We should reclaim, with pride and with humility at our frailties, as much of our identity as we can. But we should expect and willingly acknowledge the differences between us, in our senses of who we are and what constitutes our woman-identity, without succumbing to the temptation to justify our own identity by denying our sisters'.

We should celebrate the resultant spectrum of values with its vibrant oppositions as a sign of our flourishing explosion out of the narrow confines of our traditional sphere, even when those values at the same time express an authentic preference for motherhood over competitive careerism, for nurturant woman-loving lesbian identity over heterosexual marriage, for professional involvement in social change over domesticity, and for loving our loving-men over lesbian separatism.

I would like to propose a fourth alternative that builds on the other three; it would: (1) affirm, as Beauvoir does, that some women, without false consciousness, authentically desire and value the pursuit of a career over motherhood, if they are forced to choose or even if they see both as viable alternatives. This would acknowledge Beauvoir's insight and achievement in locating within her description of women's consciousness the existence of a desire for individual achievement and for the expression of productive cultural creativity that is properly understood as not being the sublimation of a supposedly more authentic desire for a child.

My alternative would however: (2) affirm that the desire for a child can be a morally authentic desire in no way inferior to the woman's desire for individual

achievement, thus rejecting Beauvoir's claim and a claim implicit in the alternative drawn by analogy from the woman-identified-woman position, that the desire for a child is by definition morally inauthentic, or a sign of false consciousness, etc.

I would also affirm, drawing on the definitions of oppression in both Rich and Beauvoir, that: (3) oppressive institutions are those that deny women opportunities for the expressive of her individual autonomy or her maternal/nurturing values. Correlatively, (4) few women in our society experience motherhood as real choice; for this to be a reality: (a) a woman must have other opportunities for personal development and social contribution; (b) she must feel that she can choose to not be a mother without jeopardizing her identity as a woman or abrogating her social responsibilities; and (c) she must feel that she can have a child without jeopardizing their economic and/or physical survival—something which is not possible for women today, as poverty becomes increasingly the province of women and their children. Thus moral obligations are ultimately inseparable from political change.

AN EXPERIENTIAL FOUNDATION

This feminist analysis of motherhood is based on my own experience, which reflects the increasingly prevalent reality of being raised in a family where both parents hold full-time jobs. My identity as a woman comes from the many different women in my life who have nurtured me, including my friend's grandmother who taught me to crochet, an activity I still find both comforting and womanly. Because my mother worked full-time for most of my childhood, I experience my career very much as my identification with her, although my grandfather, a retired Methodist circuit preacher, encouraged me to study philosophy by saying that we were the only two members of the family with the same profession.

But I feel closest to my mother in my work as a philosophy professor, identifying with her as a teacher in working with my students, but, even more so, in the intellectual probing of life's toughest questions. For that's how she has expressed her mothering, and her teaching, with a courageous and sympathetic desire to help us analyse and understand the reality of our experience.

Too many analyses of women's experience, such as the psychoanalytic work on motherhood, fail to acknowledge the growing number of women who are daughters of working mothers, whose identities are not ideologically or emotionally shaped by the experience of having been raised by a full-time mother. Our values express that different identity; we take pride in our independence, as our mothers often did. Some of us, perhaps especially those who felt closest to our mothers during the period of their most intense, productive, joyful involvement in their careers, can feel an emotional identification with them in our career that is not documented in these theories.

We need to describe the ways in which our identity as women is challenged and sustained in this experience, to give ourselves support and to encourage

other women to trust their feelings, if they feel the desire to choose not to have children.

As long as women are mothers, it will be an element in our woman-identity, but increasingly, it will not be the only, or defining element; nor will it be an experience women will have to give up because their job had been defined by career obsessed men. One of the ways these changes are coming about is through the current pressure on the economy to provide for national health insurance, adequate day care, and equal pay for jobs of equal worth, which would enable the growing number of single mothers to provide adequate support for their children.

We have to acknowledge that, for many women, who are stuck in dead-end, alienating jobs, motherhood is far more meaningful and significant. It can also be very meaningful for women in careers they enjoy and find rewarding; the two are not mutually exclusive. What we are seeing is the expansion of roles for women and new previously unimagined activities with new challenges and opportunities. What will happen in the future if babies are grown in test tubes? Will women as we know them disappear with that role? In a sense; each generation creates its nature anew, if there's any human population around to do it. Who can tell the future? Only the young.

CONCLUSION

Ethical challenges differ within different situations which are constantly changing. Trying to define an ethics is difficult, given all the changing factors. Not just historical, political, cultural and social but also the biological and emotional dimensions of mothering vary tremendously among women already and will continue to vary, in unpredictable ways in the years to come. The positive or negative feelings one has about one's membership in a community will affect one's decision about giving birth—just as one's feelings about the future do.

Within the context of a career, the decision not to be mother is the rejection of an opportunity that has been the source of profound meaning for many women. But it is not the only opportunity for the expression of nurturing social relationships, as is evident from the examples of great social contributions made by persons who have not been mothers. Furthermore, this experience of a moral dilemma in my thirties is a new feature of moral development. It fits neither the traditional pattern of development of a young mother nor that of a career man.

Something career women can do is claim our maternal feelings with pride. One of my mother's most humiliating experiences came during World War II, when she was pregnant and desperate for a teaching job. She was forced to take off the enormous coat she wore to hide her pregnancy, so that a male school principal could decide if she 'showed' too much to be allowed in a classroom. If motherhood was a sign of our shame, we should claim it with pride.

Beauvoir is wary of the return of the romantic motherhood-mystique as a return to oppressive roles. This is a political response, complicated by the French political context in which a 'woman-identified' group was able to win in court a copyright for the MLF, the French equivalent of a Women's Liberation Movement. No wonder that Beauvoir cannot identify 'sisterhood' and maternal feelings, and thus she adamantly denies any motherhood feelings in her own life. But surely her relationship with her young student Olga back in the thirties, a friendship which continues to this day, had many of the psychological colorings of her own relationship with her mother and provided Beauvoir, through its nurturing, with lessons learned typically by a mother. But Beauvoir refuses to consider any such interpretation of her relationships, including her current close friendship with a woman in her thirties. Surely this relationship also awakens emotional memories of mother and daughter in both participants. But Beauvoir adamantly refuses to identify with mothering.

My experiences lead me to a different response. When I was in graduate school, I met my first woman philosophy professor. She was a single woman in her fifties, 'on-loan' from another university as a visiting professor. She was a wonderful teacher who loved her students, a trait which (with her specialization in 'soft-headed' Eastern philosophy and religion) earned her the contempt of the male faculty, who ridiculed her for 'sublimating her maternal instinct.' It's time we claimed our maternal feelings with pride, instead of embarrassment, and challenged those of our male colleagues who are locked into teaching by ridicule and are training their (mostly male) students in philosophical combat, to have the courage to face the very unmasculine parts of themselves buried deep within their macho exteriors. It's the least we can do for our students.

REFERENCES

Beauvoir, Simone de. 1952. *The Second Sex*. Translated and edited by H. M. Parshley. Alfred A. Knopf, New York.

Beauvoir, Simone de. 1948. *The Ethics of Ambiguity*. Translated by Bernard Frechtman. The Citadel Press, Secaucus, New Jersey.

Boston Women's Health Collective. 1971. *Our Bodies, Our Selves*. New England Free Press, Boston.

Burton, Gabriella. 1972. *I'm Running away from Home, But I'm not Allowed to Cross the Street*. Avon Books, New York.

Conger, Carol. 1983. Child abuse: a lesbian anarchist perspective. *The Lesbian Inciter* 11, (July) 1: 20–21. *The Lesbian Inciter* is available from P. O. Box 7038, Powderhorn Station, Minneapolis, MN 55407, U.S.A.

Davis, Angela. 1981. *Women, Race, and Class*. Random House, New York.

Ehrenreich, Barbara and Deirdre English. 1978. *For her Own Good: 150 Years of the Expert's Advice to Women*. Anchor Press/Doubleday, Garden City, N.Y.

Firestone, Shulamith. 1970. *The Dialectic of Sex: the Case for Feminist Revolution*. William Morrow, New York.

Friedan, Betty. 1982. *The Second Stage*. Summit Books, New York.

Rich, Adrienne. 1976. *Of Woman Born: Motherhood as Experience and Institution*. W.
    W. Norton, New York.
Ruddick, Sara. 1982. Maternal thinking. In Thorne, Barrie and Marilyn Yalon, eds,
    Rethinking the Family: Some Feminist Questions. Longman, New York.
Wolgast, Elizabeth. 1980. *Equality and the Rights of Women*. Cornell University Press,
    Ithica, New York.

WOMEN AND LYING

A PRAGMATIC AND SEMANTIC ANALYSIS OF 'TELLING IT SLANT'

Gillian Michell

Tell all the Truth but tell it slant—
Success in circuit lies
Too bright for our infirm Delight
The Truth's superb surprise
As lightning to the Children eased
With explanation kind
The Truth must dazzle gradually
Or every man be blind—

Emily Dickinson's poem inspired Tillie Olson and in turn Adrienne Rich to adopt the expression 'telling it slant' for a way of speaking they believe is forced on women in male-dominated society (Rich, 1979a: 207). It is a way of speaking that conveys a message by distorting the truth somehow, so that what is conveyed is not the whole truth. The speaker who says (1a), for example, when it is (1b) that accurately describes the situation, is telling it slant.

1. (a) Joan and Bob don't always agree with one another.
   (b) Joan and Bob fight constantly with one another.

Intuitively, telling it slant seems to fall somewhere between being truthful and lying, but it would in most cases count as a lie by Sissela Bok's definition in her book *Lying:* for her, a lie is any statement which communicates an intentionally deceptive message, a message meant to make others believe what we ourselves do not believe (Bok, 1978: 14). And she intends lying in all contexts to have a very strong negative moral tone.

I claim, however, that for women telling it slant may nevertheless be excusable. Beginning with some examples of telling it slant, I will show how they

An earlier version of this paper was presented at the Fifth Annual Conference of the Canadian Society for Women in Philosophy, London, Ontario, October 15–17, 1982. For their help in trying to make a linguist pass among philosophers I am grateful to quite a number of patient feminist philosophers but most particularly to Barbara Houston.

can be categorized, using categories that arise from a set of supposedly general and widely cited rules for rational conversation proposed by Paul Grice. In each example, one or another of Grice's rules is deliberately violated. An examination of the relationship between the violations and certain aspects of women's experience leads to my conclusion that for women telling it slant is what makes it possible to exchange information in a sexist setting.

I. EXAMPLES OF TELLING IT SLANT

In each of the following four examples, a situation is described to which the speaker responds in a way that distorts the truth.[1]

Example 1: You, the speaker, are talking to the husband of a friend about the division of housework at their house. Your friend has complained to you that her husband only goes through the motions of sharing the work, though he sees himself as the ideal feminist man. He boasts that he does the dinner dishes every night and says *his* wife has nothing to complain about. Not wanting to undermine your own credibility or your friend's hope of change by coming on to rabidly, you tell it slant by saying (2a), rather than the truth, (2b).

  2. (a) But maybe doing the dinner dishes isn't really a fair share of the house-
         work.
     (b) But doing the dinner dishes isn't a fair share of the housework.

This response downplays or softens the whole truth.

Example 2: You're playing volleyball with a mixed group from work. One of the men keeps poaching shots from your part of the court. You tell it slant by saying (3a), rather than the truth (3b).

  3. (a) You're poaching everybody else's shots.
     (b) You're poaching my shots.

This response exaggerates the actual situation.

Example 3: You're making excuses for missing a meeting to the man who chairs the committee. You had had terrible menstrual cramps, so at the time of the meeting you'd been home in bed, trying to proofread a report you'd finished the day before. You say the slant (4a), instead of the more accurate (4b).

---

[1] The examples given here are restricted in context to white, middle-class experience. Grice's rules are implicitly rules for white middle-class conversation, and the claim I am making is that they are perhaps applicable only to same sex, white, middle-class conversation. I am not in a position to describe the ways in which telling it slant might be similar or different within or across other races or classes, though Ochs [Keenan] (1974, 1976) has raised questions about the universality of Grice's rules on the basis of her studies of Malagasy society.

4. (a) Sorry I missed the meeting—I had to finish that report for the dean.

   (b) Sorry I missed the meeting—I had terrible cramps.

The excuse given is plausible but not the most salient one.

Example 4: A man in your department calls into question your judgment on a moral issue and mentions Kohlberg's claim that women are less developed morally than men. You counter with (5a), not (5b).

5. (a) There's a psychologist at Harvard whose work suggests Kohlberg's theory isn't valid because of its male bias.

   (b) There's a woman/woman psychologist/feminist/feminist psychologist/psychologist called Carol Gilligan at Harvard whose work suggests that Kohlberg's theory isn't valid because of its male bias.

This response is worded so as to obscure the sex of the psychologist in question.

These are all examples of telling slant, since in each case the truth is distorted or withheld in some way without any of them actually being completely false. But the examples differ from one another in the way they distort the truth. The next section of the paper describes an approach to categorizing the types of distortion or deception which can also, I think, be used in accounting for the practice of telling it slant.

II. GRICE'S COOPERATIVE PRINCIPAL AND CONVERSATIONAL MAXIMS

The approach comes from Paul Grice's 'Logic and conversation' (1975), derived from his 1967 William James lectures. It has been used in this analysis because its usefulness has been demonstrated previously in much insightful work in the philosophy of language and linguistic pragmatics.

Grice views conversation as rational behaviour, and he claims that a primary purpose of conversation is the maximally effective exchange of information. He recognizes that conversation is also characteristically a cooperative undertaking, and claims that as such it is governed by what he calls the Cooperative Principle, given in (6).

6. *The Cooperative Principle:* Make your conversational contribution such as is required, at the stage at which it occurs, by the accepted purpose or direction of the talk exchange in which you are engaged (Grice, 1975: 67).

Grice offers no argument for this claim, but the cooperative nature of conversation is well-established by ethnomethodological research. See, for example, Sack *et al.* (1974) and Schegloff (1982). Grice elaborates the Cooperative Principle into four categories of conversational maxims and submaxims which must be observed, he says, in order to abide by the principle. These maxims are given in (7).

7. *Conversational Maxims*

Maxim of Quantity: Make your contribution as informative as is required (for the current purposes of the exchange).

Maxim of Quality: Try to make your contribution one that is true.
(i) Do not say what you believe to be false.
(ii) Do not say that for which you lack adequate evidence.

Maxim of Relation: Be relevant.

Maxim of Manner: Be perspicious.
(i) Avoid obscurity of expression.
(ii) Avoid ambiguity.
(iii) Be brief (or avoid unnecessary prolixity).
(iv) Be orderly (Grice, 1975: 67).[2]

It should be noted at this point that there are certain assumptions behind the Cooperative Principle and the Conversational Maxims concerning the conversational participants whose behaviour they govern. Grice's Principle and Maxims take it as a necessary (though implicit) assumption that the participants are equal or matched or at least in agreement in certain essential respects. First, the Cooperative Principle refers to the '*accepted* purpose or direction of the talk exchange' [my emphasis], assuming there is no problem in gaining this acceptance from both participants. Then the Maxim of Quantity specifies that contributions to the conversation are to be 'as informative' and 'not more informative' than is required, again assuming that the participants recognize and accept the same requirements for informativeness. The Maxim of Quality assumes participants share the same perceptions of reality and recognize the same evidence as convincing. Further, although Grice mentions various potential problems concealed in the formulation of the Maxim of Relation, 'Be relevant', he does not raise the possibility that the participants might disagree on what is relevant. Finally, the Maxim of Manner, 'Be perspicuous', appears to assume that perspicuity would mean the same thing to different participants.

The assumption that the conversational participants are alike in these respects, which I will return to later, is essential to Grice's purpose in proposing the Cooperative Principle and its accompanying maxims, which is to account for *conversational implicature*. This is the process by which a speaker says something which blatantly flouts one of the maxims, and the hearer, assuming that the Cooperative Principle is being observed, interprets the speaker as having implicated another proposition. Thus, to use one of Grice's examples, a statement like (8)

[2] In his article Grice includes a second submaxim of quantity. 'Do not make your contribution more informative than is required', but he suggests, and I agree, that it may be disputable, in part because to be overinformative might be no more than a waste of time, rather than an uncooperative act (Grice, 1975: 67). In a 1981 article Grice proposed adding a fifth submaxim of manner, 'Frame whatever you say in the form most suitable for any reply that would be regarded as appropriate', to deal with some questions concerning the theory of descriptions and the theory of presupposition. He ultimately concluded that his solution would not work for the problem at hand. Since I think this submaxim is different in type from the others, I have chosen not to include it.

8. You're the cream in my coffee.

is clearly false and so violates the Maxim of Quality. What is implicated to the hearer by (8) is that the speaker is attributing to the hearer 'some feature or features in respect of which the audience resembles (more or less fancifully) the mentioned substance (Grice, 1975: 71)'. Thus certain types of metaphor can be accounted for by conversational implicature.

Another example of conversational implicature, also from Grice, is the following letter from a faculty member about a student who is a candidate for a philosophy job:

9. Mr. X's command of English is excellent, and his attendance at tutorials has been regular.

This violates the Maxim of Quantity, since the faculty member must know more about the student than is given here and knows that more is expected in such a letter. What is being implicated by what is said and what is not said, then, is that the student is no good at philosophy.

These and other examples of conversational implicature make a fairly convincing case for the existence of rules like the Cooperative Principle and the Conversational Maxims. A phenomenon that depends for its effectiveness, first, on mutual recognition of certain norms governing conversation, and, second, on mutually recognized and systematic interpretations of their violations could not be so widespread otherwise.

In summary, for conversational implicature to work, both speaker and hearer must know that a Conversational Maxim has been violated. The speaker exploits the Maxim in the breach on the assumption that the hearer will recognize this and figure out what the words actually said are intended to convey.

III. TELLING IT SLANT AS
VIOLATIONS OF GRICE'S RULES

Telling it slant uses—or abuses—Grice's Cooperative Principle and Conversational Maxims in a different way from conversational implicature. In telling it slant, the speaker wishes to be taken to be observing the Cooperative Principle and the Maxims when in fact she is not. We can get a better idea of how this is done by analysing the examples and categorizing them in terms of the Maxims they violate.

The first example, 'But maybe doing the dinner dishes isn't really a fair share of the housework', violates the Maxim of Quantity, because the speaker's contribution is not as informative as is required, given her beliefs. She is saying less than the whole truth in asserting that the proposition is only possibly true, rather than certainly true. This way of telling it slant is commonly called *understatement*.

In the second example, the speaker says, 'You're poaching everybody else's

shots', when the truth is that only her shots are being poached. This is commonly called *overstatement*, and it violates the Maxim of Quality, since the speaker is saying that for which she lacks adequate evidence. One could argue that the general maxim, '*Try* [my emphasis] to make your contribution one that is true', has been met; that is, that the speaker has met the requirement of trying, since the proposition that the man is poaching everybody else's shots, while untrue, does entail the true one, that there is someone, namely, the speaker, whose shots he is poaching. Whether this justification is accepted or not, the entailment relation between the slant statement and the one that tells it straight should be noticed.

In the third example, the speaker follows an apology for having missed a meeting with a statement about having to finish a report. This violates the Maxim of Relation in implying that the need to finish the report was relevant to missing the meeting. The statement about the report is true, of course, but it is not the true explanation that it appears to be to the hearer. We can call this way of telling it slant the *Red Herring*.

In the fourth example, the speaker tells it slant in order to obscure the sex of the psychologist whose work challenges Kohlberg's. This I consider to be a violation of the Maxim of Manner, more specifically of either submaxim (1), 'Avoid obscurity of expression', or submaxim (ii), 'Avoid ambiguity'.[3]

Some people might argue that it is not telling it slant to omit the sex of the researcher being referred to. They might even claim that it would be overinformative to specify it. I would deny this on two counts. First I would claim that under normal conditions the sex would be specified if the referent is a woman. If the speaker is a feminist, she would make a point of including the researcher's sex in the form of expression she chose. This would conform with the feminist practice of taking special care to acknowledge or even accentuate the contributions made by women, in compensation for traditional sexist nonrecognition. On the other hand, if the speaker were a traditional sexist, the sex of the researcher would still be something to be mentioned, since in the sexist view it is strange for a woman to have a profession; hence, *lady doctor*, *lady lawyer*, and so forth, which alert the hearer to something peculiar. It is to avoid this alerting that the speaker in my example suppresses the sex of the researcher, a particularly germane move where sex is central to the argument. If the speaker were to mention the sex of the researcher, it would reduce the credibility of the research findings in the mind of the hearer, a painful truth that the speaker acknowledges in telling it slant.

Again in this example, as in the last, the slant version is perfectly true, but the form of expression is carefully chosen to conceal another relevant truth. For lack of a better name I will call this way of telling it slant *Equivocation*, since the manner of expression is chosen precisely because it has two or more

[3] *Psychologist* is technically an example of vagueness rather than ambiguity in terms of sex, but I assume that an exhaustive listing of sins of manner would include vagueness with intent to obscure, along with obscurity of expression and ambiguity.

interpretations and can be expected to mislead the hearer in a predictable direction.

I have shown how each of my four examples illustrates a different way of telling it slant, and I have characterized those differences as arising from the different Conversational Maxims which each violates. One of my claims, then, is that telling it slant is accomplished pragmatically by deliberately violating the Cooperative Principle and its component Maxims, while making it appear to the hearer that they are being observed.

IV. SCALAR PREDICATES
AND TELLING IT SLANT

While my account of telling it slant has till now used a purely pragmatic approach, there is another kind of regularity which holds between propositions expressed in slant versions and propositions in the corresponding wholly true versions of a statement. This regularity is both semantic and pragmatic and is found in the understatement and overstatement categories of telling it slant. It exploits scalar predicates, which are discussed at length in Larry Horn's 1972 dissertation, 'On the Semantic Properties of Logical Operators in English'.

Scalar predicates are sets of predicates the values of which constitute named points on a continuum. The relative positions on the continuum are shown by Horn to have linguistic consequences in terms of the presuppositions, entailments, and conversational implicatures that attach to sentences using these predicates. They show up in a range of linguistic categories, of which examples are given in (9).

9. (a) *Adjectives*
      passable . . . attractive . . . pretty . . .
      beautiful

   (b) *Adverbs*
      Verb-modifying
      seriously . . . critically . . . mortally
      [wounded]
      Sentence modifying
      possibly . . . probably . . . necessarily

   (c) *Verbs*
      gloss over . . . overlook . . . ignore

   (d) *Quantifiers*[4]
      some . . . many . . . most . . . all.

---

[4] I concede, with Horn, that some if not all logicians will find it unsettling to describe quantifiers as predicates. The category they belong to is not crucial for this presentation.

Horn states that it is a general fact of natural language that scalar predicates are lower-bounded by assertion and upper-bounded by implicature (if not pre-supposition) (1972: 52). 'Lower-bounded by assertion' means that a sentence containing a scalar predicate asserts that at least that value on the scale holds or entails that propositions containing scalar predicates lower on the scale are true. Thus, if (10a) is true, (10b) must be true, but not (10c).

10. (a) The rapist was critically wounded.

    (b) The rapist was seriously wounded.

    (c) The rapist was mortally wounded.

The entailment relation between (10a) and (10b) makes a sentence like (11a) anomalous, while the lack of such a logical relation between (10a) and (10c) makes (11b) acceptable.

11. (a) The rapist was critically but not seriously wounded.

    (b) The rapist was critically but not mortally wounded.

'Upper bounding' means that if a sentence containing a scalar predicate is said, the implicature or presupposition is that stronger predicates on the same scale do not apply. That is, the use of 'pretty' to describe someone conversationally implicates that no stronger term, such as 'beautiful' or 'gorgeous' or 'stunning', applies or is appropriate.[5] The 'if not' construction in (12a) is used to suspend that implication, and its anomalous use in (12b) shows that it cannot be used to open the possibility that a weaker predicate might be more accurate.

12. (a) The rapist was critically if not mortally wounded.

    (b) The rapist was critically if not seriously wounded.

The importance of scalar predicates for my purposes is that two of the kinds of examples of telling it slant I have given can be described as exploitations of the semantic and pragmatic relationships that hold between propositions containing linguistic elements that belong to a common scale. Understatements such as 'But maybe doing the dinner dishes isn't really a fair share of the housework' and 'Joan and Bob don't always agree with one another' are true but mislead because what is implicated conversationally is that to the speaker's knowledge no stronger statement can be made, which is not true. Overstatements, on the other hand, are not strictly true but entail or presuppose a proposition that is.

---

[5] Conversational implicature is used here to describe a phenomenon somewhat different from the one Grice originally wanted to account for by proposing the Cooperative Principle and the Conversational Maxims. Horn and many other linguists have adopted the phrase to describe the pragmatic relation between what is said and what a hearer should understand the speaker to have been trying to get across that is not part of the literal meaning of the words but follows if Grice's rules are being observed.

The speaker is claiming that 'You're poaching X's shots' applies in a wider range of cases than it does, namely, to all cases instead of just her own.

In the previous section I described a method of categorizing types of telling it slant based on conversational or pragmatic rules, and in this one the nature of some of the semantic and pragmatic relations between propositions using scale predicates that speakers can use to produce two very common kinds of telling it slant, understatement and overstatement. The next section provides some description of the circumstances in which speakers, particularly women, resort to telling it slant.

V. THE CONTEXT OF TELLING IT SLANT

If an appropriate categorization of the ways of telling it slant arises from the maxims that govern rational discourse, and if telling it slant depends on violating those maxims, then an adequate account must explain, first, what it is about the context of conversation that is perceived by speakers as requiring them to violate such important maxims, and, second, what is gained by not observing the Cooperative Principle and the Maxims.

The answer to the first question can be found, I think, in two sources: the first being some unexamined assumptions behind the Cooperative Principle and the Conversational Maxims, and the second certain of the restrictions on the cultural and linguistic rights of women in patriarchal society.[6]

The unexamined assumptions behind the Cooperative Principle and the Conversational Maxims are those I mentioned earlier concerning the conversational participants whose behaviour they govern. Grice appears to assume that mutual understanding and acceptance of the parameters guiding cooperative and appropriate conversational contributions are given in any normal conversation; however, the empirical evidence indicates that they are anything but. First, the 'purpose or direction of the talk exchange'—that is, the discourse topic—is not something that is 'accepted' without work, or something that stays accepted. Topics cannot be established unilaterally by one conversational participant; they must be negotiated. One participant can introduce a topic, but it must be taken up by the other participant in order to become the established

---

[6] A third source which might be suggested is the claim that the rules for structuring polite conversation override the rules that govern rational conversation; that is, that it is more important to be polite than it is to convey information effectively. Robin Lakoff makes this claim, saying that

'Grice's Conversational Participles are usable only in case there is no possibility of conflict with the Rules of Politeness, or in situations in which polite conversation is not felt to be required' (1975: 72).

She goes on to claim that when politeness is required, which is normally the case for women, conversational implicature must be used to convey information. But telling it slant cannot be accounted for by conversational implicature, and, though politeness is certainly a requirement that restricts conversational options, the treatment Lakoff gives it is too general to make it the most useful approach to accounting for telling it slant.

topic of conversation, and at each conversational turn that topic may or may not be maintained.

The required degree of informativeness called for by the Maxim of Quantity is not necessarily obvious either. Beyond the question of whether the speaker is accurate in her or his beliefs about the hearer's background knowledge relative to the matters under discussion are more delicate questions regarding how much information the speaker may appropriately give or assume the hearer to have.[7]

Cooperativeness in making true contributions as required by the Maxim of Quality assumes shared beliefs and shared standards for what counts as adequate evidence. This is frequently not the situation in which a conversation takes place. One of the problems, for example, in discussing the pro-choice position on abortion with someone in the anti-choice camp is to find any common ground at all—starting with whether the issue is choice or the murder of the unborn.

The problem of what the 'real' issue is on abortion is also illustrative of one of the major problems in observing the Maxim of Relevance. Wilson and Sperber (to appear) define a proposition P as relevant in a context $C_1 \ldots C_n$ if and only if there is at least one proposition logically implied by the union of P and $C_1 \ldots C_n$ which is not implied by either alone, where the context is made up of previously expressed propositions as well as propositions derived from memory, observation, and inference. A statement made by a pro-choice speaker will only be accepted as a relevant contribution, then, if what is said combines appropriately with the hearer's context, which, given the content of the pro-fetal life position, it is often unlikely to do.

Being perspicuous, in accordance with the Maxim of Manner, is also a far from straightforward matter. Differences in standards regarding the component submaxims are regularly observed, for example, when a philosopher and a hard-line empiricist try to discuss a topic of concern to both disciplines from their respective disciplinary approaches. The philosopher tends to be experienced as hopelessly prolix and obscure of expression, the empiricist as recklessly ambiguous and disorderly (at least from my own perspective on the fence).

In summary, then, there are a number of assumptions implicit in the formulation of Grice's Cooperative Principle and Conversational Maxims about the extent to which conversational participants share knowledge, beliefs, and values which are not valid assumptions in many if not most settings. This is not to deny the usefulness of Grice's rules but to underline the necessity of taking account of the effect of differences between conversational participants on various dimensions on the operation of those rules.

In the present case I want to argue that the challenge to the 'normal' functioning of Grice's rules becomes critical when there are systematic disparities between the conversational participants.

---

[7] Some discussion of ways in which a speaker can give the hearer required information when it would be insulting if the speaker made explicit her or his belief that the hearer does not already have the information is included in Michell (1975).

This would be the situation in conversation between a woman and a man.[8] If we take the situation simply to be one in which any woman and any man are conversing, too many parameters remain unspecified. The situation which would most clearly illustrate the effects of sex difference on Grice's framework would be one in which as many parameters as possible are held constant, that is, have the same value for both participants, so that they will not interfere with the effects attributable to sex difference. This ought to be the case when peers or intimates are talking: students, spouses, or co-workers, for example; however, research shows that even among peers and intimates sex is a variable that has significant effects, and that these effects can be expected to have a major impact on the interpretation of Grice's rules.

One class of research findings on sex differences that has very general implications for the organization of conversation concerns the relative roles of women and men in defining or creating the culture in which we live. Anthropological, sociological, and psychological evidence attests to the fact that women have been largely excluded from creating the model of society that shapes the institutions which socialize and organize us.[9] Dorothy Smith claims that there is a circle effect in operation, whereby men attend to and treat as significant only what men say. She says:

> 'The circle of men whose writing and talk was significant to each other extends backward in time as far as our records reach. What men were doing was relevant to men and was written by men about men for men. Men listened and [still] listen to one another's [words]' (Smith, 1978: 281).

Jean Baker Miller explains some of the effects of this closed circle (1976). She argues that the maintenance of male supremacy has required men to promulgate the belief that there is only one reality which it is their position to define. Those areas which that definition of reality cannot encompass have been denied. Not by chance, these are the very areas that have been assigned to women, areas in which things go wrong, inexplicable and unpleasant things happen, and order cannot be maintained. This includes much of the reality of human experience, particularly in the area of social relations. Dale Spender calls this view of reality 'tunnel vision' and thinks it explains the cliché that men are frequently unable to understand what woman are talking about. Women's experience, by contrast, requires them to accommodate the apparent contradictions of everyday life, and this results in their having a more complex awareness of meaning and their being able to handle multiple realities that incorporate the dominant male reality as well as their own (Spender 1980: 90–96). (This of course is a very broad generalized sketch and ignores exceptions.)

---

[8] I might say that some of the points I will be making about women could be made of other oppressed groups too, but women's use of telling it slant is my interest here.

[9] A summary of this research is to be found in Spender's chapter 'the dominant and the muted' in *Man Made Language* (1980).

The situation in which conversation is set, then, is one where the maintenance of male monodimensional reality requires the rejection of women's meanings as unreal or at best trivial.

The second class of research findings which has implications for interpreting Grice's rules has to do with differences in the way conversations are regulated that depend on whether the participants are of the same sex or of different sexes. One relevant finding is that in mixed-sex conversations males control conversational topic. Fishman's ethnomethodological analysis of taped conversations between mixed-sex couples at home led her to conclude that women made the efforts in conversation, but that men controlled the choice of conversational topic by choosing whether to respond to topics preferred by the women (Fishman, 1977: 1978).

A second ethnomethodological study, by Zimmerman and West (1975), gives additional information as to how males control conversations. They observed an uneven distribution by sex of silences and interruptions in conversations between mixed-sex student pairs that did not show up in same-sex conversations. They concluded that both silences and interruptions were used by males to control topic. Silences signalled non-support for the continued development of a female-chosen topic, while repeated interruptions of the female speaker by her male partner either restricted the female's right to contribute to a male-chosen topic or resulted in the abandonment of a female-chosen topic. A point of interest about Fishman's subjects is that all professed themselves to be 'sympathetic' to the women's movement, so any bias from the choice of subject could be expected to be in the direction of egalitarian behaviour.

A final point relating to conversation concerns the amount of talk that each sex produces. Although it is a common belief that women talk too much and that they talk more than men, there is no research that supports it; however, there do exist a number of studies that show that men talk more than women. Spender explains this contradiction by positing that the amount of talk produced by women is compared not with the standard set by men but with the standard of silence. If the desired standard is silence, then any amount of talk by women is too much (Spender, 1980: 42).

To sum up this research, then, female-male conversation takes place in a male-defined culture which features a monodimensional view of reality; men expect women to do the 'chores' involved in keeping conversations running smoothly but themselves control what topics are discussed; and men do most of the talking.

VI. MALE DOMINANCE AND THE
INTERPRETATION OF GRICE'S RULES

What happens when male dominance of conversational space in mixed-sex conversation is taken into account in interpreting Grice's rules? Let's look again

at the maxims to see how each is affected by male-defined reality, male control of conversational topic, and the greater amount of male talk.

In applying the Maxim of Quantity, what might seem to a woman to be an appropriately informative contribution would seem over-informative to her male conversational partner. Telling it slant by saying 'But maybe doing the dinner dishes isn't really a fair share of the housework' gives less of the speaker's information than the straight unqualified statement would, and it is correspondingly more likely to be accepted. Note that the informativeness relates to how much information you have available, and that women are not supposed to know too much, particularly since they are not in a position to define reality. Thus, the need for a woman to hedge her statements.

An interesting example of the institutionalization of this pretence of knowing less is found in what has been called the Doctor/Nurse Game (Stein, 1967). In this setting, the nurse, because she is responsible for the primary care of patients, often has better knowledge than the doctor of what changes in treatment are called for, for example. Yet traditionally she has had to present her observations in such a manner as to make appear that it is only the doctor who can make sense of them and decide what is to be done. The nurse must present the salient facts while not giving it away that she knows what they are salient to. Of course, with the growing recognition of the professional competence of nurses, seen for example in the development of nurse-practitioners, as well as the decrease in the number of doctors, particularly women, with god complexes, this game is played less frequently these days, though it still appears to be alive and well.

The conclusion we are led to is that if a woman wishes to be seen by the dominant male as observing the Maxim of Quantity, she should probably make her contribution an understatement or qualification of what she believes.

When the Maxim of Quality is interpreted relative to male conversational dominance, we see that the dice are loaded against a woman being able to make a contribution which is true. Given that the truth is so often more complicated than a lie, it is likely to take considerably more conversational space to set out, yet a woman's smaller amount of talk and restricted ability to introduce and develop conversational topics limit her opportunity to make her point. Then, her evidence and her truth may conflict with or be outside male reality. Further, if a woman's role in conversation is to facilitate male topics by doing specific kinds of interactional work and generally 'being available' in case of need, somewhat like a block parent, then it may be that the truth of her contributions are of much less importance to the effective functioning of the conversation than it would be if the participants had equal rights.

The example I gave of telling it slant by violating the Maxim of Quantity had a woman accusing a male volleyball player of poaching everybody else's shots, rather than just her own. On the surface of it, this overstatement seems to be a gratuitous lie, in which the speaker asserts that a proposition holds in a wider range of cases than it really does. But it is in fact an example that depends on an understanding of male reality. Diller and Houston (1982) cite empirical

evidence that, in mixed-sex sports, males by preference make their plays, by throwing the ball or whatever, to other male players, even if the female players are more skilled than the males. Apparently in some sense the females don't count as players in the male world view. So to accuse a male of poaching a female player's shots would not have much impact. On the other hand, being a good team player is recognized as an important component of the male value system, so an accusation of poaching *everybody* else's shots, where 'everybody' would include men as well, would get a real man where it hurts. And he could hardly deny it by saying that he was in fact only poaching one person's shots who, being a woman, didn't count. Looked at in this light, the speaker's slant version is an effective way of making her point.

Comparable effects could be expected on interpretation of the Maxim of Relevance. Relevant contributions by a woman in a male-dominated conversation would most likely be those perceived as supportive of a male-chosen topic or facilitative of its development. Minimally a relevant contribution would have to relate to male-defined reality; hence, the problem with saying that cramps are the real reason for missing the meeting. Cramps unquestionably belong among the disorderly and chaotic things which women are responsible for and male reality ignores, and it has long been a condition of acceptance into the male world of work that women deny the importance of 'their' part of human experience and pretend male reality is their reality too. In male reality the most acceptable excuse for missing a meeting is a higher status, higher priority, job-related task. A report for the dean would meet this criterion.

The Maxim of Manner interacts with male conversational dominance predictably as well. What being brief means for a woman is clear enough, while avoiding ambiguity and obscurity of expression, and probably being orderly as well, would be achieved by not talking about anything outside male reality. The example I gave to illustrate telling it slant by violating the Maxim of Manner had the speaker refer to a woman researcher using terms that obscured her sex. This is again a concession to male-defined reality, where a professional woman's credibility is potentially suspect, and nowhere more than where her work challenges the patriarchal order. By obscuring sex and stressing research credentials the speaker makes a stronger case for the researcher's findings and her own argument.

I have attempted to illustrate here the ways in which sex differences affecting the context and content of mixed-sex conversations have a systematic influence on the interpretation of Grice's rules. The remaining task is to summarize what is gained and lost by telling it slant and by not observing the Cooperative Principle and the Conversational Maxims.

VII. WHAT IS GAINED AND LOST
BY TELLING IT SLANT

There is a common thread running through the explications of each of my examples. This is that the slant versions get the speaker's point across in a way

that the male hearer is likely to accept and attend to, while the straight versions do not. Yet one of Grice's basic assumptions is that the purpose of observing the Cooperative Principle and the Conversational Maxims is to achieve the maximally effective exchange of information. The constraints on women's linguistic and conversational rights in our society make following Grice's rules counterproductive for women in terms of achieving the end that those rules are supposed to serve. For a woman to achieve the maximally effective exchange of information in a sexist setting, to get her point across in a way that works, her only solution is the judicious and covert violation of the conversational rules that we call telling it slant. So what a woman gains by telling it slant is the means of communicating information effectively. And it is the strength of the implicit norms governing mixed-sex conversation that is recognized in the claim that women are forced to tell it slant in patriarchal society.

But there is another major gain that motivates women to tell it slant. A woman will often resort to telling it slant in order to avoid the risk of hurting her hearer. This risk weighs heavily with women, and Spender's transcripts of CR group discussions show that it is a common practice for women to 'protect' men from the inadequacies of their definitions of reality, on the assumption that they could not cope with the truth. But it is a harder claim to establish that the need to protect men from the truth is so important that it too forces women to tell it slant. Telling it slant is perhaps not a survival strategy in this case. It is a choice, and the cost of the choice must be recognized.

This brings us to the question of what is lost by telling it slant. First, telling it slant to men serves to restrict male access to the knowledge of the real complexity of human experience and consequently perpetuates monodimensional male reality. We tell it slant at the cost of perpetuating the situation that makes it necessary.

Another cost of telling it slant is that we may lose the habit of telling it straight, even with those who have no real power over us, such as our female peers. Telling it slant to be supportive, to avoid causing hurt, can withhold from someone the truth she needs to make sense of the complexities of her existence, a point made with great eloquence in Rich's 'Women and Honor'. Further, as Rich also says, 'Lies are usually attempts to make everything simpler—for the liar—than it really is, or ought to be' (1979b: 187–188).

I will finish by reviewing the major points I have tried to make in this paper. I began by showing how examples of telling it slant could be categorized as violations of conversational rules that Grice has claimed must be followed in order to achieve the maximally effective exchange of information. I argued that the constraints on women's rights and options in male-dominated conversations were such that, paradoxically, it was only by violating these rules that a woman could achieve this goal. Thus, in this sense, the claim that women are forced to tell it slant in patriarchal society is justified.

We see that women are faced with a dilemma. If we tell it straight, our truth is not communicated effectively; if we tell it slant, what is communicated effectively is not really our truth. This dilemma complicates moral choices about truth telling for women in the most ordinary of circumstances. It may be that

for a woman to tell the truth requires more courage and requires it more often than we had thought.

REFERENCES

Bauman, Richard and Joel Sherzer, eds. 1974. *Explorations in the Ethnography of Speaking.* Cambridge University Press, Cambridge, Mass.

Bok, Sissela. 1978. *Lying.* Vintage, New York.

Cole, Peter, ed. 1981. *Radical Pragmatics.* Academic Press, New York.

Cole, Peter and Jerry Morgan, eds. 1975. *Syntax and Semantics 3: Speech Acts.* Academic Press, New York.

Davidson, Donald and Gilbert Harman, eds. 1975. *The Logic of Grammar.* Dickinson, Encino, Cal.

Diller, Ann, and Barbara Houston. 1982. Women's physical education: a gender-sensitive perspective. In Postow, Betsy, ed., *Women, Philosophy, and Sport.* Scarecrow Press, Metuchen, N.J.

Fishman, Pamela. 1977. Interactional shitwork. *Heresies* 1: 99–101.

Fishman, Pamela. 1978. Interaction: The work women do. *Social Problems* 25: 397–406.

Grandy, R. ed. Forthcoming. *Festschrift for Paul Grice.*

Grice, H. Paul. 1975. Logic and conversation. In Davidson, Donald and Gilbert Harman, eds, *op. cit.* (Also in Cole, Peter and J. Morgan eds, *op. cit.*).

Grice, H. Paul. 1981. Presupposition and conversational implicature. In Cole, Peter, ed., *op. cit.*

Horn, Laurence R. 1972. On the semantic properties of logical operators in English. Ph.D. dissertation, University of California, Los Angeles.

Lakoff, Robin. 1975. *Language and Woman's Place.* Harper & Row, New York.

Michell, Gillian. 1975. A pragmatic analysis of sentence adverbs; a study with particular reference to *obviously.* University Microfilms, Ann Arbor.

Miller, Jean Baker. 1976. *Towards a New Psychology of Women.* Beacon, Boston.

Ochs Keenan, Elinor. 1974. Norm-makers, norm-breakers: uses of speech by men and women in a Malagasy community. In Baumann, Richard and Joel Sherzer, eds, *op. cit.*

Ochs Keenan, Elinor. 1976. On the universality of conversational implications. *Language in Society* 6: 67–80.

Rich, Adrienne. 1979a. Conditions for work: The common world of women. In her *Lies, Secrets, and Silence: Selected Prose 1966–78.* Norton, New York.

Rich, Adrienne. 1979b. Women and honor: Some notes on lying. In her *Lies, Secrets, and Silence.*

Sacks, Harvey, Emanuel A. Schegloff and Gail Jefferson. 1974. A simplest systematics for the organization of turn-taking for conversation. *Language* 50: 696–735.

Schegloff, Emanuel A. 1982. Discourse as an interactional achievement. In Tannen, Deborah, ed., *Analyzing Discourse: Text and Talk.* Georgetown University Press, Washington, D.C.

Smith, Dorothy E. 1978. A peculiar eclipsing: Women's exclusion from man's culture. *Women's Studies Int. Q.* 1 (4): 281–295.

Spender, Dale. 1980. *Man Made Language.* Routledge and Kegan Paul. London.

Stein, Leonard J. 1967. The doctor-nurse game. *Archs. Gen. Psychiatry* 16: 699–703.

Tannen, Deborah, ed. 1982. *Analyzing Discourse: Text and Talk.* Georgetown University Press, Washington D.C.

Wilson, Deirdre and Dan Sperber. Forthcoming. On defining 'relevance'. In Grandy, R. ed. *op. cit.*

Zimmerman, Don H. and Candace West. 1975. Sex roles, interruptions, and silences in conversation. In Thorne, B. and N. Henley, eds, *Language and Sex: Difference and Dominance*, pp. 105–129. Newbury House, Rowley, Mass.

REREADING FREUD ON 'FEMININITY' OR WHY NOT *WOMB* ENVY?

Eva Feder Kittay

Feminists have long bristled at, argued over, and offered reinterpretations of Freud's concept of penis envy. And for good reason. The concept, as it functions within Freudian theory, is crucial to Freud's conception of female sexuality. Indeed, Freud claimed that this envy was a 'primary narcissistic wound' for the woman and, as such constituted a central element in her personality formation. Without validating the notion of penis envy, I want to raise the question of why psychoanalysis has never embraced the concept of a parallel envy on the part of men which, similarly, might constitute a primary narcissistic wound for them. Such envy I designate 'womb envy', for short, meaning by the term not merely envy of the specifically named organ but of the entire complex comprising a woman's distinctive physiology and capacities as these relate to childbearing.

In this paper, I will argue that, although it is not unreasonable to think that psychoanalysis might have developed such a notion, upon careful consideration we see that such a concept is inimical to Orthodox Freudian psychology: that given Freud's androcentric conception of femininity, the concept of womb envy is rendered incoherent. As long as Freudian psychoanalysis maintains such a conception of female sexuality, it cannot incorporate a notion of womb envy.

The argument presented in this paper is a metapsychological one. I am not here adducing evidence of a clinical sort for the existence of womb envy nor presenting a theory in which womb envy might play a role.[1] Rather the paper is an effort to understand, from a feminist perspective and using the method of a philosophical critique, how a theoretician and clinician as astute as Freud could miss the significance of a concept such as womb envy. What we find is that an androcentric perspective has so strongly influenced Freud's scientific enterprise that he fails to see female sexuality as having intrinsic value and is thus led to represent her maternal capacities and desires as emanating from her deficiencies as a male. This, in turn leads him to misconstrue significant

---

[1] See Kittay (1983) for an account of an alternate theoretical framework in which to accommodate womb envy.

elements of male sexuality. What I am presenting, then, is a philosophical feminist critique designed to show how a concept which, as I will show, was, even within Freud's own time, plausible both on empirical and theoretical grounds is rendered incoherent through a distorting patriarchal perspective.

Freud's treatment of the concept of femininity is significant to philosophically-minded feminists on two grounds. First it offers a case study for the philosophical investigation of how a male-centered perspective can distort a psychology which fails to recognize its originating stance. Second, feminist philosophers cannot ignore development in psychoanalytic theory. Despite the difficulties philosophers of science have attempted to call our attention to, psychoanalysis remains the most cogent account of the development of the human personality. Chodorow (1978) has recently exhibited the power psychoanalysis can have for explaining the formation of those personality traits that a society deems necessary for the maintenance of a particular power relation between the sexes. If as Juliet Mitchell (1975) has argued and Chodorow has recently demonstrated, psychoanalysis has immense power for understanding how the internal colonization of women is maintained, then it is important that we get the theory right. This means that we subject it to critiques and analyses which help us see both how the theory, in its traditional formulation reflects male power and how it can be made truer to a complete understanding of personality and gender formation. To further these aims, I am presenting a critical analysis of the concept of femininity as it emerges in Freud's (1933) last and most elaborated essay on the subject, 'Femininity'.

There are several reasons to expect that Freudian psychoanalysis might have developed a concept of womb envy. Freud himself wrote three significant studies which involved the expression on the part of males for the desire to bear a child or to have womanly organs, viz. Dr Schreber (1911), the Wolfman (1918), and Little Hans (1909). In *Beyond the Pleasure Principle*, Freud (1928) includes amongst the painful disappointments of childhood, the child's 'own attempt to make a baby himself, carried out in tragic seriousness [which] fails shamefully.' (p. 43). Earlier, Freud (1908) had written, in regard to children's theories of anal birth, 'It was only logical that the child should refuse to grant women the painful prerogative of giving birth to children. If babies are born through the anus, then a man might give birth just as well as a woman . . . a boy [can therefore] imagine that he, too, has children of his own, without there being any need to accuse him . . . of feminine inclinations. He is merely giving evidence . . . of the anal eroticism which is still alive within him.' In addition, as early as the 1920s many prominent analysts discussed the envy men feel toward women's parturition and sexual organs; some, like Melanie Klein (1921), stressing the envy both sexes experience with regard to the sexual organs and functions of the other sex.[2] Finally, within Freudian theory itself, at least two

---

[2] These include Klein (1921), Eisler (1921), Groddeck (1924), Horney (1924), Abraham (1925) and Jones (1927). Many more studies were to follow: Reik (1931), Zillborg (1944), Edith Jackson (1950), Fromm (1951), Bettelheim (1954) among others. For a detailed review of the early literature see John Munder Ross (1975).

important doctrines would appear to demand a concept of womb envy, that of our inherent bisexuality and the positing of an 'ancient symbolic equivalence' between penis and baby.

Let us begin by considering these two Freudian theses. On Freud's view, the girl's desire for a penis is related to her initial love attachment to her mother and her desire to penetrate her mother as a man would. For boys, the postulated bisexuality might be expected to manifest itself not only in terms of the choice of a same-sex love-object at some stage in his development, but also in his identification with the opposite sex, whereby he desires the powers appropriate to women. Womb envy ought to follow as an inevitable consequence of bisexuality for just as the girl experiences the absence of a penis as a wound to her narcissism, perceiving her difference as a lack and regarding her genitalia as deficient or defective, so it might be supposed that the boy would similarly regard his differences as deficiencies and defects. He might well be expected to regard the impossibility of his body growing breasts, his lack of a genital interior opening, and perhaps most significantly his inability to produce a child from his own body, as significant lacks or defects which would similarly constitute a wound to his narcissism.

The 'ancient symbolic equivalence' between the penis and the baby posited by Freud, constitutes a significant element in his theory of penis envy and the woman's desire for a baby.[3] An equivalence relation is, of course, symmetrical, so that if the baby is to compensate the girl for her lack of a penis, the penis ought to be viewed as compensating the boy for this inability to bear a child. That is, if we are to treat the symbolic equivalence or psychical interchange-ability of penis and baby (Freud also includes within this set of interchangeable entities feces, breast and money), then we might suppose that masculine flouting of phallic power is man's compensatory move for the child which does not emerge from his own body.

We know that Freud himself never developed any of these theoretical considerations favoring the inclusion of womb envy into the heart of pscyhoanalytic theory—in spite of Freud's own case studies documenting fantasies on the part of men and boys for woman's organs and functions. In these studies, Freud denies womb envy explanatory power by reducing the apparent manifestations to symptoms of some other underlying psychological reality. I am not proposing to re-examine these cases to show that the concept of womb envy would provide us with a better analysis. Instead, I want to suggest that Freudian theory demands such a reduction.

Let us look very briefly at Freud's treatment of what appear to be manifestations of womb envy. Dr Schreber, whose autobiography provided Freud (1911) with his theory of paranoia, complained of terrible persecutions. Schreber, an educated and eminent public official, thought that these were directly related to the mission for which God had chosen him: to give birth to a new race of man which would spring forth from him after God had impregnated

---

[3] See Freud (1933) 'Femininity', p. 113, also see 'Anxiety and the instinctual life' in the same volume, p. 89, and Freud (1908) p. 34.

him with 'divine rays'. Freud ascribed Dr Schreber's paranoid fantasies to his repressed homosexual and incestuous desires for his own father, thereafter linking paranoia to repressed homosexual longings—and wrote that unfortunately Dr Schreber did not have a son unto whom he could discharge some of his homosexual libido.

The case of Little Hans, described by Freud (1909), was based on a five-year-old boy whom Freud treated indirectly through a correspondence with the child's father, a man familiar with psychoanalysis. The child had an overwhelming fear of horses which appeared to be related to Hans' fear and hostility toward his father. While the phobia was alleviated when the boy confronted these negative feelings toward his father, he was not fully 'cured' until the true facts of childbirth were revealed and assimilated by him. It is noteworthy to mention here that the child repeatedly expressed the wish to bear a child and thought that he was capable of giving birth, although he understood that he was a boy. Such desires and beliefs are indeed not uncommon in a child Hans' age and do not disappear until the child is cognitively capable of understanding the process of childbirth (see Ross, 1974). The desire to give birth was here somehow related to the horse phobia as the ultimate 'cure' of the boy's condition suggests. The case is treated by Freud as one of castration anxiety and strong incestuous feelings toward his mother, exacerbated by the birth of a sister. (The sister is both a rival and a 'castrate,' as she is in the case of the Wolf Man as well.)

The case of the Wolf Man, a case so named for the significant and recurrent dream of Freud's patient in which wolves appear sitting upon a tree, a dream Freud (1918) took to signify the young child's witnessing of the 'primal scene,' the lovemaking between his parents, concerns a young man who exhibited a 'feminine' stance, particularly towards his father. Freud attributes all indications of the patient's 'feminine' stance to expressions of repressed homosexual libido. Of this case Freud writes:

> 'The wish to be born of his father (as he had at first believed was the case), the wish to be sexually satisfied by him, the wish to present him with a child— . . . at the price of his own masculinity, and expressed in the language of anal eroticism . . . in them homosexuality had found its furthest and most intimate expression.' (1918: 294).

In both the case of the paranoid Dr Schreber and that of Little Hans, Freud relates the striving for a child to anal eroticism, an association made powerful by virtue of the child's theories about how babies are born and attempts to produce babies while producing feces. In the cases of the Wolf Man and Dr Schreber, Freud attributes all indications of the patient's apparently feminine characteristics, such as passivity and desires to 'give birth', as expressions of repressed homosexual libido.[4] Womb envy has no explanatory function in the

---

[4] For an interpretation of Schreber's illness which is more amenable to the notion of womb envy, see Macalpine and Hunter (1953).

behaviors, fears, and wishes expressed by these men and boys, since in all these analyses, the difficulties are presented in autoerotic or homosexual terms, i.e. only in terms of *male* sexuality.

In an article presumably written in collaboration with Freud, Ruth Mack Brunswick (1940) speaks of the 'two great wishes of childhood: the wish for a baby and the wish for a penis.' But the significance of the former becomes tied to a desire for a passive receiving of a gift (of the baby) from the father. The possibility that the desire for a baby on the part of the child is a wish to have the *active* capacity of the mother for giving birth is obscured by having *activity* granted to the male role of impregnation. Again the presumptions underlying the Brunswick's discussion are androcentric, with the result that the significance of womb envy fails to emerge.[5]

In relating the sexuality of men largely in terms of a man's own constitutional character and his relation to his father, Freud places the entire emphasis of the developmental period on the Oedipal relation. This is essentially a *triangular* relation where the father plays perhaps a more significant role than the object of the boy's love, the mother. While Freud came to recognize that he had greatly underestimated the impact of the pre-Oedipal maternal relation with a daughter, he did not revise his thinking vis-à-vis the boy. Without such revision, Freud could not recognize the contribution made by womb envy, for the desire to achieve motherhood must be formed in the pre-Oedipal identification with the mother.[6]

Amongst the other analysts who called attention to the wish to bear a child on the part of men and boys, most did not recognize womb envy as an underlying psychological reality which may have explanatory value. One analyst who understood that the boy's wish for a baby was related to his identification with his mother, still writes, 'These ideas are side issues of the phallic development and gain importance only in pathological cases.' (p. 285). Penis envy, contrariwise, is not regarded as a 'side-issue'.[7]

A blindness to the potential significance of womb envy outlined above, even in the light of some recognition of the pre-Oedipal identification of the boy with his mother, has its source (in the case of Freudian theory) in the conception of femininity which significantly misconceives woman's sexuality, and ultimately

----

[5] The wish for a baby, Brunswick claims, has its origin in the child's identification with the mother and has an active and a passive form. See the text below for a further discussion of this article.

[6] Freud does recognize the boy's identification with the mother in the 'inverted' or negative Oedipal complex, where the father is the love-object rather than the mother and where the boy assumes a feminine stance toward the father. But this identification is not pre-Oedipal but rather follows the simple, positive Oedipal relation in which the mother is the love-object. (See Freud, 1923, pp. 21–24.)

[7] See Kestenbert (1956). For another example of such handling of the issue see Eisler (1921), who, while providing good clinical material documenting womb envy, subtitled his paper in accordance with the treatment he gives the material: 'A clinical contribution to anal-eroticism.' Boehm (1930), while offering a striking account of what he calls men's 'femininity complex,' concludes:

'But I do not think the material I have quoted in this paper enables us to decide with any certainty whether the man's envy is as closely related to narcissism as the woman's or . . . whether it is substantially influenced by a passive-homosexual libido.' (p. 467).

misconstrues man's sexuality. But this conception, although inaccurate as a true description of woman's sexuality, is valuable for its mythic dimensions, for its adequacy in capturing the concept of femininity to which men have attempted to confine woman's sexuality.

Auspiciously, Freud begins his essay 'Femininity' by posing 'the riddle of femininity'—to men only. To women, he says, the problem does not apply for 'you are yourselves the problem.' (p. 100). Arguing against the existence of clear biological or psychological criteria by which to distinguish femininity, Freud embarks on what appears to be a descriptive account of the creation of woman's sexuality.

In outlining the psychosexual development of women, Freud stresses here the newly uncovered significance of the pre-Oedipal period for the girl and with it her intense attachment to her mother. Since the mother is the first love-object for the girl, as for the boy, the girl must ultimately not only change the person of her later erotic attachment, she must also change the sexual identity of her first love-object. The girl's hostility to her mother, resulting from the 'discovery' of her own and subsequently of her mother's 'castration,' facilitates the transfer of the girl's love from her mother to her father. The wound inflicted in her psyche by the discovery that men possess genital organs different from her own, or as Freud would have it, her discovery that she *lacks* a penis and is therefore incomplete, deficient, defective, is one for which she can only fully compensate with the birth of a male child 'who brings with him the longed for penis'. The girl's 'castration complex' also causes her to disdain what she took to be her phallus, viz. her clitoris. This disdain facilitates the withdrawal of her libido from the clitoris and frees it for its future investment in the vagina. The feminine stance, then, requires two transitions not paralleled in men: the change in sexual orientation in transferring her love from her mother to her father and the change in the locus of sexual pleasure from the clitoris to the vagina.

In the same essay, Freud recognized the extreme difficulty such a circuitous psychosexual development presents and remarks on the 'physical rigidity' of a woman of thirty, as opposed to the 'youthful, somewhat unformed individual' we expect in the man of comparable age. He writes, 'It is . . . as though, indeed, the difficult development to femininity had exhausted the possibilities of the person concerned'. Those of us who would penetrate the recalcitrant riddle of femininity must ask, 'But why then are women made to pay this price?' Before we can understand what Freud might answer—for this would solve the riddle—we must first collect all the pieces of the puzzle.

The girl's penis envy, as we have seen, both facilitates and is causally related to transfers critical to her 'femininity'. Beyond this, compensation for the envy is intimately bound to woman's role as mother, a role expressed early in a girl's life in doll playing. While the desire to mother completes Freud's discussion of women's emergence out of a bisexual infancy, mothering *as such* is *not* for Freud an expression of femininity. Freud, noting that girls play with dolls prior to the onset of the Oedipal situation writes, 'but that play was not, in fact, an expression of her femininity: it served as an identification with her mother with

the intention of substituting activity for passivity. *She* was playing the part of her mother and the doll was herself . . . ' (p. 113).

The passage has the flavor of a paradox: the daughter, in her identification with her mother (her quintessential female role model), as her mother appears in the quintessentially female role of mother, is not expressing her femininity! What then is femininity? Here it is instructive to note that Freud seems to be implying that, by virtue of her activity (as opposed to her passivity) the child is not yet expressing her femininity. But earlier in the essay Freud rejects passivity as the defining character of femininity since a woman, in her mothering capacity is active. For Freud the question of femininity and its coincidence with passivity retained an ambivalence characterised by the above passage, an ambivalance made acute by the relation of activity and passivity to mothering.

In the article cited earlier which Freud presumably co-authored with Ruth Mack Brunswick (1940), three developmental stages are claimed for girls and boys alike: passive/active, castrate/phallic, feminine/masculine. The wish for a baby, Mack Brunswick claims, has its origin in the child's identification with the mother and has an active and a passive form. When, in the anal period, it takes on the significance of a gift, children of both sexes desire that their mother receive from them or to give to them such as offering. Given that the mother, in her mothering capacity, is viewed as active, one would assume that the passive wish is that the mother give birth to a baby which she then presents (in fantasy) to the child, and that the active wish is the child's wish to give birth to a baby which the child could then present to the mother. Here the masculine role would be passive, i.e. receiving the baby, while the feminine role would be active, i.e. giving birth to the baby. However, in Mack Brunswick's discussion, it is clear that the passive wish, which the boy must give up and the girl must assume, is the wish to give birth, while the active wish, which the boy assumes and the girl gives up, is the wish to impregnate. The severing of the active from the masculine functions and passive from feminine functions is only apparent, and remains as tied to androcentrism as are the very linguistic forms we use to speak of pregnancy, i.e. 'to be pregnant' vs 'to impregnate' (although 'to give birth' is in the active voice).

For Mack Brunswick and for Freud the truly feminine wish for a child is the passive wish as we see in the passage from 'Femininity' which comes just prior to the passage cited. Here Freud claims, 'The feminine situation is only established if the wish for a penis is replaced by one for a baby, if, that is, a baby takes the place of a penis in accordance with an ancient symbolic equivalence.' (p. 113).

But again an apparent paradox emerges. A woman's desire for a child is truly feminine only when it emerges as the compensation for not being a man! Is the riddle of femininity then to be solved by the posing of such paradoxes?

Still another quotation from this passage and we will have all the pieces of our puzzle. Freud writes: 'Not until the emergence of the wish for a penis does the doll-baby become a baby from the girl's father and thereafter the aim of the most powerful feminine wish.' (p. 113). Freud unwittingly recognized that our concept of femininity requires not merely that the daughter strive to be

like her mother in her mother's attention to her child, but that a woman's role as mother be expressive of her femininity only as a consequence of her sexual availability to a man, as having received (and note the passive voice) the baby from that man. And unless a woman changes the locus of her sexual pleasure from clitoris to vagina, and changes her love-object from woman to man, she will not have prepared the psychic ground necessary to receive a man's sexual attentions in such a way as to make his impregnation and its outcome not only possible, but desirable.

Reading Freud in this way allows us not only to see what Freud meant by femininity but to recognize it as distinctly congruent with dominant patriarchal conceptions of woman's sexuality. Furthermore, if we understand that this is Freud's solution to the riddle of femininity, we understand why he chose to address the riddle only to men and why he took femininity not to be a puzzle for women themselves. Given the facts that women mother and the particularities of male and female sexual anatomy, the problem for men is not how to make women sexually available to them and mothers in the aftermath: brute force and the force of nature could accomplish this. As men also seek loving sexual relations and mothers for their children, and as loving and mothering cannot be coerced, the problem for men is to turn women's desire toward them and their nurturance toward *their* children (that is, the children who affirm the desire of the heterosexual woman), thereby reproducing for themselves and their offspring lovers-mothers. Femininity ought not to be a riddle for women because women's very will and consciousness must be molded and at an age too young for the self-conscious awareness of the creation of that femininity.

Nonetheless, the early formation of femininity is not always entirely successful and femininity is often an enigma for the same women who are meant to exemplify it. Ideologies and psychologies of femininity fashioned by men systematically distort women's experience so that women either find themselves alienated from the doctrines and hence from the standard of 'normalcy', or they unwittingly renounce what existentialists would call authenticity, adopting other-imposed conceptions of femininity as representative of their own experience.

Penis envy, which gains its significance (as Freud seemed at times to recognize) from the dual considerations of masculine superior status and the fact of women's mothering, is central to the creation of that femininity. Freud made the 'truly feminine' wish for a child compensatory only, replacing the wish for the valued genital organ, the penis. In the concept of penis envy, a woman's sexuality becomes defined exclusively in terms of man, for she adapts her sexuality to receive the penis and to transform it into a baby.

Once again then, in Freud, we see examplified the thesis of woman as Other which de Beauvoir (1949) so lucidly enunciated: Man is the One, the Essential, the norm, in relation to which woman (and in this case, her sexuality) is defined. Women's sexuality is, on this account, nothing intrinsic in contrast to man's sexuality which, relative to the woman's convoluted development, unfolds as naturally as a flower blossoms. Even the one distinctively female function, child-

bearing, is but the outcome, psychologically speaking, of a compensatory wish to be male.

On this account, the idea of womb envy is certainly superfluous. But beyond this it is incoherent, for although the physiological organs exist in women and not in men, there is *psychologically* nothing to envy: The woman bears a child to compensate herself for the penis the man already possesses. It is incoherent to speak of an envy for the *compensation* for something that one *already* has. It is as if a rich man who owned an original Picasso were to envy a poor man's cheap reproduction of the same Picasso. As for a woman's sexuality, it is nothing but what is adopted for man—for man to envy it, is to covet that which is already for his use. Hence a wish to possess aspects of a woman's body is explained as an expression of homosexual longings for the father, and pregnancy wishes as forestallings of castration fears along with a regression to an earlier pregenital stage of sexual development (anal eroticism). Given Freud's view of femininity, there is no room for womb envy. This is why Freud, astute observer and theoretician that he was, remained blind to the significance of womb envy and why an orthodox Freudian psychoanalysis still cannot incorporate this concept.[8]

Elsewhere, I (1983) argue that a consequence of and defense against womb envy is the appropriation on the part of men of the procreative powers for themselves. Freud, in making a woman's desire for a child an expression of her repressed wish for a penis, has, in a certain regard, appropriated childbearing to men—it is, now, merely a barely acceptable substitute for being a man (barely, for Freud believed that most women could never truly be reconciled to the futility of their wish) and the child's active wish of presenting the mother with a child is not the feminine childbearing itself but the masculine prerogative of impregnation.

Necessary to this conception of femininity, in which woman's sexuality is 'other' and 'inessential', is the unwillingness to recognize as inherently desirable features of a woman's sexuality—of the physiology and capacities unique to woman in which a woman can take pride as the man takes pride in his distinctive sexuality. Feminists since Karen Horney have recognized that Freud's view, as a descriptive rendering of female sexuality, is absurd. There is no inherent reason why a girl should not take pride in her genitalia which serve to give her pleasure and comfort her as much as the boy's serve him. Beyond this, pregnancy, childbirth, lactation, experienced out of choice and in the right circumstances, have as an inherent possibility sexual as well as emotional gratification (an element of sexuality that Freud, in fact, did at times acknowledge, but which he chose to ignore in formulating his concept of femininity).

The notion of penis envy has force only in the situation of woman's subordination to man. Within the context of patriarchical male dominance, where

---

[8] Notice that my claims here are limited to Orthodox Freudian theory, particularly as it pertains to the conception of female sexuality. The theory of womb envy may be made consistent with a neo-Freudian view that gives a different account of female sexuality such as that given by Chodorow (1978). In my paper (1983), I attempt just such an incorporation.

Man is the Essential and Woman the Other, sexual differences cannot be simply differences. They take on symbolic significance as hierarchical differentia so that features of men are positively marked and those of women are lacks, defects or excesses.

If, as we have urged, penis envy derives its importance not from an innate desire for the boy's sexual organ, but from the social circumstances which invest it with particular power, ought we not to argue that womb envy is subject to the same social circumstances: those which value what is male and devalue what is female? Freud might then, after all, be justified. Just as there is not room in his theory for womb envy, the possibilities of the 'womb' may be so devalued that there is no place for envy. We may only envy what we value.

But to argue so is to ignore both the awe-inspiring miracle of creation itself and, even more importantly, the potency of the mother as the young child perceives her. It is in the identification with such a potent mother, a notion represented, within androcentric Freudianism, by the barbarism 'the phallic mother', that womb envy acquires its significance. And it is within a context of women's general subordinated status that the destructive forces of envy subvert the boy's early desires to be as fecund and nurturant as his mother.

Woman's mothering and women's subordinate status along with evidence that young boys exhibit the desire to bear children, provides ground for the view that boys perceive their incapacity as a loss and a narcissistic wound which results in subsequent envy. Although the resultant womb envy certainly has a basis in biological difference, it does not reduce to biological fact. Rather the sexual difference is elaborated into a gender difference regarding the continued nurturance of the baby, once outside the womb. The fact of woman's mothering beyond gestation gives her procreative capacity heightened significance, while the fact of her diminished social standing lends, for men, a bitter flavor to her apparent biological superiority: Why should someone inferior to me possess something that I desire? The defense of such envy issues forth in a large variety of behaviors, but all ultimately support the male dominance which fuels the envy.[9]

These last claims as well as efforts to establish the validity of womb envy and its significance in the context of male dominance require a psychological theory which focuses on the young child's identification with a potent female nurturer. The work of Nancy Chodorow and others investigating the consequences of the universal fact of woman's mothering are making substantial contributions to such a theory. Although Freud himself had begun to understand some of the importance of the child's relation to the pre-Oedipal mother, the mother experienced as powerful and independent of a male's mastery, his implicit (even if somewhat ambivalent) acceptance of woman's secondary status resulted in an unwillingness to accept the child's desire for and emulation of

[9] As Sara Ruddick pointed out (in a personal communication), woman's capacity 'inspires in men a fear that women will (a) do it virtually without them and (b) exploit the real powers they would get if they were not socially dominated (and until recently, dominated by a reproductive body which they could not harness to their own uses)'.

the mother's unique sexual possibilities. The (male) child's recourse to theories of anal birth that, Freud (1908) suggested, allowed the child to deny to women 'the painful prerogative of giving birth to children' would then parallel Freud's own contorted explanations of such masculine desires as manifestations of anal eroticism and a strong constitutional inclination to homosexuality. By so explaining the clinical evidence of such desires and the attendent envy, Freud could circumvent the theoretical need to posit woman's sexuality as something inherently valuable and thus even enviable. But if woman's sexuality is nothing inherently valuable then it seems it must be so by virtue of its failure to 'measure up' to the masculine norm and so 'penis envy' emerges as the conceptual linchpin of his theory of female sexuality, of 'femininity'. To Freud's credit, he never felt fully satisfied with his theory, holding it to be the weakest point in psychoanalytic theory; although others have perceived the falsifying distortions, they have been unable or unwilling to adequately revise the theory.

The question of womb envy emerges out of a consideration of the nature of female sexuality, which has been rendered a thing defined and even experienced by women themselves in terms of men's desires and needs. I have argued that the prevailing theory of personality formation, Freudian psychoanalysis with its biological determinism and skewed masculine orientation, has failed to recognize the significance of womb envy because its conception of female sexuality renders the concept incoherent. Philosophers of science may argue whether or not psychoanalysis is indeed a science. What is clear beyond doubt is that Freud's intention was to produce a scientific theory. But his scientific claims and efforts to uncover the truth of human personality development flounder on the bedrock of male bias, a bedrock so overgrown with privilege and seeming inevitability as to remain unchallenged by even as great a master for what is hidden as Freud himself. A challenge to such a conception necessitates an examination of what is inherent in female sexuality and the way in which an adequate understanding of a woman's sexuality will further enhance our understanding of the drives and motivations of men as they suppress their desires to identify with the potent mother of their youth, the mother 'castrated' through a devaluation of her sex.

REFERENCES

Bettelheim, Bruno. 1954, 1971. *Symbolic Wounds*. Macmillan, New York.

Boehm, Felix. 1930. The femininity-complex in men. *Int. J. Psycho-Analysis* 11: 444–469.

Brunswick, Ruth Mack. 1940. The pre-oedipal phase of the libido development. *Psychoanal. Q.* 9: 293–319.

Chodorow, Nancy. 1978. *The Reproduction of Mothering*. University of California Press, Berkeley, CA.

de Beauvoir, Simone. 1949, 1974. *The Second Sex*. Random House, New York.

de Groot, Jeanne Lampl. 1946. The pre-oedipal phase in the development of the male child. *Psychoanal. Study Child* 2: 75–83.

Eisler, Michael J. 1921. A man's unconscious phantasy of pregnancy in the guise of traumatic hysteria. *Int. J. Psycho-Analysis* 11: 255–286.

Freud, Sigmund. 1908, 1976. On the sexual theories of children. In Rieff, Philip, ed., *The Sexual Enlightenment of Children*. Macmillan, New York.

Freud, Sigmund. 1909, 1976. Analysis of a phobia in a five-year-old boy. In Rieff, Philip, ed., *The Sexual Enlightenment of Children*. Macmillan, New York.

Freud, Sigmund. 1911, 1968. Psychoanalytical notes upon an autobiographical account of a case of paranoia. (Dermentia Paranoides). In Rieff, Philip, ed., *Three Case Histories*. New York, Macmillan.

Freud, Sigmund. 1918, 1968. From the history of an infantile neurosis. In Rieff, Philip, ed., *Three Case Histories*. Macmillan, New York.

Freud, Sigmund. 1923, 1960. *The Ego and the Id*, ed. James Strachey. W. W. Norton, New York.

Freud, Sigmund. 1925, 1950. Some psychological consequences of the anatomical distinction between the sexes. *Collected Papers*, V. Hogarth Press, London.

Freud, Sigmund. 1931. Female sexuality. *Collected Papers*, V. Hogarth Press, London.

Freud, Sigmund. 1933, 1965. *New Introductory Lectures on Psychoanalysis*. Translated by James Strachey. W. W. Norton, New York.

Fromm, Erich. 1951, 1967. *The Forgotten Language*. Holt, Rinehart & Winston, New York.

Horney, Karen. 1924. On the genesis of the castration complex in women. *Int. J. Psycho-Analysis* 5: 50–65.

Horney, Karen. 1932, 1973. The dread of woman. In Kelman, Harold, ed. *Feminine Psychology*. W. W. Norton, New York.

Jacobson, Edith. 1950. Development of the wish for a child in boys. *Psychological Study Child* 5: 139–152. International U. Press, New York.

Kestenberg, Judith S. 1956. On the development of maternal feelings in early childhood. *Psychoanal. Study Child* 11: 257–291.

Kittay, Eva. 1983. Womb envy as an explanatory concept. In Trebilcot, Joyce, ed., *Mothering: Essays in Feminist Theory*. Littlefield Adams, Totowas, New Jersey.

Macalpine, Ida and Richard Hunt. 1953. The Schreber case. *Psychoanal. Q.* 22: 328.

Ross, John Munder. 1974. The children's children: A psychoanalytic study of generativity and nurturance in boys. Ph.D. Dissertation, New York University.

Ross, John Munder. 1975. Paternal identity: A critical review of the literature on nurturance and generativity in boys and men. *J. Am. psychoanal. Ass.* 23: 783–818.

Zillboorg, Gregory. 1944. Masculine and feminine. *Psychiatry* 7: 257–296.

LOVE, KNOWLEDGE AND TRANSFORMATION

Caroline Whitbeck

1. PREFACE: WHAT THE SYMPOSIUM TEACHES US ABOUT LOVE

What do we learn about eros from examining Plato's *Symposium*? Eros is presented as a divine madness. The object of the lover is a transformation. Plato's characterization of this transformation is variously translated as a 'birth in beauty', 'breeding in the beautiful', or 'the conception and generation that the beautiful effects'. It is elucidated in the following way: Eros is a divine madness which brings the lover to a final ecstatic vision of the Beautiful, the Good. This 'birth' is viewed as the culmination of the lover's pregnancy of soul. It is the expression of, and union with the divine.

What actually transpires in the *Symposium*? Socrates describes himself as a midwife, one who will help others to bring forth the Beautiful, to achieve the ecstatic bearing of the divine. (One would think that no one could overlook the envy of women and women's functions [pregnancy and midwifery] that pervades this work, but that assumption does not reckon with the ingenuity of male commentators.) Given Socrates' self-proclaimed role as midwife, one would expect to see him gently and deftly helping to deliver at least one of his cohorts into enlightenment, or at least to make some progress toward that end. Nothing of the sort occurs, however; no one midwifes anyone. What there is is a good deal of competition among the participants, particularly notable is the aggressive sparring that goes on between Socrates and Agathon.

I am indebted to Marilyn Frye and Naomi Scheman for thoughtful and insightful criticisms of the penultimate version of this paper. I regret that *Hypatia's* publication deadline made it impossible for them to see the final version before it went to press.

A version of the first part of this paper was presented March 31, 1977 at a conference sponsored by the N.Y.U. Graduate Historical Society, 'Constructing A History of Power and Sexuality,' and another version at the 1979 spring meetings of the Society for Women in Philosophy held at SUNY/ Stony Brook. I am grateful to the organizers of both conferences and to the conference participants especially (at the first conference) to G. J. Barker-Benfield for his extensive comments, and to Donna Harraway and Nancy Hartsock for their provocative reservations, and (at the second conference) to Eleanor Kuykendall.

I am also indebted to my feminist discussion group for the opportunity to discuss some of the ideas presented in the balance of this paper in their embryonic form, and especially to Nancy Werth for her comments.

Alcibiades is presented as one whom Socrates has loved, although all that is evident in the dialogue is that Alcibiades has an awkward crush on Socrates to which Socrates responds with coyness and disdain. Whatever the nature of the attachment, Socrates did not use to induce Alcibiades to pursue the beauty of virtue (which we are told surpasses the beauty of bodies and the beauty of words). Alcibiades is in fact the sorriest of the lot; history tells us (and Plato and his audience knew) that he went on to betray and die in shame.

The dialogue closes with Socrates browbeating Aristophanes, the master of comedy, and Agathon, the master of tragedy, into agreeing that the same person ought to be the master of both comedy and tragedy. We are told that they agree with Socrates only because they are falling asleep.

The theoretical insights concerning love that are presented in this dialogue are totally absent in the practice of the participants. That the discrepancy between theory and practice is generally neglected by commentators leads one to believe that the majority of scholars do not ask that theory and practice be consistent with one another. The neglect of certain types of practice in favor of theory finds some justification in Plato's scheme in the devaluation of the actual in favor of the ideal—recall that Plato alleges that concerning the actual world one cannot tell the truth, one can only tell a likely story (*Timaeus* 27C–29D). Nonetheless, the split between theory and practice regarding love remains odd, since the whole characterization of love given by Socrates/Plato is of a power that transforms the self to make it capable of grasping the ideal realm. Therefore, practical knowledge of love, knowledge of loving that transforms both oneself and others—of how to live as 'the changer and the changed' as one lyricist has expressed it—ought to be of paramount importance in Plato's view even if knowledge of nature and practices influencing the natural world would not.

I believe that one of the most exciting things about the Women's Movement is its capacity to develop new practices and/or extend the practices that have been women's. In particular, I think the movement is working out a distinctive practice and theory of love. My purpose here is to draw attention to that practice and theory and contribute to it. What I regard as the central error of masculist ways of doing philosophy, is that practice is so often ignored. This has particularly disastrous consequences for an account of love. A central feature of feminist ontology, I shall argue, is an understanding of the relation of theory and practice that is very different from the masculist representation of theory and practice as polar opposites.

2. A FEMINIST EROTICS AS AN ASPECT
OF FEMINIST ONTOLOGY

My purpose in this paper is to sketch a feminist erotics. By an 'erotics' I mean much more than merely an intellectual understanding of a type of human

engagement, erotic engagement; I mean a fundamentally different way of living the erotic engagement, which makes for a fundamentally *different engagement*. In general, a change of overall ontology involves the articulation and clarification of a different way of living and not just a different intellectual understanding of some invariant way of living. Therefore, accepting or believing an ontology is not simply a matter of what analytic philosophers call 'having a certain propositional attitude'. This way of speaking harks back to earlier senses of the term 'believe'.

The erotics that is the subject of this paper is an aspect of a feminist ontology that I have discussed in detail elsewhere (Whitbeck, 1983b). Certain features of that larger ontology will be of significance in developing this erotics. In particular, an erotics, in elucidating the desire for an other, is deeply influenced by the understanding of the self–other relation.[1]

I call this erotics and ontology 'feminist' because I find it ingredient both in many of the practices regarded as 'women's work' and a major strand of past and present feminist writing and practice. The most general characterization of these practices is that they are the practices of the mutual development or realization of people. What makes the term 'masculist' an appropriate as well as symmetric descriptor for the dualistic ontology implicit in 'Western Thought' is that the culture that produced it is male-dominated, and that, given our cultural practices, the self–other opposition is likely to fit the experience of a boy and man, particularly one of the dominant group, better than it does the experience of a woman. It is not because I believe that all and only men accept or operate with masculist ontology.

The ontology has at its core a conception of the relation of self to other(s) that is quite different from the self–other *opposition* of masculist thought and that has dominated (at least) so-called 'Western thought'. The self–other opposition of masculist ontology is primarily an opposition of *characteristics*. This opposition in characteristics usually leads either to the assumption that one term naturally dominates, or to the assumption that there is a conflict in the struggle for dominance between the two. It seems to provide the model for other distinctions and categories that are regarded as ontologically significant, which are likewise understood as dualistic oppositions. Among these are theory-practice, culture-nature, spirit-matter, mind-body, human-divine, male-female (or masculine-feminine) and therefore gay-straight, political-personal, public-

---

[1] In the case of friendship and familiar affection—setting aside charity or compassion for present purposes—the structure of the self-other relation is less central. This is particularly true with familiar affection. Fondness for an old teddy bear or not particularly charming virtuous or talented relative when explained in terms of familiarity mutes that being's otherness; we know just what to expect and that confirmation of our expectations produces much if not all of the comfort of familiar affection.

Friendship is something of a problem for an ontology based on a self-other opposition, since friendship turns on *shared* goals and understandings. One response to the difficulty is to deny that friends are distinct beings. Thus Aristotle at one point speaks of friends as one soul in two bodies. When one remembers that soul is form, it follows that Aristotle is committed to say that to be friends is close to being the same person.

private, knower-known, and lover-beloved. The feminist alternative yields a distinctive, non-oppositional and non-dualistic conception of the corresponding subjects, together with a major change in emphasis given some of these categories (for example, since the relation of self to other is not taken to be represented by gender difference, gender is neither taken to be, nor is symbolic of, an important ontological difference.) It generates a new view of the person and of ethics. (Because differentiation does not depend on opposition, the differentiation of the proposed ontology from dualistic ontologies does not require that it be interpreted as the 'opposite' view, or even the only alternative to dualism.)

It is notable that the term 'eros' or 'Eros' has a currency among speakers of English that is not equalled by 'philia', 'storge', and 'agape', the other three terms in ancient Greek that are translated by the English word 'love'. (Indeed, a number of thinkers including Freud and Jung have given their own technical meaning to the term.) It is for this reason that I employ the term 'eros' to demarcate a particular species of love. I shall not explore the meaning of 'eros' in ancient Greek, but shall take as my starting point the four-fold distinction between eros and three other types of attachment: deep friendship or sisterhood, familiar affection, and totally generous love or charity—the brief modern renderings that are commonly offered of philia, storge and agape (e.g. Lewis, 1960). The four-fold distinction provides a framework that is at least richer than that of modern individualism. Within the framework of individualism human bonding is difficult to comprehend, and in recent years the tendency has been to reduce love either to hedonistic sexual appetite or to masochistic self-sacrifice.

3. THE USE OF PSYCHOLOGICAL THEORY TO CONTRAST MASCULIST AND FEMINIST ONTOLOGY

In an early paper, I documented a remarkable constancy over the last 3000 years in the themes or motifs embodied in the theories proposed by philosophers and scientists to identify and explain sex differences (Whitbeck, 1976). That research revealed some major features of masculist ontology that are important for the present discussion. There are three themes that repeatedly recur:

(1) woman is an incomplete man;
(2) there are two opposing complementary principles, masculine and feminine, that are constitutive of reality;
(3) the strengths or virtues proper to women are defined by male needs.

In some cases a single theory exemplifies two or more of these themes. The recurrence of these themes is all the more notable when one considers that

our views about nature, scientific method and the like have undergone profound changes in that period of time. Each theme shows an androcentric bias, that is, it is the male experience that is taken as the norm.

Although the theories of Freud and the Jungians exemplify the first and second themes, and are incoherent in their treatment of *female* development, their theories of male development give major clues as to how the three recurrent themes arise in the thoughts and fantasies of little boys. In particular the view that the masculine and feminine are opposite principles that symbolize other major oppositions, especially an opposition of self and other, is one that the Jungians trace to the (male) infant's differentiation of his masculine self from the feminine primordial nurturer. It is this second theme, which dates at least from Pythagoras, that is central to masculist ontology. (It turns up even in influential theories, such as those of Aristotle and Freud, that primarily view woman as an incomplete man.) The masculine principle is taken to have whatever attributes the culture sees as appropriate to the conscious and rational self. The characteristics that are viewed as opposite are attributed to the second, the 'feminine' principle. Although the two principles are frequently held to be complementary, the association of the masculine principle with rationality leads to a hierarchical interpretation of the relationship between the principles, so that the masculine is viewed as superior and the feminine as inferior.

Often the project of constructing a feminist view is confused with the project of simply affirming the goodness or the primacy of the characteristics associated with what masculist dualistic thought views as 'the feminine principle,' or appropriate to the feminine gender, or arising from female biology. The confusion of a feminist viewpoint—by which I mean one that aims to provide concepts and models that make possible the articulation of women's experience and women's practices (or, as Marilyn Frye, 1983: xi, puts it, 'makes women's lives intelligible')—with being an advocate for what masculist thought takes to be the 'feminine' viewpoint, seems to be particularly common in feminist discussions of mothering. Thus I have recently heard feminists ape the uncritical yeasaying thought proper in the Victorian 'angel in the home' in an effort to represent the maternal viewpoint, and other feminists express the fear that any attention to maternal thinking, even in such insightful and unsentimental treatments as that given by Sara Ruddick (who clarifies the place of control in maternal thinking) (Ruddick, 1983), will provide new justification for confining women to what the Victorian world defined as 'woman's place'.[2] If we do not give detailed attention to women's actual experience and practices (and by this I mean more than repeating vague laudatory slogans regarding women's practices) feminist philosophy will be of no use to women, and no use in reorganizing

---

[2] A return to Victorian social arrangements seems a remote possibility given modern work life. A more present danger is that individualism of modern society will continue to distort our perception of human relationship and our society's responsibilities towards its children. The result will be that motherhood will increasingly be regarded as an expensive hobby that distracts people from their 'normal' career paths. This trend is reflected in the title of a recent cover story in the *New York Times Magazine* (November 21, 1982) 'Careers and the lure of motherhood'.

society organized around the practices of development or realization of people, practices which have been for the most part 'women's work'.

4. EROS, OTHERNESS AND
SEXUAL RELATIONS

Let us start with the rough characterization of eros as desire of or for an other—that which is distinct from the identified self.[3] The characterization of eros as desire of or for that which one is not is not yet specific enough, since one might desire to *possess* something in order to control it or do something with it but such a desire to possess, to treat as property, is not eros. Similarly one might desire to incorporate something (here the paradigm is food), and this too fails to be eros.[4]

Instead eros may be characterized as a desire for fusion or at least *transforming contact with the other that brings one to a turning point* (Addelson, forthcoming) *or which takes one out of one's limited self*, i.e. it produces an *ex stasis*. As such it is often taken as a means to the realization of one's deepest self, as in enlightenment. This is certainly the view that Socrates espouses in the *Symposium*. It is the basis of spiritual practice in certain traditions,[5] and, insofar as transference is the medium for psychoanalytic work, it is the means here to achieve the end-state which eclectic psychoanalysts like Fingarette identify with enlightenment.

What is distinctive about eros within feminist erotics is that it is a bond to an other who is understood as analogous to the self (where the scope and limits of that analogy are something to be discovered in each case). Since the other is not viewed as opposite as it is in masculinist ontology and erotics,[6] it is presumably possible to genuinely recognize the characteristics of the self in

---

[3] The expression 'identified self' requires clarification. There may be and usually are aspects of the self that are not recognized and owned as part of the self. Therefore, one may come to love or otherwise respond to a part of oneself by first projecting it upon another person who in fact possesses few of the projected characteristics. In such a case it makes sense to say that the other whom one loves is in fact an aspect of oneself even though it is not identified as part of oneself.

[4] Both the desire to treat-as-property, or the desire to treat-as-food are components in the infant's attachment of the primary nurturer which Freudians see as the primary sexual and erotic attachment but this only shows that this notion is not adequate even as a rudimentary notion of eros.

[5] Here I have in mind not only traditions such as the Left-handed Tantric Tradition that embodies spiritual-erotic practice as specifically sexual practice, but also those that regard eros as opening the person to transformation. In addition to Williamson's "Soaring," see Rich (1978), Raymond (1982) and Lewis (1960).

[6] The dualism of masculist ontology and erotics is illustrated in the following passage from Norman O. Brown: 'Dual organization is sexual organization. The structural principle is the union of opposites. . . . The *agon*, the contest between winter and summer, night and day is coitus' (Brown, 1966: 22–23). Standing outside the ontology based on dualistic oppositions, it is easy to recognize what is odd about the attempt to represent cyclical changes as an alteration between opposing states. If one considers the seasons, for example, we find there is nothing about those cycles that dictates what two points should be taken as the extremes of the cycle. One might select extremes of temperature, or of duration of daylight, or any number of other pairs of points.

the other. Such genuine recognition is contrasted with misattribution of one's own characteristics to the other—what the Freudians call 'projection'. The other may genuinely possess the characteristics of the self that one sees in the other, one may simultaneously learn to love oneself (or an aspect of oneself) in loving the other. The experience of learning to love oneself in *loving* (as well as in being loved by) the other appears as a frequent vehicle for development or transformation among women. The experience of this sort of transformation is vividly expressd in Cris Williamson's song "Soaring."[7] The second half of the lyrics reads as follows:

> Meeting myself in the mirror,
> Finding myself getting much clearer.
> You loved the living daylights into me . . .
> A heartbeat harmony—
> A circle symphony.
> Flying free . . .
> My heart is soaring
> My love is pouring
> Into your life.
> You came and found me
> When I was lost in a daze
> You came around me,
> And showed me my face.
> You are my mirror.
> I see myself shine.
> And when I'm near you,
> I'm in my own time
>
> Soaring . . .
>
> I am soaring . . .
>
> In my own time.

In this sort of love relationship being the lover is no longer the converse of being the beloved.

In what then does the otherness of the other lie? As Claudia Card (personal communication) has observed, surprise is erotic (if it isn't something else). The truth of this observation is explained by the underscoring of the other's oth-

---

[7] In academic circles it is common to assume a hierarchical ordering that places the insights of philosophers and other academics 'on a different plane', so that it would be unthinkable for a philosopher to quote song lyrics in corroboration of the view that there is a new and alternative ontological viewpoint being developed. I trust that that is not the case with this audience. Nonetheless, since the music as well as the lyrics are integral to the pieces of women's music from which I quote, the references will not be fully meaningful to those who are not already familiar with these songs.

erness in these circumstances: the other's otherness is most vividly experienced in the spontaneous and hence unexpected action of the other.

The unexpected character of an action turns only on its departure from what one has usually seen done. It does not require that action be unintelligible much less that it be threatenting or antagonistic. An unexpected action of an other may on the contrary appear ingenius or even just what, one judges upon reflection, one would have done had one been in the same situation. Therefore nothing in an other's manifestation of otherness in the way of distinctness and autonomy requires that the other possess characteristics that are opposite to those of the self (still less that the other's action be antagonistic to one's own purposes). This is a key feature of what I term the feminist self-other(s) distinction, namely that the distinctness of others does not require that they be counted as opposite in character to the self. (As a consequence others may be distinct from each other as well. Hence the relation is not fundamentally dyadic: it is a self-other(s) relation.)

Insofar as the those who love one another have symmetric relationship, in contrast, for example, to the relationship between an adult and an infant which though mutual is not symmetric, eros includes the elements of friendship or sisterhood. Eros is not presupposed for friendship or sisterhood, however. Indeed, the deep trust that is a hallmark of such partnership enhances one's capacity both to make a mindful choice for, and to endure, the terrors of *ex stasis*. (The Latin root of ecstacy meant terror, from the Greek word meaning to drive one out of one's senses.)

Insofar as eros is linked with sexual relationships, this new erotics provides the theoretical underpinnings for what in 1972 Alice Koller called her 'rule of chastity' which was that one have sexual relations only with a person who is first one's friend (Koller). However, the bond of eros is not limited to those linked by specifically sexual attraction, let alone engaged in sexual relationship. Therefore, the thesis for which I am arguing is much more general. It is that, to the extent that the relationship is symmetrical, the *ex stasis* of eros is entered into with one to whom one is bound by friendship.

Although the act of getting into another's body and consciousness and the receiving of another into one's body and consciousness enacted in sexual encounter is an apt metaphor, and perhaps even a common *vehicle* for the *ex stasis* of eros, it is not equivalent to it. Erotic *ex stasis* does not depend upon a sexual engagement.

Indeed, as I have argued, eros is an essential aspect of the mother-child bond and 'falling in love' aptly describes certain aspects of the maternal experience. In particular, many of the passions of maternal attachment turn on seeing in the infant qualities which exist only in potential. (Potentials are not simply absences, however.) It is the immediate filling in of a whole picture on the basis of a few perceptions that makes 'falling' an apt metaphor for the experience. The fact that incest involving the mother is extremely rare, however, supports the generalization that the mother's attachment to the child is *not* sexual in the narrow sense of seeking expression in genitally focused activity. Insofar as the girl-infant's eros toward her mother is modeled on the mother's

own attachment (because it is learned throught identification with the mother), it is likewise not sexual in the narrow sense.[8] I suspect that even the infant boy's attachment to his mother has been distorted by reading into it a great deal of the (culturally mediated) attachment of men to women.

5. KNOWING AND LOVING

In the view of the dominant culture the erotic attachment is assumed to be to an opposite other. The conventional wisdom is 'opposites attract' and in this instance being the 'opposite' sex is of the greatest significance. Freud, for example, takes homosexuality to be rooted in narcissism.

If the lover and beloved were opposite in nature, it could hardly be expected that each would be able to recognize the other for what s/he is. The disconnection between loving and knowing the beloved is an unsurprising result to the dominant culture: generations of theater-goers have accepted at face value Othello's assertion that he loved 'not wisely but *too well*', although, as Carol Gilligan recently observed (personal communication), he clearly did not know who his beloved was. The separation in masculist thought between loving and knowing or understanding a person is just one illustration of a general feature of masculist ontology, namely the presumption that the other is unlike the self until proven otherwise. This assignment of the burden of proof is reflected in a number of philosophical 'problems', such as the so-called problem of other minds (Whitbeck, 1983c). This ontological view of the self–other relation, coupled with the dictum that opposites attract, make loving and knowing or understanding one's beloved virtually contradictory!

A number of well-known thinkers, including Hegel and Norman O. Brown (1966) (see Note 6), envision a solution in the form of a synthesis or union of opposites. My point is that their solution is a solution to a masculist problem, a problem engendered by an ontology of dualistic oppositions. Similarly, some feminists who believe it desirable to create a society in which gender was not a major social category have held that it is difficult to envision such a society. Such a view of society is only natural on the non-dualistic ontology that I call 'feminist', however, and it has to some extent been realized in those subcultures, such as the Friends ('Quakers'), that have accorded full respect to women's spiritual, moral, and ontological vision. (See Margaret Fell, *Women's*

---

[8] For *some purposes* certain physiological changes or 'signs of arousal' are taken to define the sexual. Thus sex therapists may take such signs to indicate that a client who complains of an inability to become aroused, is in fact responding sexually, and then go on to teach the client how to recognize and accept his or her sexual response. I regard it as a major error for philosophers to adopt physiological criteria for the application of terms that are of significance in human life and thus to divorce the application of those terms from a consideration of human agendas in which those responses occur, however. In the case of sexuality, if it should turn out that, as it is sometimes alleged, the nursing experience is physiologically similar to sexual arousal, then among the absurdities to which we would be committed if we were to take physiological data to decide the question of the sexual character of the relationship issue, is that all nursing mothers would be said to have had incestuous relations with their children.

Speaking, 1664). In a society that fully realized this non-dualistic vision no importance could be accorded to the gender of one's beloved, even if the beloved were one's sexual partner. (What Koller called her 'First Rule of Chastity' would still be important, however, and it is an empirical question as to who is capable of friendship and with whom at any point in history.)

6. LOVE, KNOWLEDGE AND TRANSFORMATION IN THE MOTHERING EXPERIENCE

After centuries of representation of the mother from the perspective of men and occasionally the male infant, we have seen a new literature that explores this relation from the perspective of the girl. Some of these explorations, such as those of Jean Baker Miller, are carried out without recourse to dualistic categories and thus, as I have explained, these feminist psychological accounts provide a heuristic for feminist ontology (Whitbeck, 1983b).

A smaller literature has examined the mothering relation from the mother's perspective (e.g. McBride, 1972, Rich, 1976, and several of the essays in Trebilcot, 1983). I wish to consider the issue of eros in the mothering relation from the point of view of the mother, and specifically to consider the potential for transformation of both the mother and the child in this relationship. In speaking of 'the mothering experience' and 'the practice of mothering', I do not mean to suggest that it is an experience that all and only biological mothers share. It might be called 'parenting' but as matters stand throughout the world, it is the female relatives of an infant who most often have this experience and engage in this practice (Peterson, 1983).

An essential aspect of the mothering of infants is the engagement of the infant so that s/he matures into a social person, that is, a being who is capable of interpersonal relationship. A crucial element in this process is seeing the infant as a person, and therefore, often as seeing the infant as engaging in more sophisticated behavior than s/he is fully capable. This does not require that one make an intellectual error: one may know about the perceptual and cognitive limitation of infants. Yet one responds to the infant as to the person and this response communicates to the infant which of its actions are significant.

At some point, as a result of viewing the interactions of others engaged in mothering if not before, one becomes aware of the variety of interpretations as well as the latitude of responses possible. For example, the actions of an eighteen-month-old from whom the mother has been absent for two days and who responds by avoiding or refusing to look at the mother the first day of her return, may be seen by the mother in a number of distinct ways, e.g. as punishing the mother for going away, as expression of anger at her for going away, and as attempting to gain some control over her appearance and disappearance. The mother may become aware of these alternative interpretations, or if not, if she sees the child as, say, expressing anger, she is at least aware that she has a choice as to how to respond to that anger.

Since some identification with children is necessary to do a decent job of reasoning on their behalf and teaching them how to reason for themselves, there is ample opportunity for misattribution to the child of one's own conscious and unconscious thoughts and feelings. The frequency of surprises in the child's articulation of her or his experience, and the child's demonstration of new responses as a function of new capacities frequently show the mother that some of her interpretations were false. The reflective mother (or motherer) learns a great deal about herself from her perceptions and the patterns of her misperceptions.

It is not possible to avoid the risks of this process by the philosopher's frequent expedient of suspending response, since in child-rearing the absence of a response is itself a response and will communicate something to the child. Success in mothering in part turns upon learning what situations one is likely to misperceive, and in fashioning one's responses so that they will be appropriate, or at least not disastrous, even if one has to some extent misperceived the situation. The accurate assessment of what would be disastrous requires that one be able to see the situation from the child's perspective, and this of course requires that the subjectivity of the child be attended to.

My use of the terms, 'success' and 'appropriate' point to the standards of achievement for the mothering relation that set it apart from the erotic bond as represented in dualisitc thought: the development and empowerment of the beloved is essential to the process.[9] Essential to the child's experience of empowerment is the experience of being recognized as one who can perceive and influence others, especially the most significant others. The way in which such people are actually changed *by* the child is one of the most profound aspects of their participation in the child's development.

A central aspect of the empowerment of the child is the differentiation of the child's self from that of the maternal figure(s). This differentiation is played out in the varying access that each presumes to the other's person, especially, but not only, to the other's body. Among the concrete problems that a woman commonly faces that force her to make decisions regarding the infant's access to her body are the problem of what to do about the infant who bites the nipple, or that of how to respond to the hazard of little elbows at breast height. (In my observation women often discuss such matters, but men seem much less liable to share strategies about protecting their genitals from rambunctious lap-sitters.) Certainly the actual strategies chosen (for example, keeping the child off one's lap, protecting the breast, controlling the child's movement when on the lap, making the child aware of the pain caused by getting elbowed in the breast), together with the ages at which they are altered, are themselves of significance in the child's development. The importance of the correlation of the child's access to the mother's body with the mother's access to the child's body for the child's development of a sense of differentiation of self from other

---

[9] There are many views about what powers are the most important, that is, what are or should be the characteristics that make a person fit for life.

is frequently overlooked, however. (I explain this as due to the culture's silence about the tasks of mothering.) It is sometimes necessary in caring for children to force them to undergo painful procedures, say the removal of splinters. On these occasions I observe that mothers often balance the intrusions on the child's person by allowing the child more unrestricted access to her own body. The *mutuality* of such temporary dissolution of boundaries is overlooked by those who accept the dualist dogma that the choices are confined to egoism and self-sacrifice. Such people are liable either to regularly intrude upon their children or let their children intrude upon them, and so rear children who are either unsure of their own rights of and capacity for privacy, or who act as petty tyrants (or alternate between the two)—with varying results depending on their position of privilege. As the ground-breaking empirical studies of Carol Gilligan, Nona Lyons (1983) and others at the Harvard School of Education show, many women think about ethical matters in ways that are strikingly free of the assumptions of masculist ethics that pervade the thinking of men with similar backgrounds.

The empowerment of the child, to be successful, must give the child the skills for influencing others besides the mother. Thus, maternal love not only leads the mother to a deepening knowledge of both her child or children and herself, but more poignantly, to the preparation of the beloved child to go her or his own way which is likely to produce physical separation. Although there may be those who do a good job of mothering who are somewhat possessive of their children in their early years, as the child grows older possessive aims frustrate or are frustrated by the aim to empower the child.[10]

7. CONVERGENCE IN FEMINIST THOUGHT ON A NEW EROTICS

The acknowledged feature of maternal love, that it needs to be non-possessive is a feature of eros between adults in a growing number of feminist representations. For example, the refrain of Holly Near's 'Golden Thread' admonishes:

> . . . You can't possess a woman, no
> You can't possess a woman
> If you love her so
> you've got to let her go
> And she's got to let you let her go

'Love them and let them go' is the phrase that Gini Clemens takes from a Buddhist injunction regarding children, to be the title of a song in which she

---

[10] As Naomi Scheman (1983) pointed out, the culture's emphasis on motherhood as the sole vocation for the middle-class woman, makes it extremely difficult for her to be non-possessive in the way required for good mothering.

asks her friends to love her and let her go. (Because those Clemens addresses are identified as friends it is less clear that what is involved is specifically eros rather than friendship, however.)

In her extended account of the contrast between a loving and an arrogant attitude toward the other, the 'loving eye' as contrasted with the 'arrogant eye', Marilyn Frye (1983) gives a detailed account of the centrality of the recognition of the other's independent existence in the loving attitude. She says, 'The loving eye makes the correct assumption: the object of the seeing is *another* being whose existence and character are logically independent of the seer and who may be practically or empirically independent in any particular respect at any particular time.' (p. 173). (This passage taken by itself might seem to be as much a characterization of respect—see Addelson, forthcoming—or of charity, rather than eros, but there are other passages that explicitly discuss the need of the seer for the beloved.)

An explanation of this agreement on the nature of love (eros) on the part of feminists writing in a variety of formats from a variety of life experiences is that as we free ourselves of the residues of masculist theory and practice, we find ourselves living in terms of a different self–other(s) relation. We need to understand this self–other(s) relation and the erotics that is being lived by women in a variety of relationships, usually but not only, with other women. Reflection both on Frye's account and on her practice in philosophizing, further clarifies the character of this erotics. (Frye's stated purpose in her book is 'to say something clearly enough, intelligibly enough, so that it can be understood and thought about' (1983: 173). In choosing this purpose as well as in carrying it out with such success, Frye demonstrates feminist practice as well as contributing to feminist theory in a way which helps to heal the division between theory and practice that is common in philosophy and other academic pursuits.)

8. CONCEPTS OF A LESBIAN, FEMINIST ONTOLOGY AND LISTENING TO WOMEN

Frye connects seeing with the loving eye and being a lesbian. Indeed, the ability to see women with the loving eye, to recognize women, and in particular to recognize women's ability to author perception is central to the characterization that she gives of a lesbian (Frye, 1983: 172). Frye's project is to give new life to the word 'lesbian' and to make it an adequate term of self-description for at least some women who presently find no descriptors adequate for themselves. Therefore, she does not simply accept any of the customary definitions, such as 'female homosexual'. Nonetheless, although in her view the property of having sexual relations with women does not constitute a necessary or sufficient criterion for the application of the term 'lesbian', it is a core property.

There are many reasons for being concerned with the project of redefining the term 'lesbian' as Frye (1983), Ferguson (1981), Addelson (1981), Hoagland (unpub'd), Raymond (1982), Rich (1980), Zita (1981) and others have, and/or

with using the term in one of these new ways. Liberation movements from at least Christianity to Marxism have taken the most despised roles and identities within a society and reappraise the society or human life in terms of the virtues and perceptions available to those who occupy those identities and roles. New uses of language are frequently important in carrying out the larger project of seeing women and/or of making women's lives intelligible.

If, or to the extent that, we take the goal of seeing women, of recognizing them as the authors of perception, and/or of making women's lives intelligible as the primary projects, then we need to be clear about when, or under what circumstances, other projects intended to contribute to that larger project do in fact do so. This applies to new uses of language, and to new uses of the term 'lesbian' in particular. (It also applies to doing feminist theory, and to the project of developing a feminist ontology, of course, but that is the subject of another paper.)

Frye regards the situation of a lesbian as radically different from that of other women in the following respect:

> 'Lesbians are not invited to join—the family, the party, the project, the procession, the war effort. There is a place for a woman in every game. Wife, secretary, servant, prostitute, daughter, assistant, babysitter, mistress, seamstress, proofreader, nurse, confidante, masseuse, indexer, typist, mother. Any of these is a place for a woman, and women are much encouraged to fill them. None of these is a place for a lesbian' (1983: 131).

Of course, lesbians are also mothers, secretaries, nurses, etc. and as such invited, cajoled, coerced etc. into doing what male-dominated society wants of mothers, secretaries, etc. I interpret Frye to mean that male-dominated society has reservations about a woman occupying any of these traditional women's roles if she is a lesbian. Given the new concept of a lesbian that Frye is developing, there are at least two characteristics of a lesbian in Frye's sense each of which individually as well as jointly might make her objectionable to the dominant culture, particularly in stereotypic women's roles: her feminism in the sense of her insistence that both she and other women are authors of perception, and her homosexuality. Although it is certainly part of Frye's purpose to join the two attributes in her concept of the lesbian, where the two traits have existed independently they have been responded to differently. The response to them has depended not only upon the relative importance for a given segment of society of maintaining the masculist dualistic organization that Gayle Rubin (1975) has called the 'gender-system', as compared with its homophobia, but on whether sexual relations between women were considered a serious possibility. (Queen Victoria for one held they were not, and the French writer Colette describes the belittling toleration accorded to sexual relations between women in some segments of turn of the century French society.)

Without discounting the fury with which society has sometimes punished women for homosexual relationships, homosexuality has sometimes not only

been tolerated in 'exceptional women' (of the upperclasses) who entered traditionally male professions and presumed to take on social roles that had been open only to men, it offered confirmation of their exceptional status (Smith-Rosenberg and Newton, 1981). The exemption that did and to some extent still does go with being labeled 'lesbian' by men, in many academic and professional circles, should not be overlooked. I recall one of my students who was told by her male professor that if he knew that she were a lesbian then he could give her a certain opportunity. His implication was that if and only if she were lesbian could he be assured that she would not waste the opportunity, as though lesbianism and only that would insure that she had stereotypically male career ambitions. (The issue of exemption has lost some prominence in the last decade to the extent that modern individualism is coming to regard it as only rational for everyone to want to be the sort of careerist previously regarded as a normal desire only in men. This has equally unacceptable implications for many women who do not want this Procrustean bed any more than the one designed for the stereotypic woman of the 1950s.)

To the extent that women's relationships to other women are key relationships in a woman's life, her life experience is one for which she will find scant representation in the larger culture, and to this extent she is beyond the pale (etymologically 'outside the fence') which is a place of both terror and creative opportunity.

Consider, for example, the sister of a woman as such. (We have no word at all for this very common and ancient relation.) The unspoken features of this relation are now just coming to be discussed (see for example, *Sisters* by Elizabeth Fishel, 1980) and this is a part of the growing awareness among women that none of our relations with other women and women-children have been represented to any significant extent within the dominant culture. Many women are dispelling the silence, and speaking from the experience of these relationships which are outside the masculist conceptual scheme. (See for example, Lousie Bernikow's *Among Women* (1980), or the song 'Every Woman' by Bernice Johnson Reagon of Sweet Honey in the Rock.)

Frye explains this point saying that for 'phallocratic' reality, women are the background. The role of background is to be uneventful. Therefore, events and aspects of women's lives that are not a part of events and aspects of men's lives are ignored.

Let us return to the connection between being deviant and being outside of the conceptual scheme which Frye (1983) proposes in the passages quoted above: What, if any, connection is there between being outside the conceptual scheme and being deviant? There certainly is an incompatibility between being *classified as deviant* and being outside the conceptual scheme altogether, for if, or to the extent that, one is outside the scheme one is not classified at all. Therefore, the difference between, say, being labeled eccentric, say, and being labeled deviant simply would not apply. Nonetheless, having as the central relationships in one's life relationships about which the culture is silent certainly does give one a different perspective, and if one speaks out of that perspective

one will certainly seem odd, *whether or not* these relationships are classified as deviant.

In their paper 'The mythic lesbian and the new woman: power and sexuality', Carroll Smith-Rosenberg and Ester Newton (1981) shed some light on the question of the connection between the concept of a lesbian and deviance from the point of view of the dominant culture. They adduce historical evidence to show that the term 'lesbian' was first used by Havelock Ellis and other male sexologists and only subsequently came to be a part of the description and self-definition of some among the second generation of feminists. (They point out that it had *not* been a part of the self-description of the first generation of feminists—regardless of their sexual practices—many of whom never married, however, and therefore counted as deviant by Victorian society.)

What this suggests is that in spite of being silent about women's love for one another, the dominant culture in reacting to the multiple anomalies posed for dualism by the feminist movement (and to influential new theories concerning the role of sexuality in the development of the personality) found a need both to talk about sexuality and to find a way of rationalizing the anomalous behavior of nineteenth-century feminists.

It is worth recalling here that at least in Victorian times the tendency of the dominant culture was to think of male homosexuality as involving at least one partner taking on a stereotypically female or feminine role. (The same misinformation is explicitly stated in some popular books on sex such as *Everything You Always Wanted To Know About Sex*.) Thus in the nineteenth-century, British Naval regulations laid down extremely harsh penalties for homosexual activity which was *defined* as anal intercourse between men. Oral-genital activity between men was not considered. I hypothesize that this was because anal intercourse seemed to them analogous to vaginal intercourse which they took to be the paradigm of sexual activity between a man and a woman.

I hypothesize that the male sexologists who generated the term 'lesbian' did so in a conscious or unconscious attempt to contain or rationalize the deep threat that feminism posed to the social order, by constructing a category of deviance consistent with the framework of gender dualism. What they did was to explain the existence of women who behaved in ways that do not fit the stereotypically feminine behavior within the dualistic framework by creating a special category of women who were understood as women-who-act-like-men or, to put it more dramatically, 'men in women's bodies'. Women who were perceived as fitting into this category, and only these women, were to some extent exempt from the expectations usually placed upon women, but the exemption carried the price of being labeled deviant.

(I subscribe to the philosophical position that most concepts of interest are not adequately rendered by giving a definition of the corresponding term. Therefore, I regard the generalizations that the male sexologists thought true of lesbians were as much a part of their concept of a lesbian as their explicit definition of the term.)

My hypothesis about the concepts of homosexuality and lesbianism in mas-

culist thought finds further support in the prevalence of the confusion of homosexuality with transexualism, as though sexual preference were indicated by, and a sure indicator of, gender identity. (Contrast this with the more refined categorization of the Mohave Indians—discussed in Ferguson, (1981)—who maintained their gender structure with a category of deviance for members of one sex who took on the social role of the opposite sex, but who did not confuse homosexuality with taking the role of the member of the opposite sex.) It is also supported by the observation that, as Frye puts it 'Queerly enough, one appears heterosexual by informing people of one's sex *very* emphatically and *very* unambiguously' (1983: 24). This shows that not only is homosexuality confused with transexualism, but to neglect or refuse to proclaim one's gender according to the established social convention is *not* interpreted as a sign of refusal to cooperate with the dualistic gender system, but as a sign that one fits into the special categories of deviance within that system. One is then usually assumed to fit the stereotype of one gender in spite of having the body of the other sex.

I am not, of course, suggesting that anyone *should* use the term 'lesbian' in the way that its original authors did, because the function of that use or sense is to defend an inadequate ontology and an inhumane social structure. What I am saying is that the category, lesbian, both in the minds of its male inventors and as used in male-dominated culture is that of a physiological female who is in other respects a stereotypical male, and that is important for those who want to know when the projects of redefining the term 'lesbian' or of using it in a new sense serves the larger goal of recognizing women and making women's lives intelligible, and when they do not.

Outside of the confines of a few academic environments, I have found large numbers of women who are still reluctant to call themselves 'feminists' because they are afraid of being labeled as 'lesbians'. (In my experience this includes a significant number of women who not only have a sexual preference for women but who reside and spend their life [except for their paid work] with other women many of whom share the same sexual preference and lifestyle. When some of them have said [to me] that they are not 'lesbians' what they meant is that they are not men in women's bodies, and they are right!) I have encountered the problem of how to find words with which to share feminist views, and in particular the idea that we can (and indeed do!) live in ways that the dominant culture never envisioned for either men or women. To find a solution I have needed to come to terms with the way in which they understand the term 'lesbian'.

I have come up with two basic strategies in speaking with women who think of a lesbian as a stereotypic man in a woman's body. One is to explain myself in other terms, and the other is to give some time to redefining the term, 'lesbian'. My own pieced together strategy in such situations is to take the first approach if I know the women with whom I speak to be heterosexual, and the second if I know them to be homosexual, and when I don't know, or am dealing with both, I take the first approach if I have not yet gained the group's trust,

and the second if I have. (I welcome comment on this practice as well as the theoretical reflections presented here.)

9. REFOCUSING ON LOVE

So far in this paper I have suggested the thesis for which I have argued elsewhere, which is that individualism or what I call 'the rule of the sons', has largely replaced patriarchy or 'rule of the fathers' as the structure of the dominant culture. (My view is similar, though not identical to an earlier view of Ehrenreich and English (1978).) As I remarked earlier, individualism has a difficult time making intelligible any human bonding other than that based on contract—what so many 19th century British and American writers called 'the sacred contract'—or on appetite. I argue that it is because sexual desire lends itself as representation as mere appetite (lust) that sexual relationships are taken as the uniquely intelligible personal relationships in modern society. A correlative assumption of modern society is that only the sexual couple or perhaps the nuclear family, is a viable form of human bonding.

It is very likely that for most of the women in history and for most of the women in the world today, the closest relationships are not sexual relationships. This is not to deny that they are physical—who but philosophers could think they were not physical—but as the example of the mother and child illustrates, some of the most intimate physical relationships are not sexual. Although the receiving of another into one's body and consciousness enacted in sexual encounter is one metaphor, and perhaps even a common *vehicle* for the *ex stasis* of eros and for transformation, so may be other human relationships as well as meditation, prayer, therapy, and various forms of massage and body work.

Jacqueline Zita has given careful attention to the consequences of various projects to redefine the term 'lesbian' for the larger project of hearing women (Zita, 1981). I agree with many of her observations, but I wish now to consider one that I think is an oversimplification. Zita suggests that a 'genital homophobia' often lies behind the use of terms such as 'woman-loving' rather than 'lesbian' in these contexts. I am not entirely sure what is meant by this expression, but assume it is something like an irrational fear of the genitals of, or genital contact with homosexuals or with homosexuals of one's own sex. I do not find this convincing, in part because in my experience, many women shun the label 'lesbian' for other reasons, and in part because I think the women's health movement has made many feminists comfortable with all aspects of their own and other women's bodies. I recognize that it is important both to get women over the fear of being called 'lesbian', and to dispell the taboo on sexual relations between women, and using the term 'lesbian' sometimes furthers both of these projects. I think it is dangerous to *assume* that women are afraid of doing something just because they are reluctant to focus on it, however, because

that puts the burden upon them to prove their authority with regard to their own experience. I am reminded of the male rationalization, brilliantly exposed in a series of Jules Feiffer cartoons in the sixties, in which a man explained some women's lack of sexual interest in him as fear of his masculinity.

Suppose, however, that it were true that most feminists who don't use the term 'lesbian' were fearful of, rather than uninterested in, genital contact with women. We would still need to decide under what circumstances it would be of the greatest priority to bring this hang-up to their attention, and in what circumstances would it be more important to do other things.

In the light of my own experience it does seem odd to suggest that loving women without sharing sex with them leaves the relation incomplete. This suggestion is made by some proponents of the idea of a 'lesbian continuum' when they speak of 'consummated' and 'unconsummated' love for women, by which they mean relationships that do and do not include sexual activity. Among the relationships to which I have devoted considerable energy in the last few years is my relationship to my sister. It does not seem to me that that relationship is well described as 'unconsummated' just because the consummations of that relationship are other than sexual. It seems to me that the same is true of many other love relationships among women, so that whatever advantages there are to using the notion of a lesbian continuum in some contexts, the labeling of non-sexual relationships as 'unconsummated' is only confusing.

The incapacity of this society to recognize the transformative potential of any human relationships other than sexual and therapeutic relationships is re-markable. It is important to avoid perpetuating this over-emphasis on sex in feminist thought. I recall in the 1960s the people (usually white women) who told me that my commitment to civil rights and overcoming white racism would be more complete if I had a black lover. (In those days it was assumed that the lover would be male.) Neither political action nor non-sexual friendships with black women and men were supposed to have the same potential. Then too, there were those who held that the quintessential psychological break-throughs required engaging in group sex.

Although no doubt many are sincere in recommending to others what they see as a crucial step in their own journey, and although sexual experience *may* be an important vehicle for making radical steps toward self-realization, it is not the unique means for doing so. Therefore, women are not missing something essential in not learning to express in a sexual way the deep love that they feel for one another, any more than they are missing something essential in not becoming mothers. Indeed, in my observation some feminists who do have sexual relationships with other women, have non-sexual relationships with women which are of equal or (especially in the case of daughters) greater intimacy and significance in their lives.

A new society requires more than a shift in the individuals who are a party to various relationships; it requires different types of relationship, and different ways of loving than those to which our society has given much attention. It is this that many feminists are creating and this deserves to be the focus of our attention.

REFERENCES

Addelson, Kathryn Pyne. 1981. Words and lives. On 'Compulsory heterosexuality and lesbian existence' defining the issues. *Signs* 7 (1): 187–199.

Addelson, Kathryn Pyne. Forthcoming. *Respect, An Essay on Abortion and the Social Organization of Morality.*

Bernikow, Louise. 1980. *Among Women.* Harper & Row, New York.

Boulding, Elise. 1977a. *Women in the Twentieth Century World.* Sage Publications, Beverley Hills, CA.

Boulding, Elise. 1977b. *The Family As a Way Into the Future.* Pendel Hill Publications, Wallingford, Penn.

Brown, Norman O. 1966. *Love's Body.* Random House, New York.

Chodorow, Nancy. 1978. *The Reproduction of Mothering, Psychoanalysis and the Sociology of Gender.* University of California, Berkeley.

Christ, Carol and Judith Plaskow. 1979. *Womanspirit Rising, A Feminist Reader on Religion.* Harper & Row, New York.

Clemens, Gini. Love them and let them go. On *Long-Time Friends.* Open Door Records, Chicago.

Collins, Margery and Christine Pierce. 1976. Holes and slime: sexism. In Gould, Carol C. and Mary Wartofsky, eds, *Women and Philosophy: Towards a Theory of Liberation.* G. P. Putnam's Sons, New York. First published in *Philosophical Forum* 5 (1 and 2), 1973–4.

Condren, Mary T. 1982. Patriarchy and death. Paper presented at the American Academy of Religious Meetings, New York, December.

Ehrenreich, Barbara and Deirdre English. 1978. *For Her Own Good: 150 Years of the Experts' Advice to Women.* Anchor Press/Doubleday, New York.

Fell, Margaret. 1664. *Women's Speaking.* In *Works.* London: 1710.

Ferguson, Ann. 1981. Patriarchy, sexual identity, and the sexual revolution. In On 'Compulsory heterosexuality and lesbian existence' defining the issues. *Signs* 7 (1): 158–172.

Fingarette, Herbert. 1963. *The Self in Transformation, Psychoanalysis, Philosophy, and the Life of the Spirit.* Basic Books, New York.

Fishel, Elizabeth. 1980. *Sisters.* Bantam, New York.

Freire, Paulo. 1973. *Pedagogy of the Oppresses.* Myra Bergman Ramos (trans.). Seabury Press, New York.

Freire, Paulo. 1974. Education as the practice of freedom. In Freire, Paulo, ed., *Education for Critical Consciousness.* Seabury Press, New York.

Frye, Marilyn. 1983. *The Politics of Reality: Essays in Feminist Theory.* The Crossing Press, Trumansburg, N.Y.

Gould, Carol, ed. 1983. *Domination. New Pespectives on Women and Philosophy.* Rowman and Allanheld, Totowa, N.J.

Gould, Carol C. and Mark Wartofsky, eds. 1976. *Women and Philosophy: Toward A Theory of Liberation.* G. P. Putnman's Sons, New York.

Griffin, Susan. 1981. *Pornography and Silence: Culture's Revenge Against Nature.* Harper & Row, New York.

Harding, Sandra and Merill B. Hintikka, eds. 1983. *Discovering Reality.* D. Reidel, Dordrecht, Holland.

Hoagland, Sarah. Lesbian epistemology, unpublished manuscript.

Holmes, Helen B., Betty Hoskins and Michael Gross. eds. *The Custom-Made Child?: Women-Centered Perspective.* (Vol. 2 of the edited Proceedings of the conference on Ethical Issues in Human Reproduction Technology: Analysis by Women.) Humana Press, Clifton, N.J.

Koller, Alice. On female sexuality, unpublished manuscript.

Lewis, C. S. 1960. *The Four Loves.* Harcourt Brace & World, New York.

Lindemann, S. K. and Elizabeth Oliver. 1982. Consciousness, liberation and health delivery systems. *J. Med. Philosophy* **7** (2): 135–152.

Lugones, María and Elizabeth V. Spelman. 1983. Have we got a theory for you! Feminist theory, cultural imperialism and the demand for 'the Woman's Voice'. *Hypatia* **1** (1): *Women's Studies Int. Forum* **6** (6): 573–581.

Lyons, Nona. 1983. Two perspectives: on self, relationships and morality. *Harv. Educ. Rev.* **53** (2) May: 125–145.

McBride, Angela B. 1972. *The Growth and Development of Mothers*. Harper & Row, New York.

Miller, Jean Baker. 1976. *Toward A New Psychology of Women*. Beacon Press, Boston.

Miller, Jean Baker. 1982. *Women and Power*. The Stone Center for Developmental Services and Studies, Wellesley, Mass.

Near, Holly. Golden thread. On *Fire in the Rain*. Redwood Records, Ukiah, CA.

O'Faolain, Julia and Lauro Maritines, eds. 1973. *Not in God's Image: Women in History from the Greeks to the Victorians*. Harper & Row, New York.

Ortner, Sherry B. 1974. Is female to male as nature is to culture? In Rosaldo, Michelle Zimbalist and Louise Lamphere, eds, *Woman, Culture and Society*. Stanford University Press, Stanford, CA.

Peterson, Susan. 1983. Against 'Parenting'. In Trebilcot, Joyce, ed. *Mothering Essays in Feminist Theory*. Rowman and Allanheld, Totowa, N.J.

Plato. *The Symposium*. 1961. Translated by Michael Joyce in *The Collected Dialogues of Plato*. Edited by Edith Hamilton and Huntington Cairns. Princeton University Press, Princeton, N.J.

Rawlinson, Mary. 1982. Psychiatric Discourse and the feminine voice. *J. Med. Philosophy* **7** (2): 153–177.

Raymond, Janice. 1982. A geneology of female friendship. Trivia, **1** (Fall): 5–26.

Reagon, Bernice Johnson, Everywoman. On Sweet Honey in the Rock. Redwood Records, Ukiah, CA.

Reuther, Rosemary Radford. 1979. Motherearth and the megamachine: A theology of liberation in a feminine, somatic and ecological perspective. In Christ, Carol and Judith Plaskow, eds, *op. cit.* First published in *Christianity and Crisis*, 12 April 1972.

Rich, Adrienne. 1976. *Of Woman Born: Motherhood as Experience and Institution*. Bantam Books, New York.

Rich, Adrienne. 1977. The meaning of our love for women is what we have constantly to expand. Reprinted in *On Lies Secrets, and Silence*. W. W. Norton, New York.

Rich, Adrienne. 1978. *The Dream of A Common Language*. W. W. Norton, New York.

Rich, Adrienne. 1980. Compulsory heterosexuality and lesbian existence. *Signs* **5** (4): 631–660.

Ringelheim, Joan. Communities in distress: Woman and the holocaust. Unpublished manuscript.

Rosaldo, Michelle Zimbalist and Louise Lamphere, eds. 1974. *Woman, Culture, and Society*. Stanford University Press, Stanford, Calif.

Rubin, Gayle. 1975. The traffic in women: Notes on the political economy of sex. In Reiter, Rayna, ed. *Towards an Anthropology of Women*. Monthly Review of Books Press, New York.

Ruddick, Sara. 1983. Maternal thinking. In Trebilcot, Joyce, ed., *Mothering: Essays in Feminist Theory*. Rowman and Allanheld, Totowa, N.J. First published in *Feminist Studies* **6** (2): 213–230 (1980).

Scheman, Naomi. 1983. Individualism and the objects of psychology. In Harding, Sandra and Merill B. Hintikka, eds, *Discovering Reality*. D. Reidel, Dordrecht, Holland.

Smith-Rosenberg, Carroll and Ester Newton. 1981. The mythic lesbian and the new

woman: Power and sexuality. Delivered at the Berkshire Conference on Women's History, Vassar College, June.

Trebilcot, Joyce, ed. 1983. *Mothering: Essays in Feminist Theory.* Rowman & Allanheld, Totowa, N.J.

Warren, Mary Ann. 1980. *The Nature of Woman, An Encyclopedia and Guide to the Literature.* Edgewood Press, Michigan.

Whitbeck, Caroline. 1976. Theories of sex difference. In Gould, Carol C. and Marx Wartofsky, eds, *op. cit.* First published in *Philosophical Forum* 5 (1 and 2) 1973–4.

Whitbeck, Caroline. 1982. Women and medicine: An introduction. *J. Med. Philosophy* 7 (4): 119–133.

Whitbeck, Caroline. 1983a. The 'maternal instinct'. In Trebilcot, Joyce, ed., *op. cit.* First published in *Philosophical Forum* 6 (1 and 2): 1975.

Whitbeck, Caroline. 1983b. A different reality: Feminist ontology. In *Beyond Domination, New Perspectives on Women and Philosophy.* Rowman & Allanheld, Totowa, N.J.

Whitbeck, Caroline. 1983c. Afterword to the 'maternal instinct'. In Trebilcot, Joyce, ed., *op. cit.*

Whitbeck, Caroline. 1983d. The moral implication of regarding women as people: New perspectives on pregnancy and personhood. In Bondeson, William B. Tristam H. Engelhardt Jr., Stuart F. Spicker and Daniel Winship, eds., *Abortion and the Status of the Fetus.* D. Reidel, Dordrecht, Holland.

Williamson, Cris. Soaring. On *Live Dream.* Olivia Records, Oakland, California.

Zita, Jacquelyn N. 1981. Historical amnesia and the lesbian continuum. In On 'compulsory heterosexuality and lesbian existence' defining the issues. *Signs* 7 (1): 172–187.

Part III

Beauvoir and Feminist Philosophy

Introduction
Margaret A. Simons

"Why should we read *The Second Sex?* It's out-of-date, male-identified, and just Sartrean anyway!" That was the response of a friend of mine, a feminist philosopher, when I asked if she might use a book I'm writing on *The Second Sex* and contemporary feminism.

Her reaction reflects the feelings of many feminist philosophers asked to teach *The Second Sex*. For many of us, *The Second Sex* was the only text we had available for the first women's studies and feminist philosophy courses. So it's not surprising that we should have become acutely aware of its limitations and frustrated by its shortcomings. No one book could, or should, ever again be expected to fill such a role.

The Second Sex gave us a start; it gave feminist theorists and philosophers a starting point for defining research issues. As a foundation of feminist philosophy, it became a baseline for our philosophical differentiation. But in giving us something to push against in shaping our own perspectives, it came to be defined negatively in our feminist consciousness. "Who I am" began with "How I'm not like her."

Many feminists experience Beauvoir as their feminist mother, as Iris Marion Young's dream imagery in the first essay in this part reveals. But it may be an especially common experience to feminist philosophers. Coming to terms with Beauvoir, understanding and accepting her limitations and insights, can be as difficult for a feminist philosopher as coming to terms with her own mother. But it is work that must be done if we are to assure a future for the feminist philosophical tradition.

The essays that made up this special issue of *Hypatia* were selected from among those presented on the philosophy program of the 1984 University of

Pennsylvania conference "After *The Second Sex:* A New Beginning." They reflect a wide range of feminist philosophical perspectives and methodologies, but they all reflect a commitment to working with Beauvoir's philosophy and defining its relevance to contemporary feminist philosophical concerns.

The criticisms raised by my feminist colleague, that Beauvoir is "out-of-date, male-identified, and just Sartrean anyway," reflect some of the most serious scholarly problems that researchers interested in Beauvoir's work must address—and overcome—insofar as they are seen as justifications for ignoring her work. All of them are addressed in this collection of essays.

Many of the essays make some reference to the problem of historically situating Beauvoir's work in *The Second Sex,* although few address it directly (Charlene Haddock Seigfried and Ann Ferguson raise the issue most centrally). Most of the authors, as well, interpret Beauvoir as working within a Sartrean philosophical framework, without bringing that interpretation radically into question (Linda Singer's paper is a major exception here).

A problem all of the authors address—and the one I allowed to shape the organization of this issue of *Hypatia*—is that of Beauvoir and woman-identification. Young, in the first essay, frames the problem historically as a confrontation between two opposing feminist positions. The first is what Young characterizes as Beauvoir's humanist feminism marked by a dualism that identifies human values with male values and devalues the female. A second, opposing, position which emerged with the second wave of feminism is gynocentric feminism.

Young sees gynocentric feminism as marked by a respect for differences and a valuing of female experience, which thus overcomes the phallocentrism of Beauvoir's humanist feminism. But Young is troubled by the essentialism of gynocentric feminism, its conservative view of woman's nature as mothering and reproduction, and its shift from political involvement to cultural discourse. In her conclusion she calls for a synthesis of the two positions: an appreciation for differences and a revaluation of humanist feminism (and, implicitly, Beauvoir's perspective), acknowledging the effectiveness of its analysis of women's oppression.

Alison M. Jaggar and William L. McBride seem to proceed in a direction much like that suggested by Young in her conclusion. Situating Beauvoir's analysis of so-called reproduction in the socialist context established by Marx and Engels, they criticize her dualist and naturalist view for its devaluing of women's experience. They provide an extensive analysis of the traditional Marxist concepts of production and reproduction, concluding that the differentiation of reproduction from production is unjustified and sexist. They propose eliminating the concept of reproduction entirely, thus forcing male-dominated socialist ideology to acknowledge women's traditional work for the productive labor that it actually is.

Proceeding in a different direction and shifting the focus from woman's mothering to her eroticism, Arleen B. Dallery defends gynocentric feminism, represented by the French feminist perspective known as *écriture féminine*, against the charge of essentialism leveled by Young and Beauvoir herself. This criticism,

she argues, mistakenly identifies the *écriture féminine* perspective with a biological naturalism, ignoring their insight that "woman's body is always mediated by language."

Tracing the development of a French feminist analysis of woman's eroticism, Dallery describes the masculine bias in the phenomenological descriptions of sexuality by Merleau-Ponty and Sartre, and the failure of Beauvoir to make up for this "lack of a woman's voice." But, interestingly, Dallery senses a tension in Beauvoir's description of woman's sexuality and the presence of a sub-text in *The Second Sex*.

She finds there woman's sexuality seen not as a quasi-political reaction to patriarchal control of woman's sexuality as some of Beauvoir's critics suggest, but as description of woman's difference, her "impulsive libido." "Read across the grain, what Beauvoir describes is not woman's dependent or alienated sexuality, but rather, woman's repressed eroticism," an "erotic embodiment that cannot be fully subjectively lived within the confines of the dominant submissive model of patriarchal sexuality: it is still to be spoken and written."

Ann Ferguson focuses her discussion on the historical emergence of the modern concept of lesbian women-identity, through the historical creation of the lesbian community. While crediting Beauvoir for having defended the authenticity of lesbianism against Freudian attacks, Ferguson criticizes Beauvoir's analysis on three main grounds: its individualism, idealism, and naturalism. In *The Second Sex*, Beauvoir's individualist ethics fails to acknowledge the historical, social foundation of individual choice and lesbian identity. Her idealism leads her to falsely universalize about lesbian experience, and her naturalism leads her to a position antithetical to feminist political change. Ferguson wonders as well why, since Beauvoir saw lesbianism as a more "natural" sexual relationship for women in patriarchal society, she didn't question the possibility of authentic heterosexual relationships.

Claudia Card voices a similar concern in her essay, which gives a close, analytic reading of the ethical issues raised in Beauvoir's chapter on the lesbian. Card's paper focuses on the ethical questions of authenticity and taking responsibility for one's sexual orientation, and addresses Beauvoir's failure to extend her analysis of choice and responsibility to the heterosexual.

Beauvoir's was a radical position on lesbianism for its time; why did she stop short of bringing heterosexuality into question? "It seemed not to occur to her in that context that there was any choice involved." Card suggests that such a step would have provided Beauvoir with a critical perspective on the problematic Hegelian dualisms and on Hegel's view of the fundamental hostility of human consciousness. In her conclusion she calls for an assessment of lesbian relationships and lesbian attitudes.

In commentary on the two preceding essays, Marilyn Frye addresses the ethical issues of determinism and responsibility raised by Ferguson and Card, remarking that Beauvoir's concern in her chapter "The Lesbian" is less with lesbians than with "women, conceived as heterosexual." "Beauvoir's lesbian feels to me like a logical construct composed by turning various categories inside out and upside down to see what might fall out." Her focus, then, is on

the problem of reconciling an acceptance of the social determinants of women's perspectives and senses of self-identity, Ferguson argues, and an acknowledgment of the ethical obligation of being responsible and holding other women responsible for choices of perspective and identity.

In her detailed analysis of the very problematic biology chapter in *The Second Sex*, Seigfried addresses the issue of naturalism and woman's biological femaleness—her eroticism and mothering—which play such a role in gynocentric feminism and the definition of woman-identity. Interestingly, her philosophical perspective, based on pragmatism, seems sympathetic to the humanist feminist position of uniting rather than distinguishing male and female.

Seigfried terms Beauvoir's descriptions of woman's biology "obsolete and irredeemably flawed." She criticizes Beauvoir's male-as-human value structure endemic to both existentialism and science. But she finds Beauvoir's characterization of the body not as thing but as situation to be an insightful nondualistic model not only for cultural explanation but for biological explanation as well. She thus sees Beauvoir's treatment of woman's biology and its relation to the social, historical, psychological dimensions of woman's experience to be theoretically innovative and of contemporary relevance to the fledgling feminist theories of science.

Singer offers the most radical reinterpretation of Beauvoir, in her reading of *The Second Sex* and *Ethics of Ambiguity* as not Sartrean, but as establishing a gynocentric ethics, oppositional to that of Sartre. Singer sees Beauvoir's ethics not as reflecting a Sartrean idealism of absolute freedom, but descriptive of freedom emergent from a situation of relatedness and affinity. In reading Beauvoir's work as "the voice of the ethics of otherness" and an ethics of commitment, Singer thus returns to the project suggested by Young, of reconciling humanist and gynocentric feminism. But locating one such historical synthesis within Beauvoir's thought, Singer reclaims this important mother of feminist philosophy for contemporary feminists.

HUMANISM,
GYNOCENTRISM AND
FEMINIST POLITICS

Iris Marion Young

December 1978. At a mostly male conference I hug, chat, eat, drink, listen with my sisters in philosophy. My body avalanches from its recent maternal swellings to the plateaus of a folded uterus, milkless breasts. I left my baby daughter in Chicago, who used to suckle 90 minutes at a time while I read *The Women's Room.* For the first time in fifteen months that warm red flow moves through my clitoral canals. No quiet transition, but a body revolution throbbing my back and neck. Clouded in this privately womanstate, I glide around the chandeliered ballroom finding one woman's face and another and another. Fervently we converse about the day's papers and each other's questions. We catch up on the news about each other's lovers or children or jobs.

That night in my restless sleep I dream. A ballroom filled with women, hundreds under the chandeliers, a reception after business at the Society for Women in Philosophy. I flit from one group of women to another, in smiling comfort. As I turn to find another friend I see her tall figure across the room, as though overlooking the sisterly crowd: Simone de Beauvoir. Then, just before I wake, a single object, shimmering: a glass of milk.

No other woman can occupy our dreams as the mother of feminist philosophy (who in her time, in her view, could only be a writing mother by leaving her body out of mothering, and I think she was right). Yet most feminists in the U.S. today find irredeemable flaws in Beauvoir's story of women's oppression and her hope for liberation. What has happened between the childhood and puberty of our feminist revolution?

In this essay I explore the shift in feminist thinking from a Beauvoirian sort of position which I define as humanist feminism to an analysis which I call gynocentric feminism. Humanist feminism defines women's oppression as the inhibition and distortion of women's human potential by a society that allows the self-development of men. Most feminists of the nineteenth and twentieth centuries, including feminists of the early second wave, have been humanist feminists. In recent years a different account of women's oppression has gained influence, however, partly growing from a critique of humanist feminism. Gynocentric feminism defines women's oppression as the devaluation and repres-

sion of women's experience by a masculinist culture that exalts violence and individualism. It argues for the superiority of the values embodied in traditionally female experience, and rejects the values it finds in traditionally male dominated institutions. Gynocentric feminism, I suggest, contains a more radical critique of male-dominated society than humanist feminism. But at the same time, especially within the social context of anti-feminism backlash, however, its effect can be quieting and accommodating to official powers.

I

Humanist feminism consists in a revolt against femininity. Patriarchal culture has ascribed to women a distinct feminine nature by which it has justified the exclusion of women from most of the important and creative activity of society— science, politics, invention, industry, commerce, the arts. By defining women as sexual objects, decorative charmers, and mothers, the patriarchal culture enforces behavior in women that benefits men by providing them with domestic and sexual servants. Women's confinement to femininity stunts the development of their full human potential, and makes women passive, dependent and weak. Humanist feminism defines femininity as the primary vehicle of women's oppression, and calls upon male dominated institutions to allow women the opportunity to participate fully in the public world-making activities of industry, politics, art and science.

Women's liberation, on this view, consists in freeing women from the confines of traditional femininity, and making it possible for women to pursue the human projects that have hitherto been dominated by men. Any assumptions that women are not capable of achieving the excellence that men have attained must be suspended until women are allowed to develop their full potential. When gender differences are transcended in this manner, persons will be able to choose whatever activities they wish to pursue, will be able to develop their full human potential as individuals. Women's liberation consists in eliminating a separate women's sphere, and giving women the opportunity to do what men have done. This implies that men will have to do more of the work traditionally assigned to women.

I call this position humanist feminist because it defines gender difference as accidental to humanity. The goal of liberation is for all persons to pursue self development in those creative and intellectual activities that distinguish human beings from the rest of nature. Women's liberation means sexual equality. Sexual equality means bringing women and men under a common measure, judged by the same standards. We should judge all by the standards according to which men have judged one another: courage, rationality, strength, cunning, quick wittedness.

Humanist feminism, in one version or another, has dominated feminist accounts for most of the nineteenth and twentieth centuries. The feminist classics of Wollstonecraft, Mill and Taylor, as well as the views of many of the suffragettes in nineteenth-century England and the United States, exhibit the main

outlines of humanist feminism. Until recently humanist feminism was also the dominant strain in contemporary feminism. Simone de Beauvoir's description of the oppression of women and her vision of liberation in *The Second Sex* (Beauvoir, [1952] 1974) stands as one of the most theoretically grounded and thorough articulations of humanist feminism.

Beauvoir's account of women's oppression depends on the distinction between transcendence and immanence. Transcendence designates the free subjectivity that defines its own nature, and makes projects that bring new entities into the world. The free subject moves out into the world, takes initiative, faces the world boldly, creates his own individualized life. According to Beauvoir, patriarchal society allows only men such transcendence. Masculinity entails no particular attributes, but in patriarchal society is identified with transcendence, free activity that fashions artifacts and history. A man is confined to no particular nature, but has all manner of projects open to him—he can be a soldier or an artist, a politician or a chef, a scientist or a gambler. To be sure, Beauvoir understands the class and race oppression that puts more limits on the possibilities of some men than others. Gender does not restrict oppressed men, however. The possibility of action is still open to oppressed men, in the form of wiley sabotage or open rebellion. Masculinity entails individual existence, where the person defines his own individual projects and creates his own nature.

Patriarchal culture confines women, on the other hand, to immanence. Immanence designates being an object, a thing with an already defined nature lined up within a general category of things with the same nature. Femininity is an essence, a set of general attributes that define a class, and which restricts women to immanence and being defined as the Other. Whereas a man exists as a transcending subject who defines his own individual projects, patriarchal institutions require a woman to be the object for the gaze and touch of a subject, to be the pliant responder to his commands.

Beauvoir discusses several respects in which femininity confines women's existence to immanence and the repetition of the species rather than individual existence. She finds female biology itself as in part responsible for rooting women in immanence; women's reproductive processes limit her individual capacities for the sake of the needs of the species. But gender determines women's oppression more significantly than biology. Whatever might be her position in the world, and whatever her individual accomplishments, a woman is appraised first *as a woman*, and only afterwards for her individual position or accomplishments. Others will evaluate her beauty or lack of it, ascertain whether her clothes are tasteful and becoming, whether her smiles, gestures and manner of speech exhibit charm. Whether a woman conforms to the requirements of feminine attractiveness, is indifferent to them, or rebels against them, both her and other people's attitudes toward her will be determined by this definition. Women have been barred from the important business of government and commerce, or from fashioning products that achieve recognition, and instead have been expected to expend most of their energy keeping a home for husband and children. From early childhood women learn that the world of individual achievement is closed to them and that their primary vocation is

to please and serve men. Thus women learn to be deferential, accommodating, and attentive to the desires of others.

The expectations of femininity which circumscribe the lives of women inhibit the development of their human possibilities. Beauvoir describes how in their childhood girls learn early that the world of action and daring is closed to them, and learn not to move freely and openly and do not develop an ability to fight (cf. Young, 1980). Women's sexual being is clouded with masochism (cf. Bartky, 1984), a desire to love the strong actor but not be actors themselves. Women often become timid and lacking in confidence, or fear that success will conflict with their femininity.

More than merely inhibiting their human possibilities, in Beauvoir's account femininity often produces mutilated or deformed persons. In my view this is the most ingenious aspect of Beauvoir's account. She explains characteristics that many have found undesirable about women as the effects of imprisonment in femininity. Despite the culture's denial, women are human subjects, full of creative energy, intelligence, and the desire to make their mark on the world. Patriarchal institutions, however, restrict their recognized activity to caring for their appearance, for a household, and for children. Women thus channel their creativity into these activities. They try to make a human project out of turning themselves into mannequins, keeping a house clean, orderly and pleasing, and raising children. These activities, however, belong to immanence, to objectification and mere life maintenance. Trying to make them the freely chosen projects of a transcending subject only produces a monstrous caricature of expressiveness and individuality: the haughty vanity of a woman preoccupied with her image in the mirror; the shrewish women who will not allow living action to occur in her house, for fear it will soil the rug or knock over a plant; the clutching mother who tries to mould her child's life according to her own plan.

To summarize, Beauvoir defines women's oppression as the confinement and mutilation of women's human potentialities by patriarchal requirements that she be a pleasing and deferent object for men. Unlike femininity, masculinity does not entail confinement to an essence or nature, but the freedom to make oneself and assert oneself in the world. Women's liberation consists in freeing women from the confines of traditional femininity, and making it possible for women to pursue the human projects that have hitherto been dominated by men.

While Beauvoir's book remains one of the most sensitive, thorough and theoretically grounded descriptions of women's oppression under patriarchy, most feminists today find it deeply marred by at least two related factors. Beauvoir does not call into question the definition of being human that traditional Western society holds and she devalues traditionally female activity in the same way as does patriarchal culture.

Beauvoir fiercely rails at the male privilege that restricts such transcendence to men, but she does not question the value of the activities through which men compete with one another and achieve recognition. Power, achievement, individual expression, rationality, mastery of natural processes, are for her as

for the patriarchal culture she criticizes, the most human values. She is a socialist, of course, and therefore asserts that the achievement of full humanity by both men and women requires the elimination of capitalist domination. She calls for a participation of women in these public world making achievements, but does not question the prominence male-dominated society gives to achievement itself, and to public activities of politics, competition and individual creativity.

Beauvoir's humanism identifies the human with men. She points out herself in several places that whereas women experience a contradiction between being human and being feminine, men do not experience such a contradiction. The other side of her impressive and often sympathetic account of how patriarchy has victimized women is her descriptions of the free subjectivity she claims it gives to men. Boys roam, climb, play rough, and very importantly for Beauvoir, learn to fight.

> 'Violence is the authentic proof of each one's loyalty to himself, to his passions, to his own will; radically to deny this will is to deny oneself any objective truth, it is to wall oneself up in an abstract subjectivity; anger or revolt that does not get into the muscles remains a figment of the imagination. It is a profound frustration not to be able to register one's feelings upon the face of the world' (p. 371).

Men are allowed, encouraged, to be daring, to reach out and accomplish a project. Men are supposed to be rational, inventive and creative. Thus, the great achievements of humanity have been accomplished almost entirely by men: exploring the world, charting and mapping it, formulating theories of the universe, writing great plays, developing constitutions and ruling cities and states. Even less renowned or accomplished men have a privilege not accorded to women, the privilege of being in public; they can achieve some public recognition in the workplace, among comrades or cronies at the bar. Men's situation allows or encourages them to be free subjects, transcending the given to bold new futures, confronting other subjects as equals.

The distinction between transcendence and immanence ensnares Beauvoir in the very definition of woman as a nonhuman Other which her brilliant analysis reveals as patriarchal. Defining humanity as transcendence requires setting human being in opposition to non-human objects and in particular nature. Fully human, free subjectivity transcends mere life, the processes of nature which repeat in an eternal cycle without individuality or history. Thus risking life and being willing to kill are cardinal marks of humanity, for Beauvoir as for Hegel. Taking control over one's needs and fashioning objects to satisfy them, confronting and mastering the forces of nature that threaten one's life or comfort, these are the aims of human projects (Hartsock, 1983, Appendix 2). Humanity achieves its greatest freedom, however, in the creation of moral ideals and works of art. For these express a wholly new and un-natural way of being in the world. Beauvoir's ontology reproduces the Western tradition's oppositions of nature and culture, freedom and mere life, spirit and body.

With those distinctions Beauvoir brilliantly shows that patriarchal culture has projected onto women all those aspects of human existence that participate in mere life. She does not, however, as Dinnerstein (1976) rereading her later does, call upon a transformation of culture in the direction of a greater acceptance of life, the body, and mortality. Instead, she herself devalues women's lives insofar as she finds them closer to nature and the body than men's.

Beauvoir mirrors patriarchal culture in her exposition of the experiences of the female body. The young girl finds her puny clitoris less glorious than the boy's more apparent penis. At puberty girls react to menstruation with shame and disgust, though Beauvoir asserts this is due to the social status of femininity rather than to any natural reaction. Female sexuality is passive and masochistic (see Fuchs, 1980):

> 'Feminine sex desire is the soft throbbing of a mollusk. Whereas a man is impetuous, woman is only impatient; her expectation can become ardent without ceasing to be passive; man dives upon his prey like the eagle and the hawk; woman lies in wait like the carnivorous plant, the bog, in which insects and children are swallowed up. She is absorption, suction, humus, pitch and glue, a passive influx vaguely feels herself to be' (p. 431).

Pregnancy is an 'ordeal' (p. 559) in which the woman submits to the species and must suffer limitations on her capacity to individualize herself. Beauvoir expresses with understanding and sympathy how many women take pleasure in pregnancy and nursing. But clearly she regards such pleasures as examples of women's resignation to their condition of immanence, one among many ways women agree to relinquish their freedom (O'Brien, 1981: 67–76). That pregnancy itself can be a human project (Young, 1984) is impossible in her ontological framework.

Beauvoir also devalues traditionally feminine activity, such as housework and mothering. The woman is imprisoned in her home, and since she is deprived there of activity, she loses herself in things and becomes dependent on them. Though she recognizes that housework and mothering are arduous and important tasks, in her account they have no truly human value. Housework has a negative basis: one gets rid of dirt, eliminates disorder, and in performing it the woman is condemned to endless repetition that issues in no product, no work. Beauvoir finds cooking to be something of an exception here, and explains that women thus rightly take pride in culinary achievements; but even these are only to be consumed, not to stand as lasting artifacts.

As a wife, the woman is abjectly dependent, not in control of her life. This makes her dangerous for raising children, since she tends to be smotheringly possessive or brutally resentful. Even the best of mothers, on Beauvoir's account, do not attain transcendence—that is, full humanity—by caring for and loving their children; they only make it possible for their children to do so. Beauvoir thus devalues women's reproductive labor (Jaggar and McBride, 1985; Young, 1979).

Beauvoir's concrete descriptions of women's lives are full of insights, sym-

pathy and an understanding of the variations in each individual existence. (She does not, however, systematically examine variations in women's situation due to structural considerations such as class and race.) The over-all picture she offers, however, portrays woman only as victim—maimed, mutilated, dependent, confined to a life of immanence and forced to be an object. She rarely describes the strength that women have had and the earthly value of their work: ways women have formed networks and societies among themselves, the lasting beauty of the caring social values women often exhibit. While she expresses outrage at the selfishness, blindness and ruthlessness of the men who benefit from the mutilation of the personhood of half the human race, she finds little to criticize in the modern humanist conception of individuality and freedom.

II

Gynocentric feminism defines the oppression of women very differently from humanist feminism. Women's oppression consists not in being prevented from participating in full humanity, but in the denial and devaluation of specifically feminine virtues and activities by an overly instrumentalized and authoritarian masculinist culture. Unlike humanist feminism, gynocentric feminism does not focus its analysis on the impediments to women's self-development and the exclusion of women from spheres of power, prestige and creativity. Instead, gynocentric feminism focuses its critique on the values expressed in the dominant social spheres themselves. The male-dominated activities with the greatest prestige in our society—politics, science, technology, warfare, business— threaten the survival of the planet and the human race. That our society accords these activities the highest value only indicates the deep perversity of patriarchal culture. Masculine values exalt death, violence, competition, selfishness, a repression of the body, sexuality and affectivity.

Gynocentric feminism finds in women's bodies and traditionally feminine activity the source of more positive values. Women's reproductive processes keep us linked with nature and the promotion of life to a greater degree than men. Female eroticism is more fluid, diffuse and loving than violence-prone male sexuality. Our feminine socialization and traditional roles as mothers give to us a capacity to nurture and a sense of social cooperation that may be the only salvation to the planet. Gynocentric feminism thus defines the oppression of women quite differently from the way humanistic feminism defines it. Femininity is not the problem, not the source of women's oppression, but indeed within traditional femininity lie the values that we should promote for a better society. Women's oppression consists in the devaluation and repression of women's nature and female activity by the patriarchal culture.

In distinguishing between humanist feminism and gynocentric feminism I intend to mark out two tendencies or poles of feminism, which are held in various forms and degrees by different feminists. Feminism of the nineteenth-century in the United States was marked by an oscillation between humanist

and gynocentric feminism. For most of the period of the suffrage movement the humanist position prevailed, but the movements of moral motherhood and social housekeeping had a more gynocentric cast. In contemporary feminism both tendencies have been present, often in uneasy union. Nevertheless I think it is appropriate to distinguish periods of contemporary feminism when one of these tendencies has been stronger. Until the late 1970s feminism in the U.S. was predominantly humanist feminism, but in the mid and late 1970s feminism has shifted more in the direction of gynocentrism.

The distinction between humanist feminism and gynocentric feminism cannot be mapped onto the more commonly held way of classifying feminism into liberal, radical and socialist (Jaggar, 1983). The set of position often referred to as liberal feminism is indeed a species of humanist feminism, and to the degree that these positions are still held by many feminists, humanist feminism is sill a strong tendency among feminists. Many of those who called themselves radical feminists in the early and mid-seventies, however, asserted something similar to the humanist feminist position I have identified as Beauvoir's. They found women's oppression as located primarily in confinement to femininity, which they claimed made women dependent on men and inhibited women's self-development, and they often called upon women to develop skills and attributes traditionally associated with men—physical strength, mechanical ability, assertiveness, etc. Similarly, until recently most feminists who called themselves socialist feminists held humanist feminist positions like that of Beauvoir. They took socialism as a necessary but not sufficient condition of the self-development of all human beings, and took the goal of feminism to be the elimination of gender differences and the requirements of femininity which inhibit the full development of women's human capacities.

Starting about the mid- to late-seventies, many of those called radical feminists and those called socialist feminists increasingly moved toward a more gynocentric feminism and several of the writers treated in this section are self-identified socialist feminists. Those calling themselves radical feminists moved toward gynocentric analysis first, but by the late seventies this mode of feminism had become increasingly influential even among those who might in other ways be called liberal feminists. In the herstory of the contemporary women's movement I find at least three factors that have produced this shift from humanistic to gynocentric feminism: anti-feminist reaction to feminism, the emergence of black feminism, and the development of women's history and feminist anthropology.

Anti-feminists have identified feminism solely with humanist feminism. In their perception feminists eschew femininity, devalue traditional womanhood and want to be equal to, that is, like, in identity with, men. Anti-feminist women have sneered at such a naïve claim to eliminate difference, and have argued without difficulty that treating men and women equally will often lead to injustice for women (Wolgast, 1978). Early during the second wave of the women's movement, moreover, anti-feminists protested what they regarded as feminist denigration of women. Many women take pride in the homes they decorate and bring warmth to, and regard their caring for children as a noble

vocation, they claimed. They dress well and do their hair to please themselves, not because men require it of them. How dare you feminists claim these activities lack value, entail imprisonment, they exclaimed. And furthermore, they asserted, we don't want to be like men, competitive, unfeeling, getting high blood pressure and ulcers at the office or cancer in the factory. Anti-feminists still screech this line, even though contemporary feminism has changed considerably in response to such protests of anti-feminist women.

One of the first jobs of black feminists was to attack the victim/dependent image of women's situation that held sway in the women's movement in the early 1970s. Our women, they said, have rarely had the luxury to be housewives, kept relatively comfortable by men, having their capacity to act smothered by diapers, corsets and girdles. On the contrary, to survive, black women typically learned to be tough, physically strong, clever, but usually also warm, sexy and nurturant. Black women have suffered endless injustice and humiliation, but it has not maimed their spirits, for they have acted with brilliance, courage and righteousness (Stack, 1975: Davis, 1981). Through such discussion the women's movement learned that the typical account of femininity as entailing weakness and dependence had a class and race bias.

The work of feminist historians also promoted awareness of the differences in women's situations and the historical specificity of bourgeois femininity, as well as a sense of women as active participants in history. We discovered the mother rulers of Mycinae and the wisdom of the witches. We found that in most cultures women's work contributes as much as or more than men's work to the subsistence of the family and village, and we recovered the contributions women have made to agricultural development, diplomacy, healing, art, literature, music, philosophy. We reconstructed the lives of peasant and proletariat women and saw them as providing crucial strength and foci of resistance for dominated classes. From the protests of some feminists against the humanist image of women as forced to be inactive, less than human, and from these concrete studies of women's lives and action, a new focus on the positivity of women's culture was born.

Gynocentric feminism has received a number of expressions in the U.S. women's movement in recent years. Artists and poets have been among the leaders of developing the images of celebration of this more positive understanding of women's history and contemporary self-understanding. Judy Chicago's *The Dinner Party*, for example, laboriously and beautifully recovers whole aspects of women's history and locates them within images of female genitalia and objects that rely on traditionally female arts.

Within the sphere of political activism, gynocentric feminism perhaps is best represented in the feminist anti-militarist and ecology movements of the last five years. In the Women's Pentagon Action or the action at the Seneca Army Depot, for example, a major aspect of the political protest has been the use of symbols and actions that invoke traditional labor, such as weaving, spinning, birthing, mothering. Feminist anti-militarist and ecological analysis has argued that the dangers to the planet that have been produced by the nuclear arms race and industrial technology are essentially tied to masculinist values (Blu-

menthal, 1981; Young, 1983). The burgeoning movement of feminist spirituality entails a similar analysis, and promotes values associated with traditional femininity.

A number of prominent recent theories of contemporary feminism express a gynocentric feminism. I see Susan Griffin's *Woman and Nature* (1978) as one of the first written statements of a gynocentric feminism in the second wave. It shows that one of the first steps of gynocentrism is to deny the nature/culture dichotomy held by humanists such as Beauvoir, and affirmatively assert the connection of women and nature. Daly's *Gyn/Ecology* (1978) I see as a transition work. In it Daly asserts an analysis of the victimization of women by femininity that outdoes Beauvoir, but she also proposes a new gynocentric language.

Carol Gilligan's critique (1981) of male theories of moral development has had a strong influence on the formation of gynocentric analysis. She questions dominant assumptions about moral valuation and affirms forms of moral reasoning associated with traditional femininity. Following Chodorow (1978), she argues that gender socialization creates in women a relational communal orientation toward others, while it creates in men a more oppositional and competitive mode of relating to others. These gender differences produce two different forms of moral rationality, a masculine ethic of rights and justice, and a feminine ethic of responsibility and care. Traditional moral theory has ignored and repressed the particularistic ethic of care as pre-moral. Women's moral oppression consists in being measured against male standards, according to Gilligan, in the silencing of women's different voice. The dominance of those male centered values of abstract reasoning, instrumentality and individualism, moreover, produce a cold, uncaring, competitive world. Both the liberation of women and the restructuring of social relations require tempering these values with the communally oriented values derived from women's ethic of care (cf. Gould, 1983). While Gilligan herself would reject the label of gynocentric feminist, her work has exerted an enormous influence on feminists in fields as diverse as mathematics and philosophy, providing the foundation for a revaluation of attributes associated with femininity.

Mary O'Brien (1981) articulates a gynocentric critique of traditional political theory starting from the biological fact that the reproductive process gives women a living continuity with their offspring that it does not give men. Women thus have a temporal consciousness that is continuous, whereas male temporal consciousness is discontinuous. Arising from the alienation from the child they experience in the reproductive process, masculine thought emphasizes dualism and separation. Men establish a public realm in which they give spiritual birth to a second nature, transcending the private realm of mere physicality and reproduction to which they confine women. Patriarchy develops an ideology of the male potency principle, which installs the father as ruler of the family and men as rulers of society, and substitutes an intellectual notion of creativity for the female principle of life generation. The contemporary women's movement has the potential to overturn such a conception of politics that is separated from life continuity because out of female reproductive consciousness can come a politics based on women's experience of life processes and species continuity.

Nancy Hartsock's theory (1983) of the feminist standpoint from which she analyses patriarchal culture is a more sweeping version of gynocentric feminism. She argues that the sexual division of labor provides men and women with differing experiences that structure different standpoints upon nature and social relations. Based on Chodorow's theory of the development of gender personalities, Hartsock argues that men experience the relation of self and other as one of hostility and struggle. The sexual division of labor also removes men from the needs of the body, from the vulnerability and basic demands of children and the aged, and provides men with an instrumentally calculative relation to nature. This division of labor, she argues, produces a way of thinking about the world Hartsock calls abstract masculinity, which organizes experience and social relations into binary oppositions in which one term carries greater value than the other. This standpoint of abstract masculinity has determined the primary structure of Western social relations and culture. This male dominated culture's values are both partial and perverse. It embodies sexuality where desire for fusion with other takes the form of domination of the other. Masculine consciousness denies and fears the body and associates birth with death. The only sense of community generated by abstract masculinity, moreover, is the community of warriors in preparation for combat.

From women's experience Hartsock claims we can both criticize masculinist values and conceptualization, and develop a better vision of social relations. The gender personalities women develop in relation to their mothers give them a propensity to feel more connected with others than men. The experiences of menstruation, coitus, pregnancy and lactation, which challenge body boundaries, give women a greater experience of continuity with nature. Women's labor in caring for men and children and producing basic values in the home, finally, gives them a greater rootedness in nature than men's work gives them, a more basic understanding of life processes. These attributes of women's experience can ground, Hartsock argues, a form of conceptualization which does not depend on dichotomous thinking and which values connections among persons more than their separation, as does abstract masculinity.

While Sara Ruddick (1980, 1983) is careful to claim that any recovery and revaluation of traditionally feminine attributes must be infused with a feminist politics, her notion of maternal thinking provides another example of a gynocentric feminist analysis. She argues that the specific daily practices of mothering generate specific modes of thinking motivated by the interests in preservation, growth, and the acceptability of the child to the society. Maternal practice is not restricted to mothers, but exists wherever such nurturing and preservation interests prevail. She suggests that maternal thinking provides anti-militarist values that feminists can use in promoting a politics of peace.

Writing within a very different intellectual current than American feminists, using rather different assumptions and style, several women in France in recent years have developed distinctive versions of gynocentric feminism (Jardine, 1982). I shall mention only Luce Irigaray and Julia Kristeva. Like a number of other contemporary French thinkers, Irigarary (1980, 1981a, b) describes phallocentric culture as preoccupied by a metaphysics of identity dominated

by visual metaphors. Male thinking begins by positing the One, the same, the essence, that generates binary oppositions in which the second term is defined by the first as what it is not, thus reducing to its identity. Phallogocentric discourse defines the opposition male/female in just this way, woman is only not a man, a lack, a deficiency. Preoccupied with the straight, the true, the proper, men establish relations of property and exchange in which accounts are balanced. Women in the phallocentric system have been silenced and separated, exchanged as goods among men. Irigaray proposes that women must find and speak the specificity of female desire, which has completely different values from those of phallic thinking. Women's eroticism is neither one nor two but plural, as women's bodies themselves experience arousal and pleasure in a multiplicity of places that cannot all be identified. Touch, not sight, predominates, the auto-eroticism of vaginal lips touching clitoris, of intimate bodies touching. A genuinely feminine language moves and twists, starts over again from different perspectives, does not go straight to the point. Such a language can displace the sterility and oppressiveness of phallogocentric categorization (on Irigaray, see Gallop, 1981; Berg, 1982; Kuykendall, 1983.)

Kristeva, (1980, 1981a, b) also focuses on language, and the repression of specifically female experience. Language has two moments, the symbolic, the capacity of language to represent and define, to be literal, and the semiotic, those elements of language that slip and play in ambiguities and nuance. Certain linguistic practices, such as poetry, make most explicit use of the semiotic, but for the most part the playful, musical, in language is repressed in Western culture and the symbolic, rational, legalistic discourse rules. For Kristeva this repression concerns the repression of the body and the installation of order, hierarchy and authority. Repression of the body and the semiotic entails repression of the pre-oedipal experience of the maternal body before the subject emerges with a self-identical ego, as well as denial by the culture of the specificity and difference that the female body exhibits. Challenge to the dominant oppressions, to capitalism, racism, sexism, must come not only from specific demands within the political arena, but from changing the speaking subject.

Kristeva finds in the repressed feminine the potential for such change, where feminine means at least two things. First, women's specific experience as female bodies, the daughters of mothers, and often mothers themselves, an experience of a decentered subject. Second, the aspects of language and behavior Western culture has devalued and repressed: the poetic, rhythmic, musical, nurturant and soothing, but also contradictory and shifting ways of being, that fickleness the women have been accused of. This revolution of the feminine Kristeva finds in a number of male avant garde writers. The women's movement, however, also carries the possibility of displacing the rigidity of a subject that loves authority, provided that women do not fall into that humanist feminism by which they simply demand getting in on the masculinist power game.

To summarize, humanist feminism defines femininity as the source of women's oppression, and calls upon male dominated institutions to allow women the opportunity to participate fully in public, world-making activities of industry, politics, art and science. In contrast, gynocentric feminism questions

the values of these traditional public activities that have been dominated by men. Women's oppression consists not in being prevented from participating in full humanity, but in the denial and devaluation of specifically feminine virtues and activities by an overly instrumentalized and authoritarian masculinist culture. Femininity is not the problem, for gynocentric feminism, and indeed is the source of a conception of society and the subject that can not only liberate women, but all persons.

III

The polarity between humanist and gynocentric feminism might be considered part of the logic of feminism itself. Feminism consists in calling attention to and eradicating gender-based oppression. Humanism and gynocentrism are the two most obvious positions to take in that struggle. Either feminism means that we seek for women the same opportunities and privileges the society gives to men, or feminism means that we assert the distinctive value of womanhood against patriarchal denigration. While these positions need not be mutually exclusive, there is a strong tendency for both feminists and non-feminists to make them so: Either we want to be like men or we don't.

I think that contemporary gynocentric feminism has a number of aspects that make it a better analysis than humanist feminism. At the same time, I think the swing toward gynocentrism has left behind some important elements of feminist politics that humanist feminism has emphasized. We need to rethink our analysis, not to form a synthesis of the two, but to cook up a better mixture out of some of the old ingredients.

Since it was first uttered in the eighteenth century, humanist feminism has assumed the liberation of women as an extension of the values of liberalism. The ideal of universal humanity, that all persons have equal rights whatever their station or class, should be extended to women. To be sure, many humanist feminists, such as Beauvoir, have been socialists, and have called for radical transformation of economic and political institutions. The argument for such socialism, however, is that only publicly controlled and democratic economic and political institutions will make it possible to realize the ideal of equality and self-development promised by liberalism. Even socialist versions of humanist feminism, then, stand in continuity with the modern humanist tradition insofar as it seeks to realize the values articulated by that tradition for all persons, including and especially women (Eisenstein, 1980).

Gynocentric feminism confronts humanist feminism on one of its core assumptions, namely, that the ideal for feminists is a universal humanity in which all persons equally realize their potential for self-development. Nearly every term in this sentence can be put to gynocentric feminist critique, but I will restrict myself to the notion of universal humanity. On the humanist feminist view uttered by Beauvoir, differences between men and women are socially enforced oppressions. In their humanity there is no essential difference between

men and women, and we look forward to a society in which sex difference will make no difference.

Gynocentric feminism can reveal this ideal of universal humanity as both unrealistic and oppressive. This ideal proposes to measure all persons according to the formal standards of rationality and rights. But the material differences among persons determined by history, region or bodies continue to operate, so some will measure differently. Only an explicit affirmation of difference and social plurality, gynocentric feminism suggests, offers the hope of overcoming sexism, racism, ethnic oppression. Such affirmation of difference is difficult and threatening, however, because it challenges modes of individual and community self-identification.

As I already pointed out in discussing Beauvoir, humanist feminism focuses its investigation primarily on women's situation and criticizes patriarchy because of its specifically destructive effect on women's lives, without questioning the dominant culture's basic assumptions about the good human life. Gynocentric feminism, on the other hand, takes a much broader look at our society. It seeks to uncover and throw into question some of the most basic assumptions of the Western tradition of thought of which modern humanism is a part—the distinction between nature and culture, spirit and body, the universal and particular. Gynocentric feminism links masculinist culture's equation of humanity with rationality, on the one hand, to the repression of life spontaneity and the development of an oppressive web of social controls and organizational hierarchy, on the other. In these ways it is similar to and stands in the same category with critiques of Western culture uttered by Nietzsche, Adorno and Horkheimer, Foucault and Derrida.

As a result of its greater comprehensiveness, gynocentric feminism broadens its critique of our society beyond focus on specifically sexist institutions and practices and specific damage to women. Because it brings feminist critique to basic assumptions of the society as a whole, gynocentric feminism offers for the first time distinctively feminist analyses of social structures and forms of symbolization not tied to women in particular—such as racism, classism, the military or the state. This has produced a broadened politics in which feminists participate as feminists in ecological, anti-militarist, anti-racist struggles. Unlike humanist feminism, that is, gynocentric feminism has developed a perspective from which to criticize any institution or practice in our society, even if it does not distinguish women's specific oppression.

While gynocentric feminism is deeply radical in these ways, it also harbors some dangers to radical politics. Turning to femininity as the source of values by which to criticize patriarchal culture and form the image of a better society seems to lead to a disturbing essentialism. By 'essentialism' I mean an account that theorizes women as a category with a set of essential attributes. O'Brien states that she describes the structure of womanhood in her articulation of the female mode of reproductive consciousness. Hartsock acknowledges historical and situational differences among women, but claims feminist theory requires identifying common attributes of women's experience. Gynocentric feminists find these attributes in the same place as has patriarchy—in women's repro-

ductive biology and the activity of mothering. Feminist anti-militarist and ecological analysis finds women more in touch with nature than men because of
the cycles and changes of our bodies, and more peaceloving because our nurturing impulses foster in us a love of life.

French theorists explicitly criticize feminist tendencies toward essentialism.
On this account many of them reject the label 'feminist'. They fear replacing
humanism, where universal humanity is projected as an ideal, with universal
womanhood. 'Woman' is a fiction, a metaphysical attempt to bring multiplicity
into unity. The French theorists I have referred to nevertheless share some of
the essentialist tendencies of gynocentric feminism in the U.S. They rely on
an opposition between the masculine and the feminine, even where, as in
Kristeva, they do not necessarily associate these with men and women. Though
these theories explicitly question Western dichotomous thinking, their use of
the opposition of masculinity and femininity retains its traditional dichotomous
terms, in revaluated form: the masculine is power, discursive rationality, cal-
culation, abstraction, while the feminine is desire, sensuality, poetic language,
the immediacy of contact with nature. Like their counterparts across the ocean,
these French theorists tend to reduce women's specificity to reproductive biology and the function of mothering (Stanton, 1983), though in some of her
writing Irigaray reaches toward a woman-to-woman relation beyond the mother/
daughter cycle.

Gynocentrism's most important contribution is its affirmation of difference
against humanism's claim of a universal humanity. Gynocentric feminism, however, still tends to see gender difference as a relation of inside and outside.
We need a conception of difference that is less like the icing bordering the
layers of cake, however, and more like a marble cake: where the flavors remain
recognizably different, but thoroughly in-sinuated in one another.

Gynocentric feminism has rightly restored dignity to the character of women,
shown how within our confined roles and despite often severe domination by
men, we have made new things, contributed to historical events, struggled
actively against our oppression, and formed networks of solidarity. It has been
especially necessary to topple the stance of women as victims, weak, passive
and only partial human beings.

In its effort to recover self-respect, agency and authentic subjectivity of
women by finding greater value in traditional women's culture than the dominant masculinist culture, however, gynocentric feminism tends to swing too
far away from understanding women as confined or enslaved. It rejects too
completely the Beauvorian claim that femininity inhibits, distorts and mutilates
women's lives. Gilligan's accent on women's traditional sovereignty in the private realm where she cares for each person in her particularity, for example,
fails to note how this ethic of care often leads women to a sacrificing stance
that can make us easily hurt.

The gynocentric revaluation of traditional femininity can weaken the claim
that women are oppressed. If women's labor has been as creative or moreso
than men's labor, if women's networks and relations with children have been
the source of values more life giving than the public activities of men, if female

desire is more playful, less rigid than male desire, then what warrants the claim that women need liberating? To be sure, all gynocentric feminists find that men rule society and in so doing devalue and repress this feminine sphere. Such a way of conceptualizing male domination, however, mutes the outrage against injustice that humanist feminism exhibits because it claims that women are not simply devalued, but damaged, by male domination.

Gynocentric feminism, moreover, tends to reject too categorically the value of the activities and ambitions associated traditionally with masculinity. Men have traditionally reserved for themselves the public activities of political position, recognized artists, inventor or scientist, and have recognized only other men worthy to compete for the accolades that reward excellence. If the activities which men have dominated really are less valuable than those in which women have traditionally engaged, as gynocentric feminism suggests, then in what does male privilege consist? The other side of gynocentrism's denial of the damaging consequences of femininity is its denial of the growth promoting aspects of traditional masculinity. If we claim that masculinity distorts men more than it contributes to their self-development and capacities, then again the claim that women are the victims of injustice loses considerable force.

Within the context of anti-feminist backlash, the effect of gynocentric feminism may be accommodating to the existing structure. Gynocentric feminism relies on and reinforces gender stereotypes at just the time when the dominant culture has put new emphasis on marks of gender difference. It does so, moreover, by relying on many of those aspects of women's traditional sphere that traditional patriarchal ideology has most exploited and that humanist feminists such as Beauvoir found most oppressive—reproductive biology, motherhood, domestic concerns. Even though its intentions are subversive, such renewed attention to traditional femininity can have a reactionary effect on both ourselves and our listeners because it may echo the dominant claim that women belong in a separate sphere.

Humanist feminism calls upon patriarchal society to open places for women within those spheres of human activity that have been considered the most creative, powerful and prestigious. Gynocentric feminism replies that wanting such things for women implies a recognition that such activities are the most humanly valuable. It argues that in fact, militarism, bureaucratic hierarchy, competition for recognition, and the instrumentalization of nature and people entailed by these activities are basic disvalues (Ferguson, 1983).

Yet in contemporary society, men still have most institutionalized power, and gynocentric feminism shows why they do not use it well. If feminism turns its back on the centers of power, privilege and individual achievement that men have monopolized, those men will continue to monopolize them, and nothing significant will change. Feminists cannot undermine masculinist values without entering some of the centers of power that foster them, but the attainment of such power itself requires at least appearing to foster those values. Still, without being willing to risk such cooptation feminism can only be a moral position of critique rather than a force for institutional change.

Despite its intention, I fear that gynocentric feminism may have the same

consequence as the stance of moral motherhood that grew out of nineteenth century feminism: a resegregation of women to a specifically women's sphere, outside the sites of power, privilege and recognition. For me the symptom here is what the dominant culture finds more threatening. Within the dominant culture a middle-aged assertive woman's claim to co-anchor the news alongside a man appears considerably more threatening than women's claim to have a different voice that exposes masculinist values as body-denying and selfish. The claim of women to have a right to the positions and benefits that have hitherto been reserved for men, and that male-dominated institutions should serve women's needs, is a direct threat to male privilege. While the claim that these positions of power themselves should be eliminated and the institutions eliminated or restructured is indeed more radical, when asserted from the gynocentric feminist position it can be an objective retreat.

Gynocentrism's focus on values and language as the primary target of its critique contributes to this blunting of its political force. Without doubt, social change requires changing the subject, which in turn means developing new ways of speaking, writing and imagining. Equally indubitable is the gynocentric feminist claim that masculinist values in Western culture deny the body, sensuality and rootedness in nature, and that such denial nurtures fascism, pollution and nuclear games. Given these facts, however, what shall we do? To this gynocentrism has little concrete answer. Because its criticism of existing society is so global and abstract, gynocentric critique of the values, language and culture of masculinism can remove feminist theory from analysis of specific institutions and practices and how concretely they might be structurally changed in directions more consonant with our visions.

REFERENCES

Bartky, Sandra. 1984. Feminine masochism and the politics of personal transformation. *Women's Studies Int. Forum (Hypatia Issue)* **7** (5), 323–334.
Beauvoir, Simone de. [1952] 1974. *The Second Sex*. Translated by H. M. Parshley. Random House, Vintage Books, New York.
Berg, Elizabeth L. 1982. The third woman. *Diacritics* **12** (2): 11–20.
Blumenthal, Lyn. *et al.*, eds. 1981. *Heresies: A Feminist Publication of Art and Politics* **4** (1).
Chodorow, Nancy. 1978. *The Reproduction of Mothering*. University of California Press, Berkeley.
Daly, Mary. 1978. *Gyn/Ecology*. Beacon Press, Boston.
Davis, Angela. 1981. *Women, Race and Class*. Random House, New York.
Dinnerstein, Dorothy. 1976. *The Mermaid and the Minotaur*. Harper and Row, New York.
Eisenstein, Zillah. 1980. *The Radical Future of Liberal Feminism*. Longman, New York.
Ferguson, Kathy E. 1983. Feminism and bureaucratic discourse. *New Political Science* **11**: 53–73.
Fuchs, Jo-Ann. 1980. Female eroticism in *The Second Sex*. *Feminist Studies* **6** (2): 304–313.

Gallop, Jane. 1981. *The Daughter's Seduction*. Cornell University Press, Ithaca.

Gilligan, Carol. 1981. *In a Different Voice*. Harvard University Press, Cambridge, MA.

Gould, Carol C. 1983. Private rights and public virtues: Women, the family and democracy. In Gould, Carol C., ed., *Beyond Domination: New Perspectives on Women and Philosophy*. Rowman and Allenheld, Totowa, NJ.

Griffin, Susan. 1978. *Woman and Nature: The Roaring Inside Her*. Harper and Row, New York.

Hartsock, Nancy. 1983. *Money, Sex and Power: Toward a Feminist Historical Materialism*. Longman, New York.

Irigaray, Luce. 1980. When our lips speak together. *Signs: A Journal of Women in Culture and Society* 6 (1): 69–79.

Irigaray, Luce. 1981a. The sex which is not one. When the goods get together. In Marks, Elaine and Isabelle de Courtivron, eds, *New French Feminisms*. Schocken Books, New York.

Irigaray, Luce. 1981b. And one doesn't stir without the other. *Signs: A Journal of Women in Culture and Society* 7 (1): 60–67.

Jaggar, Alison. 1983. *Human Nature and Feminist Politics*. Rowman and Allenheld, Totowa, NJ.

Jaggar, Alison and William McBride. 1985. 'Reproduction' as male ideology. *Women's Studies Int. Forum (Hypatia Issue)* 8 (3): 185–196.

Jardine, Alice. 1982. Gynesis. *Diacritics* 12 (2): 54–65.

Kristeva, Julia. 1980. Motherhood according to Giovanni Bellini. *Desire in Language*. Columbia University Press, New York.

Kristeva, Julia. 1981a. Woman can never be defined. In Marks, Elaine and Isabelle de Courtivron, ed., *New French Feminisms*. Schocken Books, New York.

Kristeva, Julia. 1981b. Women's time. *Signs: A Journal of Women in Culture and Society* 7 (1): 5–12.

Kuykendall, Eleanor. 1983. Toward an ethic of nurturance: Luce Irigaray on mothering and power. In Trebilcot, Joyce, ed., *Mothering: Essays in Feminist Theory*. Rowman and Allenheld, Totowa, NJ.

O'Brien, Mary. 1981. *The Politics of Reproduction*. Routledge and Kegan Paul, Boston.

Ruddick, Sara. 1980. Maternal thinking. *Feminist Studies* 6 (2): 342–367.

Ruddick, Sara. 1983. Preservative love and military destruction. In Trebilcot, Joyce. ed., *Mothering: Essays in Feminist Theory*. Rowman and Allenheld, Totowa, NJ.

Stack, Carol B. 1975. *All Our Kin: Strategies for Survival in a Black Community*. Harper and Row, New York.

Stanton, Donma. 1983. The maternal metaphor and the problematics of difference. Unpublished, University of Michigan.

Wolgast, Elizabeth G. 1978. *Equality and the Rights of Women*. Cornell University Press, Ithica.

Young, Iris M. 1979. Is there a woman's world?—Some reflections on the struggle for our bodies. Proceedings of *The Second Sex*—Thirty Years Later, a Conference on Feminist Theory. New York Humanities Institute. Mimeograph.

Young, Iris M. 1980. Throwing like a girl: A phenomenology of feminine body comportment, motility and spatiality. *Human Studies* 3 (1): 137–156.

Young, Iris M. 1983. Review essay, feminism and ecology. *Environmental Ethics* 5 (2): 174–179.

Young, Iris M. 1984. Pregnant embodiment: Subjectivity and alienation. *J. Med. Phil.* 9 (1): 45–62.

'REPRODUCTION' AS
MALE IDEOLOGY

Alison M. Jaggar
and
William L. McBride

For many people, and especially for many men, the most outrageous feature of the women's liberation movement that erupted in the late 1960s was its insistence that the personal was political. This was the claim that feminists used to justify their critique of male behavior in the innumerable 'unofficial' or informal encounters of daily life: in the kitchen, on the bus, at the table, on the street, in bed. Men felt first bewildered and then betrayed by feminist political analysis of what men conceived as private life, that part of their lives in which they felt entitled to indulge what they saw as their personal tastes and idiosyncrasies and simply to 'be themselves,' undisturbed by the considerations of propriety or principle that regulated so much of their so-called public lives. All sorts of explanations may be given for the discomfiture and resentment that the new feminist critiques aroused in so many men. One source of these feelings must certainly lie in the fact that the new feminists were offering a direct challenge to a way of thinking about social life that had prevailed for hundreds and even thousands of years.

At least since the time of Aristotle, the western tradition in political theory has been characterized by its insistence on a distinction between the public and the private, the political and the personal realms of human existence. Different theorists within the western tradition have marked that distinction in different places but none has abandoned it entirely. Western political philosophers have always assumed that some human activities fall outside the proper domain of political theory and are not susceptible to rational evaluation in terms of political ideals and principles.[1] No matter how they have defined the so-called private sphere, moreover, western theorists have always included within it the activities called reproductive: the activities of conceiving and

---

[1] This separation of the public and political from the private sphere is a very salient theme, for example, in the thought of Hannah Arendt, even though in so many other respects Arendt wished to break with the tradition of western political thought (see Parekh, 1981: 131–132).

bearing children, of rearing them, of caring for the sick and old and of maintaining the healthy and mature. After centuries of almost undisturbed existence,
this notion of a private realm was rudely challenged by the feminists of the late
1960s. These feminists claimed that the organization of the activities that had
been protected hitherto from critical scrutiny should now be judged by the
same political standards that were used for evaluating activity in the so-called
public world. No wonder many men were upset: their comfortable lives and
their comfortable concepts were simultaneously under attack.

In this paper, we propose to continue that attack by taking a critical look at
the concept of reproduction. As we have just remarked, so-called reproductive
activities traditionally have been seen as the heart of the private realm. We
want to discover the rationale for excluding these activities from the domain
of politics and to consider the validity of that rationale. Our focus will be on
the treatment of reproduction first by Marx and Engels and second by Simone
de Beauvoir. We shall argue that these theorists make certain unwarranted
assumptions about the naturalness of the so-called reproductive realm. Consequently, they conceptualize it in a way that obscures its historicity and especially obscures the social possibility of alternatives to past and present modes
or organizing these aspects of life. We shall conclude by questioning whether
there is any rational justification for separating out certain human activities
under the concept of reproduction. In our view, the very distinction between
production and reproduction, at least as it is made by the theorists we examine,
is an invidious and male biased distinction. The traditional concept of reproduction is part of an ideology of male dominance.

1. PHENOMENOLOGY OF
'REPRODUCTION'

Before we begin our critique, let us turn our attention briefly to that area of
life that has been designated theoretically as reproduction. Let us remind ourselves of how so-called reproduction is experienced as an everyday phenomenon
in our lives apart from elaborate theoretical frameworks. The core of these
activities, of course, is pregnancy and childbirth, but no one can seriously
maintain that pregnancy and childbirth exhaust the domain of activities required
to ensure that human life will go on. They are only the beginning.

Beyond this beginning we need to remember, first, the vast array of tasks
that are usually facilely categorized and equally facilely dismissed under the
heading of 'childrearing'. What this means in concrete contemporary experience
is, of course, constant feeding, including procuring food, preparing it and cleaning up after the meal; it means guiding infants to the stage of self-control over
excretory functions and assuming responsibility for diapering and related chores
up to that point; it means constantly monitoring infants and children to protect

them from the numerous complex dangers—fast vehicles, electrical outlets, etc.—that abound in our modern physical environment; and it means perpetually renewed activities such as cleaning, ensuring continued fuel supplies, either oneself repairing or commissioning someone else to repair damaged household appliances, and so on, in order to keep the physical environment in safe operating condition.

Children's needs are not only physiological; their psychological needs are equally important. It is now well established that, in order to thrive, children must not only be fed and protected from physical danger; they must also receive affection and be taught the incredibly complex series of skills necessary for functioning in adult society. Nurturing and constant social interaction are what create fully human beings out of helpless infants. These sophisticated but ill-defined and often unrecognized activities are the most crucial of all the child-rearing tasks and also the most difficult, requiring vast reserves of sensitivity, patience, good humor and intelligence. They constitute the most basic kind of education, in addition to which children in industrialized nations are also required to attend school. The additional enterprise of academic education often requires that the labor of teachers be supplemented by that of parents and guardians who are frequently involved in arranging for or actually providing transportation, in some of the school activities themselves, etc. Involvement in children's educations may last even more years for some adults with child-rearing responsibilities, but under current laws in many parts of the world it is bound to last a minimum of 15 or 16 years for every single child.

The types of activities that we have just summarized so briefly involve an enormous proportion of the resources, both human and material, of our society. Most of them also, by any measure of energy-expenditure, constitute some of the hardest work that it is possible to undertake. Only those who themselves have engaged in childrearing are fully aware of the exhausting demands that it may make not only upon one's physical endurance but also upon one's character, one's intelligence and one's emotions. Childrearing draws on one's patience, one's imagination and even one's integrity to an extent equalled in few other types of activity. In short, childrearing is a lot of hard work. Moreover, the activities involved in childrearing may be carried out in all kinds of ways and with a wide range in quality, from successfully to disastrously—although of course as with all qualitative judgments there can be numerous disputes about the standards to be employed. Nevertheless, it is sheer prejudice to deny that various aspects of childrearing can be performed more or less well—in other words, that childrearing can be accomplished with excellence and even, to use the twentieth-century buzzword that is often said to epitomize what activities of reproduction cannot achieve, with *creativity*.

Beyond the awesome variety of activities that are encompassed within the domain of childrearing, there are numerous others which, it seems to us, should also be counted as essential parts of the reproduction of human society. To speak in general terms, the nourishment and other care, especially health care,

of mature adults and the special services that must be furnished to the handicapped and to the elderly are vast additional domains of work, carried out by millions of individuals, which are also properly seen as reproductive in nature. By definition, the severely handicapped and those among the elderly who are most in need of care are often not capable themselves of even the routine tasks of personal maintenance; as long as society affirms a collective commitment to sustain the lives of such individuals, a comprehensive description of the reality denoted by 'reproduction' must encompass the many activities associated with this sustenance, as well.

The 'services', as they are often called, of this vast congeries of reproductive activities are performed, in our society, in a great variety of settings and under a variety of economic arrangements: from parenting activities in the nuclear family, where there is seldom if ever a question of monetary compensation; to volunteer work in hospitals, or with groups that provide meals to persons unable to leave their homes or to cook, or in other settings; to day-care performed by usually low-paid, but nevertheless salaried, professionals; to salaried teaching in the schools; to social service occupations, some of which involve functioning in large governmental bureaucracies. Regardless of how they are performed, three features of reproductive activities as we have described them are especially salient and worth noting: first of all, the majority of them, both in domestic and public settings, are performed in fact by women; secondly, these activities are often unpaid and, even when they do receive monetary compensation, this is usually very low; thirdly, both popular literature and official job classification lists rate this work as being of low value by comparison with most other categories of activities.[2] The coincidence of these features is, one should suspect, no accident.

This, then, in a very broad outline, is the everyday reality of so-called reproduction in the modern world. It can be said at the very least to make up a large proportion of the total quantity of human work. It raises interesting and obvious problems for the critical social theorist because of its contradictory qualities of being at once so important and so much undervalued, so central to the fact that there continues to be a human race at all and yet so disproportionately carried out by one sex. What we hope to have done with this preliminary description is to have laid the groundwork for understanding how the conceptualizations of reproduction that have prevailed in most of our traditional social theory tend to distort reality and hence why they have ultimately been harmful to the feminist goal of overcoming the unequal treatment of women. Often such distortive conceptualizations have characterized even philosophical traditions that in principle are sympathetic to this goal. We shall

---

[2] The U.S. Department of Labor's *Dictionary of Occupational Titles* (1965), for instance, assigned a rating of 8-7-8, with 8-8-8 being the 'lowest' possible, to the jobs of homemaker, foster mother, child-care attendant, and nursery-school teacher, with the 8s standing for 'no significant relationship' to data and to things, respectively, and the 7 representing 'serving', the final category prior to 'no significant relationship' with respect to people (see A. B. McBride, 1976: 169).

now analyse two of these, the Marxian tradition and the work of Simone de Beauvoir.

2. THE TREATMENT OF REPRODUCTION IN CLASSICAL MARXISM

Within traditional Marxist theory the two most important types of human activity are production and reproduction. The categorial distinction between these activities is fundamental to the Marxist account of women's subordination. Very simply, Marxists believe that, throughout history, women have been primarily responsible for reproduction whereas men have engaged primarily in production. With the emergence of class society, production came to dominate reproduction and so men came to dominate women. Male dominance can be ended, on the classical Marxist view, only if women can achieve full participation in the heretofore male sphere of what Engels calls 'public' production.

In the next few pages, we shall examine more closely the assumptions that underlie the classical Marxist analysis of women's subordination, especially the way that this analysis links women's subordination with women's responsibility for reproduction. We shall then look at the attempted feminist revision of this analysis by Simone de Beauvoir. Finally, we shall critique the assumptions about reproduction shared both by Marx and Engels and by Beauvoir and suggest an alternative way of conceptualizing so-called reproductive activity. We contend that this alternative is more useful to feminist theory and more faithful to social reality.

One of the first things to notice about the Marxist concept of reproduction is that it is gender-defined. Reproduction is primarily a female activity. Of course, men participate to some extent in reproduction; at a minimum, they must feed and clothe themselves and, as Marx and Engels point out, they must participate in the so-called 'sexual act' in order that the next generation may be conceived (Marx and Engels, 1979: 51). What Marx and Engels regard as the original division of labor in the sexual act is of course, a division *within* reproduction; it is followed immediately by another division of labor, this time, *between* production and reproduction. On the classical Marxist view, this division of labor, like the first, has always been sex-defined. Engels writes of a sexual division of labor in very early communities and asserts that this took the form of the women's looking after the household while 'it was the man's part to obtain the food and the instruments of labor necessary for the purpose' (Engels, 1972: 119). As we have noted already, the orthodox Marxist view is that this ancient division of labor persists into the present, with women assigned the primary responsibility for reproduction and excluded from full participation in the 'male' sphere of production.

A second important feature of the Marxist concept of reproduction is that it acknowledges 'reproductive' activity as a fundamental necessity of human life.

In *The German Ideology*, when Marx and Engels list 'the premises of human
existence', they include the need 'to make other men, to propagate their kind'
(Marx and Engels, 1979: 49) and assert that this need is an aspect of human
social activity that has existed 'since the dawn of history and the first men, and
which still asserts [itself] in history today' (Marx and Engels, 1979: 50). Engels
takes up this theme again in the definition of historical materialism that he
gives in his famous introduction to *Origin* (1972):

> 'According to the materialist conception, the determining factor in history is, in
> the final instance, the production and reproduction of immediate life. This, again,
> is of a twofold character; on the one side, the production of the means of existence,
> of food, clothing and shelter and the tools necessary for that production; on the
> other side, the production of human beings themselves, the propagation of the
> species. The social organization under which the people of a particular historical
> epoch and a particular country live is determined by both kinds of production:
> by the stage of development of labour on the one hand and of the family on the
> other.' (pp. 71–72).

From what has been said so far, we might suppose that production and reproduction are equally valuable activities. After all, both are directed towards ends
that are equally necessary to human survival. We might surmise that the distinction between production and reproduction is simply that they are directed
toward different purposes: production is activity directed towards the creation
of goods suitable for human consumption and reproduction is activity directed
towards the creation and maintenance of human beings themselves. As Marx
and Engels conceptualize production and reproduction, however, these activities differ not just in their products but also in their processes; not just in the
goals towards which they are directed but also in the sorts of activities that
they are. One way of expressing this difference is by saying that Marx and
Engels conceptualize production but not reproduction as a full form of human
labor.

The concept of labor is absolutely central to the Marxist conception of human
nature and historical development. Labor is the conscious and purposive social
activity through which human beings transform nature so that it will satisfy
their needs and in the course of which they also transform themselves. Labor
draws on the experience of past generations but takes different forms in different
historical periods. The specific form and organization of labor at any one time,
which Marxists call the prevailing mode of production, ultimately determines
the human and social possibilities of that time. Labor is the precondition for
and the expression of all human creative potential. It is labor that makes us
human.[3]

In the ordinary, non-Marxist, sense of the word, much if not all of the re-

---

[3] We now feel that a more extended analysis of this notion of labor, in its bearing on the topic
at hand, is called for at some future time.

productive activity that we outlined earlier would certainly count as labor. As we noted earlier, those who participate at all fully in reproductive activity discover very quickly that reproduction is a lot of hard work. Marx and Engels nowhere provide the sort of phenomenological account of reproduction that we gave earlier, but there is no reason to suppose they would deny our contention that reproductive activity is often physically strenuous and may be mentally or emotionally demanding as well. As we saw earlier, Marx and Engels also acknowledge that reproductive activity is socially necessary. Even so, they do not view it as labor in the full historical sense. When Engels writes that 'the social organization under which the people of a particular historical epoch and a particular country live is determined . . . by the stage of development of labour on the one hand and of the family on the other,' his formulation is revealing. His distinction between 'labour' on the one hand and the family on the other reflects a fundamentally different evaluation of the ontological status of productive and reproductive activity.

A clue to the reason for Marx and Engels' differing evaluations of production and reproduction may be found by looking again to that passage in *The German Ideology* (1979) where Marx and Engels talk in general terms about the basic requirements of human life. When they talk about production, they say that the act of satisfying the biologically-based needs for food, shelter, clothing, etc. leads immediately to the production of new needs and so history is set in motion. When they talk about reproduction, however, they do not say that this activity gives rise to new needs and so to new possibilities of social organization. Their asymmetrical treatment of production and reproduction clearly suggests that Marx and Engels view production as an activity that gives rise to far greater possibilities of historical progress and development than does reproduction. Reproduction, on the other hand, sounds as though it is relatively unchanging throughout history.

If reproduction is relatively unchanging, it cannot constitute a motor of historical progress; if anything, it would seem more likely to constitute a brake on historical change. In the definitive Marxist account of reproduction, Engels' *Origin*, reproduction is treated in just this way. Engels does indeed recognize that there have been historical changes in reproduction; he traces the early development of the family through several forms, identifying changes not only in the social organization of sexuality (who might have sexual relations with whom) but also in the social organization of household work. In particular, Engels focuses on the emergence of monogamous marriage, which gave the husband control over his wife's sexuality and which also transformed household work from a collective project performed by women for the benefit of the entire community to a private service performed by his wife for the benefit of a single man. As Engels explains these changes in reproduction, however, they do not result from any developments within reproduction itself; they do not have their own internal logic. Instead, changes in reproduction result from or are generated by an 'external', nonreproductive cause. They result from developments in the sphere of production. Thus, although reproduction is just as fundamental

a social activity as production in the sense of being just as necessary to human life, it exerts less of a causal influence on the shape of human society and so is less fundamental in an explanatory sense.

Because Marx and Engels view reproduction as less fundamental than production in this latter sense, they give it very little direct attention. The main focus throughout their work is on the so-called sphere of production, which they analyse exhaustively. We are left to speculate on just what it is about reproduction that makes it such a historically repetitive activity, so relatively insusceptible to historical progress. We are also left to speculate on why it has been assigned universally to women. Nevertheless, given our background knowledge of how reproduction has been conceptualized throughout the western tradition, and given the few offhand remarks about reproduction that are scattered throughout the Marxist corpus, a plausible explanation may be reconstructed. According to this reconstruction, Marx and Engels view reproduction as less variable than production because they see it as more rigidly determined by human biology. Similarly, they assume that there are biological reasons why most reproductive activity is always performed by women.

Biological determinist explanations do not accord well with the general spirit of Marxism (W. L. McBride, 1977: 124; Jaggar, 1983). The whole point of the historical materialist method is that it seeks fundamental explanations not in terms of biological givens but rather in historically alterable modes of organizing labor. On the classical Marxist view, indeed, biology itself is socially shaped; Engels (1968) writes: 'The hand is not only the organ of labour, *it is also the product of that labour*' (p. 359). The Marxist approach postulates a dialectical relationship between nature and culture, a relationship mediated by labor, so that nothing in human society is ever totally natural in the sense of being totally determined by human biology.

Nevertheless, in spite of the general anti-determinism of their world view, Marx and Engels (1979) write consistently that the sexual division of labor is 'natural.' For instance, discussing the division of labor in *The German Ideology*, they write that it was 'originally nothing but the division of labour in the sexual act, then that division of labour which develops spontaneously or 'naturally' by virtue of natural predisposition (e.g., physical strength, needs, accidents, etc.)' (p. 51).

On the following page, they refer again to 'the natural division of labour in the family.' (p. 52). These remarks are not just youthful slips. In his mature work, *Capital* (1961), Marx several times repeats the suggestion that there is a sexual division of labor in the family that is natural. For instance, he writes about the 'spontaneously developed' system of organizing labor in 'the patriarchal industries of a peasant family, that produces corn, cattle, yarn, linen, and clothing for home use.' This family, according to Marx

> 'possesses a spontaneously developed system of division of labour. The distribution of the work within the family, and the regulation of the labour-time of

the several members, depends as well upon the differences of age and sex as upon natural conditions varying with the seasons' (p. 78).

Later in the first volume of *Capital*, Marx repeats the point: 'Within a family . . . there springs up naturally a division of labour, caused by differences of sex and age, a division that is consequently based on a purely physiological foundation' (p. 351).

None of the passages quoted above is explicitly deterministic. It is possible that Marx and Engels do not have in mind a biological determinist meaning for such terms as 'natural', 'spontaneous' or 'based on a purely physiological foundation.' However, Marx and Engels do not specify any alternative interpretation and the biological determinist interpretation is in accord with the whole western tradition which has consistently viewed men and production as cultural, women and reproduction as natural. Ultimately, perhaps the main ground for attributing a biological determinist view of reproduction to Marx and Engels is not so much the way they explain the sexual division of labor in production and reproduction as the way they fail to explain it. They do not seem to see it as a fact that requires explanation. For them it is a given, simply 'natural.'

If reproduction is an activity that is biologically determined to such a large extent, it is not a very appropriate topic for political analysis. It will not make much sense to talk about the 'means' or 'forces' or reproduction, except by a stretched analogy with production. Certainly there will be no possibility of distinguishing different 'modes' of reproduction and no political reason to distinguish conceptually between different aspects of it. It will be closer to an animal process than to fully human labor. While it may undergo superficial changes, as a result of changes in the mode of production, reproduction cannot be totally transformed. So it cannot constitute the ground for a constantly greater development of human creative potential. In consequence, those who are engaged in reproduction will be, to a large extent, outside history. Where their reproductive work is subject to historical development, it will ultimately be as a function of production and so they will not be able to control their own destiny through a collective transformation of the mode of reproduction.

Although Marxism does not draw these implications explicitly, since it deals with reproduction primarily by ignoring it, they are implicit in the Marxist strategy for women's liberation. As we have seen, that strategy is to bring women to participate fully in production. Traditional Marxists do not make the converse call for men to participate fully in reproduction, and now we can see why not. Some reproductive activity is such that only women are biologically capable of it; the rest is repetitive and unfulfilling, more likely to limit than to expand the creative potential of men.

The classical Marxist conception of reproduction obviously was influenced deeply by the traditional western distinction between the public and the private, the political and the personal realms of human existence. Marxism, in its

turn, has influenced contemporary conceptualizations of this dichotomy. Let us turn now to see how reproduction has been treated in the contemporary theory of a pioneering twentieth-century feminist, Simone de Beauvoir.

3. 'REPRODUCTION' IN BEAUVOIR

In an early chapter of *The Second Sex* (1952), Simone de Beauvoir discusses what she calls 'The Viewpoint of Historical Materialism', that is, the orthodox Marxist perspective on women. There, she explicitly criticizes Engels for slighting the function of reproduction—'[woman's] reproductive function is as important as her productive capacity, no less in the social economy than in the individual life,' Beauvoir says—and for proposing an abstract solution, simply 'the abolition of the family', to the problem of women's oppression (pp. 64–65). But even in this context, which at first sounds promising for our purposes, Beauvoir goes out of her way to stress the very sharp distinction, as she sees it, between *reproduction* and *work*. Indeed, in the paragraph following the one from which we have just quoted, she seems to identify reproduction with 'gestation'—a very abstract and unphenomenological move, as we have already shown—and to say that this activity cannot simply be equated 'with a *task*, a piece of work, or with a service, such as military service.' (p. 65).

It is in the following chapter, the first of her short and very depressing sketches of the oppression of women across history, that Beauvoir first makes full use of certain Hegelian theoretical concepts, as she interprets them within her existentialist framework, to reinforce her sharply dichotomous way of thinking about reproduction and production. It seems ironic, when one reflects on what is known about the high mortality rates of women in childbirth during primitive nomadic times, the period about which Beauvoir is writing, that she begins her conceptual misadventure here by contrasting childbirth with the life-risking adventures in which males engaged in these societies. 'The painful ordeal of childbirth seemed a useless or even troublesome accident,' she writes. 'But in any case giving birth and suckling are not *activities*, they are natural functions; no project is involved; and that is why woman found in them no reason for a lofty affirmation of her existence.' (p. 71). At least, it should be noted, she mentions that nomadic childbirth was painful!

Nomadic men, on the other hand, regularly did just what Hegel, in his Master-Slave dialectic, tells us must be done in order to achieve self-consciousness and full humanity: they *risked their lives*. Now, it must be conceded that the wild animals against which the nomadic male was locked in mortal struggle were also risking their lives; in fact, must of the time, as we know from empirical evidence, the animals lost. The difference, Beauvoir asserts, is that animals have no projects—they never had and never will—, whereas human males from nomadic times on *have* had projects. As for human females, they have always, as human, aspired to the transcendence over the mere playing

out of the life cycle that characterizes the forming and implementation of projects, but they have been thwarted and relegated by men to that cycle of unending repetition. The historical male-female relationship better accords with some aspects of Hegel's dialectical analysis, Beauvoir says, than do historical master-slave relationships (p. 73).

One can legitimately take issue, even on grounds internal to the Hegelian framework, with the implications that Beauvoir draws here. Yes, she is right in suggesting the applicability of the master slave dialectical analysis to the history of male dominance. But then consider, as she does not here, the outcome of that analysis in Hegel's *Phenomenology* (1967): the slave, initially anxious and in fear for her very existence in her relationship to the master, eventually comes *through labor and service* to recognize that in reality it is the master's consciousness that is the dependent one, and hers that is independent. While Marx's criticism of Hegel concentrated, as we know, on the fact that the resolution proposed by Hegel was a resolution merely in consciousness and not in the actual social world, Alexandre Kojève (1969) stressed the vital role here attributed to *labor* by Hegel in reinforcing his claims about the strong influence of the latter's thinking on Marx's basic outlook.

Beauvoir, on the other hand, while certainly familiar with all of this later history, deliberately ignores it because it fails to accord with her clearly-stated conviction that reproduction, the traditional activity of women, is in no sense labor or service at all. Hence, there is absolutely no aspect of triumph, such as that which comes to Hegel's slave at least within that slave's own self-consciousness, to Beauvoir's historical woman; and women are consigned, quite explicitly, to the level of mere animal consciousness (assuming, for the purposes of argument here, that this is a correct characterization of animal consciousness!)—with the one difference that women have never-fulfilled *aspirations* to something higher.

More significant, no doubt, than the demonstration of her misuse of Hegel for understanding the ultimate impact of Beauvoir's treatment of women through history is a careful re-reading of the identifications that she establishes between what she herself calls 'the male principle', on the one hand, and the historical role of women as she conceives it, on the other. Consider this sentence, which comes from her description of the evolution of early agricultural societies: 'Spirit has prevailed over Life, transcendence over immanence, technique over magic, and reason over superstition' (Beauvoir, 1952: 16). She unhesitatingly identifies 'the male principle' with the first term of each pair. It is this set of contrasts, together with the fundamental and all-pervasive emphasis on production over reproduction, that sets the tone for Beauvoir's view of the whole of past history, right up to her own century (see Seigfried, 1984). It is to her great credit that she dedicated herself to the seemingly quite impossible task of somehow overcoming her own sexual fate, as she had characterized it, and realizing all the positive qualities—transcendence, reason, productivity, and the rest—that she presumably thought to be the historical tasks of men alone. Moreover, we think it unnecessary to pay further tribute to the intel-

lectual inspiration that Beauvoir provided for the contemporary women's movement. *But*—was hers the conceptually most fruitful path to take? May it not
rather be the case that Beauvoir's penchant for dramatic dichotomies, for sometimes treating limiting case concepts as if they actually constituted the real, in
fact has been a liability in both feminist theory and practice? We think so, just
as we think that the original Marxist dichotomy between production and reproduction, which Beauvoir, far from questioning, has rendered starker and
less ambiguous, is such a liability. We shall now proceed to discuss why this
is so.

4. PROBLEMS IN THE MARXIST CONCEPT OF
REPRODUCTION

The main focus of Marxist theory, as we noted earlier, is on production rather
than on reproduction. At first sight, the conceptual distinction between these
two types of activity seems quite unproblematic: one is concerned with producing goods, the other with producing people. On closer examination, however, the clarity of the distinction blurs. Later we shall argue that this
conceptual fuzziness results inevitably from the social reality that so-called
productive and reproductive activity in fact are continuous and only artificially
separable. For the moment, we shall concentrate on the way in which Marx
and Engels conceptualized the distinction between them.

Several feminist authors have pointed to ambiguities in the Marxist concept
of production. Linda Nicholson identifies three distinct senses in which Marxists
use the term. First, in its broadest meaning, 'production' refers to all activities
necessary for species survival: it is a transhistorical category more or less synonymous with 'labor.' In its second and narrower sense, 'production' refers to
those activities that result in objects; in this sense, production is distinguished
from so-called reproduction, that is from those activities concerned with creating and caring for human beings. Finally, Marxists employ a third sense of
'production' which cuts across the second sense; in this third sense, 'production'
refers to activities resulting in commodities, that is, in goods and services that
are bought and sold (Nicholson, 1984: Chap. 6).

The concept of reproduction in Marxist theory is at least as ambiguous as
the concept of production, but the distinctions between the various senses of
'reproduction' do not correlate with or match the distinctions between the
various senses of 'production.' In its broadest meaning, 'reproduction' is that
aspect of production which is devoted to replacing the means of production;
for instance, it includes the production of seed-corn or replacements for existing
machinery. Reproduction in this sense is part of the economic foundation of
society: seed-corn and machine replacements are produced through the same
physical and social process as corn and machines for exchange on the market;
the 'mode of reproduction' in this sense is identical with the mode of production.
Marxists also use 'reproduction' in a more restricted sense to refer to those

institutions that maintain and reproduce the social relations of production. In contemporary society, Marxists construe these as capitalist social relations. In this second usage, 'reproduction' is taken to include entertainment, education, advertising, in short, the whole realm of culture and ideology—what Marxists sometimes call the superstructure of society, as a contrast with the economic foundation.

There is, of course, still a third sense of 'reproduction', the sense that we characterized roughly at the beginning of this paper. The third sense is still not very precise since it includes not only the activities of childbearing and childrearing but also the work involved in caring for adults, both those who are disabled and those who are sometimes called the temporarily abled. It is this third sense of 'reproduction' in which we are primarily interested, since it is the activity included under this heading that Marxist theory construes as typically female and links with women's subordination. In particular, we are concerned with the theoretical and practical consequences of conceptually stigmatizing this activity by labeling it 'reproduction' *in contrast with* the supposedly primary activity of production.

Before addressing these consequences directly, we should note a complication in the Marxist way of conceptualizing women's procreative and nurturing work. This is that, although Marxist theory ordinarily contrasts production with reproduction, yet it construes much of women's work *simultaneously* as reproductive and as productive. Although women's procreative and nurturing work is referred to ordinarily as reproduction, it is obvious that most if not all of this work is also production in the broadest sense of being activity necessary to human survival. Moreover, it may also be production in the third sense, if it falls within the confines of the market. Increasingly, indeed, such work does not fall within the market. Not only has the production of food and clothes been industrialized, but laundering and the final stages of food preparation continue to move outside the home. Health care, including emotional care and the care of the elderly and the permanently disabled, is performed increasingly by paid workers and so is the care and education of children. As we saw earlier, most of those who do this work are still women, but the social relations within which they do it have now changed. Their work has become a commodity and the women who perform it are now producers of surplus value.

At this point, we might begin to wonder about the rationale for continuing to conceive of women's procreative and nurturing activity as reproductive rather than productive. Why does Marxist theory maintain the second sense of 'production' and continue to make a distinction between the production of people and the production of things, especially if this no longer correlates even roughly with the distinction between home and market production or with the distinction between the production of use values and the production of exchange values? We contend that there is no valid point in maintaining this distinction. In our view, the Marxist distinction between production and reproduction distorts the reality of women's work and encourages us to think about that work in a way that devalues it.

One possible rationale for labeling women's procreative and nurturing activities as reproduction is that women do indeed reproduce that most important means of production, labor power. Thus they are reproductive in the first sense identified above. If women's activity is viewed as reproductive in the first sense, then it must be part of the economic foundation of society. However, one might still question why at least part of women's procreative and nurturing activity is not conceived as production rather than as reproduction, since prevailing demographic trends show that women do not simply replace the existing stock of labor power but also increase the supply. In some parts of the world, indeed, the rate of increase in the available labor power is so fast as to be called explosive.

Women's procreative and nurturing activity might also be construed as reproductive in the second sense that we identified earlier, namely, the sense of reproducing the social relations of production. If it is understood in this way, then women's procreative and nurturing activity does not appear as part of the economic foundation of society, but only as 'superstructural'. The treatment of the family by Engels and also by contemporary Marxists indicates that Marxist theory in fact conceptualizes women's procreative and nurturing activities as reproduction in the second sense and thus as peripheral rather than central to the prevailing mode of production. When 'reproduction' is interpreted in this way, then we can see that to categorize women's activity as reproductive is to devalue its historical significance. It is to suggest that the system of production is created and changed by men and that women merely reproduce or maintain it. Men seize fire and women keep it burning.

To characterize women's procreative and nurturing activity as reproduction is to deny its creativity in an even more fundamental way. As we have seen earlier, this characterization suggests that what women do is to repeat essentially similar activities from generation to generation. They push the 'everlasting broom across the everlasting floor' or dandle a baby eternally on their lap. In our opinion, this suggestion seriously undervalues the variability and the complexity of women's procreative and nurturing activity as well as its possibilities for historical development.

In what follows, we shall not spend time considering the social and technological developments in women's health care and other nurturing activity. Once one is willing to acknowledge such developments, it is obvious that they decisively refute the ideological stereotype that so-called reproduction is biologically determined and unchangeable at least in these aspects. Rather than discussing women's more evidently historical activities, therefore, we shall focus directly on the acticity surrounding the conception, bearing and early rearing of infants. This is the activity that is seen as the core of reproduction, and this is the activity that is conceptualized as most rigidly determined by biology. It is also the activity that seems most obviously to justify the claim that, simply in virtue of their biological constitution, women are better suited to procreative and nurturing activity than men. It is in this area that the assignment of reproduction to women seems most 'natural.' If we can show that the activity of

producing and caring for infants is no more determined biologically than the activity of industrial production and distribution, then we shall have undercut the most influential rationale for assigning this productive activity to a special category called reproduction.

5. CLASSICAL BIOLOGICAL DETERMINISM VS CONTEMPORARY SOCIAL REALITY

At several points in *Capital* (1961: 232, 403 and 427; 1962: 838), Marx refers to an unchangeable, natural component of the production process: it has to do with the chemical and physical characteristics of muscles and other human anatomical features that together set a limit to the length of the working day. These remarks appear as, so to speak, slight qualifications to the general contention of the entire book, namely, that what constitutes socially necessary labor will vary enormously according to changing technical possibilities. (It is in some of these passages, and virtually only there, interestingly enough, that Marx employs the conservative terminology of the 'nature of man.') But, as was implied earlier when we pointed out the lack of consistency between biological determinist explanations and the general spirit of Marxism, Marx should have considered whether even these qualifications may not be exaggerated. After all, muscle capacity, for example, may itself be altered greatly in a single individual by the use of drugs and/or certain types of physical training. Moreover, some of the most important contemporary industrial activities—as distinguished, perhaps, from many of those heavy industries which were beginning to dominate in Marx's nineteenth-century—are very little reliant on capacities for physical endurance much beyond the ability to stay awake and alert. Our point is that the element of ineluctable never-changeable biological determination even in those types of activities that Marx regarded as paradigmatic of production must be considered as negligible to the point of vanishing.

Is the case different with respect to procreation, regarded as the core of traditional 'reproduction'? We think not. The twentieth-century availability of more reliable methods of birth and fertility control has substantially altered the nature and meaning of procreation. The event of procreation has come to be, in the main, the outcome of human decision—sometimes that of a mother, at least in part, but often also that of agencies of social control, the possibilities of which have been greatly increased by new technologies. At any rate, procreation can no longer reasonably be seen, as it still was in Marx's day, as being in large measure an 'act of God.' Similarly, developments in obstetrics and infant pediatrics, as well as advances in public health and hygiene, have dramatically changed what childbirth and infancy are and what they mean; once again, abuses of this technology are at present widespread. An improved comprehension of nutritional and psychological aspects of young infants has introduced many new possibilities, both for better and for worse, into the field of childrearing; on the one hand, children's behavior may now be controlled by

drugs as well as by persuasion or threat; on the other hand, mystical accounts, e.g. the existence of some alleged sacred or biological bond between a mother and her child, have given way to more plausible, realistic understandings, e.g. the young child's need for regular care by one of several primary caregivers whom she or he will recognize. Just as industrial developments of the past two centuries have destroyed many once firmly-held myths about limitations on the human capacity for achievement, so such changes in the practices of procreation, the core area of what traditional and Marxian and Beauvoirian thought has characterized as 'reproduction', have also destroyed many myths, including the myth of 'reproduction' as a timeless and hence radically different set of activities. In male-dominated society, these activities invariably remain alienated and exploitative just as, for example, work in the factories of new 'high tech' industries remains alienated and exploitative, despite the dramatic changes signified by the existence of those industries (Jaggar, 1983: 307–317). But neither type of activity should be seen as subject to an unalterable biological destiny.

This is especially clear if we look to imminent possibilities in the area of procreation. These possibilities, as we all know, have already begun to be realized; taken as a whole, they amount to absolute denials of such once 'common-sensical' propositions as that children can only come about through a male's directly impregnating a female, that an infant cannot survive unless borne in a womb almost to term or that the ovum from which a given child has developed must necessarily have been that of the woman who carries and gives birth to that child. Even the claim that a child, in order to exist, must have been conceived and, at least for a certain time, carried within a woman's body is itself no longer, by anyone's reckoning, a statement of what was once called 'physical necessity'; the technology of in vitro fertilization is already being implemented.

Let us straightforwardly acknowledge then that the activities surrounding procreation, like the other activities that Marxists characterize ordinarily as reproductive, differ from those that Marx and Beauvoir designated as 'production' in no socially or conceptually significant way. They involve no fewer of our distinctively human capacities and they are equally susceptible to historical transformation. As feminists have pointed out, they are also equally susceptible to exploitation and degradation. In our society, the entire range of human activities, including those that have been ideologically isolated as belonging to the allegedly special sphere of 'reproduction', are deformed both by capitalism and by male domination. In the case of procreation, this is clearly manifested in the current for-profit and male biases of the medical industry. The price now being extorted by that industry for its administration of the technological advances of which we have just spoken is a system wherein mostly male doctors insist on totally controlling all those aspects of procreation which are most lucrative for them. Nevertheless, from a conceptual standpoint this current situation simply reinforces our finding that what has been singled out traditionally as a separate and somehow inferior sphere called 'reproduction' is simply one form of human labor. We shall conclude by mentioning some major implications of this finding.

6. CONCLUSION: RECONCEPTUALIZING 'REPRODUCTION'

Every society is sustained on a daily basis by continual procreative and nurturing activity. In every society, so far as we know, this activity has a lower status than other activities such as hunting, war or the performance of religious rituals, even though these other activities are often less basic to social survival. In every society too, so far as we know, this activity is performed by women. Contemporary industrial society is no exception to the general rule: among us, as apparently everywhere else, the direct, routine, face-to-face care of adults and children has a relatively low status; among us too, as apparently everywhere else, this procreative and nurturing activity is performed by women. In the preceding pages, we have looked at some problems in the way that this activity has been conceptualized in the classical Marxist tradition and by the influential feminist, Simone de Beauvoir. In what follows, we want to sum up our criticisms of this way of conceptualizing women's activity and to suggest the outlines of an alternative conceptual approach. This alternative is designed to retain the Marxist emphasis on the primacy of human labor but to incorporate the feminist insight that women's so-called activities are full forms of human labor.

In our view, there is no good reason for theoretically separating procreation and nurturing from other forms of creative human activity by assigning them the label of 'reproduction.' As we have seen already, procreation and nurturing are production in the broadest Marxist sense of being necessary to human life and they are increasingly productive in the capitalist sense of falling within the market. We can find no adequate rationale for insisting on a theoretical distinction between the production of things and the production of people. Things, after all, are produced for the use of people and for this reason their production may just as appropriately be viewed as a part of 'reproduction.' Moreover, much of what is counted as reproduction in fact consists in the final stages of producing things for people's use: cleaning or even sewing clothes, preparing food, etc. In our view, the activities that have been conceptualized respectively as production and as reproduction in fact form part of a continuous process and we can see no reason to make a conceptual break in this continuum.

If the distinction between so-called production and so-called reproduction is indeed arbitrary, then one might ask why it has been so widely accepted, accepted even by theorists such as classical Marxists and Simone de Beauvoir, who have had a genuine interest in women's emancipation. We cannot engage here in a reconstruction of the motives of these theorists, but we can look at some results of their making this distinction.

The most obvious result of the theoretical distinction between production and reproduction is that it effectively separates women's from men's work and makes women's work appear to be less fully human and less important in accounting for historical change. Women's activity then seems to be less interesting from the point of view of the political economist and a rationale is provided for relegating it from the public or political to the so-called personal

or private realm. Men thus have a pretext for refusing to take seriously women's demands for a reorganization of procreation and daily nurturing. Women's work remains invisible and men continue to benefit from it both directly and indirectly. Directly, men gain increased leisure time and an improved quality of life from women's procreative and nurturing activity; indirectly, because women are handicapped by their responsibility for 'two jobs,' men gain an advantage over women in the competition for jobs and professional advancement. In this way, the categorization of procreation and nurturing as reproduction rather than as production functions to obscure the way in which women's labor is exploited by men and so promotes men's interests at the expense of women's.

In this paper, we have argued that the activities categorized as reproduction are just as fully forms of human labor as is agriculture or manufacturing. Procreative and nurturing activities are no more determined by human biology than any other activities and are equally susceptible to social control and historical transformation. We have not argued that specific modes of organizing procreation and nurturing are as fundamental in shaping society as are specific modes of producing food, clothing and shelter, but such arguments have been made convincingly by a variety of feminist theorists who take the subordination of women to be a central rather than a peripheral feature of contemporary society. All this is obscured when procreation and nurturing are conceptualized as reproduction, and this is why we assert that the concept of reproduction, as it is used by the classical Marxists and by Simone de Beauvoir, is a key piece of male ideology. We suggest that 'reproduction' should no longer be used in this way and that procreation and nurturing should be theoretically conceptualized as forms of human labor and more or less fully realized social expressions of human creative ability.

We are not sure what is the best way of linguistically designating this admittedly broad category of human activity. 'Human activity' itself is too broad; we want to exclude consumption and other types of activity that do not make an easily recognizable social contribution. 'Labor' and 'production' are obvious candidates, but some feminists have objected to these terms as being too much imbued with nineteenth-century or male or capitalist values. 'Labor' is sometimes interpreted as drudgery, as activity that is not playful or creative, that is undertaken from necessity rather than for its own sake. 'Production' is often interpreted in a similar way: as expressing a male preoccupation with tangible products rather than a feminist interest in the process itself. Joyce Trebilcot has suggested that our category be labeled 'reproduction', as a way of emphasizing both traditional female values and the reality of social continuity. We are attracted by this idea but think that the word 'reproduction' is too strongly suggestive of the sort of ahistorical, transgenerational repetition that is more characteristic of animal than of human activity (see Jaggar, 1983: 307–317).

Another promising candidate might be the word *poiesis*, which received its philosophical credentials primarily from Aristotle. In the *Nicomachean Ethics*, Aristotle associated *poiesis* with art or applied science and distinguished it from (non-productive) action, *praxis* (Aristotle, 1962, 1140a: 151–152). Aristotle,

whose own systematic misogyny is notorious, would certainly not concur with our suggestion that so-called 'reproduction' should be considered as a form of *poiesis*, nor would we concur with his very sharp distinction between *poiesis* and *praxis*. Nevertheless, we think 'poiesis' might come to be an acceptable alternative to 'production' for some people, since it lacks the unpleasant associations that capitalism has attached to the latter. In the meantime, and in the absence of a fully satisfactory alternative, we shall use the term 'production' for the remainder of this paper. However, we wish to emphasize that we are using it in the broadest Marxist sense of the activities necessary for species survival and enhancement and not because we wish to assimilate all activity to industrial production or women's traditional work to men's.

The conceptual revision that we suggest would encourage a more comprehensive understanding of what Marxists call past and present modes of production. Procreative and nurturing activities would be taken into account by theorists attempting to identify modes of production, the classes that characterize them, and the causes of their historical transformation. A large proportion of human survival activity would not be necessarily excluded for our conception of the economic foundation of society and it would become possible to investigate the reciprocal influence of modes of organizing procreation and nurturing on the organization of other human activities. Such an enlarged conception of production promises to provide a more social and less biologistic understanding of women's historical and continuing subordination and so to suggest political ways of ending it.

To enlarge our conception of production in this way is not necessarily to create a category so all-inclusive that it obscures distinctive features of specific human activities. Within this category, it would still be possible to distinguish various moments, aspects or modes of production. But enlarging the category of production as we have suggested might show that some of our earlier ways of distinguishing aspects of production were inadequate because male-biased. For instance, the inclusion of procreation and nurturing within production, together with reflection on the ways in which these activities historically have been organized, might well lead us to question traditional, sex-blind definitions of the ruling class. We might well conclude, as a number of feminist theorists have done already, that ruling classes are characteristically male. Similarly, when we looked at the history of procreation, we might question traditional ways of demarcating one mode of production from another. In these sorts of ways, an enlarged conception of production might lead us to an understanding of human social organization that was more specific as well as more comprehensive.

Just how we chose to reconceptualize production would depend, of course, on our predominant political and theoretical purposes, and our conceptualizations might change as these varied. For instance, instead of trying to make a once-and-for-all distinction between economic base and super-structure, we might make the notion of economic base relative to specific political and theoretical problems. Thus, we might see the mode of organizing procreation as

basic to understanding women's subordination but as less fundamental, though still not irrelevant, to an understanding of racism or industrialization. Our theory would thus reflect our primary questions and our political priorities.

To reconceptualize procreation and nurturing as production, construed in the broad sense that we have indicated, rather than as reproduction is not just to recommend a linguistic change. How we describe the world affects as well as reflects how we perceive and act upon it. To conceptualize procreation and nurturing as production rather than as reproduction is to bring them into the realm of politics, to make them available both for political criticism and for political reconstruction. So-called women's issues could no longer be dismissed as merely personal or even as simply 'women's issues' and women's labor could no longer be devalued or ignored.

Over the past 15 years, feminists have engaged in sustained critique of our modes of organizing procreation and daily nurturing; in the process, they have expanded our conceptions of coercion, of alienation and of exploitation. This feminist critique must be continued as new forms of procreative exploitation emerge, such as the recent development of so-called surrogate mothering, where a woman is paid to gestate a child which is then adopted by an infertile couple. As well as criticizing, however, it is also time to start thinking seriously about alternatives to prevailing ways of organizing to satisfy these basic human needs. So far, most of the alternatives have taken the form of individual experimentation and many Marxists have dismissed these experiments contemptuously as 'lifestyle radicalism,' personal indulgences that are irrelevant to genuine social transformation. As individual experiments, lifestyle radicalism is indeed utopian but reflection on its failures may point the way to a more thorough-going and deeper transformation of the prevailing male dominant and capitalist mode of production than any that has yet taken place.

REFERENCES

Aristotle. 1962. *Nicomachean Ethics*. Translated by M. Ostwald. Bobbs-Merrill, Indianapolis & New York.

Beauvoir, Simone de. [1952] 1974. *The Second Sex*. Translated by H. M. Parshley. Random House, Vintage Books, New York.

Engels, Friedrich. 1968. The part played by labor in the transition from ape to man. In Karl Marx and Friedrich Engels, *Selected Works*. International Publishers, New York.

Engels, Friedrich. 1972. *The Origin of the Family, Private Property and the State*. International Publishers, New York.

Hegel, G. W. F. 1967. *The Phenomenology of Mind*. Translated, with an introduction and notes by J. B. Baille. Harper and Row, NY.

Jaggar, Alison M. 1983. *Feminist Politics and Human Nature*. Rowman and Allenheld, Totowa, N.J.

Kojève, Alexandre. 1969. *Introduction to the Reading of Hegel*. Translated by J. H. Nichols. Basic Books, New York & London.

Marx, Karl. 1961. *Capital*, Vol. I. Translated by S. Moore and E. Aveling. Foreign Languages Publishing House, Moscow.

Marx, Karl. 1962. *Capital*, Vol. III. Translated by S. Moore and E. Aveling. Foreign Languages Publishing House, Moscow.

Mark, Karl and Friedrich Engels. 1979. *The German Ideology*. International Publishers, New York.

McBride, Angela. B. 1976. *A Married Feminist*. Harper & Row, New York.

McBride, William L. 1977. *The Philosophy of Marx*. Hutchinson, London.

Nicholson, Linda. Forthcoming. Feminism as political philosophy. Columbia University Press, Columbia.

Parekh, Bhikhu. 1981. *Hannah Arendt and the Search for a New Political Philosophy*. Humanities Press, Atlantic Highlands, N.J.

Seigfried, Charlene. 1984. Gender-specific values. *The Philosophical Forum*. Forthcoming.

United States Department of Labor. 1965. *Dictionary of Occupational Titles*, 3rd edn. U.S. Government Printing Office, Washington, D.C.

SEXUAL EMBODIMENT

BEAUVOIR AND FRENCH FEMINISM

(écriture féminine)

Arleen B. Dallery

In this paper, I am going to be looking at the deployment of woman's sexuality in Beauvoir's *The Second Sex* and in the writings of Irigaray, Cixous and Kristeva, proponents of *écriture féminine*. My thesis is that Beauvoir constructs differences between male and female sexuality, using male sexuality as the norm, whereas these feminists enunciate women's sexuality as radically other and heterogeneous. In my analysis of the texts on sexuality in *The Second Sex*, I shall argue that Beauvoir is *almost* a French feminist! Although she alludes to woman's sexuality or eroticism as distinctively different from the male norm, she never adequately describes it. After a brief exposition of some of the major themes in *écriture féminine* I shall address the 'anti-essentialist paranoia' which is rampant in current feminist theory, as it seeks to come to grips with French feminism.

Phenomenology has sought to restore the primacy of the lived-body as the center of philosophical reflection. The lived body or embodied consciousness has been described in its primordial structures of perception, movement, gesture, desire and erotic perception. But phenomenology has never adequately or explicitly articulated gender-specific structures of embodment. The lived body is presumably gender-free, a human body. Yet, Sartre's and Merleau-Ponty's descriptions of embodiment in the modes of sexuality and desire, although intended as gender-free descriptions of human experience, actually presuppose male norms of sexuality and desire. Desire is always structured by intentionality towards the other *as* woman, constituting the other's body as erotic object.

In Merleau-Ponty, for example, the sexed body (*corps sexué*) is really a masculine body and erotic perception *is* a masculine experience. Merleau-Ponty quite explicitly acknowledges a genderized subject:

> 'In the case of the normal subject a body is not perceived merely as an object;
> this objective perception has within it a more intimate perception. The visible
> body is subtended by a general schema which is strictly individual, emphasizing
> the erogenous areas outlining a sexual physiognomy and eliciting the gesture of

the *masculine* body which is itself integrated in this emotional totality.' (Merleau-Ponty, 1962: 156).

Woman's own erotic embodiment is nowhere accounted for in this chapter except in brief reference to the deficient mode of frigidity.

Woman's sexual embodiment cannot be the subject of phenomenological description, because she is the other against whom male desire and erotic perception are constituted with this projection of a sexual schema. We cannot just substitute woman's erotic perception for men's, since woman's sexual embodiment does not necessarily presuppose any other, constituting an other's body with erotic meaning.

It would appear, then, that Beauvoir's description of female sexuality in *The Second Sex* ([1952], 1961) would finally make up for this lack of a woman's voice, a woman subject in the phenomenological accounts of desire. Yet, when interpreted closely, Beauvoir's appropriation of the Sartrean categories of transcendance and immanence, being for one-self and being for others, belie these expectations. If Woman is Other, then her sexuality is only a complement to male desire, her immanence and passivity the counterpart of his transcendence and agency. As Fuchs has pointed out (1980), Beauvoir's descriptions of woman's erotic body are really expressions of *alienation* from one's body, its wetness, sponginess, oozing mollusk-like qualities; it is the body as seen by others, feared by others, repulsive to oneself (Beauvoir [1952] 1961: 362).

Her sexuality, too, is constituted by the desire of the other; he installs her in the circuit of desire. Woman's desire, unlike the man's, is not intentional; it encloses her body; engulfs her. It does not constitute another with sexual meaning. Woman's sexuality is not a linear project, a style of conduct, as in Sartre and Merleau-Ponty, but a spell in which woman swoons, not wanting it broken by the agency, or too obvious manipulations of the other (Beauvoir [1952] 1961: 372). And while woman's eroticism transcends the genital to encompass the whole body in an unsegmented way, it is still limited to the realm of sexual intercourse, a heteronomy of desire.

Here are some key descriptions of woman's dependent sexuality, of her total immanence in her body, refusing action, control and transcendence.

'The young girl needs a man to reveal her own body to her, she is more deeply *dependent*.' Beauvoir [1952], 1961: 356).

'All voluntary effort prevents the feminine flesh from being taken; this is why woman spontaneously declines the form of coition which demands effort and tension on her part; too sudden or too many changes in position, any call for consciously directed activity whether word or behavior—tend to break the spell.' (Beauvoir [1952], 1961: 355).

'Sex pleasure in woman, as I have said is a kind of magic spell, it demands complete abandon, if words or movement oppose the magic of caresses, the spell is broken.' (Beauvoir [1952], 1961: 372).

Sartre and Merleau-Ponty described stages of erotic embodiment. Merleau-Ponty begins with erotic perception and comprehension of the other; Sartre describes desire, the caress, the orgasm. Beauvoir, however, examines woman's erotic embodiment always and already in the throes of libidinous experience. She emphasizes the abandon and rapture of woman's libidinous experience, the fact that it has no definite goal, that it is not fully satisfied by orgasm. Again the comparison is always with male desire and the opposition.

> 'Male sexual feeling rises like an arrow; when it reaches a certain height or threshold it is fulfilled and dies abruptly in the orgasm; Feminine enjoyment radiates through the whole body it is not always concentrated in the genital organs; because no definite term is set, woman's sex feeling extends towards infinity . . .' (Beauvoir [1952], 1961: 371).

It is not just that Beauvoir's account shows woman's sexuality in the mode of passivity, the pleasure of submission, but she is already described in the libidinous experience, in the erotic embrace, which is seemingly non-intentional. She never has to or never gets to constitute herself as an autonomous desiring subject, as transcendence. Although Jo-Ann Fuchs, for example, claims that Beauvoir posits woman's sexuality as a form of 'mindlessness' (1980: 309), it could be read quite differently. What is submissive, passive, or immanent from the perspective of gender-biased phenomenological categories is *libidinous* from the perspective of Freudian categories, where subject/object and active/passive distinctions are irrelevant, or blurred. Instead of the intentional libido as aim or want, 'the impulsive libido produces a collage of contradictory images . . . the phantasm, . . . the impossible . . . which smites . . . and captivates you.' (Lingis, 1978: 7).

Al Lingis, in a recent paper critical of phenomenology, drew this distinction between phenomenology's intentional libido and Freud's impulsive libido. While Lingis does not explicitly use these terms to describe genderized sexuality they do seem to fit. He describes a libidinal body beneath the functional, agent body, an orgasmic body beneath the body-organism when the other is not alien to self. 'In the kisses and caresses one feels oneself existing as a voluptuous subject afflicted with phantasmal identities . . . and this alien presence is not distinguishable from the intensity of one's feelings' (Lingis, 1978: 18). Could the opposition between male and female sexual desire, according to Beauvoir, be characterized as that between the male intentional libido which constitutes the other with erotic meaning, signifying the other as a 'lure for caresses and copulation' (1978: 3) and woman's impulsive *libido*?

That is, what I see is a *tension* in Beauvoir's text. Using male sexuality as the norm, woman's sexuality seems unfocused, undirected, deficient, a variant, a spell, an atmosphere. She rejects male manipulation of her body towards orgasm because it structures a subject/object split; it breaks the spell of phantasm, the desire for libidinous fusion. Is this sexual passivity really a quasi-political reaction to patriarchal control of woman's sexuality like the listlessness of Southern slaves (Fuchs 1980: 309)? Or, is it to be read differently: woman's

sexuality is far more erotic than male genital sexuality and never fully expressive in the dominant submissive mode.

Feminist critics of Beauvoir, like Fuchs, have charged that her existentialist analysis of female sexuality really represents a specific, historical form of patriarchal control of woman's sexuality (Fuchs, 1980: 308). Sexuality and one's relation to one's body are social and cultural constructions. While I agree with this criticism, I want to present a different reading of the text in terms of a sub-text, which is signified by one of the last statements in *The Second Sex* (p. 688) where Beauvoir claims that woman's sexual world is different from a man's. But, from our reading of chapter fourteen, Beauvoir never reveals this truly different feminine sexual world, since female sexuality is already qualified by male desire and domination. Unless we go back to the earlier descriptions of 'magic spell' 'rapture' and 'abandon' and construe them as *not* negative, not mindless, not even passive, e.g. deconstruct their meaning. We can read them as woman's *impulsive* libido seeking to subvert (unsuccessfully) male manipulation and conquest, intentionality as negation. But Beauvoir's analysis has already *masked* or hidden these meanings by viewing woman's sexuality through the signifying practices of male sexuality, that *intentional* libido for whom woman's body is constituted as 'erotic lure for caresses and copulation.' Female eroticism is effectively and linguistically repressed and, therefore, devalued in the metaphors of 'mollusk,' 'bog,' 'nature,' 'swamp,' 'hole' and 'slime.'

Read across the grain, what Beauvoir describes is not woman's dependent or alienated sexuality, but rather, woman's repressed eroticism. At any rate, Beauvoir never voices the subjectivity of woman's eroticism. Since Beauvoir only shows us that woman's erotic embodiment can not be fully subjectively lived within the confines of the dominant submissive model of patriarchal sexuality: it is still to be spoken and written.

Écriture féminine

While Beauvoir describes woman's eroticism as mediated by male desire, French feminist writers, like Cixous and Irigaray, through their discourse, reveal woman's eroticism as autonomous. The concern is not the phenomenological one of how we live our sexual body, but how we *speak it*, symbolize and represent it, separate from the categories of phallocratic thought.

French feminism or *écriture féminine* is essentially a deconstruction of the phallic organization of sexuality and its code which positions woman's sexuality and signified body as a mirror or complement to male sexual identity. And, correspondingly, it is a discourse on the genuine multiple otherness of woman's libidinal economy—her eroticism—which has been symbolically repressed in language and denied by patriarchal culture.

The two themes that I want to outline in this brief exposition are (1) the displacement of the male economy of desire for a feminine economy of pleasure or *jouissance*, (2) the displacement of a dualistic, oppositional, hetero-sexuality for feminine structures of erotic embodiment where self and other are continuous, in pregnancy, childbirth, and nursing.

Before discussing French feminist discourse on the body it might be helpful to point out Beauvoir's early reaction to French feminism. In an interview with Peg Simons, Beauvoir accepts this new valorization and appropriation of woman's bodily experiences in pregnancy, childbirth, menopause, the transcendence of bodily alienation in feminist praxis (Simons and Benjamin, 1979: 342). But she strongly resists a cultism, a narcissism or a mysticism of the body (Simons and Benjamin, 1979: 342). Yet, her pronouncements on French feminism seem to be deliberate misreadings as if 'writing the body' was only a new biological reductionism, an essentialism, based on some ontological difference of woman's body or, what Beauvoir calls, the 'construction of a *counter-penis*' (Simons and Benjamin, 1979: 342).

What she neglects to note is that woman's body is always mediated by language; the human body is a text, a sign, not just a piece of fleshy matter. Clearly, Irigaray and Cixous are not so philosophically naïve as to make this Hegelian move to an abstract opposite. The structures of language and other signifying practices which code woman's body are as equally oppressive as the material/ social structures which have tended to mediate one's awareness of one's body and self and erotic possibilities. For this reason, some filmmakers, according to Mary Ann Doane (Doane, 1981), have refused to film woman's body so layered has it been with the male gaze, with male signification. In these comments, Beauvoir completely ignores the roots of *écriture féminine* as a response to Lacanian psychoanalysis which claims that sexual differences cannot be reduced to biology, since woman's body is constituted through phallic symbolization.

Deconstruction of differences to otherness

These differences are already at work in phenomenological accounts of desire and erotic perception where woman's body is already constituted, or sexualized as the object of desire, fragmented into erogenous zones. Cixous refers to Beauvoir's description of woman's dependent sexuality as the old fool's game: 'I will give you your body and you'll give me mine' (Cixous, 1981a: 256). I will incarnate you in flesh and you will reveal my flesh for me. Woman's body is already colonized by the hegemony of male desire; it is not *your* body.

These sexual differences are also constructed, according to Lacan, when the boy child reads the girl child's anatomy as a Lack, the absence of the phallus. The boy's sexual identity is based on perception of the other—she who lacks, who is only absence. The phallus, the symbolic meanings of the penis, is the transcendental signifier, constituting difference in sameness.

In response to Lacan, Cixous claims that

> 'sexual difference is not determined merely by the fantasized relationship to anatomy, which is based on the point of view, therefore upon a strange importance accorded (by Freud and Lacan) to exteriority (the seen body of one's own and the seen body of another) and to the *specular* in the elaboration of sexuality. A voyeur's theory, of course' (Cixous, 1981b: 95).

By speaking the body, *écriture féminine* reverses the hierarchy of male and female sexuality, this male identity-in-difference, by showing that woman's sexual embodiment is the general model of sexuality and male sexuality is a variant of it, a prolonged utilization of the phallic stage. Jonathan Cullers has noted this deconstructionist strategy of French feminism; instead of lack, woman's body is over supplied: 'With her, two sexual organs, one male and one female, is the general model of sexuality.' (Cullers, 1983: 172).

As Irigaray expands: 'woman has sex organs just about everywhere,' (Irigaray, 1981: 103). Woman's sexuality is not one but two or even plural, the multiplicity of sexualized zones spread across the body.

> 'She is neither one nor two she cannot strictly speaking be determined as one person or two. She renders any definition inadequate. Moreover she has no "proper" name. . . . ' (Irigaray, 1981: 101).

Irigaray posits woman's autoeroticism as plural, based on the primacy of *touch*.

> 'She experiences pleasure almost everywhere, even without speaking of the hysterization of her entire body, one can say that the geography of her pleasure is much more diversified, more multiple in its differences, more complex, more subtle than is imagined . . . (p. 103). Woman finds pleasure more in *touch* than in sight and her entrance into a dominant scopic economy signifies, once again, her relegation to passivity' (p. 101).

In constructing the radical otherness of female autoeroticism, *écriture féminine* displaces the male economy of desire, the gap between desire and its object, the nexus of need, absence and representation, for the feminine economy of pleasure or *jouissance*.

> 'No, it is at the level of sexual pleasure (*jouissance*) in my opinion that the difference makes itself most clearly apparent in as far as woman's libidinal economy is neither identifiable by a man nor referrable to the masculine economy' (Cixous, 1981b: 95).
>
> 'How do I experience sexual pleasure? What is feminine sexual pleasure; where does it take place; how is it inscribed at the level of her body, of her unconscious? And then, how is it put into writing?' (p. 95)

Woman's erotic embodiment is separate from the scopic economy of male desire which posits a dualism, an opposition of self and other, and then seeks to reduce the other to sameness or complement.

This concept of *jouissance* is central in Kristeva's writings on pregnancy and Motherhood; It is the orgasmic pleasure of sexual continuity with the maternal body, of libidinal fusion. Feminine *jouissance* takes place on the linguistic level of the semiotic, between physiology and speech, nature and culture, the pre-symbolic, before the separation of self and other. Through motherhood one comes in contact with one's own Mother before the fear of castration. 'By giving

birth the woman enters into contact with her Mother; she becomes, she is her own Mother. They are the same continuity differentiating itself' (Kristeva, 1980: 239).

This split subjectivity or elision of self and other also exists between Mother and child in pregnancy when the pregnant woman may enjoy the heft of her body and sensations within her belly, of otherness within the self. Despite the purification and idealization of motherhood by religion and patriarchal culture, pregnancy, childbirth and nursing are dimensions of woman's erotic embodiment. The autonomous erotic aspects of these realms are more difficult to repress or censor in patriarchal culture, since women preside over them. In this regard, Iris Young has insightfully pointed out that the pregnant woman is not usually sexually objectified by the male gaze (Young, 1984). Maternity offers what heterosexuality, as it is now historically constituted, cannot: libidinal fusion.

These, then, are the overall themes of the discourse on woman's body:

(1) Writing the body celebrates women as sexual subjects not objects of male desire. It undermines the phallic organization of sexuality by retrieving a presymbolic level of speech where feminine *jouissance* is disclosed. Writing the body celebrates woman's autonomous eroticism, separate from a model of male desire based on need, representation and lack. This *jouissance* is prior to self/other dualisms; it expresses the continuity of self and other.

(2) Otherness of woman's body: through *écriture féminine* woman's distinct bodily geography and forms are progressively disclosed, outside the categories of binary thought and the signifying practices of male perception. 'Woman's body is not one nor two. The sex isn't *one*, not a unified identity'. This articulation of woman's erotic body is secured through a deconstruction of sexual differences, based on phallo-morphism *à la* Freud and Lacan. Through writing the body, woman's body is liberated from the objectification and fragmentation of male desire.

(3) This discourse traces out an archeology of woman's body from the preoedipal stage. The erotogeneity of woman's body, its multiple sex organs, is repressed in the development of symbolic language, since there is no one to speak it. In the beginning, the boy child interprets the girl's body as lack, as absence. Through this scopic economy he constituted his own sexual identity, based on her difference—lacking the penis. Meanwhile, as Mary Rawlinson has noted, we never hear the feminine voice in Freud's analysis; there is no *positive* reading of the feminine somatic constitution (Rawlinson, 1981: 166). The silent girl remains a partial man, seeking a penis-substitute in her desire; her body only a complement to his. In speaking woman's body, Irigaray and Cixous signify these bodily territories which have been kept under seal, suppressed in the phallic development of male and female sexual differences.

Writing the body is both speech and praxis.

'Write yourself, your body must be heard. . . . To write an act which will not only realize the decensored relation of woman to her sexuality, to her womanly

being; it will give her back her goods, her pleasures, her organs, her immense bodily territories which have been kept under seal . . . ' (Cixous, 1981a: 250).

'Writing is precisely the very *possibility of change.* The space that can serve as a springboard for subversive thought, the precursory movement of transformation of social and cultural structures . . . women *seizing* the occasion to speak, hence her shattering entry *into history*' (Cixous, 1981a: 249, 250).

Critique: Essentialism?

What, then, are the implications of woman's differentiated erotic embodiment for feminist theory? Is it liberatory for women to own their pleasure? (1) Does *écriture féminine* posit an essentialism: (a) an ahistorical nature of woman; (b) a definition of woman, (c) a *natural* body and, therefore, innate differences between men and women? Does woman's erotic body, alone make her radically other in all respects? Is that bad? Isn't the body or our relation to our body also socially mediated, open to historical shaping? (2) On the other hand, where or how may this discourse on the body suture gaps in feminist theory, repeal the silences in feminist theory?

(1) Both Kristeva and Irigaray reject any definition of woman, any representation or categorization of woman, any Platonic universal. Writing the body, then, does not mirror a Platonic essence. But the charge of essentialism is broached in a different sense: a paranoid reaction based on what patriarchy has done to women, that is, reduce women to their biology or bodily difference. *Écriture féminine* is playing into the hands of the enemy—notwithstanding the valorization of woman's erotic embodiment—because it is a reductionist doctrine.

But the anti-essentialist forgets that the body is a sign, a function of discourse, in *écriture féminine.* Here, I think Mary Ann Doane's response to the anti-essentialists is on target: for want of a stake, representation is not worth anything (Doane, 1981: 29). There is a risk, a stake in writing the body in its specificity, in its autonomous symbolic representation. Is it fear of otherness?

Does *écriture féminine* succumb to what Monique Wittig calls 'the myth of woman' or 'woman is wonderful' (Wittig, 1984: 150)? Here, I would submit that this kind of essentialism might characterize the conservative feminist theories of Jean Elshtain and Carol McMillan. (Elshtain, 1981; McMillan, 1982). According to both 'neo-feminists', woman's body and its biological imperatives, reproduction and sexuality, must be clearly demarcated from the male realm of production and political life, and described as essentially different but, human, natural processes. Both writers are discouragingly mute and silent on female eroticism and sexual politics. Both writers illustrate what Kristeva has called the repression of the female unconscious in unitary categories and binary forms of thinking: private/public; production/reproduction. McMillan, for example, describes the intentional and ethical structures of childbirth, but she never dwells on the erotic aspects of these forms of embodiment. To make woman's natural experiences parallel to the male norm of rational activity in

the public world, McMillan (and Elshtain) have de-eroticized them. So, the charge of essentialism is misapplied to *écriture féminine*.

(2) In what ways can *écriture féminine* suture the gaps and repeal the silences in feminist theory? Socialist/feminist writings, although premised on the patriarchal control of woman's sexuality and woman's labor as the causes of woman's oppression, are silent on woman's erotic embodiment. Since control of woman's labor is the fundamental tenet in socialist feminism, even woman's body is positioned as an instrument of labor in patriarchy. In Hartsock's recent essay (Hartsock, 1983: 299), woman's work is described as both mental and bodily or sensuous; in pregnancy the body is an instrument of production. For socialist feminist theory, the structures of embodiment are subsumed under the primacy of the division of labor and mediated by economic, technological and other historical factors. Woman's body is a *material* subject, but never erotic subject of its own discourse. Does sexuality belong to the realm of the *material* or to *ideology*, the realm of signification?

CONCLUSION

So we have moved from woman's sexuality as controlled and constituted by male desire in Beauvoir's *The Second Sex* to woman's autoeroticism as reappropriated by woman's writing and discourse. Furthermore, the characteristics of women's writings are somehow based on the significations of woman's body: the otherness *within* the self in pregnancy, two lips of the labia, both ones, yet other, signify woman's openness to otherness in writing, her split subjectivity; her multiple, polyvalent speech as homologous to the multiple sexuality of woman's body. It is this isomorphism between woman's body-form and woman's writing which I find troublesome, a sort of misplaced concreteness.

Perhaps, it is best to locate *écriture féminine* historically and subversively as Cixous suggests. *Écriture féminine*, speaking and writing the body, is really up against the signifying practices of a culture, its advertisements, TV, films, pornography—all the images of woman's body which reduce it 'homologous to a male speaking body' through fetishizing, fragmenting, and degrading woman's body. Against the dominant perception, the male gaze, or the scopic economy, *écriture féminine* celebrates the radical otherness of woman's erotic embodiment. As such it poses an enormous threat to the philosophical tradition of gender-free humanism and to the treasured ideal of *androgyny*, itself based on fear of otherness.

REFERENCES

Beauvoir, Simone de. [1952], 1961. *The Second Sex*. Translated by H. M. Parshley. Bantam Books, New York.
Cixous, Helene. 1981a. The laugh of the Medusa. Translated by Keith Cohen and Paula

Cohen. In Marks, Elaine and Isabelle de Courtivron, eds, *New French Feminisms*. Schocken, New York.

Cixous, Helene. 1981b. The newly born woman. Translated by Anne Liddle. In Marks, Elaine and Isabelle de Courtivron, eds, *New French Feminisms*, Schocken, New York.

Cullers, Jonathan. 1983. *On Deconstructions*. Cornell University Press, Ithaca, New York.

Doane, Mary Ann. 1981. Woman's stake: Filming the female body. *October* 17: 22–36.

Elshtain, Jean. 1981. *Public Man, Private Woman*. Princeton University Press, Princeton, N.J.

Fuchs, Jo-Ann P. 1980. Female eroticism in *The Second Sex*. *Feminist Studies* 6 (2): 304–313.

Hartsock, Nancy M. 1983. The feminist standpoint. In Harding, Sandra and Merril B. Hintikka, eds, *Discovering Reality*. Reidel, Dordrecht, Holland.

Irigaray, Luce. 1981. This sex which is not one. Translated by Claudia Reeder. In Marks, Elaine and Isabelle de Courtivron eds, *New French Feminisms*. Schocken, New York.

Kristeva, Julia. 1980. *Desire in Language*. Edited by Leon S. Roudiez. Translated by Thomas Gora, Alice Jardine and Leon S. Roudiez. Columbia University Press, New York.

Lingis, Alphonse. 1978. Intentional libido, impulsive libido. Unpublished manuscript.

MacKinnon, Catherine A. 1981. Feminism, marxism, method and the state. In Keohane, Nannerl, Michelle Rosaldo and Barbara Gelpi, eds, *Feminist Theory: A Critique of Ideology*. University of Chicago Press, Chicago, IL.

McMillan, Carol. 1982. *Woman, Reason and Nature*. Princeton University Press. Princeton, NJ.

Merleau-Ponty, Maurice. 1962. *Phenomenology of Perception*. Translated by Colin Smith. Routledge & Kegan Paul, London and New York.

Rawlinson, Mary. 1981. Psychiatric discourse and the feminine voice. *J. med. Philosophy* 7: 153–177.

Simons, Margaret and Jessica Benjamin. 1979. Simone de Beauvoir: an Interview. *Feminist Studies*. 5 (2): 330–345.

Wittig, Monique. 1984. One is not born a woman. In Jaggar, Alison M. and Paula S. Rothenberg, eds, *Feminist Frameworks*. McGraw-Hill, New York.

Young, Iris. 1984. Pregnant embodiment: Subjectivity and alienation. *J. med. Philosophy* 9 (1): 45–62.

LESBIAN IDENTITY
BEAUVOIR AND HISTORY

Ann Ferguson

I. INTRODUCTION

Simone de Beauvoir's monumental work, *The Second Sex*, was a ground-breaking work of feminist theory when it was published in 1949. Her central project is to use a feminist appropriation of an Existentialist metaphysic to analyse motherhood as a biological, economic and social institution which perpetuates male dominance cross-culturally. In this way her work is an important corrective to the orthodox Freudianism and the economistic marxism of the European left of her day in their treatment of 'the woman question'.

Beauvoir is the first presumably non-lesbian in Western philosophy to claim that lesbianism is a mode of resistance to male domination. The lesbian, her argument suggests, is more likely than the heterosexual woman to have escaped the social and biological traps that female existence finds in a patriarchal society: the alienation from one's body characteristic of biological motherhood and the patriarchal control of a husband in marriage. Consequently, lesbians are less likely to fall into the characteristic inauthentic stance of most women: accepting a definition of self as an *object* to be defined by a *subject* (man) and seeing oneself as relative and inessential in relation to (an) other(s) who are defined as essential. As she says,

> 'Even when she has a good figure and a pretty face, a woman who is absorbed
> in ambitious projects of her own or one who simply wanted liberty in general
> will decline to abdicate in favor of another human being: she perceives herself
> in her activities, not merely in her immanent person: the masculine desire that
> reduces her to the confines of her body shocks as much as it shocks the young
> boy . . . (desired by the pederast)'. (Beauvoir, 1974: 457).

One can read Beauvoir's chapter as supporting a Radical Feminist argument that lesbians are a feminist vanguard whose choice of sexual love object is a quintessential act of resistance to patriarchal domination:

> 'Women's homosexuality is one attempt among others to reconcile her autonomy
> with the passivity of her flesh. And if nature is to be invoked, one can say that
> all women are naturally homosexual. The lesbian is, in fact, distinguished by

her refusal of the male and her liking for female flesh; but every adolescent female fears penetration and masculine domination, and she feels a certain repulsion for the male body; on the other hand, the female body is for her, as for the male, an object of desire'. (Beauvoir, 1974: 454).

Beauvior's thesis that women are naturally homosexual finds support in the contemporary writing of Adrienne Rich. Rich agrees with Beauvoir that women are originally homosexual and suggests that all female resistance to patriarchy can be classified along a 'lesbian continuum':

'I mean the term *lesbian continuum* to include a range through each woman's life and throughout history—of woman-identified experience; not simply the fact that a woman has had or consciously desired genital sexual experience with another woman. If we expand it to embrace many more forms of primary intensity between and among women, including the sharing of a rich inner life, the bonding against male tyranny, the giving and receiving of practical and political support; if we can also hear in it such associations as marriage resistance and the "haggard" behavior identified by Mary Daly. . . . ' (Rich, 1980: 648–649).

While I agree with Rich and Beauvoir that lesbianism is in part a political phenomenon related to feminism, I disagree with their universalized assumptions about sexuality and sexual identity. In this paper I shall raise several related criticisms of Beauvoir's analysis of women's sexuality. First, her Existentialist approach confines her to a dualist metaphysics of self vs other, will (or consciousness) vs body and transcendence vs immanence. This dualist stance leads her on the one hand to a type of naturalism which overemphasizes the biological limitations of women's bodies in restricting our individual freedom; and on the other hand underemphasizes the historical and social conditions that help to shape and define our choices, sexuality and sense of self.

Her ambiguity about how determinate biological and social limitations are on women's choices results in an individualist and idealist approach. That is, she suggests the key problem for women is 'bad faith' or inauthenticity (taking oneself to be an Object not a Subject) rather than sexist social structures. She thus is led to several problematic conclusions: first, that lesbianism is merely one individual solution among others to the 'problem' of women's Otherness; and second, that heterosexual relationships can be equalized by individual redefinitions of the value and meanings of masculinity and femininity. In both of these conclusions she overlooks the *social:* i.e. the social implications of lesbianism as well as the social structures underlying patriarchal ideologies which must be challenged before heterosexual relations between men and women can be equal.

My final criticism of Beauvoir concerns her use of the dualist couple transcendence/immanence. This leads her uncomfortably close to the suggestion that heterosexual relationships are on a higher level of development than lesbian ones since they demand a constant struggle to define oneself as transcendent in opposition to the other. Lesbians by contrast can merely admire our self

reflection in the other, thus facing the danger of settling for a merely immanent state of consciousness.

After I develop these criticisms of Beauvoir, my project will be to salvage some important 'partial truths' from her thinking.[1] These I will argue can only be corrected by historicizing our understanding of human sexuality and sexual identity—an approach I shall outline in the last part of this paper.

II. NATURALISM AND DUALISM IN
BEAUVOIR'S THOUGHT

In Beauvoir's view, the centrality of the different bodily experiences of men and women due to their respective functions in biological reproduction are one key to the persistence of male domination. The human female is subject to natural processes, e.g. menstruation and pregnancy, in which she is likely to perceive herself to be the unwilling victim of external forces. These latter include the biological cycles of her own body and the development of an entity within herself which is and is not part of herself, which may or may not have been chosen as a consequence of heterosexual coitus.

It is not merely these natural processes of reproduction which set the female at a disadvantage in comparison to the male, but also the *act* of coition itself which is alienating for her:

> 'Even when she is willing or provocative, it is unquestionably the male who *takes* the female—she is *taken* . . . in this penetration her inwardness is violated, she is like an enclosure broken into . . . his domination is expressed in the very posture of copulation—in almost all animals the male is *on* the female. . . . Thus, though the female plays a fundamentally active role in procreation, she *submits* to the coition, which invades her individuality and introduces an alien element through penetration and internal fertilization'. (Beauvoir, 1974: 24).

These and other passages suggest that Beauvoir has fallen into a naturalist presupposition that mere description of the biological differences between men and women imply negative or positive values of the sexed body in relation to the distinctive human goal of transcendence, viz. the possibility of setting and achieving individual projects in the world. Beauvoir tries to avoid this charge by speaking of human bodies as mere *instruments* whose ultimate value rests

[1] I consider this task analogous to that which Wilhelm Reich (with imperfect success) attempted to do with the Freudian perspective. He rejected Freud's view that the Oedipus complex was a universal phenomenon and attempted to understand the differential gender development which perpetuated male dominance as a feature of a particular form of the patriarchal nuclear family characteristic of Western capitalist development. Reich's work is flawed because he ultimately retains a heterosexist and naturalist approach to understanding what he calls 'the sexual economy.' Nonetheless feminists can correct and appropriate his insights. With respect to Beauvoir, to historicize her views requires a 'denaturalization' of her description of female alienation in biological reproduction and in heterosexual sexuality and, hence, a de-romanticization of lesbian sexuality.

on values defined by human made economic, political and social orders (cf. Beauvoir, 1974: 39). Ultimately, however, I would argue that Beauvoir does succumb to a naturalist bias by assuming that biology has functions which can be ascertained and described independent of human values. Thus, she persists in describing men's sexual selves as more 'privileged' because of their luck in having the aggressive rather than the passive biological role.

Consider these two quotes from chapter XIV ('Sexual Initiation').

> 'For men, erotic pleasure is objectified, desire being directed toward another person . . . erection is the expression of this need; with penis, hands, mouth, with his whole body, a man reaches out toward his partner, but he himself remains at the center of this activity, being on the whole, the *subject* as opposed to the *objects* that he perceives and *instruments* that he manipulates . . . the feminine flesh is for him a prey. . . . ' (Beauvoir, 1974: 414–415).

> ' . . . The privileged position of man comes from the integration of his biologically aggressive role with his social function as leader or master; it is on account of this social function that the physiological differences take on all their significance.' (Beauvoir, 1974: 419).

Although Beauvoir might be defended as having said that the social gives the significance to the biological, her discussion of the 'biologically aggressive' and 'passive' roles and her statements that the female is a 'prey of the species' suggest she thinks biology has an implicit meaning which social arrangements either support or must work to overcome. This is the sense in which Beauvoir's naturalistic attempt to discuss the 'biological facts' as a material condition of culture is essentialist, for it assumes there is ultimately some way to 'read' biological differences independently of their cultural meanings.

A thought experiment will demonstrate this. Consider the 'womb envy' reading of biological sex differences: in heterosexual coitus, women's vaginas devour and use men's semen to create children as a part of women's bodies, thus alienating men from their seed (O'Brien, 1981). In orgasm, they suck the life out of the male organ thus sapping their virility. Women, on the other hand, are able to make love at will, even when not fully aroused. Many of us who have had heterosexual sex can probably think of experiences which are better read phenomenologically along the O'Brien 'womb envy' model than they are along the Beauvoir 'penis envy' model. The point is, then, that it is implausible to think there to be one and only one correct reading of the significance of the biological differences for men and women in heterosexual coitus.

The conclusion I would draw from this line of argument is that a de-mythologizing of the biological facts demonstrates that the notions of masculinity and femininity have no fixed referents. Instead we should think of them as dependent for their content, value and meaning on the gender division of labor in *other* aspects of life in addition to the sexual, e.g. men's and women's work in parenting, productive labor, political and leisure activities.

A consequence of Beauvoir's view that biology contains implicit meanings leads to some ambiguous political conclusions. On the one hand, her chapter

on marriage suggests that heterosexuality itself as it has been developed through the institutions of patriarchal marriage, motherhood and sexual service by women to men is an institution which oppresses women. Given this, the lesbian-feminist of today asks, why not critique the choice to engage in heterosexual relations as itself inauthentic and prescribe a lesbian sexuality as the only authentic sexual interaction?

At this point Beauvoir waffles in her analysis. Instead of persisting in a social analysis which would bring out the social and material conditions which limit women's choices of sexual preference/identity, she falls back into an individualist stance. Adopting the developmental language from the very psychoanalytic mode of thought she criticizes early in the book, she suggests that sexual masochism 'belongs to the juvenile perversions' and is no mode for solving women's sexual dilemma, but a mode of 'escaping from it by wallowing in it' (Beauvoir, 1974: 44).

In this discussion Beauvoir opts for a 'blame the victim' analysis. We are given no reference to the social and economic dependence of women on men that still keeps women in battering relationships with men, nor of the power of the media to use pornography, romance and sexist advertising to shape a 'dual gender' ideology where 'real' men are sadistic subjects and 'real' women are masochistic objects. The mature development of female eroticism, she suggests, is up to the individual *will* of each woman: 'Such full development requires that—in love, affection, sexuality—woman succeeds in overcoming her passivity and in establishing a relation of reciprocity with her partner' (Beauvoir, 1974: 448).

Beauvoir's way of talking in these passages suggest that individual men and women can overcome the unequal implications of dual gender ideology merely by respecting each other. There is no real need to challenge dual gender ideology and with it compulsory heterosexuality itself. Somehow masculine and feminine gender roles themselves get a different *meaning* just by changing one's attitudes about them (not necessarily the roles themselves):

> 'This unlikeness, which too often isolates them, becomes the source of their enchantment when they do unite. The woman see in the man's virile impetuosity the reverse aspect of the passive fever that burns within her; the man's potency reflects the power she exercises on him; this life-engorged organ belongs to her as her smile belongs to the man who floods her with pleasure. All the treasures of virility, of femininity, reflect each other, and thus they form an evershifting and ecstatic unity.' (Beauvoir, 1974: 449).

A more fully social theory of the workings of patriarchal dual gender ideology in heterosexual relationships would have to incorporate a *structural* analysis of the problem of overcoming subject/object ways of thinking about male/female relationships.

In order for particular heterosexual relations to be equal, an act of will or an individual 're-reading' of the established social values of masculinity and femininity is not sufficient. Rather, the heterosexual couple must attempt to

break down the gender division of labor in the *other* social practices of their lives, e.g. parenting, men's vs women's work in wage labor, the home, etc., which reinforce the psychological meanings of 'penis' as subject, virile and aggressive, and 'vagina' as object, frigid and passive. Even the elimination of the gender division of labor for the individual couple is not sufficient to deal with the social meanings still associated with the heterosexual liason, e.g. that the man 'owns' the woman but not vice versa. Only in countercultural feminist networks can the social expectations of one's male and female peers be changed so as to facilitate this shift. Beauvoir, as an individualist, does not see the extent to which an individual's gender and sexual identity is defined by her community of peers.

III. BEAUVOIR ON LESBIAN IDENTITY

When we turn to what Beauvoir has to say about lesbian sexuality, there is much to agree with in her analysis. However, I shall argue, the weakness of her approach is to ignore the social and historical meaning of a lesbian identity in order to focus on the individual choice of sexual preference. My point is *not* that individuals do not make choices about their sexual identities, but rather that lesbian identity as we understand it today has only become an existent social option it the twentieth century in Western industrial societies. This development has political implications which Beauvoir's individualist and ahistorical approach to lesbianism ignores.

One of the commendable aspects of Beauvoir's analysis is that she is one of the first writers to have argued against the psychoanalytic approach to homosexuality. This sees homosexual preference as an infantile fixation, a neurosis, indeed an arrested state of development that is psychically unhealthy. On the contrary, she argues:

> ' . . . as a matter of fact the lesbian is no more an "undeveloped" woman than a "superior" one. . . . Homosexuality can be for woman a mode of flight from her situation or a way of accepting it. The great mistake of psychoanalysis is, through moralistic conformity, to regard it as never other than an inauthentic attitude.' (Beauvoir, 1974: 453).

Although this passage suggests that individual health cannot be determined by a general standard of normality but must be ascertained in the context of an individual life, her very next paragraph contains the quote I have at the beginning of the paper which reverts to the naturalistic mode and intimates that homosexuality is a more 'natural' choice than heterosexuality.

If, indeed, homosexuality is more natural for women, why isn't it a more authentic choice for women? As an Existentialist who holds that there are no objective values Beauvoir cannot consistently come to such a conclusion. More importantly, she can give us no historical understanding of how important the

development of the modern notion of lesbian identity has been for broadening the sexual and value options open to women.

To fully incorporate the social into one's theory of patriarchy requires an understanding of the way that historically changing relations of production and reproduction create new social and material conditions for defining one's sexuality that simply weren't present in different historical periods. While Beauvoir's views about lesbianism are mistaken if taken to be a cross-cultural generalization about possibilities for feminist resistance to patriarchy, it is true that lesbianism in advanced capitalist patriarchal societies is an important resistance to patriarchy. But this is because lesbianism as a successful resistance to patriarchy is best understood not as a universal but as a contemporary historical phenomenon connected to the weakening of the two previous historical forms of heterosexual marriage, *father* and *husband* patriarchy (Ferguson, 1984a), characteristic of precapitalist rural production and competitive capitalism, respectively. A lesbian lifestyle as we understand it today is an individual choice made possible only by the economic and social changes connected to capitalism: the lessening importance of children as an economic support in old age, urbanization, wage labor for women and the consequent weakening of women's economic and social dependence on fathers and husbands. It is the *social bonding* of women into an oppositional subculture economically and socially independent of men in domestic life that makes possible the contemporary concept of a lesbian *identity*, of a community of woman-identified women cutting across class and race/ethnic lines. And it is this *collective* and *social* lesbian identity (and identity not possible until the contemporary period), and not merely the courageous defiance of heterosexist assumptions about sexuality by *individual* women who love women, which constitutes the radical nature of contemporary lesbian-feminism.

A historical approach to the origin of the modern notion of a gay and lesbian identity can be found in Foucault (1978), Weeks (1979, 1981) and Faderman (1981). Although there have clearly been lesbian *practices* (women making love to women) from the beginning of human history, these authors argue that such practices in earlier periods were symbolically quite different than they are today. In the late nineteenth century sexologists, particularly Freud, isolated and typed a particular type of character disorder called 'inversion' or homosexuality, which was one of the types of sexual perversion. The sexologists' discourses on sexual perversion created the possibility of a social identity organized around homosexual object choice which had not existed earlier. Furthermore, the change in material conditions in capitalist societies at the beginning of the twentieth century—increasing wage labor opportunities for women, urbanization, cheap mass produced birth control devices, the liberalization of divorce, the development of mass media sexual advertising—all place more weight on the individual to consider the options which allow separating sexuality from marriage, from childrearing, indeed from heterosexuality altogether.

The development of urban lesbian enclaves takes part in Western societies later than the rise of gay male networks. This is not surprising because of the

social and material conditions limiting women's sexual independence. The historical studies of Carole Smith-Rosenberg (1975) and Lilian Faderman (1981) of nineteenth-century women's friendships explain part of the reason. Victorian sexual morality defined women as assexual and spiritual, and thus did not stigmatize close female friendships even when they were erotic. It was only when the concept of a specifically *sexual* and nonspiritual lesbian identity was created by the sexologists that women could come to see their involvements with each other as something that might come into conflict with their sexual duties to men (as present and future husbands). Lesbian practices thus acquire the political meaning of resistance to men which in turn influences sexologists to emphasize the biological and psychic defects that such women must have (Jackson, 1983). Ironically then, it was in part precisely the development of a stigmatized lesbian identity that allowed women the greater social possibility of defining ourselves more independently of men in more aspects of our lives.

Obviously there have been big changes in the meaning of a lesbian identity in the twentieth century. One of the first conceptualizations defined lesbians and gay men as Uranians, i.e. as a 'third sex' which was conceived as a genetic deviance from biological masculinity and femininity—something like a biologically based psychological hermaphrodism (Faderman, 1980). Betsy Ettorre (1980) has documented the differences between the 'old lesbian' subculture's attitude toward itself: 'we're sick, but not sorry' (symbolized by Radcliffe Hall's *The Well of Loneliness*) and the contemporary lesbian-feminist subculture's 'sorry, but we're not sick!'

The romanticization of lesbianism as a vanguard feminist choice by Radicalesbians (1971) and the concept of the 'woman-identified woman' was an important phase of the turnabout in validation of self made possible to lesbians by feminism. Indeed, the centrality of sexuality itself as a key component of personal identity characteristic of the culture of advanced capitalist societies has caused what Dennis Altman calls the 'homosexualization of America' (Altman, 1982), i.e. the position of homosexual subcultures as vanguards of the 'sex for pleasure' movement that affects everyone regardless of their sexual orientation. Lesbians and gays are thus subconsciously admired, as well as deeply resented, for our violation of sexual taboos, our supposed 'liberation' from the onerous tasks of marriage and childrearing to which heterosexuals must subordinate sexual interest.

What does this view of the historical development of the concept of lesbian identity suggest about Beauvoir's theory of lesbianism? First, it validates her criticism of the Freudian and sexologist schools which define homosexuality as a perversion and as a state of arrested psychological development. But Beauvoir's own theory does not make the historical distinction between lesbian practices and a lesbian identity that I and others have argued for here and elsewhere (Ferguson, 1981; Foucault, 1978; Weeks, 1979, 1981). Thus, her tendencies toward naturalism lead her to suggest a universal meaning to lesbianism as the more 'natural' choice for women. On the contrary, I would argue that lesbianism as a political choice for feminists can only be validated in a concrete historical context, specifically by reference to relative strengths and

weaknesses of existing feminist networks within the lesbian vs heterosexual subcommunities available to particular individuals. From this it would follow that there is no universal answer to the question of whether feminists *should* choose lesbianism or heterosexuality.

We can find a way to reconstruct Beauvoir's claim that homosexuality is more natural for women. The neo-Freudian perspective of Nancy Chodorow (1978) maintains that the crosscultural constancy of mother-centered infant care makes the mother the primary love object for both boys and girls. Women thus could be expected to have deeper homoerotic attractions for their own sex than do men. Such initial feelings provide a psychological base for the development of a lesbian orientation in most women.

One might argue that Chodorow's analysis suggests an argument for lesbian-feminism as a contemporary political choice. After all, lesbian relationships may provide *safer* possibilities of egalitarian sexual relationships than heterosexual ones in a male dominant society. This argument is unfounded for the following reasons. First, not all women's economic and social situations (family, community, class, race/ethnic) create a lesbian choice as a live option. Furthermore, every woman has the right to take risks with her sexual choices. From the fact that heterosexuality is more *risky* as a feminist sexual practice than is lesbianism, it does not follow that it is politically incorrect (Ferguson, 1984b). Indeed, I think of heterosexual feminists as doing important political work in struggling to equalize their relationships with men. What is dangerous is romanticizing the task, or falling under the spell of a complementary ideology of sexuality that suggest that the self/other *differences* in a good heterosexual relationship are somehow at a higher stage of psychological development than the more 'narcissistic' relationships of lesbians, a suggestion that creeps into some of Beauvoir's passages.

IV. CONCLUSION

I have argued in this paper that Beauvoir's Existentialist assumptions plus her naturalist treatment of the biological difference between men and women tend to leave sexuality at the level of individual choice. Thus the specific social ways in which compulsory heterosexuality operates in different ways at different historical periods cannot be clearly understood. Her approach thus limits us in judging the importance of the development of the modern lesbian identity and of the rise of a lesbian-feminist movement as social factors which have made all women's sexual choices more free.

In spite of these failings, we should not forget the strengths of her analysis. Given the existence of our current patriarchal and heterosexist ideology which defines the masculine role as superior and the feminine role as the complementary inferior, lesbians can indeed be seen as Beauvoir suggests, as rebels from an oppressive and unfree set of sexual practices.

It is fitting to conclude with one of those insightful passages from Beauvoir

in which she suggests how lesbianism as an individual political practice in contemporary society can point to the breakdown of gender categories:

'The woman who turns lesbian because she haughtily declines male domination is often pleased to find the same proud amazon in another . . . the common feeling that united them against the privileged caste enabled each to admire in a friend the impressive being whom she idolized in herself; in their mutual embraces each was at once man and woman and each was enchanted with the other's androgynous qualities.' (Beauvoir, 1974: 467).

REFERENCES

Altman, Dennis. 1982. *The Homosexualization of America*. Beacon Press, Boston.

Beauvoir, Simone. 1974. *The Second Sex*. Random House, Vintage Books, New York.

Chodorow, Nancy. 1978. *The Reproduction of Mothering*. University of California Press, Berkeley.

Etorre, E. M. 1980. *Lesbians, Women and Society*. Routledge and Kegan Paul, London.

Faderman, Lillian. 1980. *Lesbian-Feminism in Turn of the Century Germany*. Translated by Birgitte Eriksson. Naiad Press, Weatherby, MA.

Faderman, Lillian. 1981. *Surpassing the Love of Men*. Junction, London.

Ferguson, Ann. 1981. Patriarchy, sexual identity and the sexual revolution. *Signs* 7 (1) (Autumn): 158–172.

Ferguson, Ann. 1984a. On conceiving motherhood and sexuality: a feminist materialist perspective. In Trebilcot, Joyce, ed., *Mothering: Essays in Feminist Theory*. Rowman & Allenheld, Totowa, NJ.

Ferguson, Ann. 1984b. Sex war: The debate between Radical and Libertarian Feminists. *Signs* 10 (1): 106–112.

Foucault, Michel. 1978. *A History of Sexuality*, Vol. 1. Pantheon, New York.

Hartsock, Nancy. 1983. *Sex, Money and Power*. Longmans, New York.

Jackson, Margaret. 1983. Sexual liberation or social control? *Women's Studies Int. Forum* 6 (1): 1–17.

O'Brien, Mary. 1981. *The Politics of Reproduction*. Routledge and Kegan Paul, Boston and London.

Radicalesbians. 1971. The woman-identified woman. In Koedt, Ann *et al.*, eds, *Radical Feminism*. Quadrangle, Chicago.

Rich, Adrienne. 1980. Compulsory heterosexuality and lesbian existence. *Signs* 5 (4).

Reich, Wilhelm. 1972. *Sex-Pol*. Random House, New York.

Reich, Wilhelm. 1974. *The Sexual Revolution*. Simon & Schuster, New York.

Smith-Rosenberg, Caroll. 1975. The female world of love and ritual: Relations between women in 19th century America. *Signs* 1 (1) (Autumn): 1–29.

Weeks, Jeffrey. 1979. *Coming Out: A History of Homosexuality from the 19th Century to the Present*. Charles River Books, Boston.

Weeks, Jeffrey. 1981. *Sex, Politics and Society*. Longman, New York.

LESBIAN ATTITUDES AND
THE SECOND SEX

Claudia Card

In the chapter on the lesbian in *The Second Sex* Simone de Beauvoir asserted that 'homosexuality' is neither a deliberate perversion nor a physiologically, psychologically, or economically determined fate but, rather, 'an attitude *chosen in a certain situation*—that is, at once motivated and freely adopted' (Beauvoir, 1969: 424).[1] This choice, she maintained, must be evaluated according to its 'authenticity'; it can be 'a mode of flight' from one's situation or 'a way of assuming it' (p. 406).[2]

What do these claims mean? What are their implications? How much truth is there in them? Is flight from reality, failure to take responsibility for oneself, most likely to be a danger for the lesbian? How else might we evaluate lesbian attitudes?

There is a lot of truth in Beauvoir's claims about what 'homosexuality' is. Her proposal makes good sense of the contemporary radicalesbian position that one can take responsibility for one's sexual orientation. She exaggerates about the choosing but not, I think, importantly. More seriously, she failed to appreciate the implications of her claims about the lesbian for what else she had to say about women in that book. Although it is unclear just what attitude 'homosexuality' is (it may be several), the idea that it is *attitudinal* is clear enough that we can see a range of interesting implications regarding *heterosexuality* which Beauvoir missed.

Flight from reality is not the most likely danger for the lesbian, although there are realities from which she would do well to flee. If anything, lesbians are more likely than heterosexual women to have learned to take responsibility for themselves. A more probable danger for the lesbian is her temptation to exploit other women's conditioning to service and nurturance.

I may not be able to defend all these claims adequately. But I will try to say something interesting about as many of them as I can, beginning with Beauvoir's fantastic failure to catch the implications of her own position.

Beauvoir's views about lesbians were revolutionary in 1949, four years prior to the 'Kinsey Report' on women. Since the American Psychiatric Association

---

[1] Further page references are to this work, unless otherwise indicated.
[2] Parshley translated *'l'assumer'* as 'accepting it,' which is not the same.

removed homosexuality from its list of mental disorders in 1973, her position seems less revolutionary to us. However, her claim that the lesbian 'makes herself lesbian' remains a radical view.[3] Since the beginnings of 'gay' activism in the 19th century, male sex researchers have quarreled over whether homosexuality has an inherited basis or is entirely acquired (and recently have challenged that dichotomy), but they have generally agreed that it is not something for which 'homosexuals' are responsible. The 'gay is good' slogan of the late 1960s paved the way for embracing responsibility here. It has not been 'gays' who have gone that way, however. It has been radicalesbian feminists.

Beauvoir is no radicalesbian. She is an Existentialist dissatisfied with Marxian determinism. To acknowledge and affirm the implications of her views about the lesbian for women in general, she would had to have written a far more radical book than *The Second Sex*. That book was not intended to rock the heterosexual boat but, on the contrary, to calm it. Her concern was to show that the 'battle of the sexes' was not fated to go on forever and to consider what is required to substitute cooperation for battle between women and men. It was only incidentally, in applying the Existentialist concern with responsibility to the case of the lesbian, that she happened to formulate the position quoted above. She saw the implications and drew them out—for the lesbian.

A great paradox of *The Second Sex* is its failure to draw the appropriately analogous conclusions about heterosexuality. Beauvoir seemed not to see that if 'homosexuality' is a choice, heterosexuality is likewise a choice. To put it in her more specific language, it is an attitude which is not physiologically, psychologically, or economically determined and which can likewise be evaluated according to its authenticity. Except in the chapter on the lesbian, *The Second Sex* does not treat heterosexuality as a choice at all. Even in that chapter, it is treated only as a choice rejected by the lesbian, not as a choice embraced by the heterosexual woman. And what of heterosexual women? In the Introduction to *The Second Sex* Beauvoir wrote:

> 'The division of the sexes is a biological fact, not an event in human history. Male and female stand opposed within a primordial [*originel*] *Mitsein*. . . . The couple is a fundamental unity with its two halves riveted together . . . [Woman] is the Other in a totality of which the two components are necessary to one another' (pp. xix–xx).

'The couple' in this context is clearly a heterosexual couple. Beauvoir argues in Book One that women's *subordination* to men is not necessitated by physiological, psychological, or economic conditions. However, she appears to have concluded at the outset that the *opposition* of the sexes is a straightforward consequence of the biological *division* of the sexes, given the nature of human consciousness, on which she refers us to Hegel:

---

[3] Parshley translates '*la femme qui se fait lesbienne*' as 'the woman who turns lesbian' (Beauvoir, 1969: 419).

'Following Hegel, we find in consciousness itself a fundamental hostility toward every other consciousness; the subject can be posed only in being opposed— he [sic] sets himself up as the essential, as opposed to the other, the inessential, the object' (p. xvii).

Thus we are presented with the primordial soil in which the 'battle of the sexes' can grow.

Only in the chapter on the lesbian did it strike her that the requirement of two sexes for human reproduction does not entail an *attitude of heterosexuality* on the part of the animal. More specifically, it does not entail that we structure our significant or on-going relationships to others around heterosexual attitudes, that we be 'heterosexually oriented.' Even in that chapter, however, she takes the negative heterosexual attitudes (or presumably attitudes of heterosexual indifference) of the lesbian—to whom she refers, significantly, as 'the invert'— to need special explanation: 'What must be explained in the female invert [*l'invertie*] is not the positive aspect of her choice, it is the negative' (pp. 407– 408). The heterosexual woman's negative or indifferent homosexual attitudes are not acknowledged, much less thought in need of explanation: '[The lesbian] is distinguished not by her taste for women but by the exclusive character of this taste' (p. 408). Granted that 'women have always loved women' (Stambolian and Marks, 1979: 353), heterosexual women frequently manage not to let their lesbian attitudes determine their sexual orientation in a major way, and Beauvoir does not think to ask why not. Throughout the rest of *The Second Sex* her focus is on women whose heterosexual orientation is utterly taken for granted. Thus the chapters on sexual initiation and on the mother do not discuss lesbian sexual initiation or lesbian motherhood, and the chapter on married women does not discuss lesbians who marry men.

The Second Sex's positions on lesbians and heterosexual women contradict each other doubly. First, Beauvoir's view is, I take it, that any woman *can* choose a lesbian orientation, although only some are moved to do so. On her own understanding of what being a lesbian entails, this implies that any woman *can* reject a heterosexual orientation, although only some are moved to do so. That sounds incompatible with the claim that the heterosexual couple is a 'fundamental unity with its two halves riveted together.' Second, if a lesbian orientation is sometimes chosen *authentically*, how could it be that Woman is part of a primordial heterosexual *Mitsein* and that Man is necessary to her? Choosing a lesbian orientation sounds like denying, rather than assuming, her situation as a member of such a couple. Perhaps a way out is to deny that lesbians are women. According to Marilyn Frye (1983), that is just what phal-locratic culture has done.[4] In Beauvoir's terms, however, one would have to say that the lesbian *chooses* not to be a woman. That sounds like saying her attitude is not authentic, that it is a 'flight from her situation' rather than 'a way of assuming it' (p. 406). But Beauvoir asserted in the chapter on the lesbian

---

[4] See her last essay, 'To See and Be Seen: The Politics of Reality,' for analyses of the contra-dictions in the sexist understanding of 'lesbian'.

that it was a great mistake of the psychoanalysts to regard the lesbian attitude as always inauthentic (p. 406).

Had she noticed these contradictions, Beauvoir might have questioned Sartre's pessimism about human relationships in a very different way from the way she did in *The Second Sex*.[5] Instead of identifying *human* relationships with *heterosexual* relationships and assuming that the significant Other for any consciousness is probably an Other of the 'opposite' sex, she might have challenged Hegel's assumption of an original hostility in human consciousness toward others and raised the question how the sexes never *came to be* 'opposites.' Following up her own observations about the consequences of the 'special circumstances' of lesbian liaisons, she might have considered whether the tendency of any consciousness to regard another *a priori* as an object of hostility is not rather a *consequence* of oppressive institutions than among the conditions giving rise to them. The 'special circumstances' of lesbian relationships on which she comments consist in the absence of social institutions and conventions sanctioning and regulating the relationship:

'[Lesbian liaisons] are not sanctioned by an institution or by the mores, nor are they regulated by conventions; hence they are marked by especial sincerity. Man and woman—even husband and wife—are in some degree playing a part before one another, and in particular woman, upon whom the male always imposes some requirement' (pp. 419–420).

The same institutions and conventions responsible for the absence of such sincerity in heterosexual relationships may be responsible for the 'oppositeness' of the sexes as well.

Acknowledging that institutions and mores present obstacles to the development of sincerity in heterosexual relationships should raise the question whether a woman's heterosexual orientation can be authentic in such a context. Beauvoir does more than acknowledge such obstacles. Her long chapter, 'The Woman in Love' (with a man, of course), documents copiously the contradictions involved in a woman's attempt to be a subject and at the same time attract and keep a male lover under the rules of femininity. Yet she does not raise the question whether the choice to persist in heterosexuality under such conditions is an authentic choice. It seemed not to occur to her in that context that there was any choice involved.

It might briefly appear natural for a feminist theorist to take the position that although the lesbian freely chooses to be a lesbian, the heterosexual woman does not freely choose to be heterosexual, because heterosexuality is compulsory—as Adrienne Rich (1980) and others have amply documented—and lesbianism is surely not. Both choices, however, confront the same woman. Is she free, or is she not? The lesbian may appear to be free just because her choice is a defiance of convention; the heterosexual woman not free because

---

[5] Sartre (1956) concluded, in the section entitled 'Concrete Relations with Others,' that human beings in relationships are doomed to alternate between sadism and masochism.

hers appears determined by it. The compulsoriness of heterosexuality does not, however, imply that women are forced to choose it. Heterosexuality is compulsory in the sense that severe penalties are attached to its rejection. One can choose to live with many of those penalties. Lesbians are not free from them. The question is whether they are so severe as to render only the heterosexual option tolerable, in which case the lesbian's 'freedom' is simply the 'freedom' to be irrational, or perhaps, heroic.

The truth may be that lesbians are *choosing to be free* of convention, to be relatively autonomous, self-determining (Beauvoir: she makes herself lesbian), whereas heterosexual women are *choosing to be determined* by convention, relatively less autonomous. Whether the latter choice is inauthentic, however, may not be determinable independently of a consideration of the nature of the conventions by which she is choosing to be determined.

The idea of choosing to be or not to be determined by conventions or institutional requirements is unproblematic. That is, I think I understand what it means. Choosing a lesbian or heterosexual orientation does not seem that simple. I am less sure that I understand what that means. If Beauvoir is right in her assertion that 'homosexuality' is 'an attitude chosen in a certain situation,' I doubt that the attitude is simply an attitude toward conventions or institutions. But then, what attitude is it? And what does it mean to say it is chosen?

Part of the uneasiness one may feel about Beauvoir's position on lesbian choice may be due to her neglect to distinguish between 'choice' as an *option* (of which one may or may not be aware) and 'choice' as the *act* of choosing from among options (which presupposes one's awareness of them). Gay Rights activists and heterosexual feminists are no doubt often right in their insistence that they did not choose their sexual orientations but, rather, discovered that they already had them. That admission, of course, does not touch the claim that other options exist, that there are still (possible) choices. Beauvoir has in mind the *act* of choosing, not simply the existence of an option. This may account for her failure to see relevant analogies between lesbian and heterosexual women. Since it easy for women not to appreciate the existence of a lesbian option in a severely sexist society but impossible to be ignorant of heterosexuality, it is more likely the lesbian than the heterosexual woman who has *actually exercised* choice in the matter of her sexual orientation. It is, however, also possible for lesbians not to have *chosen* the lesbian *orientations* that they have developed as a result of their more specific choices. Being committed to a lesbian orientation goes beyond simply having one.

A different sort of uneasiness about Beauvoir's position may be due to unclarity about whether sexual orientation is the kind of thing that can be an object of choice. One may be able to take various attitudes *toward* one's sexual orientation—for example, be proud of it or ashamed of it—but can one choose the orientation itself? A popular view of sexual orientation is that it is simply a matter of taste and that there is no accounting of tastes, and, *a fortiori*, no accounting for them in terms of one's choices. Another version of the sexual mystique likens sexual orientation to right- and left-handedness, calling attention to the 10 per cent incidence of both left-handedness and homosexuality

and the difficulty of changing either kind of habit. Who knows what this suggestion means? There is no consensus regarding the origins of right-and left-handedness either. Beauvoir's approach is more interesting. She suggests an answer which makes good sense of various sides of the controversy: the object of choice, as she presents it, is an *attitude*. If being lesbian (and, similarly, being heterosexual) is a matter of one's attitude, it is easy to see why there is no consensus on the question of choice. It is also possible to argue that those who maintain that there is a choice are closer to the truth than those who hold that there is not.

To describe adequately the processes by which a woman's sexual orientation becomes either lesbian or heterosexual, a more generous vocabulary is needed than is provided by the dualism of 'freely chosen' on the one hand and 'fated' or 'determined' on the other. As Aristotle saw (E.N. III), not everything that is voluntary is chosen, and not everything that is not voluntary is *in*voluntary. The area of conduct for which one can be responsible includes the voluntary in general as well as the chosen in particular and can also include conduct that was not voluntary but could have been had one reflected or paid attention. Attitudes seem to fall within this area.

What is an attitude? An attitude is a pose, a position, a stance, a disposition. Originally a technical term from the Arts of Design (according to the O. E. D.), it has come to be a psychological term referring to a complex of behavior and valuation. Attitudes, like emotions, have objects: they are held *toward* things (or people, situations, etc.). They also tend to have valences, i.e. to be positive or negative, favorable or unfavorable, pro or con. And they tend to have foundations, bases, which can be either reasoned or unreasoned judgments or valuations together with perceptions and beliefs based upon those judgments and valuations. Because of the epistomological content of the bases of attitudes, attitudes are often modifiable through insight and understanding. Because of the behavioral aspect of attitudes, attitudes like habits, can outlive the judgments upon which they were originally based. Both of these possibilities are claimed for sexual orientation in the experiences people report. Attitudes sometimes dissolve with the ignorance or misinformation upon which they were based, and at other times are remarkably stubborn.

Can an attitude be chosen? We speak of cultivating attitudes, getting over them, refusing to get over them, encouraging and discouraging them, falling or lapsing into them, snapping out of them, persisting in them, adopting or striking them, and so on. Most of this is the language of agency. Clearly, there are things we can do that contribute to the production, modification and elimination of our own attitudes, and thereby to the production, modification, and elimination of our own tastes as well. If attitudes are not themselves directly the objects of choice, choices are among their causes, including such choices as the choice to acquire certain attitudes.

If attitudes are not objects of choice, there is nevertheless much about them that is voluntary. Behavior manifesting attitudes is typically voluntary, even if exhibiting an attitude was not (say, because one was unaware of having the attitude). As Elizabeth Telfer (1971) has observed about friendship, however,

one has not really chosen it unless one has *affirmed the pattern* exhibited by the particular acts that one has chosen. Frequently we discover our attitudes rather than choose them. Yet we tend to hold ourselves responsible for them anyhow. Probably we judge people as often by their attitudes as by their specific acts. We expect people to take responsibility for their attitudes. If sexual orientation is an attitude, then the idea of taking responsibility for one's sexuality (Trebilcot, 1983) belongs to that general expectation. Taking such responsibility requires developing habits of noticing things about oneself, identifying one's attitudes and determining whether they are well-founded or not. One can choose to do or not to do these things. Once those choices have been made, one's resulting beliefs may no longer be subject to one's control. To the extent that one's attitudes are based upon beliefs not within one's control, the attitude themselves seem involuntary.

Even if attitudes are not chosen, they can still be evaluated as authentic or inauthentic. They can be honest or dishonest, responsible or not responsible. What is required for such evaluations is that *like* choices, attitudes be capable of being based upon beliefs and judgments, not that they be themselves direct objects of choice. What matters is that we can be responsible for them.

Is 'homosexuality' an attitude? If so, what attitude is it? Is there some attitude the lesbian has that distinguishes her from others? According to Beauvoir, what distinguishes the lesbian is a certain *heterosexual* attitude, a negative attitude toward men. It was on this that Beauvoir fixated when she came to assess the authenticity of some lesbian choices. Thus she reviewed in relatively favorable terms lesbians like Gertrude Stein ('rather rare,' she noted) who are so assured of their virile powers that they want only men as friends and companions. (This is hardly fair to Gertrude Stein, whose closest friend and companion was Alice Toklas.) And she looked askance, even with horror, upon those who form their own clubs, rejecting men socially as well as sexually (pp. 422–424). The only way I can make sense of her judgments in these cases is by supposing that she assumed that the dyke separatist, unlike Gertrude Stein, bases her attitude toward women upon her negative attitude toward men, rather than the other way around. So understood, the separatist is reduced to a case of Nietzschean *ressentiment:* sour grapes. Beauvoir offered no reason for thinking this is the separatists' motivation; she did not consider separatists' attitudes toward women at all. What about the lesbian's *lesbian* attitudes? What about her attitudes toward women?

In pursuing the claim that it is not the lesbian's 'taste for women' that distinguishes her from other women, Beauvoir mentioned a kind of case which I would be inclined to evaluate as a good example of inauthenticity in lesbian behavior. 'Disappointed in man,' she tells us, a woman 'may seek in woman a lover to replace the male who has betrayed her. Colette indicated in her *Vagabonde* this consoling role that forbidden pleasures may frequently play in woman's existence: some women spend . . . their whole lives in being thus consoled' (p. 418). Others use women lovers for regeneration until they are able to deal with men again. The kind of 'inauthenticity' that strikes me about such cases as these is not what Beauvoir thinks of as 'inauthenticity,' not the

kind involved in *self*-deception and failing to take responsibility *for oneself*. It is possible that such failures are also involved.[6] It seems more likely that the woman in these cases, who would probably say she is 'bisexual,' has her situation very well in hand, from the point of view of taking charge of her own life. The kind of 'inauthenticity' that strikes me about these cases is the kind involved in what Aristotle distinguished as friendships of utility and friendships of plea-sure, by contrast with true friendship (E.N. VIII). In the latter, the 'object' of love is the friend; in the former, the utility or pleasure. Anticipating Witt-genstein's idea (Wittgenstein, 1958: Part I, paras 65–67) of a 'family resem-blance' among things rightly enough called by the same term but which do not possess any one characteristic in common, Aristotle said of friendships of utility and friendships of pleasure that they were both called 'friendship' only because of their resemblance (different in each case) to true friendship, which is also normally both useful and pleasant. Something similar is true of the lesbian liaisons formed by women who are still in important ways basically heterosex-ually oriented: their attitudes are 'lesbian' insofar as they resemble genuine lesbian attitudes, which also normally include receptivity to regeneration and nurturance from women.

In the consolation/regeneration case it is not just that the *woman* is being inauthentic: her *lesbianism* is inauthentic. What was it that Beauvoir intended in saying that 'the choice of the lesbian' must be evaluated according to its authenticity? Which choice? The choice of a particular relationship? The choice of *women* as lovers? At times she seems to mean no more than that lesbians are subject to *exactly* the same sorts of inauthenticity as other folks:

> 'The association of two women, like that of a man and a woman, assumes many different forms; it may be based upon sentiment, material interest, or habit; it may be conjugal or romantic; it has room for sadism, masochism, generosity, fidelity, devotion, capriciousness, egotism, betrayal: among lesbians there are prostitutes and also great lovers' (p. 419).

And

> 'Like all human behavior, homosexuality leads to make-believe, disequilibrium, frustration, lies, or, on the contrary it becomes the source of rewarding expe-riences, in accordance with its manner of expression in actual living—whether in bad faith, laziness, and falsity, or in lucidity, generosity, and freedom' (p. 424).

These comments assess lesbian relationships simply as human relationships, not as specifically lesbian. What is being commented upon is not a lesbian attitude as such, and not the choice to be lesbian. All that need have been chosen for these evaluations to be appropriate is a particular lover or relation-

---

[6] See, e.g. Ulmshneider, 'Bisexuality' (Myron and Bunch, 1975: 85–88) for discussion of this combination of exploitation and failure to take responsibility.

ship, not a sexual orientation. As close as Beauvoir comes to assessing what really looks like a choice to be lesbian is in her comments on the dyke separatists, and there she simply assumes inauthenticity rather than seeing the possibility of Amazon creativity and playfulness.

There are, actually, some fairly distinctive and characteristic lesbian attitudes, which it would be interesting to examine in terms of the temptations they present and the possibilities they offer. In studying the history of lesbian culture in predominantly White Western civilization, I have been struck by three kinds of attitudes. One is represented by the Amazon, who tends to be physically competent and economically independent. Another is the Sapphist, poetic and sensual, often significantly older or younger than her lover.[7] Third are the patterns of romantic friendship, often highly passionate and erotic, like Sapphic attitudes, but also remarkably enduring and not necessarily sensual.[8] The study of woman-loving women in other cultures will no doubt reveal further patterns. The relationships among such attitudes as these suggest a Wittgensteinian 'family resemblance' analysis of the idea of a lesbian attitude. Such an analysis seems also congenial to Adrienne Rich's suggestion of the 'lesbian continuum,' which recognizes lesbian attitudes among women whose general sexual orientation is not particularly lesbian (Rich, 1980).

One of the implications of the view that being lesbian is a matter of attitude is that lesbians do not form a natural kind. And for the same reasons, neither do 'heterosexuals.' That insight about lesbians may be Beauvoir's most important contribution to the subject.

REFERENCES

Aristotle. 1925. *The Nicomachean Ethics*. Translated W. D. Ross. Oxford University Press, London.

Beauvoir, Simon de. 1969. *The Second Sex*. Translated by H. M. Parshley. Modern Library, New York.

Faderman, Lillian. 1981. *Surpassing the Love of Men; Romantic Friendship and Love between Women from the Renaissance to the Present*. Morrow, New York.

Frye, Marilyn. 1983. *The Politics of Reality; Essays in Feminist Theory*. The Crossing Press, Trumansberg, N.Y.

Myron, Nancy and Charlotte Bunch, eds. 1975. *Lesbianism and the Women's Movement*. Diana Press, Baltimore, MD.

Rich, Adrienne. 1980. Compulsory heterosexuality and lesbian existence. *Signs: Journal of Women in Culture and Society* 5 (4): 631–660.

Sartre, Jean-Paul. 1956. *Being and Nothingness*. Translated by Hazel Barnes. Philosophical Library, New York.

[7] See Elaine Marks, 'Lesbian intertextuality' (Stambolian and Marks, 1979: 353–577), for discussion of Amazonian and Sapphic models in French lesbian literature.

[8] See Faderman (1981) on 18th and 19th Century romantic friendship in and out of literature, mostly English and American.

Stambolian, George and Elaine Marks, eds. 1979. *Homosexualities and French Litera-*
        ture; Cultural Contexts/Critical Texts. Cornell University Press, Ithaca, N.Y.
Telfer, Elizabeth. 1971. Friendship. *Aristotelian Society, Proceedings 71:* 223–241.
Trebilcot, Joyce. 1983. *Taking Responsibility for Sexuality.* Acacia Books, Berkeley, CA.
Wittgenstein, Ludwig. 1958. *Philosophical Investigations.* Translated by G. E. M. An-
        scombe. Blackwell, Oxford, England.

HISTORY AND RESPONSIBILITY[1]

Marilyn Frye

It may be a good thing for Beauvoir to have claimed that it is not necessarily neurotic to be a lesbian, in a world where almost everyone thought it was. It may have been a help to me (but then again it may have been a hindrance) as a long overdue not-yet-lesbian in my late twenties to read in *The Second Sex* the chapter on 'The Lesbian.' Be that as it may, to my way of thinking, the title of that chapter gives away much of what is not so good about Beauvoir's contribution here.

What would you expect if, in an ambitious book about American Scholars and scholarship written entirely in the generic masculine, you came upon a chapter entitled 'The Feminist'? She would be defined, would she not, in terms of her reaction to the forms and conditions of normal scholarship, and she would be presumed to treat her special subjects and objects much as academics generally treat their normal subjects and objects, only with some interesting twists due to the narcissistic possibilities of being a female studying females.

The grammatical construction combining the definite article and a general term, 'The X,' abstracts from individual variety and speaks of a species as though it were an entity. The distance at which Beauvoir holds The Lesbian is striking. So also is the air of fiction about her characterization. Beauvoir's Lesbian feels to me like a logical construct composed by turning various categories inside out and upside down to see what might fall out. My sense of it is that the discussion of The Lesbian is not in fact meant to shed any light on lesbians, lesbian sensibility or lesbian experience, but to further illuminate, by the device of contrast, the experience and situation of *women*, conceived as heterosexual.

If, as Card suggests, Beauvoir's concern was to show that the battle of the sexes is not fated to go on forever, then it may be wrong to see the chapter on The Lesbian as a tactical maneuver at the level of diplomacy. Trying to persuade the man to engage in a ceasefire, one points out that things in marriage and motherhood are *so bad* that it is not unreasonable for the women to begin thinking they might better become lesbians and be done with it. 'At least a lesbian has half a chance at autonomy and fulfillment,' a woman might say to

---

[1] This is a transcription of informal remarks made by way of commentary on the papers of Claudia Card and Ann Ferguson, at a session of the conference 'Beyond The Second Sex: New Directions.'

her man in the heat of a dispute. It is a threat. A threat of abandonment. Probably an idle threat. But with respect to real live lesbians, it is either irrelevant or exploitative.

So I am surprised, not unpleasantly, to find that a creative reading of Beauvoir on The Lesbian turns up some interesting questions. I am not surprised that in the end those questions seem to have relatively little to do specifically or importantly with lesbians to lesbianism. The interesting questions, as I hear these two papers, have to do with determinism and responsibility. My own feeling is that the fascination of connecting these moral and metaphysical issues with lesbians in particular is a fairly accidental result of the historical and contingent fact that in this era we tend to find sex particularly sexy. The very important and interesting issues about determinism and responsibility could just as well be discussed, for instance, in terms not of what we do with our bodies but what we do with our money.

Let me sketch the problem of responsibility and history as it has come up in my own work.

As some brand of radical feminist, I am committed to the view that the oppression of women is something women do not choose. Those of our activities and attitudes which play into women's oppression are themselves strategies we are forced into by the circumstances of oppression we live with. A woman may continue to live with the man who batters her, but the choice to remain is not a free one; it is a choice among evils in a severely constrained situation, and she has not chosen that situation. The oppression of women is something consisting of and accomplished by a network of institutions and material and ideological forces which press women into the service of men. Women are not simply free to walk away from this servitude at will. But also, it is clear that there has always been resistance to female servitude, taking different shapes in different places and times. The question of responsibility, or rather, *one* important question, is this: Can we hold ourselves, and is it proper to hold each other, *responsible* for resistance? Or is it necessarily both stupid cruelty and a case of 'blaming the victim' to add yet one more pressure in our lives, in each others' lives, by expecting, demanding, requiring, encouraging, inviting acts and patterns of resistance and reconstruction which are not spontaneously forthcoming?

We sometimes tell ourselves that we must respect each woman's own knowledge of herself and her situation and permit, accept and applaud what*ever* kind and degree of resistance she puts up within the historical and material particulars of her own situation, and that we must not impose upon her the requirement that she cultivate forms of resistance which *others* find possible and effective in *their* lives. There is obviously much truth in this, and as we have worked over the last few years to meet each other through and across the great diversities of our lives, this approach has come increasingly to recommend itself. Many of us have been learning important lessons in the recognition of and respect for kinds of living and resistance other than our own, and respect for other women's understandings of their own historical and material circum-

stances. But there is a tension between this stance of respectful laissez faire and a certain understanding of the liberation of women from service to men as a *political* project.

Many feminists have thought of the liberation of women from this servitude as something to be achieved by an enormous, global, political movement—as a matter of massive and historical strategies to *change* precisely the historical, material and ideological conditions which have molded us and which we have resisted, both, in so many subtle and overt ways. To change these conditions, it has seemed that we cannot simply trust to random and disorganized stubborness, sabotage, explosions of rage and so on, but must organize politically to pull *together*. When one is thinking along these lines, it seems right for all of us to think together, constructively and critically, to devise collective strategies of resistance and revolution and to try to convince and persuade each other about these things. And it seems right to require or demand of each other changes of values and characters and attitudes—central, vital, life-shaping changes. In particular, it has seemed that we must require of each other the most fundamental change, namely, a shift of our primary loyalty from its attachment to the masters and their institutions to an attachment to our sisters and our liberation.[2] Loyalty and identity are so closely connected as to be almost just two aspects of one phenomenon, so if we are right in expecting or requiring such things of each other, we must be assuming that humans, that women, are capable of choice and of change at the level of our very identities—of what and who we are—in spite of the coerciveness of oppression.

It sometimes seems to me that the call to historicity and the rule against cultural parochialism occur as a coded version of these claims: we cannot demand or expect profound redefinition of ourselves or other women, or hold ourselves or others responsible for such change, because we must respect the fact that our and others' beings are conditioned by the historical and material circumstances of time and place; if a woman says in her own vernacular, 'This is who and how I am . . . ,' she must, simply, have the last word; another woman must not think how that woman could be otherwise (or really is or was otherwise) or could be another, nor presume to require or demand such change (or presume to be disappointed), for that would be missionizing, colonizing, patronizing and otherwise generally direspecful.[3] I do think I understand the truth there is in such a view; but if it is the whole truth, there is no politics and no hope. The hope and possibility of profound change for women on this planet lies precisely in the fact that our being is *only* historically determined . . . and not given in nature. For then it is a contingent fact that I am

---

[2] Reference to such a shift may be most salient in the cases of women who by race, caste or class are connected with the men of ruling or dominating groups in their particular country or culture.

[3] In the case of a woman who has been shaped by race or class privilege, the requirement or demand that she not be racist or classist is likely to strike her more as unjust or unreasonable. Either she cannot see that there is anything wrong with those ways someone expects her to mend, or she feels she is being required simply to be someone other than whó she is (which says a good deal about a great many things, but that belongs in other papers).

who and how I am, and thus it *could* be otherwise, I could be otherwise. That is precisely the logical space needed to make it thinkable to assume responsibility for changing history (and our selves).

What does not make sense and can only be abusive is requiring of each other superficial changes that bring certain aspects of our behavior into line with reasoned strategies of liberation, but out of line with identity and the circumstances in which that identity is formed and maintained. This would be requiring dishonesty, or bad faith—yet another mask to suit yet another propriety. That sort of thing is, and should be, resented. But that seems to me to be different from assuming responsibility and wanting others to assume responsibility for the profound reconstruction of our Selves and (inseparably from that) for changing the historical determinants which shape the possible. Perhaps, in our requirements and expectations on each other, we err only when we ask too little: changes that are both superficial and noncongruent with what is historically determined as possible. Perhaps what we have to ask is that all women assume responsibility for choosing things and constructing selves that are *not* possible.

Let me bring this back down to the very sticky case at hand. As I have said before in my paper 'To Be And Be Seen' (Marilyn Frye, 1983), being lesbian or being heterosexual are not simply matters of sexual preference or bodily behaviors. They are complex matters of attachment, orientation in the world, vision, habits or communication and community. They are matters of what Card has discussed here as *attitude*. Choice and responsibility in matters of attitude are very unlike choice and responsibility in matters of selection of items from the lunch menu. Attitude is a way of being, not an act or set of acts. In my own case, being lesbian is an attitude evolved over perhaps fifteen years— from my earliest awareness of aptitude for passionate connection with women to a way of being which actualizes that possibility. That is how long the primary choosing took, as I constructed both my self and my environment toward certain configurations of being. It would have been 'inauthentic' to act the lesbian in certain ways too early in that process. It now would be inauthentic *not* to, in certain ways and certain situations. I assume responsibility for that choice, as I do for the choice I made of lifework, and for my continuing choices not to revise such choices. I think it is not logically, morally or politically wrong to assume others are responsible in the same way for making such choices about how to be, even in the midst of circumstances of oppression, and against historical odds.

To assume responsibility is not to claim that what one has decided is ultimately right, that all one's choices are right. If assuming responsibility meant claiming perfection, if it meant inviting blame and having to experience guilt for everything in which one is or proves to be morally or politically imperfect, then of course being asked to assume responsibility seems false and abusive. But being responsible can simply mean one does not passively and unconsciously submit to the winds of time and culture; it means primarily that one is living, throughout one's life, as an *agent* in the matter of who and how one is and the matrix of circumstances that conditions that; and it means recognizing and caring about

the fact that who and how one is has consequences for others. That kind of responsibility, one can live with. In some situations it comes down to nothing more onerous that making it clear to another (and to yourself) just what the limits are on your trustworthiness and comradeship.[4] Such clarity is sometimes the first step of change, for in some cases the naming of such a thing makes it obvious that it is intolerable. But also, in some cases, it is a matter of knowing and letting it be known that one will rest, at this point, with one's imperfections, or that one will rest, at this point, with a disagreement about what it would be to be correct or perfect.

Post Script: A fine resource for thoughts on choice, responsibility and perfectability is *The Sovereignty of Good* (Iris Murdoch, 1971). She works out an understanding of moral progress achieved through a kind of *work*, over time and in history. This work responds both to a desire to be decent or become a person who is just (in a sense), and to a sense of responsibility to others, and it changes one's attitude, one's perception.

REFERENCES

Fry, Marilyn. 1983. *The Politics of Reality: Essay in Feminist Theory.* The Crossing
    Press, Trumansburg, New York.
Murdoch, Iris. 1971. *The Sovereignty of Good.* Schocken Books, New York.

[4] Mutual clarity about such limits, as a result of our taking responsibility for them, has contributed greatly to some of the working friendships I have with heterosexual women.

SECOND SEX: SECOND THOUGHTS

Charlene Haddock Seigfried

It is not surprising that Simone de Beauvoir opens *The Second Sex* (Beauvoir, [1952] 1974) with a discussion of 'The Data of Biology'.[1] Plato, too, in chapter five of the *Republic* ([1937] 1963), precedes his arguments for the desirability of women sharing fully in the life of the city-state with a proof for its possibility. To put it bluntly, if women are by nature inferior, no change in social, political, or economic arrangements are going to produce parity. Like Beauvoir, Plato argues that, except for procreation, individual differences outweigh gender differences in respect to any tasks one might be called on to perform as a member of society. The biological facts that only women bear children and are, in general, physiologically weaker than men, are accepted by both, as is the irrelevance of such facts to the degree of success attainable in the arts, sciences, politics, and military life. Both criticize the sex-differentiated societal roles of their time, in which women appear inferior to men, as conventional but un-natural, and both view their radical proposals for change as unconventional but not unnatural. However, whereas Plato's tripartite definition of human nature is static and hierarchical, Beauvoir's category of the individual is dynamic and egalitarian.

The facticity of being in the world, according to Beauvoir, includes, but is not limited to, biological facts. The totality of actual relations—time, place, country, education, age, etc.—in which any woman finds herself both makes possible a range of actions and limits them. These historical, material conditions, however, can be transcended by the act of freely choosing one's self by engaging in projects which take up and transform one's situation. As usual, Beauvoir brilliantly registers the plight of women as simultaneously free and not free, as caught up in a mesh of relations and expectations not of their own choosing, of resistance to and acquiescence in their situation, as sometimes revolting and sometimes indoctrinating others in conventional behaviors. The very astuteness and comprehensiveness with which she has patiently followed up one strand after another of the threads society weaves in assigning women their places has contributed to the increasingly numerous psychological, sociological, anthro-pological, literary and historical studies of the last decades which have con-firmed the myriad ways in which women become differentiated from men. It

---

[1] All page references in text are to this edition, unless otherwise specified.

is absolutely necessary for the freedom and dignity of women that such female evolved behavior is not completely determinate of their possibilities for being in the world. Transcendence, for Beauvoir, must be absolute in the midst of constraint or it is not transcendence. In so far as one has no choice, one is dehumanized. What, then, is the relation of that most stubborn of factual givens, the biologically female, to being human, to being a woman? Since the biological seems least amenable to societal tampering, and therefore is often appealed to both by those who wish to change and those who wish to retain social arrangements, it is very important to be clear about just what constitutes biological femaleness.

Although no one has denied that biologically men and women differ, there continues to be profound disagreement not only over what such differentiation consists in, but over what follows from such biological facts. If, as John Stuart Mill already pointed out in *The Subjection of Women* (Mill and Mill, 1970), the factual inequity of women's and men's positions characteristic of patriarchal societies are attributed to nature rather than nurture, if stereotypical differences are biological, then differential treatment can not only be justified, but commendable. Those oppressed by such supposedly biological differences can also be tempted by the resentment Nietzsche postulates (Nietzsche, [1886] 1967) as the driving force of Christian slave morality in opposition to Greco-Roman values. This would be a situation in which, on the supposition that biological differences are unchangeable, weakness is luxuriated in rather than overcome, merely by a revaluation which calls weakness a strength, humility a virtue, pride a sin, and inhibition really self-discipline. Given the continued strength of sex stereotyping in most if not all societies, one suspects that the motivating force behind the current interest in brain dimorphism between men and women, and in detecting sex-linked differences in mathematical ability, is less than benign. A tempting reaction is to simply deny any relevance whatever to biological research. Those trained in the social sciences, especially, will be understandably leery of any claims to biological facticity given the problematic relationship of what is observed to what is expected, valued, desired, etc. However, unless one rejects out of hand any possibility of distinguishing testable data from make-believe, biological facts will continue to function as a court of last resort in disputes over what distinguishes women and men. Given the high stakes involved, a recognition of the values and theory dependency of observation should make us even more anxious to scrutinize the biological record rather than less.

In the introduction to *The Second Sex* Beauvoir reports that women's distinctive femininity has been thought to be due either to biology—'something secreted by the ovaries'—or to an essential Platonic difference—'a product of philosophical imagination' (p. xvi). She firmly rejects the notion of a fixed essence in either a biological or philosophical sense, not only because both the biological and social sciences have dismissed the existence of such fixed entities, replacing them with contextual, functional definitions, but more profoundly, because fundamental to her analysis is the belief that 'every human being is always a singular, separate individual' (p. xvi). Real differences between women

and men remain, however, and these are attributable primarily, but not ex-clusively, to the situations of dominance and subordination in which women and men find themselves.

The present differences between women and men, then, are due to the unjust situations in which we find ourselves. What precise differences may remain in a context of emancipation is presently unknown. It is axiomatic for Beauvoir that sexually-based differences will remain despite any situational changes (p. 813). Since she rejects essentialism, there must be some cause in women and men that remains constant, changes nonconvergently between the sexes, to assure differentiation throughout situational change. The one constant is dif-ferential female/male eroticism. Since this cannot be wholly due to the situa-tions in which we find ourselves—otherwise it could cease to be differentiated in a sufficiently changed context—such sex-segregated eroticism must be due to something nonsituationally dependent. For Beauvoir this constant seems to be based in the body as disclosed to us in biology and psychoanalysis. Since the phenomenon of human consciousness assigns meaning and value, and sub-jectivity consists in unconstrained transcendence, our situated embodiment, no matter how much of a burden, can never abrogate freedom. Biology is not destiny. Furthermore, the sciences of biology and psychoanalysis have been as much distorted by patriarchal attitudes as have all cultural, social, and eco-nomic projects.

Nonetheless, though really free (transcendent), we are also really embodied (immanent), and though such embodiment gets transformed, it also helps struc-ture the transformation. What is it, then, about woman that will always remain womanly and not manly? What accounts for the differentiation even in a sought-after world of fully emancipated women and men human beings? It will be felt most profoundly in each individual woman and expressed uniquely by each of us, but as a reality and no illusion it will also be accessible to scientific study. It is in fact to the scientific record that Beauvoir turns for guidance, using it as a baseline, so to speak, from which she can then register the myriad human interpretations of such differentiation: philosophical, i.e. historical materialism and existentialism, mythological, historical, literary, sociological, etc. This pa-per will be limited to biology, but with the understanding that for Beauvoir inexpungible sexual differentiation is due to both biological and psychological factors.

In her use of the biological record to establish the physiological basis of woman's being-in-the-world Beauvoir realizes that she is at a disadvantage, since the record itself has already been distorted: 'The male projects his fears and misogyny onto female animal behaviour and then reads such behavior back onto women' (pp. 3–4). Oddly enough, her own report of biological findings concerning male and female suffers from the same distortions. Of what use to us, then, of examining once again a sad tale of female inferiority? Studies of the impact of science and technology on women are numerous and the topic is constitutive to any elaboration of Marxist-Feminist theory. But feminist theo-ries of science are in their infancy compared to the remarkable gains made by feminist sociology, literature, psychology, history, etc. (See Stimpson and Bur-

styn, 1978; Hubbard *et al.*, 1979; Harding and Hintikka, 1983). In examining Beauvoir's use of science in *The Second Sex* in order to determine how it should be modified in view of current research, some insights emerged which could be helpful in furthering feminist critiques of science. Especially in light of the fact that Beauvoir's concern to argue for women's authenticity and against patterns of oppression did not prevent her from incorporating misogynist views in her own account, the presuppositions which undermined her conscious intentions should be made explicit so they can be avoided in contemporary accounts.

The fundamental problem is that Beauvoir recognized only the distortive use of biological facts by various interpreters and did not consider whether the research programs from which the biological facts emerged were also distorted by these same cultural prejudices. Add to the naïve acceptance of the neutrality of biological facts, her adoption of an interpretive model—Hegel's dialectic of male as spirit, female as flesh (p. 26)—which already incorporated a negative assessment of woman, and Beauvoir's own misogynist biological explanation can be accounted for. The presuppositions which led to it, however, are shared by many philosophers of science. The positivist program of dichotomizing sense data facts and theory or interpretation of facts is reinforced by the existentialist disjunction of immanence—bodily being-in-the-world as a set of limiting conditions—and transcendence—engagement in freely chosen projects expanding into an indefinitely open future (cf. p. xxxiii). Although this strict distinction of facts and values, of sensed objects and theories about such objects, is still widely held, particularly among working scientists, it has also come under severe attack in the thirty years since *The Second Sex* was published (See Hanson, 1971; Hollis and Lukes, 1982).

Beauvoir's own exposition unwittingly demonstrates the impossibility of maintaining such a strict dichotomy. Despite her intention of distinguishing between irreducible facts of observation and the myths which overlay them, her own descriptions of biological data incorporate value judgments. A few examples among many are: the vertebrate female organism is '*subservient* to maternity' (p. 23), in lower forms of life both the male and the female is '*enslaved* to the species' (p. 19), in mammals 'the female is the *victim* of the species' (p. 23), her inwardness is *violated* but the male 'finds self-fulfillment' (p. 24), 'only after menopause is woman delivered from the *servitude* imposed by her female nature' (pp. 34–35), (all the italics are mine). The conclusion of her 'physiological' survey is that in 'woman's subordination to the species,' she is 'most profoundly alienated' (p. 36). Leaving aside for the moment the negativity of the assessment of the female biological organism, one must conclude that the factual and the evaluative overlap. It should also be obvious that one aspect of her program, the premise that 'every biological fact implies transcendence' and 'every function involves a project' (p. 10), negates the possibility of isolating 'irreducible fact[s] of observation' (p. 6).

If it is true that facts take on all their meaning from within value creating projects, then there is no meaning left over discernible to mere observation and description. Even scientists will acknowledge that there is a profound

difference between a non-scientist's list of observed characteristics of, for example, deers in a clearing, and a biologist's list. One major difference is that the biologist's list is not random, but constrained by a disciplinary matrix which sets up an explanatory system and designates appropriate methodology, testing procedures, and reporting protocols (Kuhn, 1970). Within the disciplinary matrix the individual scientist is testing her own narrower hypothesis which directs which observations are relevant and which not, i.e. which are meaningful and why. The non-scientist is also filtering observations through her own project, which differs from the former only in its non-theoretical rigor. Certain items will catch her attention and others will be ignored, depending on her own set of interests, previous experience, purposes, etc.

The distinction being made is not one between neutral observation, Beauvoir's appeal to 'an irreducible fact of observation,' and interpretation of such observational facts. Neither the scientist nor the lay person simply observes. Nor does the scientist's paradigm nor the lay person's belief structures simply distort. Both bring points of views, beliefs, expectations, values, in short, interests, to a situation. Such interests are the focusing of attention which allow the world to appear as it does. As William James puts it: 'Out of all present sensations, we notice mainly such as are significant of absent ones; and out of all the absent associates which these suggest, we again pick out a very few to stand for the objective reality *par excellence*' (James, [1890] 1981: 1, 275).[2] The scientist's interests differ from the casual observer's in the explicitness of the paradigm applied, including protocols of verification and disconfirmation, but not as being factually observant as opposed to being interpretively observant, or as being simply an observation of facts as opposed to an interpretation of facts. There are levels of interpretation, of course, and it is certainly true that an essayist or journalist who interprets scientific findings is adding yet another layer of interest to such findings. One should speak here of degrees.

Why, then, did Beauvoir seek to maintain a distinction in theory which she could not sustain in practice? She did so for the same reason that many scientists would today. As Evelyn Fox Keller put it in 'Feminism and Science': 'The intellectual danger resides in viewing science as pure social product; science then dissolves into ideology and objectivity loses all intrinsic meaning. In the resulting cultural relativism, any emancipatory function of science is negated, and the arbitration of truth recedes into the political domain' (Keller, 1982: 117). Collapsing the distinction between observation and interpretation seems to trivialize the distinction between objective results arrived at through a carefully worked out and tested set of protocols definitive of science and subjective results arrived at spontaneously, whimsically, propagandistically, or any which way. The objective-subjective distinction simply breaks down, and along with it the possibility of designating results as the outcome of a series of value-neutral operations performed on raw data. In William James's terms, all data are 'cooked' already for human consumption. Science can no longer function

---

[2] See also James, 1981, 1: 273–278 and 2: 917–951.

as judge and jury legitimating and dismissing cultural beliefs, since it would itself be operating within such beliefs.

To avoid the 'nihilist retreat' into ideology Keller would retain the objectivity of science, but would also reconstruct the meaning of scientific objectivity by pointing out the distortions introduced into it by the historical linkage of objectivity 'with autonomy and masculinity, and in turn, the goals of science with power and domination' (Keller, 1982: 118). Drawing on 'that branch of psychoanalytic theory known as object relations theory' she argues persuasively how this masculinist ideological constellation of values came to be identified with science. Her solution is to replace this dominant view of science with one recognizing the 'thematic pluralism' actually operative in the history of science. Both knowledge in general and scientific knowledge in particular operate within a dialectic alternating between a desire to obtain mastery over and to unite with nature. While the poles of dominating versus conversing with nature are operative in both male and female scientists, Keller intimates that feminist scientists, freed from masculinist ideology, can bring a whole new range of sensitivities to their work and contribute toward reconstructing both scientific theory and practice as an interaction with, rather than opposition to, nature.

I would like to build on and extend Keller's insights, but from the philosophic perspective of Pragmatic radical empiricism. Criticism needs to be made of the masculinist ideology 'that asserts an opposition between (male) objectivity and (female) subjectivity and denies the possibility of mediation between the two' (Keller, 1982: 118). But one does not save scientific rationality by encouraging the illusion that one can neatly separate ideology 'from that which is universal in the scientific impulse.' The very appeal to universality is a remnant of a pre-Cartesian rationalism that denies the centrality of the self to any appropriation of reality. From the Kantian transcendental ego that accompanies all empirical knowing to Kuhnian paradigm shifts and Quine's comparison of science to 'a field of force whose boundary conditions are experience,' (Quine, 1963: 43ff), modern philosophy has been developing ever more elaborate arguments against the possibility of distinguishing in knowledge claims what is given to us by reality and what we bring to it by way of interest, pre-dispositions, neurological functions, language structures, ect. In fact, Keller's own hopes for a feminist reconstruction of science presupposes that relevant differences in one's point of view allows for different disclosures of reality. In James's words: 'That theory will be most generally believed which, besides offering us objects able to account satisfactorily for our sensible experience, also offers those which are most interesting, those which appeal most urgently to our aesthetic, emotional, and active needs' (James, 1981: 2, 940).

If by 'ideology' Keller means a false perception of reality, then, of course, one ought to distinguish between ideology and truth. But if by 'ideology' she means pre-dispositions we bring to a situation, such as she seems to mean in contrasting the coupling of dominance and scientific attitude with the coupling of eroticism and science, then one can still reject inappropriate ideologies, but only by replacing them with appropriate ones. A discussion of what constitutes appropriateness in constellations of values influencing what we take to be good

science can supply the check to relativism that so often seems to follow inevitably from the collapse of the subjective-objective distinction or of the fact-value distinction. Though undeveloped thematically, a set of such values can be gleaned from Keller's own article. In addition to universality, there is thematic pluralism, a feeling for the organism, interactionist theories, eroticism, and ecstatic communion, to name a few.

Whether one thinks that such values, which influence one's scientific theories and praxis, are preferable because they lead to true findings about reality, or one thinks that such values are preferable because the set of beliefs and actions in which they eventuate disclose a more desirable world, i.e. permit warranted assertions in John Dewey's sense, scientific objectivity is clearly distinguishable from other forms of ideology by its specific characteristics. Acknowledgement of the transactional character of the scientific enterprise abrogates the assumption that scientific propositions somehow mirror reality, in a simplistic assertion of truth, but it also undercuts nihilistic relativism by consciously specifying protocols of objectivity. Scientific objectivity has been linked, for instance, to its methodology of testing procedures, thus allowing for refutation or confirmation of claims. In fact, it is such a 'dialectics of experimentation' that is described as 'a quiet conversation with Nature,' in a quoted passage in Keller's article (Keller, 1982: 123).

What are the biological facts which Beauvoir appeals to as though they could function as a neutral foundation for existentialist values? After surveying the biological record, Beauvoir comes to two major conclusions which continue to inform the remainder of *The Second Sex*. She gives as 'the most striking conclusion' of the survey the realization that because of her subordination to the species, woman is the most profoundly alienated of all mammalian females and most resists this alienation (p. 36). She has also gleaned a constellation of 'undeniable' facts concerning woman's biological being, all of which can be summed up as a constitutional 'weakness.' Biologically, woman is weaker, fragile, unstable, and lacks control. Consequently, her grasp on the world is more restricted, she is less able to carry out her projects, and in short, lives a less richly individual life than man's (p. 38). These conclusions will be criticized, first, from the perspective of current biological findings and, secondly, from feminist analysis of distortions arising from equating human characteristics with male characteristics. Finally, I will appeal to Beauvoir's own characterization of body not as thing but as situation, as providing a better model not only for cultural explanations, but for biological explanations as well.

Given Beauvoir's understanding of the body as the instrument of our grasp on the world (p. 38), it is especially disconcerting to read that 'the male *is* his body' (p. 29), but woman and her body are one only after menopause (p. 35). Since male and female are basically equivalent—'Numerically equal in the species and developed similarly from like beginnings, the fully formed male and female are basically equivalent' (p. 17)—what accounts for such a divergent assessment? Functional differences do, and thus it happens that the female vertebrate's maternal functions account for what Beauvoir consistently describes as woman's enslavement to the species. Since the male investment in

reproduction is so much less than the female's in 'higher' life forms, he can develop all those transcendent qualities definitive of the individual.

It is ironic, indeed, that for evolutionary biologists in the more than hundred years since Darwin, only the contribution of females and males to successful reproduction counts as biological 'success.' In direct contrast to Beauvoir, such success is the ultimate value. Since, according to Beauvoir, women are so much more responsible for reproductive success than men, on biological grounds alone, she should have concluded that the female of the species is much more favored than the male. She is blind to this more defensible reading of the biological record because she is obviously perceiving it from the perspective of the transcendent individual as ultimate source of value. What *is* consistent in both the history of biology and Beauvoir's account is the disproportionate ascription of male superiority in the functions most valued. Whereas Beauvoir deplores woman's excessive involvement in the maintenance of the species because it lessens her opportunity for transcendent activity, the female's role in evolutionary development, ever since Darwin's *The Descent of Man* ([1871], 1981), has been minimized by biologists because parental contributions to reproduction are highly valued inasmuch as they affect whatever improvement accrues to the evolutionary process. Even without the assumption that evolutionary change means progress, the ability to pass on one's genes is the operant definition of evolutionary success. This is one more example of the way in which a predisposition to overvalue men's achievements and undervalue women's has led to diametrically opposed interpretations of biological 'facts.'

Biologically, the dichotomy of 'enslavement' to the species vs individuality is meaningless. Since Darwin, the genetic component and behavioral outcomes of female and male organisms in sex-differentiated species are of interest only insofar as they contribute to a common goal. According to the founding paradigm for evolutionary biology, 'the diversity of present-day living organisms had been generated by "descent with modification" from one or perhaps a few primeval forms,' and 'natural selection' is 'the principal mechanism by which this modification had been brought about' (Bendall, 1983: 34). Natural selection is glossed as 'success in leaving progeny' by Ernst Mayr, quoting Darwin's *Origin of Species* ([1859] 1979) (Bendall, 1983: 34). Both the female and the male gain whatever interest they have for evolutionary biology in terms of success in producing viable offspring. On this model not only is the female not unilaterally 'enslaved' to the species, but species survival is interpreted as maximal success, rather than as an unfair burden.

This is not to argue that Beauvoir should not have criticized the illegitimate extension of the biological model as determinate of human behavior. One should criticize this biological model insofar as this functional research program, set up to account for speciation, is illegitimately extended as an explanatory model for human behavior. William James, for instance, strenuously argued against Herbert Spencer's claim that explanations about the survival of the species, which Spencer erroneously called adjustment to the environment, can adequately encompass human development once consciousness has evolved. According to James: 'The social affections, all the various forms of play, the thrilling

intimations of art, the delights of philosophic contemplations, the rest of religious emotion, the joy of moral self-approbation, the charm of fancy and of wit—some or all of these are absolutely required to make the notion of mere existence tolerable; and individuals who, by their special powers, satisfy these desires are protected by their fellows and enabled to survive, though their mental constitution should in other respects be lamentably ill-"adjusted" to the outward world' (James, 1978: 13). But this argument for the priority of human interests over determinism, of 'projects' in Beauvoir's terms, in any account of human development, unites rather than distinguishes male and female. Beauvoir is, of course, aware of this in her arguments for woman's autonomy as a transcendent being. But this is also true of the biological descriptions of female and male, and not just of cultural descriptions based on the former. James argues for the reconstruction of biological and physical descriptions themselves, incorporating the real difference consciousness and valuation make, while Beauvoir mistakenly wants to reconstruct society's use of biological data by overriding, rather than re-thinking, the data produced by biological and psychological research programs.

Already in 1875, three years before the James article, Antoinette Brown Blackwell in *The Sexes Throughout Nature* (1976), challenged the biological basis of both Darwin's and Spencer's accounts of male and female.[3] She argues that Darwin's assumption of male superiority distorted his account of male and female behavior and shows how according to his own theory, natural selection could not select for the 'superiority' of the male of the species without selecting for the 'superiority' of the species as such, including, of course, females. Many nineteenth- and twentieth-century feminists have challenged ideological distortions within biological evolutionary theory and practices. It is not accidental that Beauvoir locates the cause of both alienation, i.e. enslavement to the species, and weakness, i.e. a more restricted grasp on the world, in female sexuality taken in the widest possible sense of female anatomy and all the processes leading up to birthing and all the processes following from it. Beauvoir's linkage of maternity with disability is as old as Aristotle. She correctly perceived that this jaundiced view of a powerful female ability persisted in the biological literature of the day. What she failed to appreciate is that the fact of maternity did not cause women to be judged as less capable in most other human affairs, but that prior assumptions of male as valued, female as disvalued, negatively affected assessments of maternity. Such differential valuations persist to the present day and can be discerned in the theoretical frameworks and working hypotheses of the various sciences.

Two approaches have been adopted by feminist scientists to correct such distortions. One is to demonstrate how females have been left out of consideration in research, as when female rats are excluded from animal studies, or male populations alone are included in psychological studies, and then the findings are illicitly extended to include the entire populations. The solutions

[3] Virginia Lohner first drew my attention to nineteenth century American feminists and biological controversies in 'Darwinism, feminism, and the unscientific uses of science,' class paper (1982).

advocated seek to redress the balance by concentrating on female experiences, either exclusively or by including females in all such studies, and also including women scientists in projects to counter male bias. Conceivable not only will this change the empirical data available, but also the theoretical frameworks adopted. This procedure is partially based on an empiricist assumption that raw data influences theory. The second approach is to change the disciplinary paradigms as their patriarchal biases become explicated, through substituting feminist values. This approach assumes that values help determine theory and that facts and theories are co-determinate. These two approaches are not mutually exclusive.

A primatologist, Sarah Blaffer Hrdy, in *The Woman That Never Evolved*, exemplifies primarily the first approach, and I would like to examine its strengths and weaknesses as a contemporary effort to bring a feminist perspective to the issues Beauvoir raised (Hrdy, 1981).[4] She works within the standard evolutionary paradigm: 'In evolutionary terms, the only pay-off that really matters is better-than-average representation in the gene pool of succeeding generations.' As applied to sexual selection, Robert Trivers's formulation is that since the female invests the most in the production and rearing of offspring, they become the 'limiting resource,' 'hence, male competes with male to tap the reproductive resources of females' (H: 22). By carefully examining female primate behavior Hrdy both critiques traditional explanations of male dominance and begins to fill in the large areas of misinformation and lack of information resulting from both male biologists' exaggerated self-importance and their limited interest in female primates 'except in their capacity as mothers' (H: 14).

Since, on the traditional model, intensity of competition leads to increasing evolutionary pressures selecting for favored characteristics (H: 23), one strategy for redressing the balance is to demonstrate that females, too, share in the competitiveness. Thus, Hrdy seeks to show that 'the two most salient forces at work in the social arrangements of primates are competition among individual females and cooperation among related females who are competing with other groups of related females' (H: 95). Although not as overt as male competition, among primate species 'every female is essentially a competitive, strategizing creature' (H: 96–97). Like males, females also set up dominance hierarchies to maximise their success in leaving progeny. 'The vision of assertive, dominance-oriented females differs radically from existing stereotypes of female primates as nonstop mothers whose perennial preoccupation with nurturing offspring keeps them out of politics' (H: 127). In fact, given the strength of the evidence in every well-documented species of primate, Hrdy questions the lack of sociological evidence for competition among females of the human species and attributes this both to sexual stereotypes and the lack of models for quantifying the less obvious hierarchies in which women have a stake.

Hrdy also examines the primate origins of female sexuality and is able to

---

[4] Page references in the text to this volume are preceded by 'H'.

account for the evolutionary value of two female sexual characteristics usually thought to be non-adaptive: (1) estrus or sexual solicitation prolonged beyond the time needed to successfully copulate coupled with hidden ovulation and (2) clitoral eroticism. Estrus behavior both induces females to mate with many more partners than are necessary for conception and females may be especially assertive when they cannot conceive, as in the phenomenon of pseudo-estrus during pregnancy. Hrdy hypothesizes that nonreproductive sexuality in primate females is nevertheless adaptive in several ways. Low-ranking females can have access to dominant males in addition to their low-ranking mates. In multi-male troops copulating with as many males as possible promotes infant survival because of intense selection pressure against males attacking their own offspring, although there are incentives for destroying infants sired by others and replacing them with one's own. In species with some male investment in infant care, it is also advantageous for the female to have as many males as possible feel that they are the father. Especially in those situations where male infanticide is a significant hazard, both increased female sexual activity and concealment of ovulation increases the chances for survival of one's infant by increasing the number of sexual partners, both resident and invading males, any one of whom may be the actual father.

The female orgasm brought about by clitoral stimulation, but not usually by intercourse alone, has long been a biological puzzle, since it does not seem to have much purpose beyond sexual stimulation. Hrdy adopts the same approach to this aspect of female sexuality by providing evidence for its reproductive advantage. Despite earlier denials, there is increasing evidence that orgasms occur in other primates (H: 172). It was long thought that females' reproduction rates were constant, that they would reproduce optimally in their fertile years, under normal conditions. Since males had to compete for access to females and therefore reproduced disproportionally, their success was over-emphasized as the most significant factor in determining the genetic pool. But Hrdy points out that primate females do not reproduce optimally and reproductive success differs widely among females. Females actively compete for reproductive success, for instance by the socially-dominate female suppressing ovulation in her subordinates, excluding rivals from choice food sites, and actively harassing them and inducing abortions. The mother's social rank has important consequences contributing to her reproductive success, including 'the availability of food and helpers, protection from predation and from other members of her own species' (H: 173).

Given the importance for reproductive success on the tolerance of nearby males, the advantages of an active, promiscuous sexuality becomes obvious rather than anomolous. The assumption of a monogamous context for early hominid society has obscured the evidence. 'The physiology of the clitoris, which does not typically generate orgasm after a single copulation, ceases to be mysterious if we put aside the idea that women's sexuality evolved in order to "serve" her mate, and examine instead the possibility that it evolved in order to increase the reproductive success of primate mothers through enhanced survival of their offspring' (H: 176). In sum 'A highly assertive female sexuality

marked by a potential to shift from cyclical to situation-dependent receptivity constituted the physiological heritage that prehominid females brought to [the] evolutionary experiment' (H: 158–159).

Hrdy works within the paradigms and methodology of her discipline, but by consciously applying them evenhandedly to women, the results she gets are strikingly different from the traditional ones. She suggests, for instance, as the most plausible hypothesis to account for the existence of female orgasm, the one which can demonstrate its reproductive advantage (H: 167). But she also draws on feminist values and theory, both to criticize distorted views of women and women's sexuality which are read into animal behavior, and to interpret the little data that is available. She refers to the feminist insight, for instance, that 'female solidarity provides crucial leverage against males' to both recognize in the first place, and then to explain, behavior of polygamous primate females who 'provide each other with indispensable support' (H: 100). Given the lack of adequate data on reproductive strategies for virtually every species of primate (H: 136), and our own self-interest in the outcome, the proliferation of biased explanations is perhaps greater than usual in other areas of science. The paucity of data, rather than leading to constraint in postulating explanations, has led to an exaggeration of cultural biases in the explanations given.

How does Hrdy avoid the accusation that she is herself just introducing one more biased reading into the record, one favoring women this time, rather than men? First of all, she is explicit about the values she is introducing, in contrast to those who surreptitiously introduce patriarchal bias into supposedly neutral reports of natural events. Secondly, her hypotheses follow from a strict application of the relevant disciplinary paradigms and seek to encompass as much data as possible. She dismisses, for example, Burley's and Alexander's hypotheses to explain continuous receptivity and nonreproductive sexuality as forcing a male to focus on a single mate, because although it could adequately account for concealed ovulation in our species, it cannot account for the same phenomena in non-pair-bonded primates not living in a communal context and not consciously engaged in birth control (H: 143–144). Ultimately only the success of a hypothesis in explaining the phenomena will count. But the very interest she, as a feminist, brings to investigating a primate female lineage that can contribute somehow to understanding female human biology can be disclosive of aspects otherwise ignored or misinterpreted.

Beauvoir's and Hrdy's biological female are diametrically opposed. The weak, unstable, passive, female animal, overwhelmed by pregnancy has been replaced by the assertive, lusty, dominance-oriented female who revels in reproductive success. Whereas Beauvoir read back into the biological substrate some of the contemporary cultural, economic, and political crippling of women, Hrdy's own investigations have built on the legacy of woman as transcendent and the insistence on reciprocity between women and men that have evolved out of *The Second Sex*. But both Beauvoir and Hrdy still work within explanatory models that confuse human accomplishments with patriarchal values.

Beauvoir unwittingly takes over the individual as male as the model for the valued human characteristics called transcendent. Echoing Aristotle's equation

of female with matter and passivity and male with spirit and activity, Beauvoir likewise concludes that women biologically are deformed males. There is a long list of traits females lack, coupled with superior traits males embody simply by being male—such traits being valued as preeminantly human: 'She does not seek to affirm her individuality; she is not hostile to males or to other females and shows little combative instinct' (p. 25); she doesn't choose her mate but accepts whoever is around; though 'sometimes' equal to the male, she renounces her accomplishments to perpetuate the species; the male keeps himself apart and maintains his individuality, is aggressive, directs sexuality, actively surmounts and penetrates the female, manifests 'the power of life' (p. 25). dominates, has a will to combat (p. 26), is autonomous, more adventurous, more independent, more masterful, imperious, commands (p. 27); the male creates while the female only maintains (p. 27); the female is possessed by foreign forces (p. 28); pain, weakness, and fatigue are constantly associated with the female body, especially in its sexual aspects, while exuberance is associated with the male's (pp. 25–33). Overall, in comparison with the female, 'the male seems infinitely favored' (p. 36).

By contrast Hrdy's female primates instantiate the favored male traits. She aggressively solicits mates, seeks to dominate in female hierarchies, is a fierce fighter, is strongly competitive, initiates and enjoys sex, supports herself and her offspring by food gathering, and is a full participant in the evolutionary struggle for survival. Such a revision of the biological evidence is long overdue, and we shouldn't lose sight of the fact that it still does not represent the dominant view. But while Hrdy obviously disagrees over the conclusions that can be drawn from the biological record, mostly because of changes that have taken place in the meantime, she by and large accepts the same value structure that Beauvoir does, but only within the biological explanatory matrix. Beauvoir, drawing on existentialist theory, and Hrdy, drawing on evolutionary biological theory, both uncritically rank aggression, dominance and individualism over co-operation and interdependence, either as primate strategies for survival (Hrdy) or as transcendent characteristics (Beauvoir). The development of feminist theory since *The Second Sex* enables Hrdy to avoid falling into the same trap that Beauvoir did, that of favoring dominance and aggression over cooperation and interdependence as desirable human strategies just because they are advantageous according to the prevailing biological disciplinary matrix. She emphatically disassociates the values espoused by the feminist woman from those recorded in primate studies: 'The female with "equal rights" never evolved; she was invented, and fought for consciously with intelligence, stubbornness, and courage' (H: 190–191).

But a more radical critique of biological theory itself is called for, and not just of its misappropriation. Both Beauvoir and Hrdy criticize the reductionist determination of woman's nature from observations of animal behavior. In this Hrdy's claim that 'of all females, the potential for freedom and the chance to control their own destinies is greatest among women' (H: 188), echos Beauvoir's claim that 'woman is of all mammalian females . . . the one who most violently resists . . . alienation' (p. 36). But Hrdy is in better position than Beauvoir to

criticize her own discipline of sociobiology, and not just insofar as it distorts female primate behavior and woman's accomplishments, but in its very foundational presuppositions, which incorporate masculinist values while purporting to be neutral.

The overwhelming connection of aggression, dominance and individualism with a patriarchal point of view and value system should provide sufficient incentive to question their place in disciplinary matrixes. It is no accident that the words, 'disciplinary matrix,' were introduced by Kuhn to distinguish global paradigms as the 'constellation of group commitments' that characterize disciplines as a whole from particular paradigms as smaller organizational units (Kuhn, 1978: 181ff). While Kuhn may not have been aware of it, the word, 'matrix,' which he uses to designate the community of scientists who share interests and beliefs, originally meant in Latin 'womb' or 'pregnant,' by a change of suffix from *mater,* 'mother.' The conjunction 'disciplinary matrix' designates the co-operation and interdependence intrinsic to science as an enterprise, indeed, constitutive of it, as a replacement for the distortive imagery of science as individualistic, as domination of nature, and as transcending beliefs and values. It is noteworthy that the replacement of the concept of science as domination by the concept of science as interacting with nature, is signaled by the word, matrix, since one can argue that the mutual interdependence that is experienced by mother and child can account for the tendency to view science as a cooperation with, rather than opposition to, nature.

However, if the second feminist approach is adopted, that of reconstructing disciplinary paradigms by substituting different values, then both Hrdy and Beauvoir already have within their differing systems the means to transform their fundamental explanatory frameworks. Beauvoir's characterization of the body as situation, as the expression of the complex of relationships that comprise everyday reality, combined with the realization that meaning and value are assigned to events through the projects adopted, would comprise the core of such a reinterpretation. Her nonreductive stance is still relevant to current biological debates. The claim that societal ways cannot be deduced from biology makes her sound inimical to the sociobiologist program, were it not for the fact that one of her premises is that the body and its functions do influence conscious choices. Even though values and meaning take up and transform biological facts, such facts in turn exercise a limiting function on the range of options available. For humans, choice is decisive, but does not work in a vacuum, but out of actual situations.

This position is compatible with contemporary versions of sociobiology, according to which biological patterns provide ranges of behaviors, but different cultures, and within cultures, individuals, differently value and manipulate these patterns. On a scale illustrating the relative strength of biological and cultural forces, from the sociobiologists for whom biological patterns are more determinative and cultural options largely epiphenomena, to those for whom biology provides a wide range of options and culture is barely constrained, Beauvoir should be placed at the far end of the scale where culture predominates

but doesn't entirely negate biology. I am here understanding culture not merely as its products and processes, which for Beauvoir are part of the not-self and can be oppressive, but as the individual who participates in creating her own self in the world and is therefore the ultimate source of culture.

Beauvoir is absolutely correct that the 'facts of biology' should be viewed 'in the light of an ontological, economic, social, and psychological context' (p. 41). Biological facts do not define either what a woman is nor what she can become. But she is also right in seeing that a biological understanding of the female body as such and in its evolutionary development is a necessary part of understanding that aspect of self as body, viewed not merely as a physiological organism, but as a situation, as a way of being in the world. The failure of the biology chapter in *The Second Sex* results from Beauvoir's adopting the scientific positions of her day rather than criticizing them. This accounts for her uncharacteristic slipping into essentialism in her explanation of the biological evidence. In addition her acquiescence in the male-as-human value structure endemic both to existentialism and science, resulted in the misogynist conclusions carried over into later chapters whenever she brings in the strictly biological: 'As we have seen, the two essential traits that characterize woman, biologically speaking, are the following: her grasp upon the world is less extended than man's and she is more closely enslaved to the species' (p. 59).

But when Beauvoir considers biological facts within the value and meaning giving structure of a woman's own transcendent project and that of others, she successfully reconstructs them. Among the principles that constitute the meaning of 'project' are: 'The peculiarities that identify her as specifically a woman get their importance from the significance placed upon them' (p. 809), and 'Woman is determined not by her hormones or by mysterious instincts, but by the manner in which her body and her relation to the world are modified through the actions of others than herself' (p. 806). Within this more defensible interpretive framework her assessment is more satisfying and challenging. 'There will always be certain differences between man and woman; her eroticism, and therefore her sexual world, have a special form of their own and therefore cannot fail to engender a sensuality, a sensitivity, of a special nature. This means that her relations to her own body, to that of the male, to the child, will never be identical with those the male bears to his own body, to that of the female, and to the child; those who make much of "equality in difference" could not with good grace refuse to grant me the possibility of differences in equality' (p. 813). These insights should be extended to biology as itself a human project and not just to those aspects of biology that are explicitly concerned with women's and men's biology.

Consequently, the strict dichotomy of transcendent projects vs immanence—factual being in the world—would have to be reworked into an interactive model (See Seigfried, 1984). Notice, above, that 'project' encompasses both the meaning I as subject assign to things and other's assignments, including actions that impinge on mine. Some aspects of Beauvoir's work already depend on such a model. Her unique contribution to existentialist theory, for instance,

in her admission of the possibility and actuality of oppression as distinct from one's inauthentic acceptance of the role of victim, already transcends the strict either/or intrinsic to the transcendent-immanent model. The quote just given on women's eroticism also illustrates the necessary blurring of the transcendent-immanent boundaries that occurs when considering the body as situated from within a project. The whole first chapter on biology is obsolete and irredeemably flawed, but not the role it plays in relation to the rest of the book. The effort to rethink female biology in light of feminist theory still remains a top priority.

Without belittling the substantial contribution Hrdy has made to primate studies by her thesis that 'the central organizing principle of primate social life is competition between females and especially female lineages' (H: 128), what would happen if co-operation and interdependence became central organizing principles in evolutionary biology? Hrdy is well aware that 'by and large, how-ever, the emphasis in recent years has been on documenting the degree to which women cooperate' (H: 224, n43). Her own research provides many ex-amples of co-operation, from females helping mother-infant pairs to female cohorts. Rather than the individual as favored unit, the object of observation in primate studies, after all, is the whole primate colony and how interactions take place within it and between it and other primate groups. In order for cooperation and interdependence to be seen as human strengths and not dis-valued as female weaknesses, however, they have to become incorporated into the evolutionary models used, and not only function in explanatory paradigms of female behavior. Dawkin's theory of the selfish gene which uses its host organism merely as a carrier is the *reductio ad absurdum* of the competitive individualistic model. Barbara McClintock's interactionist model may well be the wave of the future (See Keller, 1982: 124–126).

Some striking and promising changes are already taking place within evo-lutionary biology and the individual competitive model as the sole driving force of evolution has already been challenged. A perusal of *Evolution From Mole-cules to Men* (despite its sexist title), an edited version of the 1982 centennial conference which deliberately took a 'wide-ranging . . . view of the present state of Darwinism,' yields the following hopeful signs, not only about com-petition, but also of other interests compatible with feminist views (Bendall, 1983).[5]

Patrick Bateson: 'What is needed, therefore, is constructive collaboration between biologists and social scientists and a proper respect for the insights that the different disciplines can provide' (B: 503).

E. Novo: 'Evolutionism, the world view that considers constant change a central process of nature, always regarded organic evolution as a coevolving dialogue between organism and environment' (B: 287).

R. C. Lewontin: 'Rather, genes, organisms, and environments are in recip-rocal interaction with each other is such a way that each is both cause and effect in a quite complex, although perfectly analysable, way. The known facts of

---

[5] Page references in the text to this volume are preceded by 'B'.

development and of natural history make it patently clear that genes do not determine individuals nor do environments determine species' (B: 276).

Stephen J. Gould: 'The antiessentialism of modern thought has a host of salutory implications and consequences' (B: 362).

Other promising reinterpretations of Darwinian theory, impossible to quote in a single sentence, are to be found in Garland E. Allen's discussion of the gradual replacement of mechanistic materialistic explanations of Darwinism by holistic and dialectical ones (B: 81–102), Glynn L. Isaac's plea for acquiring more richly diverse classes of information (B: 538), including even elements of myth, providing they are testable (B: 515), and P. P. G. Bateson's rejection of reductionism (B: 503). Clearly, evolutionary biology today is fertile ground for feminist reconstruction. It would be unforgivable to lose the opportunity.

REFERENCES

Beauvoir, Simone de. [1952] 1974. *The Second Sex*. Random House, Vintage Books, New York.

Bendall, D. S. 1983. *Evolution From Molecules to Men*. Cambridge University Press, Cambridge.

Blackwell, Antionette Brown. [1875] 1976. *The Sexes Throughout Nature*. Hyperion Press, Westport, Conn.

Darwin, Charles. [1859] 1979. *Origin of Species*. Harvard University Press, Cambridge.

Darwin, Charles. [1871] 1981. *The Descent of Man*. Princeton U. P., Princeton, N.J.

Hanson, Norwood Russell. 1971. *Observation and Explanation*. Harper and Row, New York.

Harding, Sandra and M. Hintikka. 1983. *Discovering Reality*. D. Reidel, Dordrecht.

Hollis, Martin and Steven Lukes. 1982. *Rationality and Relativism*. M. I. T. Press, Cambridge.

Hrdy, Sarah Blaffer. 1981. *The Woman That Never Evolved*. Harvard University Press, Cambridge.

Hubbard, Ruth, M. S. Henifin and B. Fried, ed. 1979. *Women Look at Biology Looking at Women*. G. K. Hall, Boston.

James, William. 1978 (orig. 1878). Remarks on Spencer's definition of mind as correspondence. In *Essays in Philosophy*. Harvard University Press, Cambridge.

James, William. [1890] 1981. *The Principles of Psychology*, 3 Vols. Harvard University Press, Cambridge.

Keller, Evelyn Fox. 1982. Feminism and science. In Keohane, Nannerl O., Michelle Z. Rosaldo and Barbara C. Gelpi, eds, *Feminist Theory*. The University of Chicago Press, Chicago.

Keller, Evelyn Fox. 1983. *A Feeling for the Organism. The Life and Work of Barbara McClintock*. W. H. Freeman, San Francisco.

Kuhn, Thomas S. 1970. The structure of scientific revolutions. In *International Encyclopedia of Unified Science*, 2nd Edn, Vol. 2. University of Chicago Press, Chicago.

Mill, John Stuart and Harriet Taylor Mill. [1869] 1970. *Essays on Sex Equality*. University of Chicago Press, Chicago.

Nietzsche, Friedrich. [1886] 1967. *On the Geneology of Morals*. Translated by Walter Kaufmann. Random House, Vintage Books, New York.

Plato. [1937] 1963. *Republic* (Reprint). Harvard University Press, Cambridge, Mass.

Quine, W. V. O. 1963. *From a Logical Point of View.* Harper and Row, New York.
Seigfried, Charlene Haddock. 1984. Gender-specific values. *The Philosophical Forum*
     15 (Summer): 425–442.
Stimpson, Catherine R., and Joan N. Burstyn, eds. 1978. Women, science, and society.
     Signs **4** (1) Special Issue.

INTERPRETATION AND RETRIEVAL

REREADING BEAUVOIR

Linda Singer

This paper is written in response to a problem of intertextuality which is not best represented through an examination of texts because it is a problem of absence, the erasure of writing, and as such resists documentation. The problem is the erasure or absence of Beauvoir's work from the philosophical canon, and the resulting marginalization of her discourse within the conversation which constitutes professional philosophy. As a consequence, Beauvoir's work receives little space in the social network of journals, conferences and classrooms through which philosophical practice is concretized.

In the light of the extra-textual dimensions of the problem, it is with some irony that I propose a rereading of Beauvoir's theoretical texts in light of the philosophical contexts and conversations from which her work has been absented, and in which the professional devaluation of her work becomes justification for the community's failure to read it in the first place. My proposed reading will thus proceed by a paradoxical strategy which aims to retrieve the significance of Beauvoir's work in light of the contradictions of historical forces which have produced its peripheral position. This contradiction consists in the conjunction of reasoning according to which Beauvoir is not worth reading because she is either too far removed from the standard terrain of philosophy, i.e. too identified with the extra-philosophical turf of the feminine, or, on the other hand, because she is too closely identified with that tradition as a 'pseudo-Sartrean.' Both of these ways of not reading Beauvoir are misguided in my view, and certainly make any genuine appreciation of her work impossible.[1] My reading aims to dislodge these readings by offering an interpretation of Beauvoir as a female-identified voice who addresses the discourse of philosophy from that standpoint.

My intention is to provide a selective reading of *The Second Sex* (1952) and *Ethics of Ambiguity* (1948) (Beauvoir's major theoretical texts) which retrieves their import in the context of the ethical discourse and theory of value promised, but not delivered, by Sartre and Heidegger. In this sense, Beauvoir can be

---

[1] For a broader discussion of the relationship between Beauvoir and Sartre which argues against reading Beauvoir as a 'pseudo-Sartrean,' see Margaret A. Simons (1981).

understood as directing her discourse toward the historical tradition of ethics, and the language of freedom and responsibility privileged by existentialists, most especially Sartre. But Beauvoir's work does not stand contained or restricted to the Sartrean discourse, despite her occasional demure protestations to the contrary, because as I read her work, Beauvoir's discussion, unlike Sartre's, is identified with and emerges from the situation of femininity. Her position with respect to Sartre's work is therefore, on my reading, not complementary or supplementary, but rather oppositional and subversive, especially with respect to the concept of freedom and its position in the ethical discourse.

Beauvoir marks the site of her opposition in *The Second Sex* when she names the character of cultural representation in writing, as phallocentric.

> 'Representation of the world, like the world itself is the work of men; they describe it from their point of view which they confuse with the absolute truth.' (p. 161).

This recognition marks Beauvoir's discourse as a discourse of otherness and of difference.[2] I will be concentrating in my text on the concept of freedom as the marker of this difference. Far from being contained as a supplement within the frame established by Sartrean language and the larger conversation in which his work participates, Beauvoir's writing ruptures or disrupts the structure of the very phallocentric language and speech which claims to speak for and include the position marked as 'other.' By naming sex or sexual difference as a repressed structure of philosophical discourse, Beauvoir recasts the nature and scope of philosophy's assumptions. Specifically, Beauvoir's recognition that the sites and position from which women and men converse are different, and not only different but opposed in a way that privileges the masculine standpoint and its standards of representation, decenters the practice of philosophical signification by which some are entitled to speak for all, and where femininity comes to signify a marker created in and aimed at a position coded as alien or other.

Taking the insights of existentialism seriously with respect to its denial of a supervening perspective and its affirmation of the situational character of discourse, Beauvoir begins the project of writing the other side, giving voice to the discourse of otherness. Part of the purpose of the existential analytic of feminine development in *The Second Sex*, is to give social and historical sense to this sign of otherness, thus reconstituting femininity as an existential project with an integrity, and not just an empty sign for deferred male desire. With

---

[2] Beauvoir's discourse of 'difference' is not yet the *'difference'* of deconstruction, although I believe Beauvoir's texts have served as an unacknowledged source of that discourse. The difference which grounds signification is founded upon a preconstituted sphere of social relations, most notably that of gender caste privilege. As such the ground of signification is ruptured so that the prospect of common meaning for terms like love is impossible. Love cannot mean the same thing to both sexes, because it is positioned differently in the life worlds of men and women. See *The Second Sex*, Chap. XXIII.

the elaboration of woman as other comes the discourse of difference, the writing of female signification in its difference. Beauvoir speaks to the traditional discourse of philosophy, and to its sense of problems and issues, but she speaks to it from the other side, or the side it has positioned as other.

My efforts in this paper will focus on Beauvoir's rewriting of the discourse of freedom from the position of the oppressed feminine. The discourse of freedom has been privileged in ethical writing, but on Beauvoir's analysis, it is also revealed as a discourse of privilege. Borrowing from Elizabeth Janeway's discussion of power (1981), freedom like power, has been written, historically, from the standpoint of those who have it, and thus has been treated as a quality or attribute of persons, rather than relationships. This has resulted in a reification in theory and practice, the effect of which has been to support and perpetuate an arbitrary system of privilege. Beauvoir broaches the question of freedom from the position of the second, i.e. from the standpoint of women whose containment is secured by the traditional discourse. She engages in this discourse for the purpose of liberating those so contained. Her rewriting has the effect of shifting the locus of freedom from that of isolated autonomous individuals to freedom emergent from a situation of relatedness and affinity. This sense of a freedom which realizes itself in engagement with and for others provides Beauvoir with the basis for the morality of commitment and concern described in *The Ethics of Ambiguity*, which I read as an oppositional text with respect to the history of ethics. It is my intention to show that it is only with this reconstitution of freedom that an ethics of liberation in light of human finitude is possible.

My rereading attempts to situate Beauvoir's work within the context of the ethical discourse as the voice of the ethics of otherness, i.e. the sense and practice of value which emerges from the feminine situation. While most ethical theory presents its position as gender neutral or transsexual, recent research by Carol Gilligan (1982) provides good reason to believe that gender is a marker of difference in ethical decision making, and that men and women do in fact arrive at moral decision differently, by privileging alternate aspects of the problematic situation. This difference, Gilligan notes, is often belied by a phallocentric bias which tends to view the feminine simply as an underdeveloped mode of the masculine. Based on her research, which included extensive interviews with women, Gilligan distinguishes between two moral models which can be correlated with gender difference. The first is the masculinist model, which privileges the concept of a morality of rights predicated on equality and centered on the matter of fairness (p. 164). The feminine model, by contrast, privileges an ethic of responsibility predicated on equity and recognition of difference in need (p. 160).

While Gilligan's analysis does not address the origins or reasons for this difference *per se*, there is no reason to assume an essentialist or deterministic explanation. Read in light of Beauvoir's analysis of femininity, it is reasonable to interpret these differences in judgmental strategies as deriving from the opposed roles and situations women and men occupy in patriarchy. Those most likely to be given the power to legislate and judge will also be those most likely

to privilege these functions, while women, to whom falls the burden of care and nurture, are likely to privilege these aspects in their judgmental activities.

I will be reading the relationship between Beauvoir's and Sartre's discourses on freedom as emblematic of the opposition between these two standpoints. Considered in this light, Beauvoir is not a 'pseudo-Sartrean.' Hers is a voice of discord and resistance to the sense of freedom in isolation. Since such a view provides insufficient basis for moral responsibility, Beauvoir maps an alternative conception of freedom identified as an agency of commitment and concern. To support this reading, I will try to tie the Sartrean discourse to its displaced origins in a masculine position of privilege and then show how Beauvoir's rewriting of the feminine provides the basis for a revivified concept of freedom and responsibility and ultimately of morality itself.

To understand the relationship between these two ideas of freedom and relatedness, it will be necessary to give a brief account of Sartre's model of consciousness which is the locus for the exercise of freedom. Sartre's model of consciousness extends a philosophical tradition of dualism which positions subjects, who are conscious, and objects, which are not, in an oppositional relationship. This rift in being creates two regions which Sartre identified as regions of positivity and negativity 'without communication.' Consciousness is identified with the region of negativity since 'it is nothingness which is at the very heart of transcendence and which conditions it.' Negativity is the central structure of consciousness since positional awareness of something is only possible by virtue of a prepositional act of nihilation, a recognition that consciousness is not that of which it is conscious. Consciousness of objects is possible on this view only on the basis of the fundamental separation or difference between consciousness and its objects, which Sartre describes as an abyss of nothing. Consciousness, in Sartre's words is a 'total emptiness since the whole world is outside it.' The emptiness of consciousness is a phenomenon of absence, and it is from this sense of absence, of determination, motives or causes, that Sartre derives the view of the consciousness as radically free. Because consciousness is nothing, not a thing, it cannot be eclipsed or compromised except by being reduced to a thing in the midst of the world by another consciousness. Because consciousness is empty of objects as the condition by virtue of which there are objects for us, consciousness retains its power of transcendence, with respect to the choice of positions toward that which it positions, and thus maintains a radical sense of self-sufficiency, which marks its privilege with respect to objects. Consciousness is privileged, on Sartre's view, because the subject is free to determine or constitute objects while being free from being determined or constituted by them. The absence of content or determinations for consciousness means that consciousness lacks origins or foundations, and thus is thrown back on itself as the site of its unconditioned choices.

It is the recognition of the groundlessness of our choices which is the source of the anxiety for a radically free consciousness. This anxiety in turn motivates the flight from freedom in an act of bad faith, by which the subject endeavours to escape from the necessity and responsibility for essentially spontaneous or

groundless choices. The movement of bad faith, which attempts to decenter freedom in objects, amounts to a denial of the radical autonomy of consciousness, and a refusal to acknowledge its sovereignty over all which it is not. A consciousness defined in terms of its separation from all that is, in the Sartrean view, betrays itself in this moment of displacement. Consciousness is thus compromised by its commitments, its attachments and relationships, since such attachments serve to mask the essentially nihilating activity of consciousness from itself. A consciousness moved or motivated by its attachments is interpreted by Sartre as being in flight from recognizing its complicity with them, and its freedom to do otherwise. In allowing oneself anything other than commitments treated as groundless or arbitrary, consciousness displaces its freedom onto objects, and so itself becomes objectified.

This brief account was designed to show that Sartre's concept of freedom is such as to construe that term in a sense that is primarily solipsistic and negative. Sartre's freedom shows itself as a self-sufficient power of nihilation posed over and against a world of positivity from a position of privilege. The consequence of this conception of freedom is to compromise the prospect of freedom establishing and realizing itself in any other than solipsistic and isolated modes. The limits of this view are apparent in Sartre's discussion of interpersonal relationships, which produces rather fatalistic conclusions about the possibility of establishing affinities and identifications between freedoms.

Because the free exercise of subjectivity is always manifest, on Sartre's view, as objectification, relations with others degenerate into circular and unresolvable sado-masochistic conflicts, in which freedom seeks supremacy in the face of otherness. From Sartre's perspective, I am conscious of the presence of the other as another subject only by virtue of that subject's capacity to objectify me with the look. In the eyes of the other, I am aware of myself as a transcendence-transcended. I have been reduced to a standpoint eclipsed by the constitutive activities of a freedom which functions and is know only as a threat to my own, since its operations decenter or compromise the scope of my constitutive powers. The look of the other is a source of anxiety because it alerts me to my own lack, specifically the limits of my otherness to myself, and hence my being without foundations. In this sense, Sartre says, the other holds the secret of my being, since he is the possessor of that which I need to be my own foundation and that which I will always lack. The motive force for my relationships with others on this view is the ultimately narcissistic goal of self-completion by attempting to possess or appropriate the freedom of the other in its otherness. Such efforts, however, are ultimately futile because I can appeal to the other only by making myself an object of constitutive activity, denying my own subjectivity in the process. My efforts to capture the other's freedom through the exercise of my own also fail, since such activity reduces the other to the position of an object and hence fails to deliver the freedom I seek as freedom.

On Sartre's view, the co-presence or mutual recognition of freedoms is therefore impossible since two consciousnesses that aim for totality with respect to

their constitutive objects cannot co-exist and so must move between the equally untenable positions of sadism and masochism. Because other people function in Sartre's model as objects for consciousness, in a relationship of opposition to it, interpersonal relationships will be structured by categories of reification, displacement and deferral. Because freedom is identified with a position of solipsistic self-sufficiency without foundation in the world, freedom precludes the formation of genuine attachments with others, except as the abstract recognition of the other's constitutive powers being like my own—an ultimately empty analogy.

Given this view of interpersonal relationships, it is not hard to understand why the discussion of *mitsein* receives so little attention from Sartre in his discussion of 'Concrete Relations with Others' in *Being and Nothingness* (1953). It is also easier to understand why the ethical theory Sartre promises at the end of this text is never delivered. If freedom and relatedness are essentially opposed, one cannot construct an ethics capable of accommodating them both. Either freedom is radically unconditioned and ethical choice is indistinguishable from pure spontaneity and thus is completely arbitrary, or consciousness is motivated in the ethical moment and thus is not radically free. Given this configuration, at best this problem could be resolved by the judicial model of liberalism with its contractual models of consent and self-regulation. But it should be clear, given Sartre's position, why he found such an alternative unacceptable, as a denial of the radical freedom he took such care to elaborate. As a result, Sartre has had little to say by way of constituting an alternative discourse founded upon this view of freedom and finitude.

The task that now remains is to show how Beauvoir's discourse on freedom subverts the Sartrean conception and with it, its impasses. The core of Beauvoir's insight lies in her decision to return freedom to its roots in the patriarchal configuration of masculinity, and then to oppose to this the repressed discourse of the feminine marked by the sign of a different sense of freedom. This allows for an alternative conception of moral agency marked by a privileging of affinity and care in a way in which contributes to, rather than compromises, the integrity of moral agents or the world they constitute in common.

What is most subversive about Beauvoir's approach to freedom is her efforts to find origins, in human experience, for the very sense of freedom which is described by Sartre as anxious by virtue of its lack of origins. Sartre considers freedom from the perspective of a human subject thrown into the world with a consciousness already other than and free from the situations in which it is developed, disclosed and discovered. Even for the finite subject who exists in time, freedom is not a developmental phenomenon, on Sartre's account. It is a preestablished structure of potentiality indifferent to the occasions of its irruptions and irrevocably separate from them, hence without attachments.

Beauvoir traces the development of freedom through its embodied, social and temporal phrases, beginning with its origins in infantile vulnerability. Both male and female begin existence dependent upon and contained by mother's body. From the time of weaning, however, male and female children will be

positioned differently toward the mother, the body, and the question of origins. In childhood, Beauvoir says, the young girl seems to be favored, since she is allowed to remain longer within the protective and supportive sphere of the maternal. Young girls can be kept with mother because motherhood is their future. To remain bonded to mother is also to be bonded to a future, a future of transformation and care-taking through the medium of the body, which her patterns of play will also aim to re-identify as pleasure. The girl's sense of freedom is forged in a context of mirroring, and so her identity will come to be established for her through the refractions of approval, recognition and affinity with others.

The young boy, by contrast, is removed sooner from the maternal sphere because, as Beauvoir puts it, 'great things are in store for him,' and those great things lie outside and separate from the world of the mother. To enter the world of the fathers which operates by principles of competition and conflict rather than care, he must overcome his attachment to mother as the site of his vulnerability and original dependence. In the context of male development, transcendence is attached to this overcoming of origins, in the body, and in women, while the pursuit of foundations comes to be associated with a form of regression. His development will be marked by his movement away from protection toward self-sufficiency, or at least, the symbols of same. What will buttress this effort will be his emergence in a system of sexual difference in which he is positioned as other than and privileged with respect to the world of the mother. The young girl, who will herself be an originating body, will not seek freedom in nihilation but productivity. Her understanding of the significance of origins, connections and attachments will thus be opposed to that of the boys. This is not accidental but overdetermined since her survival and recognition will depend upon occupying this opposite pole.

It is with respect to the question of origins that Beauvoir's discussion of sexual difference in discourse takes on import with respect to the concept of freedom. In light of the difference Beauvoir names, the Sartrean idea of a freedom without foundation is recast within the frame of the distinctly masculine frame of reference which emphasizes the project of separation begun by distinguishing oneself from the mother and the socially deprivileged maternal sphere she comes to embody and represent. The male figure of freedom thus becomes associated with distance, separation and the nihilation of origins. Such distance is possible, for men, because the world of the father is a world at great remove from the world he inhabits as a child, a distance greater than that between the girl's domestic games and actual domesticity. The young man, confronted with an open future, experiences anxiety in the face of his range of possibilities. The more open the field, the more likely he is to recognize the non-necessity of any particular path, as well as to identify with his own powers of choice with respect to that situation. As a consequence he can come to feel himself to be the source of his own choices. This configuration of freedom as an autonomous choice among possibilities bespeaks a position of male privilege, since arriving at the idea of self as an agency of choice depends upon being in

a situation open to such possibilities. In patriarchy, this pluralization of possibilities is a dimension of male privilege, and thus Sartre's so-called founda-
tionless freedom is in fact tied to conditions of sociality and embodiment which
make such recognitions possible. The significance of Beauvoir's analysis of childhood can thus be read as an interpretation of the discourse of freedom without
origins, which can now be understood as a discourse of male privilege. On this
reading, the female strategy of pursuing freedom and identity in the context
of relations with others is only coded as dependent or regressive if one chooses
to normatively privilege male experience. But as feminist theory has shown,
years later, there are alternative ways to construe this difference.[3]

Beauvoir continues her analysis of female development by pursuing the configurations of sexual difference throughout the life stages of individuals. During
adolescence, for example, the course of differentiation begun in childhood takes
on particularly dramatic import with the emergence of the sexual body. For
the boy, the appearance of the markers of manhood are permeated by the sense
of entitlement he knows they confer upon him. For the girl, however, with
the emergence of her womanly attributes, the future seems to take up residence
in her body. These changes in her mode of embodiment which occur beyond
her will or complicity seem to seal her fate, throwing her into a world of glances,
expectations and desires not yet her own. Even more intensely than in childhood, the adolescent female will come to identify herself with her image as it
is mirrored and refracted through the eyes and attitude of others toward her.
Adolescence is the phase in which the confluence of pleasure and power with
the state of being looked at will take hold of the female consciousness. She will
come to associate her efficacy with the power to fascinate those who are essential. For the adolescent girl, as Beauvoir describes her, the pleasure others
take in looking at her will become inseparable and indistinguishable from her
own pleasure.

Differing from the patterns of male narcissism which aim at self-completion
through appropriation, the adolescent girl will pursue the pleasure of refracted
narcissism, which depends upon the other's glance remaining other as a source
of validation. As a consequence, her being for others will not seem to compromise her freedom, but will rather be construed as providing the most fertile
field for its exercise. Far from being an empty consciousness seeking to incorporate the other's freedom as fulfillment, the adolescent girl waits for the man
who is ready to receive and appropriate her plentitude and through this to give
meaning to her facticity. With the emergence of her sexual body, woman is
constituted in patriarchy as a locus of abundance and generosity opposed to
the emptiness and neediness of men.

'Appearing as the other, woman appears at the same time as an abundance of
being, in contrast to that existence the nothingness of which man senses in

---

[3] Gilligan's (1982) approach is a supplementary conjunction of sexual difference by which we
arrive at 'a more complex rendition of human experience' (p. 174). Mary Daly (1982) interprets
sexual difference as a principle of radical separatism, and the possibility of gynocentric values.

himself. In woman is incarnated in positive form the look that the existent carries in his heart . . . ' (p. 160).

Already marked with the look of the man who at this point has come to signify for woman the essential dimension to which she is opposed, female freedom already receives a trajectory which ties her fate to those of others. While male maturation pursues a course of separation, connection with man becomes the marker of recognition and value for women. While being seen or desired functions in the masculine discourse as a site of compromise and ambivalence, a threat to their sense of autonomy and integrity, the threat for women is the opposite, the fear of being unseen and invisible. In a world which constitutes her as other, connection becomes essential for women. The woman who is not recognized by others begins not to recognize herself. Rather than identifying with their own lack and freely seeking its fulfillment, women identify with their ability to anticipate and fulfill the needs of others. The negativities which structure her world are not gaps or separations between isolated subjects, but rather come to be seen as absences of concern, care and response. The disappointment she may experience in her relationships stems from her expectations that the other with whom she engages is as prepared to see these omissions as well as seeing her plentitude.

It is this difference in expectations that grounds the conflictual structure of interpersonal relationships, a difference which places men and women in dominant and submissive positions with respect to the larger social and historical context which forms the background for such engagements. The failure of interpersonal relationships, on Beauvoir's view, need not be understood as structurally endemic to our being for others, as Sartre seems to suggest. Rather than immersing subjects in a circular movement between the equally untenable poles of sadism and masochism, each of which necessitates the move to the opposing pole, social relationships operate in a context which already situates subjects differently by gender with respect to these positions. It is therefore not the fluid exchange of positions that compromises genuine contacts between people, on Beauvoir's view, but a social organization of sexual difference which institutionalizes and ossifies this difference as an asymmetrical opposition of supremacy and inferiority. In a patriarchal context which privileges men at women's expense, interpersonal relationships (particularly of the heterosexist variety) will always be characterized by rupture, refusal, conflict and disappointment. But in Beauvoir's analysis, as distinct from Sartre's, such conflicts are amenable to human freedom and transcendence. Rather than containing our freedom in a discourse of alienation and exile, being-for-others calls to human freedom as the agency of transformation, such that genuine human contact will be possible but only through the concerted efforts we make with others to transform the conditions which bring them about.

Beauvoir's conception of freedom which emerges from the discussion of female development qualifies as gynocentric or female-identified in a descriptive rather than normative sense. I think it is a confusion between these two senses which has led many to read and dismiss Beauvoir as male-identified and im-

plicitly misogynist.[4] This I believe is a serious misreading, which discounts the substantial contributions Beauvoir has made to the now thriving discourse of feminism and femininity. Beauvoir, when writing of women, is describing the situation of women in patriarchy, which is that of being the second sex, where femininity is a situation constituted by a patriarchal system of representation to devalue and contain it. But the naming of the moment of devaluation is also a naming of the site of opposition to that devaluation which also offers the promise of a transvaluation of value. While Beauvoir does not yet occupy the position of the valorized feminine, operative in the discourse of contemporary feminism, her writing of the oppressed feminine makes the emergence of such a position possible. By naming the freedom that emerges from the feminine situation Beauvoir articulates the very sense of freedom capable of accomplishing this movement of liberating transcendence. In this sense, Beauvoir is identified with femininity as situation, and not with the pseudo-Sartrean conflict of pure structural opposition.

The discourse which Beauvoir seems more explicitly to address in her theoretical texts, however, is that of traditional philosophy with its set of problems and issues, which is why I think it is important to read her work in that context as well. In this light, Beauvoir's developmental account of freedom can best be appreciated as providing the foundations for an ethics and politics not possible on Sartre's account, because freedom is taken to exist separate and apart from its social, historical and material origins. By articulating a freedom which arises in response to a progressively emergent body in situation, Beauvoir gives freedom what it had lacked in the traditional existentialist account, which is to say that Beauvoir gives freedom a foundation, a context, a history, and something to do. A freedom which nihilates its own past as Sartre's does, will be a freedom with only an impoverished or imaginary sense of future. A freedom that finds in connections with others only its own bad faith and flight from itself will be incapable of engaging with others to produce a situation which better facilitates its exercise. Besides, it is just this kind of faith which Sartre calls bad faith which is necessary for ethical and political change.

Beauvoir's retrieval of freedom as a developmental aspect of human existence marks a path for its engagement in a socio-historical world amenable to its efficacy while avoiding the Sartrean *cul de sac* of bad faith. Because freedom for Beauvoir is positioned on the side of the plentitude of being both imply bonds with others. Freedom, on this view, finds in others not only obstacles,

[4] Beauvoir's 'descriptive' identification with femininity consists in the recognition of writing of woman as woman. But because the situation Beauvoir describes is that of the debased feminine, i.e. femininity as represented within the frame of male privilege, much of Beauvoir's writing repeats the alienation attached to that position, and the masculinist modes of representing it. Given the absence of an intertextual support system, it is not surprising that Beauvoir speaks from a position that can now read as isolationist, or as a discourse of the 'queen bee.' But to read this textual slippage as an indication of moral ambivalence is unfair and misleading: unfair because it reduces Beauvoir too narrowly to her circumstances; and misleading, given the history of the fate of *The Second Sex*. If that text were male-identified, men would have appropriated the text for their discourse. As Simons (1981) suggests if *The Second Sex* were male identified, men would identify with it.

but also its sites of realization and recognition. Far from perpetuating the masculinist romanticism of the isolated individual, the higher particular, Beauvoir's free ethical agent recognizes the absurdity of a freedom which is inefficacious because it is in perennial flight from others when it is not seeking to dominate them. The freedom of the ethical agent, in Beauvoir's discourse, is not exercised primarily in the interests of judgment as prescribed by a morality of rights. The ethical agent is not so much free from as free for responsiveness and care in the face of the recognition of the freedom of others.

> ' . . . no existence can be validly fulfilled if it is limited to itself. It appeals to the existence of others.' (p. 67).

> 'I concern others and others concern me. There we have an irreducible truth. The me-other relationship is as indissoluble as the subject-object relation.' (p. 72).

The ethical moment Beauvoir marks in *Ethics of Ambiguity* is the moment where each subject is free to recognize the responsibility that exists toward others in non-codified form. With respect to the Sartrean discourse, which also names a moment of responsibility, Beauvoir's sense of that term takes on a radically different signification. For Sartre, responsibility involves the absurd recognition of accountability for the fate of others. Its refractions end up ultimately with the subject himself, who is thrown back on his own groundlessness and powerless with respect to the freedom of others. Because Sartre construes the scope of responsibility so widely and at the same time so abstractly, it is ultimately inefficacious as a guide for action or choice of commitments. Beauvoir's concept of responsibility which already has as its locus the needs and concerns of others, functions by contrast, as a force of positivity acting in opposition to failures of concern and indifference.

> 'Contrary to the formal strictness of Kantianism, for whom the more abstract the act of the more virtuous it is generosity seems to us to be better grounded therefore more valid the less distinction there is between the other and ourself and the more we fulfill ourself in taking the other as end. This is what happens if I am engaged in relation to others.' (p. 144).

What becomes clear in this passage is the origins of Beauvoir's ethic of concern in the feminine situation where caretaking and taking responsibility for caring is uniquely privileged. The sense of what happens when engaged with others is a reference to the distinctly female role in patriarchy. But in the context of Beauvoir's discourse, where freedom is marked by difference, female facticity is transcended without nihilation, transformed from an imposed destiny and mode of containment into an ethical appeal to the freedom and recognition of others. In this sense, female existence has itself become a normative foundation which is to say it has become ethical because, to use Beauvoir's words ethics is this very 'triumph of freedom over facticity.' (p. 44).

The significance of Beauvoir's work, marked as it is by difference can now

be appreciated as a calling to awareness of the limits and one-sidedness of the ethical problematic as it has been traditionally configured. Given a conception of freedom the integrity of which consists in its autonomy and self-sufficiency, the dilemma of freedom becomes centered on the moments in which freedoms conflict and threaten one another with annihilation or debasement. It is the privileging of conflict which engenders the judicial model of morality as an effort to garner the complicity of freedoms necessary for resolution in the form of minimization of differences. It is also clear, given their privileging of differences, why existentialists like Sartre (but also Nietzsche, Kirkegaard and Heidigger) would resist this mode of resolution. It also helps explain why existentialism was loath to construct an ethics conceived as a general set of prescriptions for social behavior.

Beauvoir's work offers an alternative way of configuring the ethical dilemma, in part because her discourse emerges from the standpoint of other where integrity is a function of interpersonal recognition and the preservation of relationships through conflict. Choice is demanded in situations which thrust upon the individual the necessity to act in light of needs of others as opposed to the abstract imperatives of autonomy which privilege the individual relative to the circumstances that call for action. Beauvoir's ethics of ambiguity constitutes a challenge to the assumption upon which the masculinist model rests, i.e. that human situations can be codified sufficiently so as to be amenable to a system of juristic prescriptions conceived independently of them. The foundation of her challenge rests with her having enfranchised freedom as a developmental potency with the power not only to transcend its situation so as to judge it, but also, and perhaps more importantly, to create and change the very social and interpersonal situations which call for its exercise. Because freedom is efficacious in the face of the world, one cannot absent oneself from complicity with the circumstance one presumes to judge, nor can one construct a position from which the force of this attachment can be neutralized. From Beauvoir's point of view, it is not clear that such a position of neutrality would be desirable, since ethical activity is conceived as motivated by care and concern, rather than by obligation and obedience to law.

Because Beauvoir writes from the standpoint of the oppressed other, she is situated so as to recognize the limits of an ethics which assumes human freedom as a birthright which need only be protected from unjustified intrusion or debasement. For those whose freedom is denied social recognition and import, an attitude of responsibility expressed through indifference and distance is insufficient. It both presumes too much, (the need to maintain the freedom which is already there for the subject) and not enough (because it fails to commit to creating the conditions for enfranchising that freedom).

As a consequence of her developmental model of freedom tied to material conditions, Beauvoir recommends an ethic of commitment geared toward a situation in which freedom ought to be mobilized in concert with others for the purpose of creating the conditions for its further development by engaging others in the recognition and exercise of their freedom. The significance of this difference lies in the fact that freedom exists primarily as a progressive force,

identified with rather than opposed to the concerns of those whose freedom is similarly directed. As opposed to an ethics of autonomy in which freedom wills the limits of its obligations to others, an ethics of ambiguity construes freedom as a will to action and commitment, where its presence to the recognition and judgment of others is endemic rather than antithetical to its integrity and power. Because she construes ethical activity as the exercise of freedom in affinity, Beauvoir can proffer a theory of value which gives freedom more than the paternal prerogative of judgment, moving freedom toward the maternal discourse of liberation aimed at freeing others toward their own possibilities through commitment and concerns for them.

Far from being male identified, Beauvoir begins the process of writing 'the different voice' both by marking the situation from which that voice speaks, and by naming its integrity as an activity of commitment and care. In Beauvoir's work, female existence, and the values emergent from it no longer remain contained within a discourse of domination but are freed for the purpose of becoming ethical, and thus changing the world, and the lives of human subjects who must make their ways there. In Beauvoir's discourse female existence triumphs in its freedom over facticity, and in so doing, marks a new path and a new future. The world Beauvoir names is our own. Her promise and vision deserve a place in it as well.

REFERENCES

Beauvoir, Simone. 1948. *The Ethics of Ambiguity*. Translated by Bernard Frechtman. Citadel Press, New York.

Beauvoir, Simone. 1952. *The Second Sex*. Translated by H. M. Parshley. Random House, New York.

Daly, Mary. 1978. *Gynecology: The Metaethics of Radical Feminism*. Beacon Press, Boston.

Gilligan, Carol. 1982. *In a Different Voice*. Harvard University Press, Boston.

Janeway, Elizabeth. 1981. *Powers of the Weak*. Morrow Quill, New York.

Sartre, Jean Paul. 1953. *Being and Nothingness*. Translated by Hazel Barnes. Washington Square Press, New York.

Simons, Margaret A. 1981. Beauvoir and Sartre: The question of influence. *Eros* 8 (1): 25–42.

CONTRIBUTORS

Azizah Y. al-Hibri is founding editor of *Hypatia*, a former professor of philosophy and author and editor of various articles and books, including *Women and Islam, Technology and Human Affairs*, and a book on deontic logic. Over the years she has been actively involved with issues of gender and race. She is an attorney with a major New York law firm.

Sandra Lee Bartky is Associate Professor of Philosophy and Women's Studies at the University of Illinois at Chicago. Her *Femininity and Domination: Studies in the Phenomenology of Oppression* is forthcoming from Routledge.

Claudia Card, a graying, vegetarian, cat-loving midwestern Sapphist of Celtic origins, professes lesbian culture, ethics, feminist theory, social philosophy, philosophy and literature, and environmental ethics at the University of Wisconsin-Madison. She is writing a book, *Character and Moral Luck*, on character evolutions under oppressive institutions.

Arleen B. Dallery is Associate Professor of Philosophy at La Salle University, where she also teaches in the Women's Studies Department. She is Co-Executive Director of the Society for Phenomenology and Existential Philosophy. Her research interests include the theme of reading in the works of Cixous and Irigaray. She recently co-edited *The Question of the Other*, published by the State University of New York Press.

Christine Di Stefano is Assistant Professor in the Political Science Department at the University of Washington. She has published articles on John Stuart Mill and Marx. Her most recent publication is "Dilemmas of Difference: Feminism, Modernity, and Post-Modernism." She is working on a study of autonomy.

Ann Ferguson is a lesbian socialist feminist who teaches philosophy and women's studies at the University of Massachusetts/Amherst. She has published articles on androgyny, the feminist sex debate on pornography, Adrienne Rich's theory of the lesbian continuum, and motherhood and sexuality. Her book *Blood at the Root: Motherhood, Sexuality and Male Dominance* (Pandora/Unwin and Hyman, 1989) develops the theory that different forms of patriarchy are based in "modes of sex/affective production"—historical ways of constructing sexuality, parenting, nurturance and social bonding. She is working on a collection of her old and new essays called *Sexual Democracy: Women, Oppression and Revolution* (Westview).

Marilyn Frye teaches philosophy and women's studies at Michigan State University. She is the author of *The Politics of Reality: Essays in Feminist Theory*.

Mary E. Hawkesworth is Associate Professor of Political Science at the University of Louisville. Her research interests include contemporary political phi-

losophy, feminist theory, and social policy. She is the author of *Beyond Oppression: Feminist Theory and Political Strategy* (New York: Continuum Press, 1990) and *Theoretical Issues in Policy Analysis* (Albany: State University of New York Press, 1988) and co-editor with Maurice Kogan of *The Routledge Encyclopedia of Government and Politics* (London: Routledge, in press).

Alison M. Jaggar is Obed J. Wilson Professor of Ethics and Professor of Philosophy at the University of Cincinnati. She is the author of many articles, primarily in social, political and moral philosophy, including philosophy of education, and in feminist philosophy. Her books include *Feminist Frameworks*, co-edited with Paula Rothenberg (McGraw Hill, 1978; second edition, 1984), *Feminist Politics and Human Nature* (Rowman & Allanheld and Harvester, 1983) and *Gender/Body/Knowledge: Feminist Reconstructions of Being and Knowing*, co-edited with Susan R. Bordo (Rutgers University Press, 1989). She is working on *Feminism and Moral Theory*, supported by a fellowship from the Rockefeller Foundation.

Eva Feder Kittay is Associate Professor of Philosophy at the State University of New York, Stony Brook. She is the author of *Metaphor: Its Cognitive Force and Linguistic Structure,* co-editor (with Diana T. Meyers) of *Women and Moral Theory* and the author of articles on philosophy of language, normative ethics, and feminist theory, including other contributions to *Hypatia*. She is writing a book on feminist critiques of the ideal of equality, *Equality and the Inclusion of Women*, with support from the American Association of University Women.

María C. Lugones is a grass-roots organizer in New Mexico. She is interested in building a grass-roots Hispanic feminism that starts from within the communities.

William L. McBride is Professor of Philosophy at Purdue University, a founding and continuing member of its Women's Studies Committee, and co-founder (with Phyllis Morris) of the Sartre Society of North America. His books include *The Philosophy of Marx* and *Social Theory at a Crossroads*.

Gillian Michell is Associate Dean of the School of Library and Information Science at the University of Western Ontario, Canada. She has a Ph.D. in linguistics from the University of Southern California. Her research focuses on aspects of gender and interpersonal communication, including psychotherapy, and on access to Canadian feminist literature and research.

Jo-Ann Pilardi has a joint appointment in philosophy and women's studies at Towson State University in Baltimore. She has a degree from the Humanities Center of Johns Hopkins University, where she wrote a dissertation on Simone de Beauvoir, *The Development of the Self in the Writings of Simone de Beauvoir: Philosophy Becomes Autobiography.* A member (and twice coordinator) of the Towson State University Women's Studies program since its founding in the early 1970s, she was also a long-time activist in the Baltimore women's liberation movement and served as an editor of *Women: A Journal of Liberation*. Her

research interests include feminist theory and philosophy, continental philosophy (particularly existentialism and phenomenology) and the political philosophy of the Enlightenment.

Ruth M. Schwartz has taught philosophy at the University of Pennsylvania, where she was managing editor of *Hypatia* in 1984. She now works for the State of New Jersey on special projects, which have included affirmative action policy, departmental codes of ethics, and prison programs. She has written on issues in normative public policy analysis, biomedical ethics and philosophy of law.

Charlene Haddock Seigfried is Associate Professor of Philosophy at Purdue University. Her many articles and books bring together feminist theory and classical American pragmatism. She has written on aesthetics, ethics, the philosophy of science and phenomenology as well as on Beauvoir. She is the author of *Chaos and Context*. Her *Radical Reconstruction of William James's Philosophy* will be published by the State University of New York Press.

Donna Serniak received her Ph.D. from the University of Pennsylvania, at which time she also acted as *Hypatia*'s first managing editor. She is Assistant Professor of Philosophy at Randolph-Macon College, where she helped form their first Women's Studies program. She wrote her dissertation on Rudolph Carnap and the origins of logical positivism. Currently, her research is on the role of affect in discourse, in feminist literary criticism and in theories of autobiography.

Margaret A. Simons is Associate Professor of Philosophy at Southern Illinois University at Edwardsville and editor of *Hypatia*. In addition to her work on motherhood and Beauvoir, she has written on racism in feminist theory and on sexism in mainstream philosophy. She is working on a book on the philosophy of Simone de Beauvoir.

Linda Singer is Associate Professor of Philosophy at Miami University, Ohio. She has published in the areas of popular culture, continental philosophy and postmodernism, and feminist theory. Her book *Erotic Welfare: Sexual Theory and Politics in the Age of Epidemic* is forthcoming from Routledge as part of its Feminism and Social Theory series.

Janet Farrell Smith is Associate Professor of Philosophy at the University of Massachusetts at Boston and has taught feminist philosophy at Smith College and Harvard Divinity School. She has published on parenting, property and reproduction, and is now working in the areas of property and reproductive technology.

Elizabeth V. Spelman teaches philosophy at Smith College. She and María Lugones also collaborated on "Competition, Compassion, and Community: Models for a Feminist Ethos" (in *Competition*, edited by Valerie Miner and Helen Longino). Her recent book is *Inessential Woman: Problems of Exclusion in Feminist Thought* (Beacon Press).

Joyce Trebilcot has been involved with *Hypatia* from the beginning, often in the background. She helped arrange for Azizah al-Hibri to become the original editor and for Margaret A. Simons to succeed her. "So I am especially gratified that the journal is flourishing," Trebilcot says, "and welcome this reprinting of essays from the first three issues."

Nancy Tuana is Associate Professor of the History of Ideas at the University of Texas at Dallas. She has written on the gender system in science, conceptions of woman's nature and feminism and sexuality. She is editor of the American Philosophical Association's *Newsletter on Feminism and Philosophy* and edited *Feminism and Science* (Indiana University Press, 1989).

Caroline Whitbeck is a philosopher of science, technology and medicine who has published widely on issues of medical technology and feminist theory. She is Senior Research Scholar at the Massachusetts Institute of Technology's Center for Technology and Policy and Senior Lecturer in Mechanical Engineering. Her research includes a study of the responsibilities of designers of medical technology and collaboration on two other projects: the design of guidelines for the conduct of biomonitoring in communities contaminated by toxic substances and a projection of the occupational risks of AIDS. She is completing a book on engineering ethics, *Designing a Life*.

Terry R. Winant is Visiting Assistant Professor in the Philosophy Department at Wesleyan University. She works in feminist philosophy and foundations of phenomenology and is writing a book on Brentano. Her most recent publication is "Rationality, Relativism, Feminism," forthcoming in *Selected Studies in Phenomenology and Existential Philosophy*, vol. 14.

Iris Marion Young is Associate Professor of Public and International Affairs at the University of Pittsburgh. She is the author of many articles on political philosophy and feminist theory. Her books include *Justice and the Politics of Difference* (forthcoming from Princeton University Press) and *Stretching Out: Essays in Feminist Social Theory and Female Body Experience*, (Indiana University Press). She has been a socialist feminist activist for nearly twenty years, working on such issues as affordable housing, intervention in Central America and reproductive rights.

INDEX

Abortion, 159

Abstract masculinity, defined, 241. *See also* Masculinity

Accidental/essential dichotomy, 75

Accidental properties, defined, 75

Adults, care of, 251–52. *See also* Reproduction

Advertisements. *See Bloodline* (movie) advertisement

Affirmative action: and Aristotle, 143; and atomistic individualism, 112, 136, 140–46, 154; and compelling state interest, 144–45; criticism of, 136, 140–46, 141*n*.10; defense of, 135–36, 146–52; defined, 135*n*.1; and equal protection, 144; purposes of, 112, 141; and reverse discrimination, 142–44; and socialized individualism, 112, 136, 146–52; and underutilization, 147, 147*n*.17

" 'Affirmative Action' Reconsidered" (Sowell), 141*n*.9

Agape, defined, 207

Agassiz, Louis, 71

Aggression, 78. *See also* Sex differences

Alienation, 24

Allen, Garland E., 321

Altman, Dennis, 287

Amazons, 298. *See also* Lesbianism

American Psychiatric Association, 290–91

"Analysis of a Phobia" (Freud), 10

Androcentrism: and Brunswick, 196, 198; and feminism, 27; and Freud, 192–93, 201; and masculist ontology, 208

Anti-feminism, 238–39, 246. *See also* Feminism

Anti-militarism, 239–40, 244, 245, 246

Arendt, Hannah, 249*n*.1

Aristotle: and affirmative action, 143; and friendship, 297; and Hobbes, 103; and nature/nurture dichotomy, 74; and voluntariness, 295. *See also specific works*

Assimilation, 24

Atomistic individualism: and affirmative action, 112, 136, 140–46, 154; characteristics of, 137–38; criticism of, 112, 152–54; and feminism, 158; and freedom, 138, 153; and Hobbes, 153*n*.22; and self-realization, 137–38. *See also* Individualism

Attitude, 295–96, 303

Augustine, Saint, 74

Austin, J. L., 55, 55*n*.4

Authenticity, 199

Autobiography (Hobbes), 103–4

Averini, Schlomo, 7, 14

Bataille, Georges, 8, 13–14, 124

Bateson, Patrick, 320, 321

Beauvoir, Simone de: background of, 161, 167, 173; and commitment, 334; criticism of, 331–32; and dualism, 228; and *écriture féminine*, 274; and femininity, 332, 332*n*.4; and feminism, 158, 159, 227, 230; and freedom, 328–31, 332–33, 334–35; and Hegel, 8, 235; and humanist feminism, 228; and lesbianism, 229; and male hegemony, 91; and masochism and sadomasochism, 124; and motherhood, 199–200; and naturalism, 228; and oppression, 332, 334; and Other, 35, 199, 334; and patriarchy, 332; and responsibility, 333; and Sartre, 228, 323, 324, 326; and sex differences, 329–31; and sexuality, 199; as socialist, 243; and transcendence, 329, 331; and Woolf, 167. *See also specific works*

Being and Nothingness (Sartre), 293, 293*n*.5, 328

Benjamin, Jessica, 6

Benn, Stanley, 7*n*.4

Bent twig hypothesis, 48, 48*n*.18

Beyond the Pleasure Principle (Freud), 9, 11, 193

Biological determinism: criticism of, 84, 86; defined, 70; and Engels, 256, 257; and eugenics, 72; and evolution, 71; and female/male dichotomy, 78; and Freud, 112, 202; and genetic theory, 72; and hormones, 72–73; and Marx, 256, 257, 263; and monogenism, 71; and nature/nurture dichotomy, 70–71, 73, 76, 78, 84, 86; and neoteny, 71–72; and polygenism, 71; and recapitulation, 71, 72; and reproduction, 263–64, 266; and sex/gender dichotomy, 86; and social Darwinism, 72

Biology, and gynocentrism, 244–45, 246

Bipedalism, 85

Bisexuality, 194

Black feminism, 239. *See also* Feminism; Women of color

Blackmun, Harry, 151

Blacks. *See* Women of color

Bloodline (movie) advertisement, 57; ambiguity of, 58–64, 60*nn*. 7, 8, 65–66, 68; and feminism, 2, 65, 68–69; ordinary discourse in, 55, 63, 65; passivity in, 62–63, 66; pragmatic analysis of, 58, 64–67; sex in, 59–63, 64, 65–66, 67; sexist discourse in, 56, 58, 64, 66, 68; speech-act analysis of, 55, 58, 59–64; standard context of, 60*n*.8, 61; victim in, 63, 64, 65–66; viewers' role in, 59–62, 63, 64, 65–66; violence in, 58, 59–63, 61*n*.9, 63*n*.12, 64, 65–66, 67; and Women Against Violence Against Women, 56–58, 61*n*.9, 68. *See also* Movies

Bloom, Allan, 36, 38